THE LIVING LIGHT DIALOGUE

Volume 18

Reproduction of the cover image of the
1972 edition of *The Living Light*

[See the appendix for a discussion of the image's symbolism.]

THE LIVING LIGHT DIALOGUE

Volume 18

Through the mediumship of
Richard P. Goodwin

Living Light Books

The Living Light Dialogue Volume 18
Copyright © 2023 Serenity Association
Through the mediumship of Richard P. Goodwin.

All rights reserved. No portion of this book may be reproduced—electronically, mechanically, or via internet transmission—without advance, express written permission of the publisher except in the case of brief quotations embodied in critical articles and reviews. No derivative work—games, supplemental material, video—may be created without advance, express written permission of the publisher. For information address Living Light Books, P.O. Box 4187, San Rafael, CA 94913-4187.

Cover design copyright © 2023 by Serenity Association
Cover photograph by Serenity Association, 2023; copyright © 2023 by Serenity Association.

www.livinglight.org

Library of Congress Control Number 2007929762
ISBN: 978-1-947199-45-3

FIRST EDITION

This volume of teachings is dedicated to the spirit friends who brought to Earth the Living Light Philosophy. With eternal gratitude, we pray that we may demonstrate these principles and continue to bring to publication these teachings.

CONTENTS

Acknowledgment ix
Preface xi
Introduction. xv
Fourth Annual World Forecast. 3
Seventh Annual World Forecast 9
Eighth Annual World Forecast 13
Ninth Annual World Forecast 17
Tenth Annual World Forecast 21
Eleventh Annual World Forecast. 27
Twelfth Annual World Forecast 39
Thirteenth Annual World Forecast 47
Fourteenth Annual World Forecast 53
Fifteenth Annual World Forecast 59
Sixteenth Annual World Forecast 65
Seventeenth Annual World Forecast 71
Eighteenth Annual World Forecast 77
Nineteenth Annual World Forecast 89
Twentieth Annual World Forecast 99
Twenty-First Annual World Forecast 113
Twenty-Second Annual World Forecast 135
Twenty-Third Annual World Forecast 153
Twenty-Fourth Annual World Forecast 175
Twenty-Fifth Annual World Forecast 199
The Lost Discourse: Giving 219
Impatient Progression 223
Control Points. 235
Discourse July 29, 1971. 237
The Fort Bragg Seminar 241
The Vacaville Seminar 267
Discourse June 5, 1972 291

Discourse June 12, 1972	293
Discourse June 19, 1972	295
Discourse June 26, 1972	297
Class July 20, 1972	299
Class July 27, 1972	305
Common Sense Meditation Part 1	311
Common Sense Meditation Part 2	317
Class October 19, 1972	323
Journey of the Living Light Discourse 1	329
Journey of the Living Light Discourse 2	331
Journey of the Living Light Discourse 3	333
Atlantean Astrology Part 1	337
Atlantean Astrology Part 2	341
Discourse January 12, 1973	343
Discourse January 18, 1973	345
Discourse January 19, 1973	349
Discourse January 26, 1973	353
Discourse February 2, 1973	357
Spiritualism and the Christian Bible	359
Class November 15, 1974	383
Stardust	405
Review #1	411
The Dog of Destiny	413
Special Discourse - The Path	415
Special Discourse - Bee	417
Private Class 1	419
Private Class 2 - The Fountain of Youth	423
Private Class 3 - The Principle of Getting and Giving	427
Private Class 4 - Sanity and Self-Concern	431
Special Discourse - Class AAA1 Human Relations	435
Special Private Class 1	441
Special Class 1	469
Appendix	487

ACKNOWLEDGMENT

Grateful acknowledgment is made to the many friends and associates for invaluable aid in compiling this book, for their helpful suggestions, for their loyal interest and encouragement.

Special acknowledgment is due to those who painstakingly and selflessly transcribed and proofread the text.

PREFACE

It was through the mediumship of the Serenity Association founder, Mr. Richard P. Goodwin, that a philosophy known as the Living Light was given in more than 700 classes over a twenty-five-year period.

To be specific, the philosophy was imparted through Mr. Goodwin by a magistrate who had lived on Earth some 8,000 years ago. The former magistrate is known to Living Light students as "the Wise One," and he narrated the journey of his soul on the other side of life, the experiences—especially the difficulties—he encountered in having to face himself, as well as the teachings he earned to help himself through the realms in which he traveled. It was his decision to share the teachings with souls on both sides of "the curtain."

Prior to the advent of the Wise One, Mr. Goodwin had prayed for a teacher from the realms of light. Mr. Goodwin, since age fourteen, had been the instrument through which spirit was able to communicate with those seeking help. But he saw that his mediumship brought only temporary solace, because the people he was trying to help soon became fascinated with the phenomena and ignored the help that spirit was imparting. He prayed for someone who would bring forth teachings that would benefit any soul seeking a path to a greater awareness of himself and of God.

His prayers were answered in 1964 when the Wise One came through for the first time. Mr. Goodwin, at first apprehensive about what this new teacher would impart, was taken into deep trance and not able to control what was being revealed through him. Upon hearing the recorded classes afterward, however, he became convinced of the goodness of the teacher and of the value of the simple, beautiful teachings. This, then, was the beginning of the Living Light Philosophy given to Earth through the mediumship of Richard P. Goodwin.

The present volume contains the Annual World Forecast series as well as thirty-nine individual classes. A world forecast was given each year, usually late in December and often on the last Sunday of the month. The forecasts often reveal events or trends of the upcoming year. No recording or transcription exists of the earliest forecasts; so, those forecasts cannot be included. The individual classes cover a very wide range of topics. In addition, because these are individual classes, the tone of the different classes is often very disparate: some are very formal; others, quite informal. Some were given to the public; some were given to a small group of dedicated students. Several of the classes have not been available in any form since the day they were given. One class is an example of what is known, in Spiritualism, as rescue work, during which a person who has passed on and is trapped in the lower realms is permitted to express through the medium in order to be helped. The individual classes are presented in chronological order, with the two undated classes first, and range in time from 1968 to 1988. Regarding the classes on Atlantean Astrology, be it in Divine order, additional teachings will be published in later volumes.

The foundation of the classes—the foundation of the Living Light Philosophy itself—is the Law of Personal Responsibility which states, in part, that we are responsible for all our experiences, and that our experiences are the return of the laws that we have established with our thoughts, acts, and deeds. Through greater awareness of our thoughts and by exercising our divine right of choice, we may choose to establish laws of greater harmony and goodness.

The Living Light Dialogue teaches that we have come to Earth to learn the lessons that are necessary to free us from the dictates and limits of our own thoughts and judgments, which are the mental patterns that we follow through our own lack of awareness and are so very potent, forceful, and limiting. These teachings guide us in making the necessary changes in our thinking in order to free ourselves from those patterns and to express our soul consciousness.

The choice of guiding the direction of our life, as stated by the Wise One when he speaks of being with a person, place, or thing, is, in essence, of being in this world and not a part of this world. He further explains that no matter what experiences we encounter, no matter what we do or do not do, we—our spirit—may view the experience in objectivity from a soul level of consciousness where peace reigns supreme.

The teachings of this volume help us to restore harmony or balance in our life by flooding the consciousness with spiritual affirmations and prayers, a few of which can be found in the appendix. When reason is restored, by balancing our sense functions with our soul faculties, we will consciously experience peace. Without annihilating our ego or our sense functions, we will find a pathway of expression for our soul. Where there was once disturbance, now there is acceptance. Where there was disease, now there is poise. And where there was hopelessness and despair, now there is reason, divine neutrality; and peace shows the way.

If you make the effort to apply these laws, such as, "If man is a law unto himself, what are you doing with the law that you are?", and demonstrate the wisdom of patience, the truth of this philosophy will be your living demonstration.

As the teacher states in CC 130, "My journey of many centuries and much experience has brought me here to Earth to share with you these simple teachings that have come as the effect of a long, long, long journey. Let not your journey be so long in the realms of illusion. For it is not necessary for you. For in your evolution, you have earned an awakening. But it is up to you to do something that is constructive and worthwhile."

INTRODUCTION

[This introduction was written by Mr. Goodwin and originally appeared in The Living Light, *which were the first teachings of the Living Light Philosophy published in book form. The entire text of* The Living Light *was republished in* The Living Light Dialogue, Volume 1.*]*

"Think, children. Think more often and think more deeply."

The teachings in this book were given as a progressive series of lessons to a group of four students who were sitting for spiritual unfoldment with me beginning in January of 1964. The communications were regular until October of that year, when nearly a seven-year silence ensued, and resumed in 1971 to the present. They were received in three ways by me as a channel. The main text was taped from a direct control of my voice in deep trance at special sittings of our group, during which I had no experience of the voice or what was being transmitted. A few scattered verses were given independently when I was privileged to see and hear our teacher clairvoyantly. I have also been a channel for this communicant when speaking from the podium at church and in answering difficult questions at our public seminars.

Nearly all we know about our teacher is contained in the lectures. He reports that he had tried for sixteen years to break through an interference barrier that the channel had to deep trance. When our conditions were in resonance with his patient wisdom, he came through ready to teach his understanding. I have seen him as an old man dressed in white with long flowing white hair. He has blue eyes, slightly smiling and deeply compassionate. I have always called him the Old Man. The students liked to call him the Wise One. He is surely one of those often called a Teacher of Light. I do not know his country, although he indicated at one time that he was from 6000 B.C., and a form of a judge in his time.

The text is often difficult, but it is complete, having been transcribed word for word from the original tapes recording the trance voice. It is presented with a minimum of punctuation to be freer for the individual interpretation of each reader. The lessons given before the long silence are phrased with many allegories often paradoxical. There are repetitions and renewals of theme, but it is explained that if an understanding is not perceived, compassion dictates that it be said again. Some of the topics have but a simple mention with little development but all are revealed, we are told, according to merit.

The Old Man is a fine teacher. He has in a hundred ways intertwined his allegory, progressive explanations, unfolding exercises, and timely references to reach a multitude of levels of individual understanding. A notable change is his more direct style of presentation beginning in 1971.

There is an endearing intimacy of person that can be felt through his lectures, a meaningful and loving encounter with a wise friend. Like an old man, he makes a mistake and conscientiously corrects himself a few paragraphs later. He listens often and carefully to our earnest discussions of his words. He consults with a group of experts on evolution and cites their learning in his lesson. His use of the direct address "children" or "my children" is not patronizing but infinitely loving and supportive.

A word must be said about the teachings. The Old Man makes clear that his lessons are not dogma, a creed or a narrow way, but simply his own understanding offered to us as a form of instruction to aid us in our own individual progression. When he speaks of Laws, he does not refer to man-made rules or moral traditions but to the cosmic and atomic way-things-are, the natural world of what-is, the universal laws of life, part of the original creative design and through which creation is fulfilled. These laws are beyond the possibility of being changed, suspended, transcended, or destroyed but they are ever a tool of mankind, not his master. First, through our awareness of the universal laws and then slowly through our developed understanding, the powers of creation are accessible to us. Not power over men's minds or circumstances, but power over whatever is selfish and imperfect in ourselves is the way up the eternal ladder of progression. When the Old Man cautions us concerning the Law of Responsibility or gives us a thinking exercise to explore the Law of Identity in a dynamic manner, he prepares us to take another step. And all move in accordance with the Law of What Can Be Borne.

Our teacher shows us how the two worlds are drawn together. In his realm, he describes, there is a great diversity of thought, many schools of understanding; but the Light is always known by the Light. Because of the interdependence of the two realms, listening to our discussions helped to clarify his teaching to others on his side of the curtain. His love and gratitude he humbly equates with ours.

The lessons to be perceived are not new, they are very old, but they are new to certain levels of our being. I would personally advise the reader, after reading this volume of discourses in full, to make a daily habit (or when there is a feeling or need) to sit quietly with the book. Open it at random and be guided to the Light by the passage that is there for the day. This technique is still used by the original students who were given the lessons and by many students after them who have studied in unfolding classes with me through these teachings.

Go beyond the words into feeling, into the immediate meanings for you. Touch into the inspiration that flows into the form of this book. It is from the Divine.

RICHARD P. GOODWIN
San Geronimo, California
June, 1972

Annual World Forecasts

Fourth Annual World Forecast

[This transcription was located in the Serenity files and appears to have been created from the notes of one or more students who attended this forecast. Unlike the previously published classes of the Living Light Philosophy, which were transcribed word for word from an audio or video recordings, no recording of this forecast has been located. The text below has been reformatted for this publication and is different from the original document in regard to slight changes in punctuation and spelling; the words, however, have not been changed.]

Good evening, friends.

It is our pleasure to bring to you the astrological and psychological effects of 1968. We should like to begin first with your United States. Your leader and President Johnson is under great strain, mentally and physically. Towards fall there will be a weakening and a visit to the hospital.

Vietnam: We see 1968 talks over a table, but no concrete or factual accomplishments. Sweden will bring about understanding to some degree, but it will receive no recognition for her efforts, but the spiritual reward will be great.

Asia: No end to the Asian situation; there will be strong conflict in Laos before the end of February. We see a great influx of troops into North Vietnam by the Chinese regulars. The Chinese regulars will take the fore in Vietnam.

United States: through the month of August will be prosperous on Wall Street. Changes from the top in Tidewater Oil. Will be much concern in June, there will be stability later in the year. We are very pleased about the mayor of San Francisco. He will accomplish much good for the poor and depressed areas and gain more federal support for San Francisco.

Gulf Coast: Great storm and destruction, but not catastrophe. More colored people will be brought into political positions. Fire in Los Angeles in the dry season. One of the greatest. The situation of war continues; it is to the best interest of country's financial positions. A great star from your theater will take her flight at the end of this year.

France: de Gaulle will have physical relapse about April. We do not see his transition in spite of his 77 years. We do see him taking his flight though mid-time of 1969.

U.S.S.R.: Scientific achievement startling and shocking before 1970. Great space achievement early part of 1969.

In the mystic country of India: It is often said before things get better, they often get worse. Famine will increase and will continue for another fourteen to fifteen months.

United States: We see no great rise in conflicts and riots this year. *[(He apologized for jumping around but he was reading from the* Book of Cause.*)]*

Sterling: It is not shaven sufficiently, there will be a rounding even more.

Finland: Great diplomat—one of the greatest the world has ever known is coming from this small country. He is a young man now and will become known to us in 12 more of your Earth years before you are aware of his influence.

The eagle will shake the Russian bear. These two countries, the U.S. and Russia, will come to terms as there is greater scientific advancement.

Russia and China: There is a split and distrust and a very deep division in ideology.

South America—Cuba: There is a great and strong desire of advisors of Fidel Castro concerning consideration for renewal of friendship with the United States. Tourism being felt out by friends of Cuba. Cuba is badly in need of dollars; rationing continues to exist. Because of the financial dependence of the past with the U.S. she is not able to adjust to another country financially. We see tourism within the next one and one-half to two years.

Agriculture: Wonderful bumper crop. We see an end to the great waste that has been going on for years and years and years. There will be a new suggestion to the farm labor of California. Good for the state and workers.

Governor of California: counseled by advisors not to run for presidency. The door is closed for this term as the vibrations are wrong. We see the door open next election year. This governor will be president of the U.S. the term after this one. We see no change in the election parties. The Democratic Party is still the strongest; race close, we see a renewal of your president.

Alaska: Mountains slip and slide. Earthquake along coast, not disastrous or great.

Now we will go along the coast to the faults of California. In the 74th year the fault opens in California.

South America: Another country, Argentina, will fly the Red Star. Reds run the country. The Red Star will fly under cover. Strong communist influence among politicians and wealthy industrialists who actually run the country. There will be talk in 1968, but really will have control before the end of 1968. In truth they have control.

Canada, Montreal: Much controversy and conspiracy among theological and religious matters. Greater and greater number to leave the Roman Church. And they will go there for a haven.

Portugal: The hand of a great queen of ancient times is over Portugal. This great and beautiful spirit has her hand over her country. Not many know Portugal had a queen. Her hungry shall be fed and new interest in those with political control will feed her hungry. Great interest and compassion.

Transportation: The Midwest; serious wreck of trains. Planes—greater safety breakthrough required by government and will become law. Act of Congress will govern safety of transportation, especially airplanes. A new type of propulsion in airplanes will bring about a faster and faster airplane. Definitely a new propulsion, no sonic booms. Old birds being set aside. And entire mechanism will be set aside. This will not be finished in '68, but development is going on.

Space Program: One failure, one success, and one greater success for the U.S. in 1968.

We see a great star on opera stage take her flight. Her flight is quick and not lingering.

Medical field: glimmers of cancer cure, but only glimmers. The year of 1975—the cure will be a reality. The transplant of artificial organs will be most successful. Other physical transplants will be successful up to a week, month or year. *[(He talked about each human organ being individual to the human being and would never be fully successful but the artificial would be and that the great medical and scientific men knew of this and they were putting their energies to the completion of artificial transplants.)]*

Italy—Vatican: We do not see a relinquish of the ruling of birth control until the end of the present pope's reign. We see this pope's transition, despite his liver condition, in six more of your Earth years.

The spirit of President Roosevelt is close over Washington. The pioneers are close to the capitol to inspire the masses to reelect present president. We see a reelection of the present president. A change would reap very bad results. The Michigan man lacks stability, stamina, character, and foresight to lead the country.

Electronics: coming in the foreground. Will startle mankind. Will be great demand and growth and will make many mistakes, but will be of great service to the world in the next two decades.

Creation of life in labs: Man, in his laboratory, shall bring about the necessary conditions for the life spark, 1971-1972.

Germany: Bad spiritual vibrations and a renewed power and force stepping forth in militant form. It will need a strong foot on it within the next five years. The pioneers are worried.

We see one passing in the Kennedy family.

We hope the courageous among you will take advantage of the first six months of 1968, which will be prosperous and like the pairs of opposites it will bring about its opposite, for the next six months.

[(He would like to continue, but the energy was waning and bid us good night.)]

JANUARY 1, 1968

Seventh Annual World Forecast

Greetings, friends.

It is indeed our pleasure to bring to you, once again, forecasts of coming events.

We read from the Books of Cause and interpret to the best of our ability the effects which are forthcoming. This year of 1971 is a year of fulfillment and totality. It is the year of nine and once in each cycle it appears. This is a year in which all things that have been thought and not yet brought into manifestation, it would be most wise to gather them together and present them in the coming year of '72, which is a beginning or a one year of the cycle.

As we look over these Books of Cause, we find that, once again, the situation in Asia in Vietnam, as was said before, shall come to an ending in the year of '73. We find, in this year of '71, almost a completion of the discord in Asia.

However, as wars have ever been amongst you, discord and strife in this world of creation and duality, we find the vibration going across the land. And new leaders with strong desires are once again rising across the land of Africa. We believe, from the vibrations set into motion, that a discord of momentous proportion will be coming forth within the coming four months.

We find that a greater stability, a greater prosperity is awakening for the country of the United States. Regardless of the prophets of doom, who are ever amongst you and have ever been, we see a greater and more prosperous vibration in this year of '71, especially after we pass the May month.

On the political scene, we find the passing of two people in high office in Washington before this year ends.

There is political and financial strife and disaster in the cancer research foundation. There have been, for the past seven years, a great deal of political vibration concerning it. This will be revealed to you before September time of this year.

Floods are welling across the Midwest as we end the year of '71.

A new law is about to be revealed concerning the drilling of oil off the California coast. There is a new seepage in the southern parts of the state, and it will be necessary for these new laws to be enforced within the coming eighteen months.

Another passing is revealed in the Roman Church. We touch the August time of the year. It is another personage of high position.

We do not wish to read to you only the seeming disasters and catastrophes, but I am sure that you realize, in creation, it is the balancing forces in nature.

We find as we go across the waters, a large ship—disaster, but many lives will be saved.

One, two, and three shall be the crashes concerned with the transportation of the air, that is, in the United States.

A wonderful breakthrough has come forth in regards to the so-called heart transplants. As we have said before, the transplants will never be successful unless they perfect the artificial hearts. We are so happy to read from these books that this artificial heart is very close to completion and perfection. And in the year of '72, the first one will be functioning in a human body. For that we are so very grateful.

This year of '71 reveals more strife concerning labor. So-called riots along the campuses, as was stated, have ceased and little more shall be heard from them. But in this year, there will be more discord and more difficulties in regards to labor and management.

[After a long pause, Mr. Goodwin speaks in his own voice. In the early classes, when the teacher spoke through Mr. Goodwin's physical form, the teacher's voice was noticeably different.]

I'm terribly sorry. Something's broke the trance. Turn on a light, please.

Not in this room, please.

I'm very sorry, friends. I don't know what's happened, but something has broke[n] my vibration.

[The recording ends].

DECEMBER 1970

Eighth Annual World Forecast

[The Serenity Spiritualist Church held its first service in the American Legion log cabin in San Anselmo, California, on May 2, 1971. While previous forecasts were given in different locations, typically, a student's home, this forecast was given as part of Serenity's devotional services.]

Greetings, friends.

It is again our privilege to bring forth to you the forecast for the coming year of 1972. We are privileged to read from this so-called Book of Cause. And in this coming year, it is the beginning of the nine cycle. Being a one year, it behooves all to consider wisely their beginnings in this coming year.

And the first of the pages that we read reveal, once again, the ending of the Vietnam situation in the year of '73. The situation in Asia will reveal many errors, in '72, on the part of the United States. However, from Washington in this coming year, there will be greater understanding and arrangements are already in process to smooth the troubled waters before the July month of '72.

We find a renewal and a continuity of the chief in your White House.

There is much concern regarding the currency of the United States, and we are pleased to reveal that within the coming six years the so-called dollar will balance out in a very stable vibration, the most stable that it has been in the past seventeen years. However, in regards to the financial market, the franc is wavering and will have to go through great changes within the coming five years.

We find quakes in the year of '72, greater ones in the year of '75. But be not disturbed, my good friends, for they are coming forth along about the October time in lower California. There is no need or concern to move from your present residence. The so-called disaster of earthquakes, you will not view in your lifetime. We are pleased to see that the scientists of your world are on the very verge of a breakthrough in the controlling of so-called earthquakes.

In regards to the heart transplant, it has been our view, from this Book of Causes, that success will be attained with the artificial transplant. We see that coming much closer to fruition than many realize.

The cure for cancer is dawning on the horizons, but is, as yet, a few years off.

On the political horizon, we see great changes in England and in Russia. As the door has opened to Red China and the world scene and in the United Nations, new changes, all for the better, are coming forth. As the Russian Bear and the eagle are drawn closer together than ever before, as they view, what they believe, a common enemy.

Floods come about along the Midwest; they are upon us. A critical shipwreck before the month of June.

The concerns over so-called depressions are without solid foundation. So-called Wall Street continues to hold its own and it shall be its brightest as we touch the November month of the coming year.

It is so interesting to read the many inventions that are sifting, so to speak, into your dimension. This so-called electronic feedback that so many are becoming interested in, in their search for truth, is but a beginning, a breakthrough into the psychic dimension. On the horizon is a new electronic instrument that will reveal to man the vibration or color of his thought at any given moment. Not only will it reveal the color but it also will reveal the sound. These instruments will serve their purpose as man seeks to free himself from the bondage of superstitious so-called religions.

Strikes reveal themselves in the southern part of England. Continued turmoil in Ireland and martial law, stronger than ever before, will become necessary before the May month of '74.

On the lines of transportation, we see a great change in an automobile known as the Volkswagen. Some time ago we read from this book that that automobile would bring forth the automatic shift. Few believed it. Today we realize it. Already the leaders of that company have been inspired that style is more important than they have realized, and therefore within the very near future a new style, so-called very sporty, shall be forthcoming.

A new religion is dawning on the horizons of your world. No matter what they call it, that who leads man to truth, that is religion. And although the parapsychologists do not yet have the awakening of the true purpose of their profession, they shall be the new ministers, the new spiritual counselors of your so-called space age. We are indeed very pleased to view that, for it will free untold numbers from their bondage and their chains of superstition.

Another bumper crop in '73. And sad, but true to view: famine and starvation once again strikes that religious country of India.

We had read before and read once again: turmoil in Africa. All that appears is not true. It will last for approximately two years and will reveal itself within the coming six months.

From out of the East of the United States comes a new system, a revelation in the field of education. Though born under great struggle, it is the seed that will revolutionize the educational system of your United States.

Two passings in high office of the Roman Church before the end of your coming year.

A change in office at the White House, most unexpected.

Problems in Georgia and Alabama on the racial scene.

My good friends, it is not always pleasant to read from this book filled with so much strife and seeming disaster, but as long as your world continues to create it, we can only read to you those effects.

A new system whereby religions will find a common ground of expression as the need becomes greater, in your year of '76, for them to unite in order to survive.

A wonderful experience from two astronauts as they go to outer space. They will reveal the absolute fact of so-called disassociation or astral flight while in space. That will be revealed to you within the coming two years.

A new material soon to come on your market, which is not only without the need for so-called ironing but has no need to dry. It will be greatly soil-resistant. It has already been brought forth, but has not yet been released. We see that coming to you within four years.

And, my good friends, in closing, it is pleasing to note that the humble potato will become king in your so-called cosmetic field.

Thank you. Good day.

DECEMBER 26, 1971

Ninth Annual World Forecast

Greetings, friends.

Once again it is our pleasure to bring to you the forecast for the coming year of 1973. As we read from this Book of Causes, we find the world entering, according to its cycles, the year of duality, the year of creation.

As was spoken many years ago, we find in this year of '73 the ending of the situation in Asia, in Vietnam.

This is a very important year for the United States, for it is a year in which decisions of great magnitude will be brought forth concerning not only the United States but concerning the Asian policy and world policies. Though there has been much discord and disturbance over the past thirteen years concerning the involvement of the United States in the affairs of other countries, we find as we touch into the year of '75, from policies that are already established, a greater withdrawal of America in world affairs. This has been brought about under divine guidance. You will be fully aware of these policies in the year of '75.

As we leaf through this Book of Causes, we find that this seeming earthquake scare that seems to be ever amongst you should not be of great concern to any in the West Coast of the United States. Though we find a tremor in the April month of the coming year, we do not see at this time any catastrophes or great quakes in the northern part of the state. There is, however, a severe tremor along about the August month in the central part.

Some time ago we read from this Book [of Causes] concerning that so-called disease known as cancer. And as we read further, we find that your scientists are indeed much closer to its cure than ever before. Within the coming seven years, you shall indeed know of it.

Again, we speak of the disturbances in that country of Africa and the Middle East. Though you have heard little, if anything, concerning it, it is like a boiling pot. And as we touch into the year of 1976, we find this strife rise to the fore. Though England has been wise in withdrawing much of her support, it will be necessary for, yea, even a greater withdrawal within the coming two to three years.

As we go forward, we touch into that country of Germany and we find a great increase in production. Indeed, it shall rise to be the second most productive country in your world within the coming eleven years. The temporary split in that country between the East and the West is not a permanent thing, and there shall be a greater understanding, a new Germany within the coming seven and one-half years.

We go now to that country of France. And there we find, in the year of 1974, a political upheaval and a great change in the governmental structure of that country.

Back again to the United States. We see a great, new educational system for your country. It is coming from the East. The country of England is indeed far advanced, and this new type of education for your schools will be made manifest within the coming three to four years.

As we go forward and touch into the land of Japan, we see new trade agreements, new contracts, a greater unity, a greater sharing between that land and the European market, especially Germany.

We touch into Canada and we find most of the medical advancements are coming through the doctors and the scientists in that country, especially in the area of Montreal, though little is known about it at this time.

Reading once again concerning earthquakes, we go now to the country of Brazil. There we find tremors and quakes within the coming one and a half years—rather severe. Be of good cheer, my children, for already the solution to so-called earthquakes is on its way. The control of these quakes will be guaranteed in your world within the coming eight years. Science is advancing very rapidly in that area.

As we touch into outer space, we find, in the year of '73 and especially in the spring of '74, a great breakthrough, so to speak, in outer space. Man shall learn, within the coming twenty-two years, that he is not the only intelligence in all the universes. He shall know that beyond a shadow of any doubt within those coming years.

In reference to the financial market of your world, we see, as we read in the areas of Wall Street, a flux and flow in this year of '73, not a wise time for investment. But go forward to your year of '75. A great wave of prosperity is coming over the United States in that year; it will be the beginning of it. Be not concerned about the gold market. It is more stable than your prophets of doom would like you to believe.

Remember, my good friends, that in your earth realm fear has long been the ruler. Many a politician has used that force to control the masses. Remember that God has given you charge over all creation. If you entertain thoughts of discord and fear, you disturb Nature herself, for she responds to energy, and thought is expressed energy. So when you hear so much of disaster in your world, you may serve the Divine by counteracting that vibratory wave with the positive one of knowledge, of faith, and of truth.

Another passing in high office in the Roman Church.

Greater support, financial and otherwise, for the seeming new profession of parapsychology. Forty-one more universities will open their doors to its study and application.

A shipwreck on the Atlantic towards the fall time of your year of '73.

A new car from General Motors—extremely economical, extremely small—which will help stem the tide of the foreign imports. It will be on your market for '74—very reliable, very worthwhile.

India continues to struggle with her famine, for the centuries are long that she has been out of balance between the spiritual and the material.

A greater restriction imposed upon imports into the United States in the coming year. In turn, England, the British colonies will follow suit.

A new government organization to replace the so-called peace movement. One that will be activated and utilized within the United States for the benefit of its own people.

A world council of religions is already being formed in our realms, and it shall bring indeed a great peace and understanding to your world in the year of '87. That is the year that we foresee it will take place in your dimension. It is indeed worthwhile and merits your thought and any effort that you may feel inclined to give it. You will hear of it within the coming few years.

Thank you.

DECEMBER 31, 1972

Tenth Annual World Forecast

Thank you, Mr. Chairman. My good friends and members.

As our chairman has stated, this is our tenth year of forecasts. And in forecasting, we must realize that the spirit reads the projections that are created in the ethereal waves by the mass thinking and acceptance of the people of this earth realm. Now there is a difference between forecasting and predictions. And that difference it will behoove us to understand in listening to whatever the spirit has to forecast for these coming years. When a forecast is read from the Book of Causes, unless there is a mass change in the thinking of the people, then the event comes to pass.

I am sure that you all realize, if you have studied to any extent spiritual matters, that the importance of the thinking of the mind can never be underestimated. *[The teacher may have misspoken. He may have intended to say "overestimated," but it is also possible that he did not misspeak.]* And when you understand when we leave this physical realm, we do take it with us. We take all the mental things that we have accepted.

And, my friends, one of the most difficult things, from the world of spirit, is to give exact dates. Those who have passed to the realms of Light return to help us to the best of their abilities. They are no longer attached to this earth realm, but they are trying to help us on our evolutionary path.

I have been asked over the years, Of what true benefit is a world forecast? If we understand what the thinking, our thinking, is doing to the world, if we find the true cause of a thing, whether it be within our own universe or the universe of this planet or the planets themselves, then it is of benefit, for wherever the cause lies, the cure is waiting.

So if you will be patient for just a few moments, I will be most grateful if I am able to be receptive to my teacher, who comes at this time of year to give you the forecasting of events.

[After a short pause, during which Mr. Goodwin goes into a trance, the forecast begins.]

Greetings, friends.

In this coming year of 1974, it is a three year, a year of manifestation and revelation of the true causes of the turmoil which seem to beset your world at this time.

Of great interest, as we look in this Book of Causes, are the political and economical events in your United States. We read from this book in the year past that the coming of 1975 would usher into your country of America a new wave of prosperity. We also foresaw at that time that the year of 1973 would not be one of the better years in your financial and economic situation.

My good friends, the political events that are taking place at this time in America are not something that have been given recent birth, but are the direct effects of policies that have been established over the past twenty-two years. There appears to be such great interest in the minds of men, at this time, with the so-called energy crisis. We foresee in this Book of Causes that with the support and the help of those who have awakened to the power of thought that the June month will be a month of great relief and release from this so-called crisis, which in truth is serving a good and great purpose in your world. Although there is much talk concerning compulsory rationing, which is not in the best interest of the country, and we do not foresee, at this time, that it will be necessary or enforced. There is a relief from the crisis come the June month.

On the Washington scene, there is an ever-increasing and growing influence and importance of the man Kissinger. His future is a golden path and will be of great benefit to the United States. However, there is a need to put a few reins of reason on his sincere but uncontrolled enthusiasm.

As we go forward with your country into the year of '76, we find a great change in the policies of the United States concerning involvement in world political affairs. The lesson of Vietnam and Asia has indeed been well learned by those who have control in government circles at this time. Be not overly concerned with the country's economy. August and onward of '74 is an excellent time for wise and prudent investment.

The United Nations are presently in process of forming an international energy council. It will serve a good purpose and we believe, from the events projected, that it will be known to your world in the May month of '75.

A new, practical method of obtaining energy is already knocking at the door of the United States. One that is not only practical but extremely economical. There has been a great need within the country to exercise a bit of control and thrift. The resources have been used over the past twenty-five years without thought of concern for the future. That, fortunately, is beginning to change at this time.

In the State of New Jersey, there is a serious condition with the governor of that state. It will affect his health, as we view the coming four months.

Back to the Washington scene: we find this so-called scandal, known as Watergate, will come to a full investigation in the sense that the causes, the true causes, for it will be revealed within the coming five years. We do not foresee at this time nor in the foreseeable future a so-called impeachment of your president. Though many mistakes and errors have been made, it has not and is not the intent of your government to undermine its people, its country, and itself. There is a great need for the support and the good thoughts and efforts of all people, for this is indeed a very critical time for the United States. With the combined prayers and efforts of her people, you will experience a greater, a better, a newer, a rejuvenation of the country of America.

As we go across the waters to that country of England, there is indeed great struggle and strife for her people. Although the Labor Party has periodically gained much support, we find a great weakening with that party as we touch into the July month of the coming year.

Before we stated, in one of our forecasts, that political disturbances were attacking the country of France. That projection remains the same in this coming year.

As we go on into the Middle East, we see a continuation of periodic flare-ups, and a great need for the coming elections in Israel, a great need for thoughts and efforts for peace within its own country. As a relatively new political country, it has strong aggressive elements. This will be revealed to you along about the June month of this coming year. We do feel, however, that the overly aggressive elements in the political structure of the country will not be effective or in control in the new elections in that country. As we go on towards the early part of 1976, we do see a great peace reign over the Middle East and a better understanding.

However, our attention is now drawn into Africa, and there a continuation of unrest is coming to the fore as we go into the latter part, along [the] September month of 1974.

Such great interest has been with the efforts to find a cure for cancer. Within the coming few years, about three to four, this cure will come to your world. And man will realize that the frustrations and the disturbances that he permits his mind to experience are throwing the body, so to speak, into an imbalance known as discord and disease.

A greater acceptance in the medical profession in England and the United States and Canada of the therapeutic benefits, the health benefits of meditation and a silent and still mind. This will be accepted more in this coming year than ever before in the history of the medical associations.

A greater effort on the part of Canada in the scientific field of outer space. We find the country and her scientists coming into the limelight as we touch the latter part of '74 and the early part of 1975.

As we cross the waters eastward to the country of Japan, we find an economic revolution taking place within that country. However, after a shaky seven to eight weeks along about the springtime of '75, we find her economy brought back into balance.

As we look forward across the shores of China, we find a greater, a more understanding relationship with the Western world, namely the United States. China is very interested in establishing solid, profitable trade relations with the United States. Although there is yet difficulty on the political scene, trade will rise above the political differences and new trade agreements will be established with China for the benefit of all concerned.

A new vaccine for animals that will be an absolute preventative of rabies. This is indeed very good news and it shall come out of the country of England within the coming two years.

Science will find, as some already have, that chocolate is not in the best interest of people, of their health. We find that it has a detrimental effect upon the emotions. Try to understand, my friends, that the mind affects the body and the body affects the mind. This will come to the fore in a small way within the coming three years.

Be not concerned or filled with fear of the so-called earthquakes and prophets of doom that are ever amongst you. Although we find some tremors in that country of Argentina and Brazil, a few more tremors in the central part of California, we do not at this time foresee any great destruction of San Francisco or the cities of California. And besides, my good friends, the technology to prevent and control so-called earthquakes is here and now. It's only a matter of months, not of years.

As we touch along the religious scene of the countries of the world, we continue to read great changes: a breaking from the old patterns. New novelties, unfortunate to say, to enter some of the churches. A great need for uniting in thought of the one Light, of the one God.

Parapsychology is making great strides in this coming year of '74–'75 and especially 1976. We view, within the coming years, services in some of the Christian churches of the so-called gifts of the spirit. Some of the Christian churches already are trying to bring into their devotional, religious services spiritual healing and spiritual communication. Although it will be a great struggle for those advanced thinkers in the orthodox Christian churches, they cannot and will not stem the tide, for that that begins is that that ends. And that that began Christianity is returning to end it, to begin it again. We do see a great, a truly phenomenal change within the structure of Christianity.

Thank you, my good friends, and good day.

DECEMBER 30, 1973

Eleventh Annual World Forecast

Good morning, friends, and welcome to the world forecast for the year of 1975.

In this coming year of '75, there will be an ever-increasing influence of stability throughout the entire United States. We read from this Book of Causes and project the effects in your world, and we see as we touch into the July, latter part of the July month, the early part of August of the coming year, that a new wave of prosperity will come over the United States, although it appears at this time to be exactly the opposite. Your present president is under excellent counsel and advice; at this time and especially in the February month, new changes will be made in Washington which will cause this prosperity to come over your country.

As we look over the United States, we do not see, for the coming year, any need or do we see any enforcement of so-called gas rationing.

Although there has been, and continues to be, political disturbance within the Republican Party, your ex-President Nixon is considering writing papers which will reveal to the world one of the greatest political games ever given in Washington. It will be much more revealing than your Watergate scandal. We see these papers in book form within the coming eight years.

A series of storms in the State of Georgia. We see this along about the October of the coming year.

Now we pass through these pages and go over to Asia. There we see great increasing trade relations between Red China and the rest of the world, especially, especially the United States. An industrial giant is indeed rising in Asia. Her name is Japan. And though there will be a great political disturbance in the December month of '76, there will be a great challenge between Japan and Germany for the world's industrial trade.

We pass now into that forlorn country of India and there we see a continuation of starvation, and we see it projected for the next five years.

Greater demands will continue to be made upon the food supply of the United States. Although it seems that the United States is an industrial giant today, her position in industry will slowly but surely decrease as ever-increasing demands are made upon her food supply.

We touch into the country of Mexico; we see various talks; agreements being made between her and the United States in reference to her supply of crude oil. Regardless of what the papers may say, we do see a harmonious agreement in reference to her oil within the coming eight months.

As we touch into the medical profession of America, we see slow but sure changes taking place in the medical association within the coming four years—an ever-decreasing dispensation of medication and pills, an increase in treatment along the lines of therapy. Photography will play a great part in medicine within the coming sixteen months. The so-called Kirlian screen photography is already being used by some doctors in research. We find this to be a great boon to the diagnosing of many, many ill people.

We touch now across the ocean into the country of France. There we see a declining in her economic situation, more so than the United States has yet experienced. And although the seeming steps to depression are recession and inflation, we do not foresee that for the country of France at this time.

We go now to the Vatican in Rome and there we see the leader of that great religious movement facing the eternal Light within the coming three years.

As we return to the United States, we see five great plane accidents within the boundaries of America. We see a new, a revamping of the federal controls of airline travel. It is long, long,

long overdue and although many must suffer from these five coming disasters of planes, great good shall come from it.

Again, we touch into the medical profession and we see within the coming two to two and a half years, the dawn of hope and cure for so-called cancer.

As we touch along the political scene in America, we see a star rising over the present governor of the State of California, and we believe from what is projected on the ethereal waves that if he will listen to the good counsel that he is receiving at present, that he indeed will be a star presented for the presidency of your United States.

As we touch into Wall Street, we find, still, a prudent time, as we stated in the year past, for wise investment. But as we touch the April month of the coming year, stocks begin to steadily but surely increase. The present high prices of the gold market is not long lasting nor enduring. Although we do not see, so to speak, the bottom falling from the gold market, we do see a decrease in its sale.

Troubles continue to plague the Middle East, but a sure cure is on its way. Be of good cheer and be of great hope, for as we view the year of 1977, we see an agreement between the Arab countries and Israel, a lasting agreement and one that will indeed be upheld.

Efforts are presently being made to establish harmonious agreements and arrangements between the United States and the country of Cuba. Although there still remains a great deal of disagreement, we do see the renewal of the tourist trade in Cuba within the coming fourteen months.

Those interested in the political scene of the United States may take note that the man Wallace will not be in the presidency. It is not for us to say at this time who will, but you may look closely at the man Reagan.

We find that the vice president of the United States is not only greatly influencing certain decisions made by the president but the influence, although behind the scenes, is a good influence, a stable influence, and the best possible counselors and advisors have been brought to the White House to bring in, to usher in this new wave of prosperity.

In reference to the cost of food for Americans today, they can indeed do their part, as some are already doing, by a much more selective purchasing, which will, in turn, help to turn the tide and lower the cost of food in your country. We see beef prices coming down, down, down, down. You have not long to wait: 'long about the twenty-third day of the coming year in the month of January, the prices will come down and down, especially in the area of meat.

And now, my good friends, I would like to share with you the reason why we give these forecasts, these shadows of coming events. The spiritual reason for doing this is to help you, as individuals, to become aware of what your attitude, your thoughts are doing not only to your personal life but, as a combined thinking of the masses, what it is doing to your world. For whenever our divine right, which is known as our divine energy, is directed downward, we guarantee the continuity of a downward experience.

We see on the world market in reference to transportation and automobiles, we see a crisis already has manifested itself in the American automobile industry. The German car market, especially the new Volkswagen, and the Japanese car market, especially the Toyota and Honda, will skyrocket in sales within the coming four years. The reason that they will do that is because the world is becoming, especially America, more concerned, more thoughtful about waste. And so it is that the American industry will begin to perceive this before another three months pass in your world, and their new, truly new, truly economy cars will go into production and, therefore, will save the American automobile industry.

Be of good cheer, my friends, you will not experience a depression in your country. You will not even experience an increase [in a] so-called recession. And the inflation has reached the saturation point. When things are the worst, there's no place left for them to go but to get better. Thank you.

I believe that our chairman had some cards [of] questions. Are those your questions?

[Students and members of the congregation were invited to write questions regarding upcoming events and submit them in advance of the beginning of devotional services.]

Yes, sir. Would you like me to read them now, sir?

Please.

The first question is, Will the world in general become more spiritual in the near future?

If you will consider thirty-five years the near future, the answer is affirmative.

The next question: What is the nature of the phenomena which exists in the area known as the Bermuda Triangle causing the unexplained disappearance of ships and planes in that area?

In reference to that question, it is a very natural phenomenon. There is a magnetic pull in that area of your world, and it is a periodic magnetic pull. And therefore, the experiences of the planes and the ships are not something that is supernatural, but something that is very natural. And within the coming fifty years, your world will know of the natural causes for it.

Thank you. The next question is: Will psychology become spiritualized and gain wide acceptance among professionals? If so, when, how, and where will the movement have its real beginnings?

Thirty-five years in the country of England.

Thank you. Next question. Will chiropractic ever gain the broad acceptance that the practice of medicine now enjoys? Will there be significant advancements in chiropractic diagnosis and treatment in the near future?

There will be significant advancements within the field of the chiropractic care within the coming six years. Photography and the use of the Kirlian screen will enter the chiropractic field and be a great boon to it. The reason for its struggle in your world, that is, the medical care known as chiropractic, is because of the dissension within its own movement, is because of its attitude of how the world looks at it. When the chiropractic association of the world stops blaming the medical profession for the position that it finds itself in and declares the great truth that nothing happens to us that is not caused by us, then the chiropractic field will indeed be well recognized in your world.

Thank you. The next question is, Who will be our next president?

We reserve the right only to reveal indications in that respect in this year; however, the star still rises over the California governor.

Thank you, sir. Next question. Will democracy in the United States return to a workable reality? And if not, what will replace it?

The truth of the matter is that democracy is already workable. Although you are experiencing what you choose to call inflation and recession, it is through its democratic policies, its democratic government, that the new wave of prosperity is coming to it in the year of '75.

Thank you, sir. Next question. An insight into the outcome of inflation, its relationship to Eurodollars, petrodollars, man-hours of labor, and gold and other basic value systems would be most appreciated.

Well, in reference to the true cause of inflation, my friends, whether we like it or not, the cause of inflation is only the people and their lack of self-control. When people, which compose a country, become so lacking in self-control, they start to experience what is commonly referred to as greed. Greed is the true cause, and the only cause, of inflation. As the country is now experiencing a new view to its values, we are not concerned with the petrodollars and etc., for they are only an effect of what the country as a whole, as a mass of people, are growing through. A greater self-control is coming into the consciousness of the American people, and through that the inflation recedes and prosperity comes to the country.

And so it is, my friends, each and every one of you within the sound of my voice can be the living demonstration and the instrument in breaking the back of inflation and recession by selective purchase, by exercising and demonstrating some degree of self-control. The cause of the problem is simply the lack, of the country, in self-control.

Thank you, sir. Next question. Is there going to be a depression? If so, when and how can we prepare ourselves for it?

The only depression that you will ever experience in the country of America is the depression of your own thoughts and your own attitudes. The country as a whole will not, I repeat, *will not* experience a depression in the year of '75, '76, '96, or 2006. A depression is not foreseeable and we are firm in our conviction that it will not, I repeat, it will not take place.

Thank you, sir. Next question. On a national level, will there be price controls on food and wages this coming year?

Although fascism in the guise of many things cares to rear its head in the country of America, price controls will not be enforced within the year of 1975. We do not see it within the coming years at all. There is no need for price control. There is no need for wage control, regardless of appearance.

Thank you, sir. Next question. Are the people of the United States gaining or losing in spiritual values?

They are gaining in spiritual values, as slowly but surely they are controlling material values.

Thank you. Are there aliens from other planets living among us on Earth?

If you consider a person an alien because you have not physically encountered them at some time during your life, in that respect, they are ever amongst us. Thank you, yes.

Thank you, sir. Next question. Will the seeming uncertainty throughout the world at this time bring us closer to a universal peace and brotherhood any time during the next twenty-five years? Or, instead, will the United States be embroiled in armed conflict with other nations or internal revolution?

There will be no internal revolution within the United States. There will be no world conflict for the United States to experience. There will be a wave of spirituality within the coming thirty-five years, a new united brotherhood for all people. Thank you.

Thank you, sir. Next question. Will we ever have peace on Earth and stop all wars?

Will we ever have peace on Earth and stop all wars? The only peace we will ever experience on Earth is the peace that we guarantee for our self, by expressing, applying a degree of self-control. Wars are ever in the world of the Earth, for there is always a war somewhere in creation. If you mean by "war," a world war, no, that is not foreseeable, but disagreement amongst people is everywhere. It is in the small family unit as well as in the large family unit, known as a country. And in that respect, you will always have disagreement. To what extent that disagreement will manifest itself will vary and therefore, to some, they will consider that a war; to others, they will not consider it a war. And in that respect, will so-called war ever be amongst the people of Earth.

Thank you, sir. The next question is, as Americans, we have grown accustomed to travel. With the present situation, should we try and avoid traveling, even when it seems essential to sanity and survival?

Travel should not be avoided except in certain areas of the world, namely in the first four months of the coming year in the Middle East. We do not recommend travel in that area. However, traveling will continue on throughout the world. And you need not be concerned about not being able to travel where you want to travel to because that will always be open for you.

Thank you, sir. The next question is, Will you please share some understanding regarding the spiritual, political, and economic future of Greece?

Revolution upon revolution upon revolution. Within the coming two years, there will be a new control in the government of Greece that will be able to grant it fifteen years of harmony and some degree of peace.

Thank you, sir. The next question is, Will the medical profession ever accept the understanding that all disease is caused by an imbalance in one's electromagnetic field?

Some few are already accepting that in the medical profession, but it will be many, many, many, many years before it becomes accepted by the entire medical association. And I can project at this time, from what we are viewing, a good thirty.

Thank you, sir. When will science make a breakthrough in proving the existence of life after death? What evidence will be presented?

The evidence that science, material science, has been looking for will never be presented, for it does not exist. The spirit, the spiritual body, is not composed of material substance. The day, however, will come when science will open its eyes to higher levels of consciousness in order that it may perceive spiritual substance or so-called Divine Energy or Light. When this happens and takes place, then science will declare the truth of spiritual communication, of life after so-called death, for they will be able to view the energy fields. And viewing the energy fields, they will be able to perceive the spirit. But what they are looking for at present is a material substance that does not exist in a spiritual body, and therefore it will be a number of years before they perceive the scientific fact of the continuity of so-called life.

Thank you, sir. The next question is, Are there still unexplored areas of medicine in which acupuncture can be used as a cure?

Acupuncture serves its purpose. It always has for many thousands and thousands of years. Acupuncture, my good friends, is like a pill, but it's not a pill. What it does is not remove the cause of the so-called disease. It simply redirects the energy into another channel. For example, if you have a pain in a part of your foot, by placing needles in a certain part of the anatomy, the sensation of the pain can and is removed, but the cause, that which caused the pain, is not removed. So therefore, acupuncture is not a cure. It is a medicine; it is a medication. It is used to redirect energy, but it does not cure, my friends.

Let us speak a moment on health. There is only one Intelligence in all the universes that grants us what we call health. When we, either consciously or subconsciously, transgress natural laws of flow, we experience what is called poor health. The cause exists within the depths of our own mind. We can go to an acupuncturist, to a chiropractor, to a medical doctor; he will work on the effect. The cause, my friends, does not exist outside of our head. And when we accept in our consciousness what the world calls God, when we accept an Intelligence that knows more than our brain, that Intelligence, flowing through our soul faculty of humility, will grant us the health that we are seeking, the health that is our divine right.

Go to that place of silence within your soul; there the greatest physician you will ever meet stands waiting to cure you of anything you call disease. Only at that silent sanctorium, at the altar of the greatest physician of all, when your head bows in humility, will your soul be freed and your body be cured. Thank you.

Thank you very much, sir. The next question is, Will psychic surgery ever be accepted by the American Medical Association?

Not within your lifetime.

Thank you, sir. The next question is, Is there a connection between John Kennedy's assassination, Robert Kennedy's assassination, Ted Kennedy at Chappaquiddick, and Watergate?

Not in the mental phraseology [in] which the question has been presented. Spiritually, there is. Mentally, physically, there is not. I repeat, there is not.

Thank you, sir. The next question is, Will there be a lasting peace in the Middle East by the end of 1975?

No.

Thank you, sir. When will the cancer cure materialize? And is it possible to foretell in what form the cure will be?

It will materialize within the coming few years. And the cure that we see is a type of medication—if you can call it a cure. And in that sense, that people will be free from the effects of cancer, in that sense, you may call it a cure.

However, the cause of cancer, the cause of all disease, the cause of all problems, the cause of all things, is in the depths of our consciousness. And there is where man must search for his health and search for his freedom.

Many, many, many centuries ago on your planet, the physician was a priest. He not only worked on your physical and mental body, he worked with you spiritually, with your soul. And so it is when this new wave of parapsychologists come[s] over your world in the coming years, they will work with you mentally, physically, and spiritually, because an effect, an experience, is a result of three levels of consciousness, not one level of consciousness. And so you must work to heal the physical body, which is the effect of the mental body, and the mental body, which is the effect of this spiritual body. Thank you.

Thank you, sir. The next question is, In one of the recent Serenity spiritual awareness classes, it was stated that a new understanding of the use of temperature would emerge in the field of medicine and this would be used in better treating illness. Can you please elaborate on this subject?

Well, in reference to temperature and its therapeutic benefits for the health of an individual, there is a great deal of research that has been taking place over this past three years in the medical profession, though you may not yet have heard about it. And it is a known fact that when the body temperature is lowered, that so-called disease and germs do not multiply as rapidly as they do when the body temperature is increased. Therefore, the research that is being done is recognizing that.

Now, my friends, let us go beyond putting ourselves into deep freeze or something else. Let us go to the cause. Certain attitudes of mind, which are the effects of thoughts, cause an increase in our body temperature. This is scientifically demonstrable. And so it is to keep a cool mind and a healthy body. If you entertain thoughts of fear, if you entertain thoughts of frustration, if you entertain thoughts that you're not getting things that you want to be getting, you increase your body temperature. And by increasing your body temperature, whatever germs or problems that you may have, they start to rapidly grow. You see, my friends, it's like a plant. You put it in a hothouse and you increase its growth cycle. You put it out in the cold and you decrease it. Thank you.

DECEMBER 29, 1974

Twelfth Annual World Forecast

As our chairman has explained to you, this is our twelfth forecast. And prior to giving way to the forecasting for the coming year, I would like to remind all of those present that a forecast is not the same as a prediction. A forecast is a viewing of the laws of causes, viewing them and their effects upon this our Earth world. So if we'll be patient for just a few moments, please.

[After a short pause, during which Mr. Goodwin goes into a trance, the forecast begins.]

Good morning, friends, and welcome to our annual forecast.

As we look over this Book of Causes, we find ourselves here in the United States of America and we see the political situation of your country. Though seemingly disturbed at the White House, it is smoothing out in this coming year. We have read in this book last year that a star was rising over Mr. Reagan, and if he continued on with the vibrations established at that time, there would be an excellent chance of his being the new president of the United States. However, we find, as we once again view these causes, that new laws are being established within his consciousness; those laws being the laws of overconfidence. And so as we view in the year of '76, we see along toward the end of the February and early part of March of the coming year that this rising star will burst, and in so doing, a renewal of your present President, Mr. Ford, is well assured.

However, ever in keeping with the laws that man alone establishes, the political situation shall not deteriorate for the United States, but a continuing and seemingly unseen wave of prosperity will continue to manifest itself in the coming year.

Be not overly concerned in reference to the diplomatic situations being established by your State Department, for as we stated before, the reins would and must be put on your man Kissinger. And so those laws have been established.

And the greatest interest in the coming year, especially along the April time, will be that boiling pot in Africa that was mentioned to you a few years ago. We see it erupt along about that time, but for a short period of almost six months, and then it will settle down as all things that rise are destined to fall.

As we look across the country of the United States, we find ourselves in the State of California, and there, laws established by your Governor Brown, though seeming drastic, will not reap an unbeneficial harvest, for these laws that Mr. Brown is establishing are in the best interest of the whole for the good of the State of California. Though seemingly drastic in reference to the police and fire departments of the cities, there will not be this seeming prophesied disturbance concerning the measures that are now in process.

We now go on into the city of San Francisco and there we find a great upheaval about to rise as the new mayor takes hold in office, for the enthusiasm generated for the laws of change for that city are not in the best interest in the way that he will try to present them. Therefore, his first two years in office will be rocky, but the city indeed will survive and learn great lessons concerning its political structure. And though seemingly small changes concerning the political structure of the city, those changes will bring about a greater interest in the public for those who govern their city.

And now we return again to the capital of the United States, to Washington. There we find the man Rockefeller ready, willing, and able to bow peacefully and quietly from the political scene as soon as possible. We believe, from what we view, that that will take place as he finishes the work that he has gone to Washington to do. He has been, though behind the scenes, a great asset to the country.

And speaking of Mr. Rockefeller, we now go into the city of New York. There, due to the corruption of the politics, the greed of the politicians in charge of the city, we find that her bankruptcy condition will continue, *will continue* to deteriorate. Although the government has made many corrective measures and steps in order to protect, financially, the city of New York, the city will not completely collapse, but the interest of the politicians who are now in charge is not an interest for bringing about a balance in the financial structure of the city. Therefore, by late November of the coming year of '76, corrective measures will be instigated by the government in reference to the financial situation in New York City.

We leave the city of New York and the United States and go on to the Middle East. There, the waters are calming more than ever before. The hand will shake from Israel to the Arab countries; the seeming impossible will take place. It will take place because there is no other way than for a friendship to be established, for the countries involved know that there is no better way. Though the seeming appearances continue to be a bit disturbing, there is a unity, a compromise, being well established and founded in that area of the world.

We now go over to Japan and the countries that surround her. As the ever-growing industrial giant, she has the growing pains of too rapid a birth. And so it is that her economy is far from balanced; that her economy will, within the coming three years, bring about some degree of balance. However, she continues to send so much of her production work to the countries that surround her, and this will prove, as it already has to some in her government, that that is not in the best interest of her own economy.

And now we return to the United States, and we see that the disturbances concerning Mexico and the Zionist movement will continue to rise as it has never risen before. Although you can be assured that those in authority of the Mexican government will make their polite apologies, the condition has risen far, far out of hand, and measures, already planned, will be enforced. However, out of the mud of Earth grows the lotus of heaven. And so lessons needed to be learned by the government of Mexico and lessons needed to be learned by the world Zionist movement shall indeed be learned and both shall benefit, in truth. Although this will take approximately two years, it shall indeed be beneficial to all concerned.

We now leave and go on into the government of Cuba. There we find a little snag that manifested in the year of '75 in reference to the tourist agreement for American tourists to return to the streets of Havana. Although it is only a temporary [situation], this seeming breakdown in negotiations, we believe from what we view that the year of '76 shall see the first tourists on Havana soil in some time.

And now, my friends, in reference to Wall Street, we find, as we touch into the April month of the coming year of '76, we find a descent in the market, to rise as a rocket as we touch into the September-October time of the coming year. However, remember, my friends, a rocket rises only to fall again. And so as we view the conditions of Wall Street, we see a steady improvement; we see the fluctuations, especially along the April time and September.

And now we view the ever-expanding consciousness of the medical profession. There we find ever-increasing interest in the power of the mind and its effects upon so-called physical diseases. There we find your scientists working diligently in the medical field to understand the chemical changes brought about by so-called meditation. A new development in reference to the degree of these physical-chemical changes wrought from the stilling or meditation process is coming to the light as we touch into the July month of the coming year.

Be not concerned again in this coming year over so-called quakes, earthquakes, in the State of California or elsewhere within the United States. Peru has a disturbance in that respect of quakes, but we do not see it within the United States. We do view a long, cold winter in this coming year. We do not see great, heavy rains, but we do view quite a bit of cold for your United States.

The greatest need within the United States, and especially the State of California at this time, is your farmworkers. This is a time in your history, my good friends, when the imbalance in your business world, in your industries, the imbalance wrought by the injustices concerning the workers in the factories and different businesses, this is a time when all of this imbalance will be brought into divine justice, for the pendulum on the clock of time swings to the right and it swings to the left. And so you will find in this coming year and the years yet to be stronger measures concerning so-called organized labor and the union empires that have been built. This will not be, *will not be* detrimental to you or to your country, but it will bring the pendulum into a neutrality where this wave of prosperity will increase and grow for the good of all concerned.

The religious movements of the world, ever seeking new ways and new things to bring in their converts, are coming about in so many different waves of entertainment and etc. Although it is a passing thing, it is bringing much disturbance to those worshippers who have become attached, so to speak, to the old ways of their churches.

Healing of a spiritual nature is gaining more respect, more interest in your world than ever before. So be of good cheer, my friends. Let the negative prophets have their way, for that is their right, but look for the good in life and the good in life will become your eternal destiny.

I believe there have been a few questions submitted.

[Members of the congregation were encouraged to write questions for the forecast and submit them to a director before devotional services began.]

Yes, sir. Are we ready at this time for more information on the Bermuda Triangle phenomena? Why are ships and planes disappearing and do they go into another dimension?

In reference to your question, do the ships disappearing over what you call the Bermuda Triangle, do they go into another dimension? They go to the bottom of the ocean. There they slowly but surely and gradually deteriorate. We have spoken before in reference to this so-called Bermuda Triangle. It is an experience in keeping with natural law. It is not something of a sensational nature where little men from outer space are capturing the planes and ships; it is a natural phenomen[on] in that particular place on your Earth—and that is not the only place—where there is a magnetic pull that takes place in keeping with laws that you do not yet understand. This magnetic pull that literally pulls these aeroplanes and ships to the bottom of the ocean is not something that is sufficiently strong enough on a continuing basis to cause every ship and every aeroplane to descend into the depths of the ocean. It is a periodic magnetic pull. And if a ship or an aeroplane is passing over that magnetic field when that field is sufficiently strong enough, that ship or aeroplane will descend. Thank you.

Thank you. What will be the extent of governmental action in saving endangered species?

The extent of governmental action in saving certain species of your planet, within the coming fifteen years, you will not recognize the laws and the strength and the power of those laws to protect the endangered species of your planet. Those laws already are being discussed in high office. They will be fully manifested within the coming ten to fifteen years.

Thank you. In the next several years, will there be any major breakthrough in improvements in automobiles?

Well, my friends, already on the drafting boards are improvements, but most of those improvements are what you call gimmicks. We are interested in what is called the electrical engine. Although there have been many problems with it, it will be, and is, the engine of the future. Its prototype is not yet fully developed or refined, but the automobile of the future will be an electrical automobile, and it will not have to use the various fuels that are now used by transportation and automobiles. It will be clean. It will be highly efficient and it will be extremely economical within the coming twelve years.

Thank you. How long will it take to finish the Alaskan pipeline?

We regret to inform you that due to political shenanigans not only in Alaska but in Washington the pipeline is being slowed down drastically. However, there will be, within the coming six to seven years, an exposure concerning those political shenanigans, and that exposure will bring about its completion.

Thank you. How did Amelia Earhart disappear? Is she still alive?

No, she has long been on our side of life. She lived where she landed. She was cared for and very ill, but she has long been with us.

Thank you. Who will be the next president of the United States?

We have already covered that question, I believe. The star is strongly shining over Mr. Ford. He will have new helpers with him, but sometimes the minds say it's hell if you do and it's hell if you don't, but he is the best that you've got in the bushel you now have. *[Many in the congregation laugh.]*

Thank you very much. That is all of my questions.

Thank you.

DECEMBER 28, 1975

Thirteenth Annual World Forecast

Greetings, friends, and welcome again to our annual forecast of coming events.

As we read from this book of life that gives indications and trends of things to come, we begin with the pages of your United States. As you enter into the year of '77, you will find an ever-increasing wave of prosperity; many new projects instigated for the public good and the public welfare. Do not be careless or foolhardy in this first initial wave of prosperity that shall reveal itself towards the latter part of the March month and early April of the coming year, for there will be a great increase in government spending under the new administration. However, the Law of Life is the Law of Balance. And though this initial wave of prosperity will bring with it much good not only to the United States but to several other countries, especially in the Far East, as secret agreements had been made in the prior administration for assistance in trade with Red China. You will find this coming to the fore in the latter part of the coming year.

Much shall be learned by your new president as he will realize in the first four months of the year that there can, in truth, only be one leader. And though his desire is to counsel with the many department heads of government and business, he will learn in those early four months that a ship can have but one captain.

However, after the initial wave of prosperity will come a balancing. There will be less union problems in the coming year than there has been in the past two, especially in the automobile industry. You will find another very economical, useful, and practical car coming from General Motors. We stated a few years ago that one would come, and you know today it has. The small-car market, which is ever increasing in the United States, shall be controlled by the United States car industry worldwide within the coming seven years.

There is no need for concern in reference to Wall Street: the normal flux and flow. A serious dip in the coming October month, but no disasters for the financial world. A very good time for investment along the July and, especially, August months.

Relations with the Middle East are going extremely well and the seeming crisis or shortage of oil will be of no future concern, or should not be, to the United States.

New developments in solar energy will reap a beautiful harvest within the coming twelve years.

And looking across the nation in reference to the weather conditions, we see great snows and blizzards in the Midwest and central United States. Some of the worst winters shall come in this year of '77. Looking across the land, especially in the State of California, we find a continued need for prayer and acceptance in reference to your great need for rain. Although there will be some, it will not be, in this year of '77, sufficient to bring back a balance to your dry state in this coming year. However, be of good cheer, for in the year of '78 there will be an overabundance of rain and water in California for all.

As all people entering a new venture must grow through the necessary seeming obstructions on their path, so it is with your man Carter in his new administration in Washington. And as we stated earlier, there can be but one leader, for too many cooks always, so to speak, spoil the soup. The lesson will be well learned. And before the year of '77 ends, there will be reins placed upon the impractical spending of [the] federal government.

We go now across the water to that country of England, who has suffered much in these past twenty-seven years. Slowly but surely the light is dawning upon the pound sterling, and within another three years the sterling pound shall be in balance and a greater security, greater trade—world trade—is coming to old England. And the many problems, financially especially, that she has had in these past few years will not plague her in the coming years.

We cross the continents and find a new, a new rising of power in Red China, not the power that you seem to think is there, but a new group of intelligent politicians are beginning to rise in that Far East country. And you will begin to see good, great good, come from Red China. Trade agreements that have already been made in secret will be revealed, but it will do much good for America and for some of the countries of Europe, namely England, Germany, and France.

Upheaval upon upheaval continues to be the shadow cast over South America. From Chile to the Caribbean there are political factions that will cause another topple of government power in Chile, Argentina, and, though not within [the] coming few years, a change in Cuba. We stated in one of our other forecasts that American tourists would once again walk the streets of Havana. This projection, in keeping with laws established, has not changed, and it will not be much longer before that will take place, for Cuba is in dire need of financial support and assistance; and her greatest asset has always been her tourist trade. And these arrangements, although temporarily bogged down this year of '76 in Washington, shall be renewed and reopened along about the June month of the coming year.

A calm is descending over the Middle East throughout Israel and the Arab countries. A great conference concerning Israel and the Arab countries will take place along about the September-October month[s] of '77. The United States and Canada shall participate in that meeting and peace shall reign for many years to come in the Middle East.

The boiling pot of Africa is not settled, and there we find, especially in Rhodesia, one change of leadership after another. A United States of Africa is what is being formulated by well-meaning people in Africa in high positions. It shall not manifest itself in the few years to come, for much turmoil and stress shall be first. But within the coming fifteen to twenty years, a new Africa shall emerge, and from it an abundance of mineral sources as the world has never before seen.

Moving along into space and so-called outer space, Russia shall make a great advancement in space shuttle travel, and by that word I mean the speed of travel of the rockets shall be so increased that it shall be known as a shuttle service from Earth to other planets.

As we look across this earth realm, we view a slow but ever-increasing spiritual awakening everywhere we view. So often we misunderstand what is known as spiritual awakening, for we view the discord and the disturbance, and do not look beyond it to see the awakening spirit rise from the mud of Earth itself. I wish to take this opportunity to encourage each and every soul within the sound of my voice, for your days ahead are brighter than you could yet imagine, for everything that is necessary is taking place to free you from any obstruction that is in your path. Look at your lives in gratitude for the opportunity that your soul has earned in its evolution, for each and every experience of the moment is a necessary ingredient for the freedom and the goodness that is awaiting you.

Begin your year with the divine principle of acceptance, and through that divine principle, ye shall rise to heavenly heights in the eternal moment of your consciousness. Accept the divine principle. Recognize and realize that each and every experience is guaranteeing your goodness and your eternal greatness. Do not permit the human mind, which is an instrument of dual, opposing creation, to dictate your joy. Free yourselves from the mind and awaken in the moment to the heaven that is in the eternal now. Do not place your heaven in the theories of tomorrow, for your heaven is in the moment of your acceptance. That is the promise of the eternal Light, known as God. And in so doing you shall know the happiness that each and every soul knows beyond a shadow of any doubt is their divine right.

I look forward to the evolution of each and every planet with the spirit of joy and the tears of happiness, for as man, his soul, enters Earth from a babe through maturity to adulthood, so does the flower that grows in the ground, so does the planet that grows in the heavens, for the Law of Change is divine law. Accept all changes in the spirit of true gratitude, and you will be free now, my children, not tomorrow. Foolhardy is the man who looks to freedom tomorrow as he holds to things that bind him today, for if the soul does not find its freedom in this the moment of its right, it shall not find it in some theory of life tomorrow.

This is the life that is yours. This is the life we have earned. Let us use it wisely, not abuse it. Do not permit your minds to flood your consciousness with need, for in so doing you deny your right. Do not look outside and say, "I desire and need that." Accept your right; you already have it. It is the curtain of delusion created by the error of ignorance of the human mind that dictates sorrow and struggle to man. It is this veil of delusion that tells you it's over there. Free yourselves, my good friends, from that veil for life is truly the kingdom of beauty and goodness.

Good day.

DECEMBER 26, 1976

Fourteenth Annual World Forecast

Greetings, friends.

In this the coming year of 1978, a year of the seven, a year of understanding. Some time ago in our forecasting we spoke to you in reference to the Mideast, to Israel, and that you would see in the forthcoming year negotiations of peace and harmony. And so it is that the dove of peace is flying not [only] over the Middle East but is also flying over the countries of Europe, of Asia, and, yea, even into South America and Africa. And so in this forthcoming year, be not concerned with the trials and the tribulations of the past years of wars and disturbances.

Though much concern has been over the so-called energy crisis in the United States, it is already before your Congress of your country and new rules and regulations governing the furtherance of solar energy shall be voted and passed upon within the coming two years.

Oil prices will hold at their present standard and within the forthcoming four years decrease, for there is difficulty and varying opinions of the oil suppliers and that will reap a good benefit for the world market in decreasing the prices of oil.

Although the eastern part of your country will bear even greater financial burdens with coal and gas heat, it shall level off within the coming three years.

In reference to the weather conditions across the country of the United States, new waves of rain and storms will flood the eastern coast. And particularly the State of California, which has suffered through a three-year drought period, will go above, in this coming year of '78, the normal rainfall. Be grateful, my good friends, for the crumbs of life, for they indeed bring to you the fullness of the loaf. And so it is there is a change in the patterns of the rainfalls in California and they shall return to the patterns of the late '30s and '40s. And so it is that, as I look forward in time, the minds of men, rarely satisfied, will complain there's too much rain, as they have complained there's not enough.

Prepare yourselves in the eastern and the midwestern part of the States for colder winters, more storms, more snow, and more rain. It will, as we stated last year at this time, be a very, very, very wet winter.

No need for Californians to be concerned over these fears of earthquakes, for we find a settlement in the geological strata and are not concerned about quakes in the coming twenty years. Though there will be a few tremors, you need have no fear, my good friends.

And so we move on in this Book of Causes and we look at the political situations in Washington, D.C. There we find your President Carter very, very busy, active, moving from person to person with so many different opinions and advices from so many different people. He is slowly but surely learning that in the final analysis he must take the fullness of the weight of responsibility for the prosperity and for the peace and the harmony of the country of which he is at present the president. And so, though fears are rising from his economic advisors in reference to the projected financial picture for the coming two years, there is no need to fear. The gold standard and the dollar bill is coming into a greater balance of adjustment than it has been in the last twelve years.

Activity in California along the San Francisco docks as new legislation will be passed by the city of San Francisco in order that it may participate more fully, economically, in the world market of shipping. Though things often move in political arenas indeed very slowly, you can be rest assured that they are moving surely for San Francisco. Though untold millions of dollars will be spent on their new waterfront, it shall reap an economical good that is badly needed for that city.

Onward we move along these pages and we view Detroit. There we find, begrudgingly, the American manufacturers of automobiles making, slowly but surely, the changes that are necessary in order to compete with the world automotive markets. You may look forward to even smaller cars, more economical cars from General Motors. Ford manufacturers have great difficulty in making the changes that are necessary and will suffer severe economical penalties by those refusals to change. And those economical sufferings will take place within the coming five years.

We move onward now to the city of New York. And there we find, viewing Wall Street and the stock market, the so-called nip-and-tuck vibrations of stock from January, up slightly in February, way down in March, leveling in April, total changes in May, balance and greater prosperity in June.

And you will see, in the larger cities of your country of the United States, more and more female mayors of towns. It is a good sign because so often one complains, from lack of understanding, why the politicians don't do a better job with your cities. And so it is, my good students, as more and more women become mayors of your cities—and rejoice, for long ago we forecast that you would indeed have a woman president. But the lessons that are being learned in these coming years from these women mayors of cities is that it is nice and it is pretty to beautify the city, but first it is necessary to convince the taxpayers that the luxury and the expense is in their best interest. And so you will hear a great deal about cleaning up the cities of the United States within the coming three years.

In the medical field, we continue to view, from these causes set into motion, a cure for your so-called disease of cancer. For there [are] ever-increasing intellectual judgments of the causes of cancer: everything from toothpaste to toilet paper, so to speak, will be added to the list of causes of that so-called disease. And when the great intellects of your scientific field[s] and medical fields have totally polluted the universe with their judgments of the causes, they will pause and view the stupidity of blaming everything outside for a simple cause that exists inside. *[Several members of the congregation laugh.]*

Now, my good friends, for many years we have spoken to you on the cause of disease, which is the absence of ease. When you are at ease, you are in an attitude of mind of peace and harmony. And when you are not at ease, or united in your consciousness, for ease only comes as the effect of unity, then you experience so-called disease or illness. The true cause of that disease, cancer, will be revealed in the coming years by your medical profession as a disturbance, a discord of frustration that affects the fluids of the body. This will be indeed a difficult pill for those minds on Earth who have judged it is everything that man creates outside.

And so we now move on in a joyful spirit, viewing an abundant prosperity for the United States in spite of the fears and negativity of so many, many people.

Across the waters in Great Britain, we see a slow but sure recovery from their financial labor crises. And we move on to France, which, at this time, is like a lotus petal on a still pond: surely not moving backward, but not advancing forward very rapidly. Germany, a spirit of activity and industry, an even greater rising of the spirit of aggression, becoming the great competitor on the world market with Japan.

Food for the world has always been the cry of the hungry. Until man changes his thinking and accepts the fullness of life, which includes food, as his divine, eternal right, you shall have hunger amongst you.

Across the waters again to the Far East, to China, there, more talks, more negotiations which have been taking place, as we stated last year. New trade agreements with Red China, prospering not only Red China but the United States. Canada has, and continues to reap, a degree of prosperity from her agreements with that country.

Times are changing, my good friends, and the law dictates that necessity is the mother of invention. And so, falling hard are the prejudices of many people. And in the best interests of your United States are these new trade agreements being settled. You will hear more about them in the September month of the coming year.

And in speaking of agreements, we look now at the Canal Zone of the Panama Canal. Regardless of the trauma and the difficulty that has been created by misunderstanding and misinformation from Washington and Panama, the Carter plan concerning the Panama Canal *will* be approved and *will* go through. The microscopic changes prior to that completion are so microscopic they have no effect on the original plan.

Cuba is rising. American dollars within the coming three years will flood into Havana. The gambling casinos of Cuba will look like Christmas trees as changes already have taken place.

In a world of creation, there are always those who accept and those who reject. And so it is that New York will experience, in the coming four months of the new year, more labor problems than it has had in the past twenty years. That will have an effect not only upon New York, whose financial situation for its city is not as good as they would like to have it be known that it is. Although government advisors have instructed them in how to handle the city finances, those politicians in control of that area are, needless to say, a bit stubborn. For to fully put into practice the advice of government officials who are trying to save that city would mean the graft that has been going on for so many years underground would be totally exposed. And so it is that you will see New York in the headlines again, concerning her money problems.

My good friends, accept this moment, in this fourteenth forecast, the essence, the very essence of the Law of Prosperity. As the son ever seeks to return to its father, so the dollar, when you stop chasing it, will start (the dollar) chasing you. Pause in your thinking; demonstrate that simple principle of prosperity. Stop thinking about money, and let it start doing the job that you have designed it to do. Do not chase it, for in so doing you establish the law and the delusion that you believe you don't have it. Stop chasing it and it will start chasing you. I speak to you, in this forecast, on that because, my good students, it is such an important thing in your material world. It is important paper because the thinking of men have made it so. When you declare the truth, you will start viewing: your importance far supersedes the importance of what you have in life created.

And so, my good students, look forward to a year of understanding, a year of prosperity, a year of abundant rain and cold, a year of goodness for each of you, for it will be, in keeping with the cycles of time, a year of understanding, a year to move forward in your business ventures, in your personal lives. Accept that all things in life have their season, and the season cannot be better than the year of '78. Opportunity, like the hands of a clock, strikes every so often. I can assure you from the vibratory waves in the atmosphere that opportunity is knocking. It is up to you to grasp it. Do not pass it by, for the cycle of seven comes, like the hands of the clock, but there are those waiting periods in between.

Step forward in this new year. Declare your right to the joy of life. Declare that right within your minds, for your mind is the vehicle that you and you alone can take control of. Control your mind and your life will be ever the joy that you choose it to be.

Good day.

DECEMBER 25, 1977

Fifteenth Annual World Forecast

Good morning, friends.

As we look forward into the year of 1979, you'll see that it is under the vibratory wave of the number eight, symbolic and meaningful that all things in this year that we face shall return unto themselves.

As we look across the United States and we see in this coming year ever-increasing floods in the winter of '79 along the Midwest and the Eastern Seaboard. In the weather conditions in the western part of the country, especially California, [there] will be an ever-increasing degree of rain in the years ahead.

The troubles and trials that have beset the United States in these past few years with the ever-increasing cost and inflation will come to a harmonious and abrupt stop as we go forward into the July month of the year of '82. However, there is no need to be overly concerned for, as we reach the September month of the coming year, new regulations will be instigated by the United States government, for inflation will, by that time, have reached its own saturation. There [are] no bleak storms of depression; a minor, a *minor* recession as we come into the summer of the coming year.

The situation, which was forecast in China some years ago here, is both a positive and a most negative vibration. For the country of China will rise as a very powerful, nuclear power in Asia. Therefore, it shall take great wisdom in the coming five years, great wisdom by the leaders of the United States in reference to her aid and supply in the fields of technology, for the giant who has slept for so long is beginning to awaken. However, on the positive side, the trade relations shall increase with the United States and Red China as never before in the history of your world. That will be instrumental, though indirectly, with a balance for the United States dollar. And the year of '82 will see much more prosperity for the United States.

A new government is in the birth and is forming in South Africa. It will take approximately ten years of your Earth time to realize the benefit of this new government, which will bring a greater freedom to the South African peoples.

Israel and the Middle East, though beset with problems and trials and tribulations, there shall be an agreement [that is] 90 percent beneficial not only for Egypt but for Israel. It shall take time, but before we pass into the December month of 1979, this agreement shall indeed be signed by both sides.

Along the political situation in the United States, we see a renewal of your present President Carter. Although there has been many, many growing pains, there has been much misunderstanding between the president and Congress, as a great power struggle, though subtle and seemingly under cover, is taking place between the Congress, the president, and the Senate. This shall, in the two years ahead, reap a beneficial harvest in many ways. And in keeping with the Law of Exposure that has been established over this past year in Washington, D. C., with the different scandals and the problems of employees of the government not properly handling the finances of the country, a greater scandal shall arise along about the May month. And it shall surprise not only the president and Washington, D. C., but it's very close to home what some of the employees within the very White House staff have been doing with the finances and misdirecting the funds.

Along the streets of New York, the famous Wall Street with its ups and downs, we see the barometer move as we enter the month of January: we see it go to its low, low, one of its lowest ebbs towards the latter part of the month, only to rise again to bring about a balance in [the] mid-time of March. And a wave, a shadow of recession along the May and April months.

Earthquakes are always predicted amongst you, especially in California. We see five minor ones in Southern California, along Palmdale, down through San Diego, but no major disasters in the foreseeable future.

Ever closer to that wonderful cure of the disease known as cancer is science, in your world, moving. Though not yet much publicized, there are doctors and scientists who have been working for years and are so close, so very close to the true cause of that disease. Therefore, you will find in the coming years more information in reference to the mind and how it is affecting the chemistry of the physical body. So much is misunderstood about health, for man does not yet understand the Law of Harmony. He has not yet thoroughly investigated the healing chemicals released in his body by harmonious thought and the poisonous chemicals released in his body by negative thought.

Russia and the United States will come closer and closer together in the years ahead. It is known as the Law of Survival. As China rises as a nuclear power in Asia, the hand of the Bear will stretch out to the Eagle. There will be agreements between the two countries, military agreements never before thought possible for the United States and Russia.

Problems along the border of Manchuria will increase, causing some conflict, but no major crises. This will take place along the October month of the coming year.

Great changes, necessary, born out of necessity, in the field of education in the schools in America. More demands placed upon qualified personnel to run the educational system. For many years, the past thirty years, there has been great waste of funds and effort. Too much time spent on what is known as liberty, but in truth has become license. Out of necessity the discipline of forty years ago will return into the educational system of the United States. Throughout all the schools and colleges, new educators are rising that know the benefit of discipline, that know for those who come to learn there must not only be guidelines but there must be some authority in order that they, as students, may move ahead, may educate themselves, and not only benefit themselves personally in life but benefit the society in which they are born.

The laws and the courts of your land, which have been greatly, greatly loosened, so to speak, in these latter years, will start to tighten up. There is great good, great benefit in the vibrations that are taking place in the judicial system of the United States. It will be for the good of all its people; it will be for the benefit not only of the country but of the entire world.

As we stated in our earlier forecast [in] years past, the United States will move more and more into the field of agriculture, for the United States, long known in history as the breadbasket of the world, will become even more so. Though it has grown to be quite a giant in industry and in the manufacture of goods, its true principle and its true benefit to all people is the agricultural system that it has developed over many years of trial and error. And through the Agricultural Department will the balance of the dollar and will its stability come about in these coming few years.

In reference to the politics of your State of California, we see no drastic changes at the state capitol or on the local levels. There is a sluggishness, a complacency that is growing; that is not beneficial, but also is not long enduring. The change of that sluggishness will take place within the coming two and a half years.

New agreements between France and England will bring greater stability to the sterling pound, greater stability in Europe. Germany, the great aggressive industrialist, will have greater competition than ever before with Japan. And as Red China rises with her industry, there will be a balance in Asia and in the world in reference to the Japanese industrial system.

Food and the constant increase [in price] is going to go through a great reversal as we enter the September month of

'79. Though prices soar until that month, there will be a turnaround, and a balance will be brought about for the many years ahead. Be not overly concerned, my friends, with the rising cost, for you shall rise with them until the balance comes about.

In the building fields, more and more apartment-type buildings, more and more so-called condominiums, and less and less and less private homes shall be built, for this is the way the building is headed in your United States. As the population continues to grow, as the demands of the people over the world continue to increase to enter the United States, the housing shortage increases accordingly.

Iran, the troubles that beset her, are the effect of twenty-some years of abuses. And although the present ruler of that country appears to have made agreements to step down, that is not his true intent. The true motive and intent is but temporarily to step down to set up a puppet government, but that is not what the Iranian people will accept. Therefore, continued riots and strife. A pause along the tenth day of the February month and more riots and more protests. And finally, with a great sigh of relief, as we enter the October month of '79, a new government. Great changes for Iran. Great lessons for the United States. She has learned, with great difficulty, not to be overly dependent upon foreign powers for her own financial success for the good of her own country.

A wave of isolationism rising within the United States to become more dependent upon herself. It is a good vibration that is being born and it will grow and benefit many, many people.

In your personal lives, look forward to the coming year. It offers to you a clear, unobstructed mirror, for it is the year of the eight, where all things return, as in cycles, unto themselves. Look at each experience objectively, peacefully, and calmly, that you may perceive the cause of all experience. And if you will look forward and make that daily effort in the coming year, you will set new laws for you into motion, and they will be beneficial and bring you a most abundant harvest of good.

In this, the cycle of eight, is that golden opportunity to demonstrate personally the greatest truth of all: the simple Law of Personal Responsibility. Take hold of those reins in this most opportune cycle that by so doing you may guide your ship of destiny into smoother waters, into the port of goodness, of abundance, of the prosperity of health, of happiness, and of wealth. If you will do that, you will not only have established new laws and experiences, you will have truly grown and perceived the lesson of life: the lesson that you came to the earth realm to perceive. In the midst of all of the seeming disasters that are around and about you, remember that your experience is dependent upon what you choose to do with your thought. Remember, my good friends, it's your thought. Therefore, you have, by that law, the divine right to choose what you do with it. And in this cycle that you face tomorrow and for a full year, choose your thought and choose it wisely, and all that you desire, you will see the law, personally for yourself, that will bring it to you.

I wish you a good day. I wish you a good year. And above all the wishes of the world, I wish you the total acceptance of personal responsibility that you may be free as never before.

Good day.

DECEMBER 31, 1978

Sixteenth Annual World Forecast

Greetings, friends. Welcome to our annual forecast.

As we share with you our understanding and our interpretation from the Book of Cause, as you enter the new year of 1980, you enter the year of totality, a year of nine, a year in which the unfulfilled and unfinished endeavors and activities could be best completed.

As we read from this Book of Cause and view the seeming turmoil and conditions in your world, we do not interpret without the light of hope and joy. As you face, and have been facing, this crisis in Iran, you will note on the sixty-third day of the hostages' captivity that a new light and a new vibration, positive, constructive, and good, will bring about the release of those souls. Some of those in control of the Iranian situation seek repentance from the United States, for in their understanding they have been gravely mistreated. Negotiations between the United States and the country of Iran, as they are presently known, will not be successful. However, we do view a change in policy in that respect on the part of the United States and on the part of Iran.

The involvement of the Union of Soviet Socialist Republics in Afghanistan is serving as a great benefit to the United States and what it is trying to accomplish in that area of your world, although it is not yet understood. By the time you enter the November month of '80, you will look with hindsight and in gratitude and see that it has indeed served a good and constructive purpose.

A new effort in the coming year by the month of June on the part of the Egyptian government to bring about a new unity with the Arab states. This will be 92 percent accomplished and successful.

Peace, as we stated in our last forecast, shall come to Israel and Egypt, and indeed a great bond of friendship between those two countries shall grow in the coming three years as never before in the history of your world.

Energy, inflation, the flux and flow of the United States dollar, those seeming disasters and prophets of doom are ever amongst you. You have been in a recession. Some people, some economists are aware of it; most of them are not. Yes, things will get a bit tighter economically, but there'll be no depression. There'll be no great, great recession. The dollar will rally before you reach the September month of the coming year. Energy and all of the problems it seems to bring is directing the leaders of your government to the various so-called synthetic fuels that are indispensable for the economic stability of the United States.

We have spoken to you before in reference to the agriculture of the United States, for it is through agriculture that America shall continue to grow and to prosper. So-called methane gas shall become most important within the coming four years. And the eyes of America shall turn, yea, even more to its wealth in agriculture; for industry, it has succeeded greatly in the world, but it is, has always been, will always be the so-called breadbasket of your world.

Peace in the Middle East by the end of the coming year. A great lesson is being perceived in the coming year by many souls. Those in charge of your government are well aware of the mousetrap that has been laid for them; to intervene strongly in a military way in the Middle East is what the giant Bear has been waiting for. Let wisdom, peace, and understanding prevail. Let pride bow to the great light of humility, for he who is willing to give shall receive without question. And so it is that the angels on high are on constant duty to encourage, to inspire that those in charge of your government may never forget, but never be so proud they cannot forgive.

As we go across the world, we look with great encouragement at the wonderful advances for the benefit of the people of

Egypt. The Palestinian situation will move from so-called hot, to warm, to cold. And regardless of the seeming predictions of the disaster prophets in your world, there will, *there will* be peace, peace in the Far East and peace in the Middle East. Peace in your world.

As we look over across the oceans, we find, by the April month of the coming year, a phenomenal increase in trade between China and the United States. You will move through this struggle of recession. You will brighten, not next Christmas, but by Easter of '81.

Japan, struggling with ever-increasing inflation, will make drastic changes, drastic changes in its political structure, for necessity is indeed the mother of invention. And it is already being discussed privately by the leaders of that country. You will be aware of some of those changes by the coming September.

Wall Street and its constant flux and flow will move into what we call a blue-ribbon state of consciousness by the month of May in the first week. What we mean by that is a secure and stable vibration, in the midst of turmoil, shall rise supreme during that month.

Medicine and the health of your world: more and more the medical profession is awakening to the great truth that nothing can affect the body that the mind has not first accepted. But remember, my friends, you come to your world with a mind, the effect of untold ages of evolution. And so you have certain tendencies to experience certain so-called diseases. It is not a working with the conscious mind; it is a working with the so-called subconscious and collective mind. But this understanding is growing each and every day and will be taught in your colleges and universities within the coming four years.

Politics in the United States: whether it's Carter or Kennedy will depend upon what action your present president takes in a situation involving the stability of your country in the October month of the coming year. At present the possibility of his reelection is 68 percent. October will reveal whether it shall move to 84 or drop to 36.

But remember, each time you encourage yourself, you encourage the world and your world becomes a better place in which to live.

Now in the field of science, so many new things in your world. Ever designed to make your life seemingly more simple, but unfortunately granting too much time for self-thought, for we all know from experience that self-thought is the most destructive. How well we feel when we think of something besides self.

No major earthquake in the coming year. Ever-increasing rainy weather in California, year after year after year. The coming months, great blizzards across the Middle West. Temperatures lower than ever before along the Eastern Seaboard. And so all of these things, all of these seeming storms of nature serve a wonderful purpose: that America may begin, *may begin* to face its great purpose in the world: to be the living demonstration of use, not abuse; to be the shining example of conservation that the generations yet to be may look at the pages of history in the spirit of gratitude that those who preceded them were so thoughtful, so kind, and so considerate.

As the American people slowly but surely and ofttimes begrudgingly move from the oil consciousness to the possibility consciousness, you'll be freed from being the victims of others. Increased oil production from South America is inevitable within the coming two years. But do not permit yourselves to become dependent, for man can only be a victim when he permits himself to be dependent.

Electronics, the pride of the United States, is at the doorway of crisis. We believe, however, that the United States government has enough wisdom and common sense to pour into that industry the necessary funds that it may remain the leader in your world, but time is running out. A decision must be made within the coming six months. We believe, we believe from the trend that it will be positive.

May the new year return to you the goodness that you think, for in your thinking shall be your act. And may it in so doing lift your consciousness to the possibility of all good, for all struggles and all crises shall pass ever in keeping with man's belief.

Good day.

DECEMBER 30, 1979

Seventeenth Annual World Forecast

Greetings, friends. Welcome to our annual forecast.

This year, being the year of one, the year of 1981 will reveal new vibrations, new events, and new endeavors not only for the world but for all people.

There has been, over this past six years, much concern over the economy of the United States. We do not foresee a depression. We do, however, foresee drastic changes in the economic policies of the United States that will take effect in the coming March month. Be not filled with fear, for there is a great need for changes not only in the domestic policies of the United States but in the international policies that have not and cannot work to the benefit of all people.

The new president and the new Cabinet entering in your new year will find, as they have already found, great difficulty in convincing the people they need to convince to make the necessary changes so that an abundant prosperity may return to the United States. However, be patient and of great faith, for we assure you, as we read the pages from this Book of Life, from the Law of Cause and Effect, that the year ahead, though offering fear to some and encouragement to others, will bring about the needed balance with trade for the United States. And as we read on, we find a great desire for friendship on the part of China, a great benefit and increase in trade agreements with China.

We also look across the land and we see a new beginning, a new start with the situation in Iran. A passing of the leader before the coming year ends. A change in their government's policy. A revolt in the northern part of the country. A stabilization in the Middle East. A wise man has been sent to that part of your world, a Mr. Kissinger. As long as the reins are kept to control him, then great good will come to your country.

A continuous upset in Israel, but not to the point of any war or any great disasters.

Stocks will balance out and stabilize by the first part of the April month. A good year for prudent and wise investments for long-term return. Remember, my friends, that we do not experience changes for the better in a country, a world, or personal life without paying the price first.

The American automobile industry is slowly but surely shrinking from outer appearances. Foreign investment within the businesses of the United States has been at a steady increase over the past fifteen years. It is entering into a dangerous, large portion of the American automobile industry, but shall not, *shall not* increase beyond the 42 percent limit of domestic balance.

No wars, [but] much turmoil in the world. A flame in central Africa growing and increasing; that will have a need for much diplomacy in the United Nations.

A balance in the financial problems and the inflation that has taken its toll in the country of Great Britain. New restrictions and limits placed upon the manufacturing of products in Japan.

As we go forward in time and we balance the budget in our personal lives, we will experience a much greater prosperity in the years ahead. Do not judge quickly the efforts of your new president. It is not his desire nor motivation to lead your country to war, but it is the wisdom of ages to stand firm on a policy of justice and good for all.

Much dissatisfaction and sadness in the civil rights movement of the United States. Much discouragement from a lack of understanding the priorities of the new administration.

The economic base of the United States must, for the survival and good of the country, go through a complete and drastic change. That will take place in the coming year. It will take approximately two years and ten months to reap the great benefit from this new economic base that will be established.

The Federal Reserve Bank will go through a very important change as one of its most important people is taken to the higher life. It is in keeping with saving the spiritual principle of America, for she has been ordained by the Divine herself to lead the world to a greater good, to a greater understanding, a greater abundance of the right for all.

Fear not the Bear of Russia, for when it knows its limits, and its limits are only known by being firm, but kind and understanding, it will not, *it will not* invade the country of Poland, for its own domestic problems have been increasing rapidly over the past two-and-one-half years.

Energy and the need to conserve. As methanol, the very energy source that will save the United States, is slowly but surely being accepted by those people in positions in your government to establish new policies of energy, methanol, not coal, not solar energy, not yet, not nuclear energy, but methanol, my good friends, will save the energy crisis.

Already we view various utility companies beginning to build plants for methanol production. Remember, rubbish is everywhere. It is a source of great energy. Whether it be the rubbish of material substance or the rubbish of mental substance, it can be transformed to accomplish great good. We encourage each and every one within the sound of our voice to encourage yourselves to encourage others that methanol will save the country. And as that slowly but surely is gaining in your country, the great need to be the victim of imported energy will decrease in the coming few years. Think not in terms of fifteen or twenty-five, my friends, for that is for those who lack the understanding of the great, the truly great inventiveness of America.

And now we look across and into South America. Do not become involved, do not become involved with imposing upon the world your standards of justice, your standards of right or wrong. A wise man cares for his own garden in his own backyard before caring for the gardens across the sea. Take care, my friends, of your home and in taking care of your home, you will become the light of the world. Take care of your country and then your country will light the path for those to follow. It is because of past errors of ignorance that the foreign policy of the United States has brought upon itself one disaster after another. The social programs will not, in the coming years ahead, be expanded in any way until the administration firmly establishes its new economic base, because, my friends, for any country or any administration to be the Santa Claus of giveaway programs, its budget cannot long endure.

[For] China, we see the light of reason, the light of joy. A great friendship will be established over the coming eight years. Great trade agreements bringing prosperity and friendship to the Far East and the United States.

Europe, the clouds of turmoil. Because Europe, still the countries are not united; even though they have the economic plans, they are not united in a single purpose. And therefore, as one country prospers, another goes in the opposite direction.

But Russia, with her ever-increasing need to care for her food shortages, to care for her energy problems, to care for the domestic turmoil and social upset of her people, Russia will be so busy in the years ahead she will not have the energy nor the interest to control the world. And that, my friends, is ever in keeping with the divine laws of natural balance.

Medical advancement is a continuous thing. And so it is good to view the cancer cure in just the years ahead. As the scientists slowly but surely reveal that it is an imbalance in the chemistry of the human body that is the true cause of disease and discord, so shall the multitudes benefit from these cures ahead.

The auto industry, of which we spoke but briefly, will be supported and sustained through its great crises of three years ahead by the American taxpayer. Not with a spirit of joy will he support the industry, but he will support it for his own good.

We do see an increase, not a decrease, but an increase in employment in the United States as we touch the latter part of the coming month of May. Remember, my friends, prosperity is the effect of an attitude of mind freed from the fallacy of judgment. And also, my good friends, be rest assured, hell only exists in past events. It cannot exist in future events. It can only exist in what has been. Heaven exists in future events, for it contains the light of hope. A wise man does not step back and forth from heaven to hell, but chooses the freedom of truth, which can only be expressed in the eternal moment of which we are consciously aware. So let us remember that prosperity is dependent upon the Law of Balance. Let us remember that for ourselves and then for those we love and for our countries.

And so this year and the coming four years ahead, filled with many changes, filled with innovation, most of them, given time, will work for your good. Be not quick to judge and you will reap the harvest of wise decision.

And so as a great tightening in respect to the habits of the American people takes place in those years ahead, so we shall all enjoy the goodness that waits for us. If we will take the necessary corrective measures of reason, if we will truly change our attitudes, then for us it shall be true.

Tremor upon tremor upon tremor in Southern California within the coming eight months. No great disasters, just the warnings of what's to come, not in my lifetime here through my channel nor in your lifetime there, but it shall come. It shall come, but we shall (you and my channel) be gone from this old mundane world.

Look ahead, my friends. There's where the light of hope lies for everyone. Be not concerned in what has gone. Be filled with the spirit of joy and acceptance of the good that is to come, for that is the way that lies ahead. And we are so grateful that the American people opened their eyes to see that a change had to be. For remember, many people have good intentions. Few are qualified to bring those good intentions into application in the

world. So when our good intentions balance our effort of application, we experience all the success we could possibly desire.
Good day.

DECEMBER 28, 1980

Eighteenth Annual World Forecast

Greetings, friends. Welcome to our 1982 world forecast.

The coming year, a year of two, a year of conflict and struggle and duality, will end a victory not only politically for the United States but economically. As the struggle increases through the end of the January month, February, especially March and April, May and June, by the twenty-sixth day of the July month of '82, we will slowly but surely begin to see the economic victory for the measures that have been taken by your present administration in Washington.

The conflict in the Middle East will flare four times in the coming year, but will not become a major crisis in the world.

The Russian Bear slowly but surely is being drained economically as her political aggressions continue to increase. Poland has, as we all know, a growing and ever-increasing rebellion in her country. It will go deeper and deeper and deeper underground and will split into two factions. There will be that known as Solidarity that will be truly controlled by the present Communist government and there will be that which is truly what they call Solidarity which will serve the motive of its true founding and go deeper underground.

This year, as your chairman has stated, we have made a bit of a change in our regular format, and I will be pleased to answer, to the best of my ability, the questions you have submitted. Please bear in mind the difference between forecasts and predictions. Forecasts are based upon the laws of cause and effect as we read here before us from this Book of Causes. And in keeping with the mass laws established shall indeed come to pass. You're free to ask your questions at this time.

Thank you. Will mass transit systems replace automobiles in the foreseeable future?

Not in the foreseeable future. And if you would understand (study) the politics of economics, you would know the reason why.

Thank you. Have we experienced the worst of the inflation and unemployment or is the worst yet to come?

Unemployment will have a marginal increase. Inflation will continue its slow but sure decrease as victory is at hand as we enter the latter part of the July month. It will be late in the year, the early part of November, when balance shall once again begin to be restored to the employment situation in your country.

Thank you. Will crime and violence continue to be a problem?

Crime and violence, called by man, shall ever be a problem to man until man awakens and demonstrates the divine Law of Personal Responsibility.

Thank you. Will America abandon nuclear power as [a] source of energy? And are more Three-Mile-Island type of experiences predicted?

America, in her present political-economic situation, will not abandon nuclear power immediately, but will gradually turn her sight, five years hence, to a much more practical and economic type of energy. In reference to Three Mile Island, no politician in office who values the office they hold will permit such a near disaster again.

Thank you. Are the United States constitutional protections and freedoms going to withstand the proposed constitutional convention?

My good friends, because the motivation of this so-called constitutional convention is contrary to the very principles of the original founding of the constitution, they shall not, for they cannot, change the freedoms that have been granted. Oh, they will try in their many subtle ways to make inroads, but fear not, for there is a greater power, there is a greater dedication from the angels on high who were the instruments in forming the constitution. They shall not let it be polluted.

Thank you. What changes are going to occur because of the expanding use and dependency of man upon the computer?

Man has, for the last thirty-five years of your Earth time, slowly but surely become more dependent upon creation for his good, for his supply, for his sustenance. He has become more and more dependent on what is outside that he may, in his judgment, feel better inside. Because of this ever-increasing dependence, you will find, as the centuries pass, that it will be less than difficult for man to do the normal, natural solving, so to speak, of problems in his everyday life. *[The teacher may have misspoken. He may have intended to say "more than difficult." Perhaps, however, he did not misspeak.]* This, of course, we know is but the effect of what you call laziness, the effect of mental laziness. We have, as a society and a civilization on Earth, permitted ourselves to become the victims of what we call convenience. And the payment of what we call convenience shall be very great. But your civilization shall survive.

Thank you. Will the inflated valuation of housing continue?

No, it will not continue. There will be indications within the coming two years of the deflation of housing. It shall never return to that that it was, of course. It shall never return to the years of the '50s and '60s, but it definitely and positively is on the down trend after the turn of two months of the coming year.

Thank you. Are banks and savings and loan associations going to experience problems similar to those of the depression era?

No, for they have taken every measure necessary that they shall not have that experience.

Thank you. Will the stock market be bearish or bullish in '82?

The stock market will feel its own youth, vigor, and growth after we touch the third day of the August month of the coming year.

Thank you. Are the environmental protectionists going to succeed in preserving open space, clean air, forests, and oceans from the threats of pollution and waste disposal?

If you call success the crumb of the loaf, then successful they will be.

Thank you. Are more hostage type of situations going to be instigated against America?

Attempted, but not successful.

Thank you. Would you please elaborate upon where mankind is headed with the changes that have and are occurring in traditional values of family, property, and education?

Man, as he pauses to think, can clearly see that moment by moment, day by day, month by month, and year by year life appears to become more mechanical, more robotical until the saturation of boredom becomes so great that he turns on the inward path to awaken his own spirit by stilling his own mind and making choices wisely and learning to act instead of react.

Thank you. Are visitors from outer space going to communicate with man?

Yes.

Thank you. Is there going to be a spiritual awakening for mankind as a whole?

Yes.

Thank you. Will the philosophy, religion, and science of Spiritualism experience a revival and be revitalized by the forthcoming satellite seances television series scheduled for '82?

In spite of all the judgments, in spite of all the negative publicity, in spite of all the fear, in spite all the hatred, in spite of all the ignorance, and in spite of the thoughts of man, they will serve as a crumb of light to open greater doors to bring a revival of the Divine Spirit to awaken man that he may know his God is the God that he worships, and worship is that which we, in our own consciousness, place ourselves dependent upon.

Thank you. Is the group called the "moral majority" going to be successful in their goal of protecting society from certain other groups, certain books, and practices?

No, they will not, for their motivation is the motive of all reformers, and they rise only to fall.

Thank you. Are we on the verge of the dawn of a new age, an age of closing the gap between science and religion?

We are on the verge, with a long ways to go.

Thank you. If it is true that extraterrestrial intelligence will prevent a nuclear holocaust, in what manner will that intervention be accomplished?

In the simplest of all manners. As the civilization of the planet Earth is yet to awaken, through the Law of Personal Responsibility, to initiate, in the light of reason, their own thought, because the civilization is yet to awaken to that divine birthright, the civilization continues to react to whatever predominant thought they have exposed their mental universe to. And because of that, we are easily manipulated, for we are the manipulators. And that that is the manipulator is in truth manipulated. And so it is they have nothing to be concerned about in the work they have to do.

Thank you. Is there going to be another war within the next twenty years for the United States?

Not the war of which you think and not the wars of which you know, but the greatest of all wars, the wars of economics, is the war America shall win. For she shall be victorious for the necessary laws in the universe are being established that she will win that great war for freedom's sake for the rights of all.

Thank you. Will our economy, such as public utilities and water, etc., eventually level out or are things going to keep rising?

Things always rise before they fall. They never fall before they rise. And so it is with your public utilities, it is necessary in order that the people may awaken. We do not awaken when we judge that all is well. We only make the effort to awaken when we are greatly inconvenienced.

Thank you. What is the responsibility, if any, of those nations that have merited great abundance to those nations who have merited other conditions?

To learn beyond a shadow of any doubt that all souls have the right, the divine right of expression; that man, in his evolution, is to help awaken not only, of course, within himself but within those who seem to be underprivileged that it is only an error in the thought of the mind; to help educate, for in educating the mind that it may see its errors, they may move into the abundant good, which is the birthright of all souls everywhere. Education is the true charity of life, for each soul has come not to be dependent upon the minds of men, but to be free to work, to live, and enjoy the abundant good of their birthright.

Thank you. Could you explain what sources of energy will be used in the future?

Methane gas, again and again, is one of the energies that is so economical and so accessible, yet you have to understand the politics of economics. But it will come. The day will dawn of a type of solar energy, but not the way you know. That is indeed in the horse-and-buggy stages, so to speak. But the day will dawn; it's going to take years. The electric cars will come. You see, that that has been discarded—the stone that was rejected shall once again return to be the cornerstone. The only reason your world does not have efficient electric cars is because of the untold millions of dollars that hold down the necessary research and development of what you call batteries. But that shall not forever endure. And within the coming seven years, you will see the economy of electric cars.

Thank you. What are the Friends' feelings in regard to artificial means of keeping humans alive with artificial organs, computer chips in our brains, extending our natural life spans, etc., and our rapid race into the computer age? How does one keep up with all this?

First, one must keep up with what they permit in their own mind before they can become qualified to keep up with what everyone else is putting into their mind. We must not deny the Law of Personal Responsibility and become the victims of what we call our destiny. Be not concerned with computer chips. They will flood your universe like a hailstorm. They will be from your toasters to your bed, from your pillows to your bathrooms. They will be everywhere. Until the day dawns and the light shines brightly in your consciousness that you may see how dependent you have permitted yourselves to become on things.

And the sadness, of course, [is] that which we depend upon becomes our master that we serve. If we depend on what you call a computer chip, then the computer chip becomes our god. And we have established the law by our own thinking: we have become so dependent upon our thoughts and experiences of the past, to lean upon in what we call the present and to be carried upon in what we call our future. And so, my friends, we have made it necessary in old creation to be the slave of computer chips and things, and it is necessary for our freedom, for our growth, for we know that we are freed in hell, but saved in heaven.

Thank you. What is a Spiritualist's responsibility to situations worldwide?

I cannot and would not speak for those who bear the name of Spiritualist, for many wear the banner of many religions. And each one understands their responsibility in keeping with what they are willing to give. If you wish me to share with you what I believe is my channel's responsibility, I will be happy to do that.

Thank you.

World events are the effects of what world we serve. And if the world we serve in our mental world is a world of contrary desires, of contradictions, and discord, then we are responsible for the vibratory wave that goes into the universe as a whole, for we are an inseparable unit of the whole and, therefore, affect, to some degree and extent, the whole itself. He who wishes to change the world must learn and wish to change himself, for the law is so clear that like attracts like in your world of creation and becomes the Law of Attachment. And when we are concerned about the world around us, our concern is ever equal to our attachment to it, ever in keeping and revealing that like attracts like. And so it is our world within our consciousness that must be worked upon. If we are not happy with the world we view, then let us be the instruments through which the world may be improved by improving ourselves. Let us do this in keeping with the law and be not interested nor concerned with what one judges, for if we judge not, we have no interest in those who do.

Thank you. Are there going to be any advances in medicine which will help some of the major diseases that are focused on in the U.S.?

There will be a cure for cancer. We have spoken on that in one of our earlier forecasts. There will be several cures for the various diseases that seem to plague mankind as the scientists of your world move closer and closer to an understanding of the human mind [and] how it really works in the electromagnetic fields in which it expresses itself. And the greatest boon to medicine and understanding the electromagnetic field of the human aura and the aura of all creation, the greatest boon it has ever known is the boon of understanding what you call electronics.

Thank you. Would you please speak on the corrective measures that may be made in reference to the ozone layer damage and when will, or have, the positive steps been begun?

It is sad that your scientists in your world, the majority of them, do not understand that the breakdown of the protective layer of life on the Earth planet is not limited to what you call your aerosol cans, but is affected, its chemistry and its breakdown, by the emanations of mental thought (on a mass [scale]) that go out into the universe. Now the actual chemical measurements of the thought released from the human aura has not [been] understood, will not be discovered for another thirty-two years of your Earth time, but it has a chemical combination that is measurable by the proper instruments. It [is] an instrument of creating or destroying. And therefore, in the coming years, as your scientists move to a greater understanding of these chemicals released by the human mind, there will be a healing take place over the ozone layers over a period of many, many, many years.

Thank you. What is taking place in the area of conservation of world resources, forests, and water?

The crumbs. Be grateful for the crumbs. Because, my friends, conservation is not a priority of the present rulers of your planet, and I speak of those yet encased in physical clay.

Thank you. How [does] the earthquake subject for California project for this year?

Not good, not bad. We see no disasters. We see four tremors. And fear not, the time is not yet.

Thank you. What levels are in control when we talk to others about imminent so-called disasters, such as earthquakes, wars, and such?

An absolute, undying faith in the righteousness of the mind.

Thank you. What, if anything, will happen in 1982 that Edgar Cayce prophesied for that year?

Shadows of reality. Time—you must be more patient for these disasters that you seek. *[A few members of the congregation laugh.]*

Thank you. In 200 years, will Nixon be viewed as a good president who made a bad political blunder or a crook?

That, in 200 years, will depend on the glory of the judgments of the minds who view him.

Thank you. Is the man [Muammar] Gaddafi the antichrist mentioned in the Bible?

Only in the minds of those who fear him.

Thank you. What is the future of our national parks and wilderness areas?

They have a future. They will survive. Do not expect them to increase very much.

Thank you. How can we help eliminate or control the growing crime and terrorism in the world?

We can do much for ourselves. We can do little or nothing for another. And by little or nothing, I mean it is dependent on their willingness to change. The blessing or benefit of suffering is that in time, when it is long endured and it is severe, intense, and painful, that it does help inspire us to accept the possibility of something different and hopefully something better.

The laws of your land and the judges and courts are moving from the pendulum of license to the responsibilities of the jobs they have of enforcing the law *with compassion*, a soul faculty, not with pity, a sense function. And that will be greatly instrumental in helping to stem the tides of so-called world terror. But try to understand, my friends, these so-called terrorist groups are not some independent entities of radical lunatics. They are simply various groups, paid and supported by various so-called governments on your planet. And when you awaken to the governments that support them, then there will be a great change in so-called world terrorism.

Thank you. Could you explain how the military intervention in Poland is in their best interest?

Indeed, indeed. The present situation in Poland is the blessing not only of the Polish people, though it is understood not at this time, but it is the blessing of the Western world. Because Poland, another satellite, will drain economically from the mother Bear all the rubles she can possibly spare. What you do not know is that the so-called country of Russia has been selling, is selling, everything it can to get hard, cold cash to try to keep

Poland economically afloat, because it is in the best interest of the government of Russia and the purpose that it has in mind to keep Poland and all her satellites economically sound. And so, like Afghanistan, which is draining on the Russian economy, and Poland, which is draining, and various other countries, which are draining and draining and draining, it is in the best interest; it is the price that must be paid for the freedom that is destined to come.

Good day.

DECEMBER 27, 1981

Nineteenth Annual World Forecast

Before getting into the nineteenth year of world forecasting, I feel it would be most appropriate to share some understanding with you concerning the process of communication. So many people do not seem to be aware or to apply the demonstrable truth of the law which reveals to us that like attracts like and becomes the Law of Attachment. And so it is with mediumship, with friendship or any other "ship." We must try to understand that.

In forecasting coming events, whether they are events concerning us directly and personally or indirectly and on through the chain of events, personally, we must understand, someday, that our world, our reality is wholly, completely dependent upon our own rate of vibration. And so it is when millions seem to be in great difficulty and struggle in this old material world, we look and see others who are not. And we justify the difference because we believe they have and we have not, but we don't seem to pause and ask our self what is the law or the rate of vibration that they have established, that they continue to establish that makes the difference in life.

One does not need to be a religionist, one does not need to be religious to apply the natural, demonstrable, divine laws of nature. Of course, it can be helpful; of course, it can be beneficial to understand, consciously, to have the awareness of the laws of nature, but it is indeed more beneficial, of course, to apply them.

We are aware of many things in life and ofttimes, after the seeming disasters, we don't feel well because we knew better: we knew what we should have done and then we had the experience of what we did do. And when the seeming disasters strike, we're not happy with our self. That unhappiness is usually expressed in anger and emotional turmoil, and it usually strikes the ones closest to us. It is rare that we run to the grocery store to express our temper and our anger. It is of no benefit, of course, to any of us to be angry, unless in the anger there is a change of attitude: so that the law that we have established, that was the instrument of making us angry in the first place, becomes the instrument through which [we make] a change in our thought, a change in our attitude, a change in our vibration, which makes a change in the law that we follow, which makes it good for us.

And so in forecasting, in a few moments, when that time comes, in making the effort to free myself from the identification to myself to try to be as clear a channel as possible, it means, like it does for any medium, all of the judgments and prejudices recorded in the subconscious mind, one must, through prayer and meditation, free themselves of the identification with the self, for that is the only place where they live.

Now we all face in this coming year various experiences. Most of us, if not all of us, are hopeful that they will be better. So often we ask for things to be better, but what we really mean is we hope they are not like they have been. And we call that asking for something better. I can assure you that an experience which has passed only reoccurs through our identification with it.

Many of us, if not all of us, have experiences we wish to forget, and we hope they do not repeat themselves. But we do not pause to think that they exist in a realm of consciousness and are awakened when we identify with the realm in which they live. Now man calls that realm of past experiences, he calls that "self." For self was the instrument through which they were born, and self is the instrument through which they live. And so if we do not want experiences that have happened in our life, if we do not want them to repeat themselves in principle, then the only way is not to identify with the realm in which they live.

If we think that times are economically tough, we establish the law, by directing energy to the judgment that we have made, to prove to our self how right we are. And yet we can use the same law to prove to our self how abundant life is for us. It is identically the same law; it's what we choose to do with it. Life is the way, our life, it is the way that we make it. It never is the way that someone else makes it. For us to permit our self to think that our life is the way someone else is making it places us in dependence to the individual, government, or society that we judge is making our life good, bad, or indifferent.

If we choose to do that, which so many of us, it seems, choose to do that, then we must be willing to pay the price of our choice. For whatever we choose in life, whatever we choose to attain, we must understand the laws of nature: there is payment for all attainment as long as we identify with creation, and self is creation.

It is not easy for any of us to identify with the formless and the free. Yet we oftentimes cry out for truth and freedom. To ask and cry for truth and freedom, we must understand truth is not form, truth is not limit, and neither is freedom. To be freedom, it must and is formless and free. To be truth, it must and is without limit, without judgment, without concept; it just is. And when we call for truth and we call for freedom, we must pay the price to attain that which we are calling for. And the price that must be paid to attain, which is by divine birth within us already, the price we must pay is the price of giving up, if only for a moment, what we understand to be self, so-called individuality, the identification with form and limit.

And now if we will just be peaceful for a few moments, I will be more than happy to share with you what I receive in reference to events in the coming year ahead.

[At this point, Mr. Goodwin goes into a trance.]

Greetings, friends, and welcome to our annual forecast.

The year of 1983, a year of harvest, a three year of manifestation, brings to your world the effects of the years preceding in the sense that you will become aware, especially in the United States, you will become aware of a turnaround, of a change, of a vast improvement in the path of economy that has been, with great difficulty, established for you. I read from the Book of Causes the passing of the months of January, February, March, April, and to the end of May, when you will see a vast improvement in the economic situation within the United States. Trade negotiations and new policies will be well established, and you will become aware of them by the early days of July.

The energy crisis which has been one of the main instruments of economic problems within the United States will make a drastic fall as the institution of OPEC begins to crumble and to fall. Ofttimes, as revealed in life, necessity, the mother of invention; and so it is that oil prices shall drop farther than ever dreamed possible in these past four years. It will benefit, of course, the United States and some of the other countries, but it will have a delayed reaction upon the Third World nations.

We go now to the pages of the White House. We see there much controversy, much discussion in reference to bringing pressure on the Federal Reserve Bank. We find, as this controversy begins to rage and becomes close, very close to interfering with that Federal Reserve [Bank], that a change, a great change will come about, and it will not become necessary, fortunately, for the Congress of the United States to dictate financial and economic stability for the nation. For it is not in the best interest of the country for those not qualified in understanding economics to interfere with policies that have become absolutely necessary for the greater good of all the people.

Storms and disasters from weather conditions will continue to sweep the Middle West. Heavy, heavy rains for California, the West Coast. And as we continue on through our pages, we view Texas, disastrous storms; New York later in January; and extreme flooding conditions in the State of California and Oregon.

We move along across to Europe. We see continued economic struggles and difficulties for England. We see another two and a half years of struggle before there is economic balance within the country.

Policies of West Germany, more friendly to the United States, but extremely sensitive and dangerous in the thinking of Russia shall create a confrontation in the early part of 1984, but it shall not be a war; it shall only be a war of words. Fear not for something greater; peace shall reign supreme.

Middle East: selfishness and greed, constant political pressures and juggling. Major countries, Russia, United States, France, Italy, selfish interests continue to stir the melting pot throughout the Middle East and Arab countries. However, there shall be freedom for Lebanon, but not without another price to pay. As we enter the coming year of '83 and move along into the November time, we see internal struggle. We see [a] small revolution, but Lebanon shall reach stability in the early part, before April, of 1985. How soon will the foreigners leave the country? Patience and more patience. It is dependent upon the United States. A change in [a] very high government office in Israel as we view the year of '83. Through that change shall the foreigners leave Lebanon and shall peace begin to grow.

World markets drop drastically in the early part of 1983, bringing about the enforcement of new trade policies, bringing about a greater prosperity for the United States. As the dollar weakens on the world market, the home economy, for Americans, shall prosper. Let us understand more fully the world trade market. Gold decreasing; slowly but surely, begrudgingly the price begins to drop and drop and drop and drop, four stages as balance begins to be manifest for the economy.

We move now to Asia, to China: an up-and-coming, growing prosperity; a major force entering the world trade market. Japan, suffering from unbearable inflation in the coming three years, shall make many changes in her economy, for without doing so, there shall be no survival.

And in speaking on the country of Japan, we are taken to Detroit and to the suffering car industry of the United States. Major agreements between auto manufacturers of the United States and Japan, bringing into the United States plants of Japanese and American ownership, will bring more work to the auto industry. New cars, already on the drawing boards, considering fuel economy, shall be highly saleable, and then drop as the prices of oil begin to fall apart. And so it is, as we have shifted to smaller, more economic cars in the United States, there will be a turn around again. And those so-called dinosaurs of luxury, some of them shall return and a great shift in the tastes of the American people, who have, by the majority, begrudgingly forced themselves into little cars, shall once again smile behind the wheels of so-called luxury.

And so it is, my friends, one day the sun shines and one day it doesn't. And wise are those who have encouraged the ability to change. For the economy turning around, tastes in the choices of automobiles turning around, and all these many changes before you, move harmoniously with them.

Medicine: vast, vast changes in the attitudes of the medical association, vast changes in their thinking, in their judgments.

Ever-increasing removal of regulations and government interference with manufacturing in the United States, with transportation in the United States. With medicine, all of the avenues through which there has been federal regulation and intervention, it is the policy of the present government of the United States, it is their firm belief and policy to remove as quickly as possible federal intervention in the free marketplace. Although there shall be, as has been, abuses of that freedom, it is in the best interest of the free market to be free. It is in the best interest of the American taxpayer to be free to use their intelligence to choose wisely what they wish to purchase in a free market. And as the United States government removes, daily, more of its interference and regulations in the marketplace, the consumer groups shall grow as never before and balance shall be maintained for the good of all.

New negotiations by certain utility companies, major companies in the United States, with Canadian natural gas [companies] will bring about a decline in the cost of natural gas. New regulations brought about by the gas industry itself within the United States, without government interference, shall bring a decrease in the cost of domestic gas. Do not expect a major change. Be grateful for the few pennies you, as the consumer, shall begin to realize.

And a return to medicine: the artificial heart which we spoke to you in our forecasts years ago shall not only be successful but it shall become the size of a 25-cent piece implanted within the body itself. This shall take over a period of eight years of continuous research and development and the funding of billions and billions of dollars. It is there, waiting, for the benefit of mankind. The heart transplant, we have always said and continue to say, medical science on the Earth planet is not yet sufficiently advanced to understand how to harmonize the organs in transplant. Consequently, from their lack of knowledge and lack of understanding, they shall not be successful. And the artificial organ implants shall be the way and the benefit for mankind.

As science continues on its rapid advancement, scientific awareness of signals from outer space shall soon be known by the layman. Not tomorrow, but within the few years, five, that are ahead. The scientists will not understand the message, but as scientists they will understand the periodic repetition and pattern of the signals; they will understand that some intelligence somewhere must be sending them. They will also understand the signals which they record were sent out into the universes centuries, centuries ago.

And so we look forward to a change in government in Argentina. We look forward to a change in government in Brazil, El Salvador, and a reconstruction of the present government in Guatemala.

We look forward to an open-door policy of trade and negotiations with mainland China, for it is a growing industrial giant; though it has far yet to go, time is passing quickly for their efforts never cease. And so China shall become a major power to reckon with in the coming ten years, as continuous research and development of atomic power is the major interest of the present government of China.

There will not be a third world war in your lifetime. There will not be a world holocaust. There will not be a nuclear catastrophe in your lifetime on Earth. There will be, and must be watched and checked closely, the small, but mentally unstable government of Libya, for it is through that area on your planet that darkness grows. It is there, revolutionist leaders are trained. It is there that a cancer is growing, spreading out in the Middle East and Europe.

Poland, much fear. So much fear. Major changes in agreements with Poland and the United States. No revolution in Poland. Suppression and suppression and suppression. For the present leaders of the government of Poland have become leaders with no alternative, for either they satisfy the country that put them in their position (Russia) or Russia moves into Poland.

Italy, the Pope, and the attempt upon his life, a political situation found necessary by Russia, found necessary from fear, for he is a strong spiritual leader, and Russia fears his influence upon his homeland of Poland that he would, though not consciously, be the instrument through which the Polish people would rise up and the government would change. Therefore, unknown discussions have been taking place over these past two months to bring about some agreement and some accord between Russia, the Polish leaders, and the Vatican. It will be many, many years before history reveals this to you.

Look forward, in this coming year, by a change of view, a change of attitude, a change of feeling, for each one, each country, their experiences are dependent upon what they believe they shall become.

Good day.

DECEMBER 26, 1982

Twentieth Annual World Forecast

Greetings, friends.

This forthcoming year, a year of stability and security, revealed numerically as a four year, will bring about a final stability in the troubled waters of the Middle East. You will become aware of that increasing stability and security in the early days of the month of August of the coming year. The so-called international troops from France, Italy, and Britain will be decreased drastically towards the latter days of the February month.

Now of interest, I'm sure, to all of you is the economic situation within your United States. First, as we have spoken before in reference to the economic plan established by your White House, there were those few years of austerity, and there is a balancing that has already shown [itself] to you. It will increase and grow and become more stabilized if conditions continue on in the forthcoming elections at the White House. We do foresee, in keeping with the laws already established, a renewal of your present president.

The fears and worries and concerns over nuclear holocaust, war, and disaster shall not come to pass. In reference to those terrible fears, the balance is being well established by those who fear and those who fear for varied or different reasons.

The nuclear energy is soon to become a page of past history as technology in your world has already developed and will continue to grow in its research and development for what is known to you as the light beam. And so energy, which has been of such concern to so many, will be less of a worry and concern in the forthcoming ten-year time.

Many changes in the civil laws within the United States. The so-called years, the twenty-five years of license or easy laws, so to speak, have come to an ending. The superior courts of your country will uphold ever more stringent laws governing the civil population. One need not be concerned over any loss of freedom unless one judges license to be freedom or liberty, for it is in keeping with laws established that there should and would be a more strict enforcement, a change of laws for the good of the whole.

Now we look through these pages in the Book of Causes at these interests and concerns with these so-called incurable diseases. Try to understand, my good friends, there is no disease without discord. Now there is no discord that does not have a beginning. It has a beginning; it has a break from the Law of Harmony. And because it has a beginning into discord or disease, it has a guaranteed ending of that. And so so-called incurable diseases are incurable only to those who do not understand the cause of the disease or discord. As we spoke to you in years past, [a] cancer cure is on the horizon for everything has been tried working with the effects. And slowly but surely technology and understanding of the disease or discord is awakening within the minds of the scientists, some of them, who are involved.

Entirely new and different trade rules and regulations. There will be an increase in this so-called sharing of industry. The United States is, by its very design and purpose, the breadbasket of the planet Earth. Its prosperity in the world is not dependent upon its industry but is in truth dependent upon its agricultural abilities. Therefore, there shall be an ever-increasing energy and attention placed upon the agriculture of the United States. The industry of the United States, by varied business arrangements with other countries and other companies in foreign lands, will come into a grand-slam awakening within the coming four years. Therefore, Americans will become more familiar with automobiles, refrigerators, toasters, appliances, televisions, and various, various manufactured products, manufactured in joint effort with other countries, especially Japan and with Korea and with China. And so, my friends, have no fear in reference to the good that comes from it, because the survival of the planet Earth is dependent upon a greater understanding, a broadening of one's horizons, of one's views in reference to cooperation of the human race for the good of all. It is through these new trade agreements, through new trade regulations, through a new, growing world economy, which someday shall be a new world currency, that this so-called fear of nuclear disaster and annihilation shall become a past page of history.

It is difficult for anyone to change identity, for it is in the belief of the identity that we find the false security to the human mind that is ever seeking to gather, to garner, and to be more and more secure. Try to remember, my friends, it is the nature of the human mind not only to gather and to garner, but to place its faith upon what it can put within its realm of domain and control.

Now these trade agreements shall increase and grow.

Fears from bordering countries such as Cuba, but, my friends, they shall not last. They shall not be a disturbance to the United States or to the countries of South America.

The Lebanon situation, the Middle East, as I said earlier, shall come to a safe and secure harbor of reason.

The Russian Bear fears more than the people of the United States. It fears from ignorance. It fears because of past experiences of so many years ago. And if you understand that this Russian Bear has such great fear, then you will more fully understand its apparent aggression; because it wants to be secure, as anyone does, but it is limited, by its past experiences, [in] how to find that security. However, it is doing everything necessary to bring about its own changes for the better of its own people. Whenever a country, no matter what country, what nation it is, places more of its resources into the defense and the security of the nation by expending more of its resources for foreign development, for defensive purposes, it is collapsing from within. Therefore, a wise nation takes care of its own backyard and, in so doing, has not to fear the next-door neighbor.

China and her industrial might shall rise, grow, and prosper. Japan has been a seeming miracle to many people with its ever-increasing industrial growth, but China shall even outdistance Japan as she moves in to become one of the greatest industrial nations in your world.

Personally, for each person, there is always a way to experience something better in life. That way, of course, is always dependent upon what you choose to think and, from your choice of thinking, are forced, by the nature of the mind, to believe. For we do become, in a mental world of self-identity, that which we believe and which we believe not. Therefore, my message to all of you for the new year—for a new year is a new life to a wise man; and a new year is the moment you choose to be consciously aware of the law that you establish moment by moment. So a new year begins, to a wise man, through an awakening that you are greater than you know, for what we know is dependent upon what we have already experienced. And so we are greater than what we have already experienced for we have, by the very nature of a past event, proven to our self the past experience has passed, but we still are.

So, beginning a new year with the understanding, and the acceptance thereof, that we are greater than all past experiences—and past experiences are the ingredients of what we know; understanding that we are greater than what we know places us on the path of becoming what we truly are. Beginning with that simple step, we will walk through evolution in a harmonious and gracious way and, by so doing, shall we grow and prosper, evolve and return to the Source from whence we have wandered.

Having left the light of reason, we are destined to return unto it. We leave the light of reason for one experience and then another, for we leave the light of reason by what we are tempted. And we are tempted by what we think we have not. We are never tempted, my good friends, by what we think we have. We are only tempted by what we think we have not. And what we think we have not is, of course, what we have in truth denied.

And so, in keeping with the purpose of our annual forecasts, of what benefit will it be to be aware of the coming changes that are inevitable in keeping with laws established if we, in the forewarning, are not forearmed by a change within our consciousness?

So much in the world of prejudice, which, of course, we all know is only prejudgment. And we, of course, prejudge in our effort to defend what we think we have that is being threatened. And so we fill our days, so often, with prejudice and do not see it as prejudice. We call it intolerance or some other name, but in truth it's prejudice. It is the root cause of all war. It is the root cause of all disaster. It is the root cause of fear. It is the root cause of disease, for it is contrary to the Law of Health, which reveals to us the goodness of harmony. Therefore, as so many changes in your world are coming into manifestation, it is important to pause, to think, and to accept something better within one's consciousness than the fear of the need to defend what we think we have. Remember, my good friends, what we think we have we guarantee to lose that we may know beyond a shadow of any doubt we have not; we are only the trustees of something greater that has, uses, and helps us to awaken.

This so-called disturbance in Europe, these fears of these missiles and things, they shall pass along the pages of history. There are no great disasters that we see.

These fears of earthquakes, especially in the western part of the United States, we see no great disaster in the foreseeable future of these few years ahead. Weather, now, we spoke to you before, shall be extremely wet and extremely cold. The weather patterns are changing on your planet Earth. They are changing in keeping with the evolution of the planet. The United States, especially, is beginning to experience the new weather patterns that shall be your winters and your summers. And it shall, of course, be much colder than you have already experienced in this past week or two. It shall indeed be more wet. But man adjusts to change, that is, a reasonable man. It is the ones who are waiting to grow who have such struggles with changes, for we find a false security in the things we think we have and especially a thought in our mind.

Now, my good friends, I want to spend a few moments more on understanding the purpose of our life, perhaps, and to share with you the inevitable journey that we're all in, for life doesn't begin, and therefore life doesn't end. But it's when we think that life is a form that physical eyes and physical senses are aware of, it's when we think that way that life begins and life ends. And so it is indeed difficult for those who believe that life is form. It is difficult for them to enter form, and it is difficult for them to leave form. But try to understand that all souls are in the process of evolution. Some are at different stages of evolution than others. Some people, they learn more quickly, and some people, they don't seem to learn at all.

And so I'm going to take a few minutes longer and let our good chairman here permit you to ask questions at this time of our forecast. And so, [Mr. Chairman], would you take care of that? *[The teacher asks the chairman to help facilitate responding to questions from the congregation.]*

Anyone who has a question, raise your hand, please. There's a hand. Would you stand, please? [The chairman asks.]

Could you elucidate on it's difficult to get into form and if it's difficult to get out of form? I didn't quite understand that.

Yes. Life is a formless, free, intelligent [Energy] that is not dependent upon form for life. Its purpose [is] to express through form, through the Law of Identity, in order to evolve, to refine the very nature of form. Therefore, one who finds—that is, one not as an individual; one as a principle establishing the Law of Struggle to enter form has the struggle to leave form. For example, if you take and pour a glass of water from a pitcher and you pour more water into the glass than the glass is capable of holding, the rest of the water, that which flows over the glass, is not contained by the glass and, therefore, is not in form an identity. And so it is with the Divine Spirit that is poured into the vessel that we call form: the human body and the human mind. Unless that which is within the vessel, and not that which overflows the vessel, unless that is all of our identity, which we often believe that it is, then we have not expanded our consciousness. We have identified with that which is within the vessel or the container—you hear?—and by so identifying, we have struggle with that which flows in the river of consciousness. I hope that's helped with her question.

Thank you.

Yes.

Any further questions? Yes, would you stand, please? [The chairman addresses a different member of the congregation.]

Yes. In tape number CC 195, the Wise One speaks of the great void. Can you please help us to understand more about that? [Spiritual awareness class CC 195 was published in Volume 7.]

Well, in reference to that particular class that speaks upon the great void, when the human mind thinks of the word *void*, it has no reference because void is not something that is limited. Try to understand, the human mind['s] stability, its stability is dependent upon limit. It is dependent upon form. Form is limit. So by its very nature, it must have limit or form in order to refer. It is when we, within our consciousness, move from the limit, from the identity to the limit, when we move from the need of that identity to limit, then we enter the void where all is. For all is nothing, for nothing—no thing, no limit, no form—is all. That is the difference between principle and personality, between formless and form, between freedom and bondage, between truth and creation.

When we pause and still our mind, we enter the great void by the stillness of the human mind, for the stillness of the human mind prevents the forms of mental substance from motion or action. It is at those moments that we move in consciousness above and beyond the limit to the limitless and view, from what is known as a realm of objectivity, all that has been, all that is to be, for it all *is*. No past and no future is the life we truly are. I hope that's helped with your question.

Thank you.

Yes, this lady here. [The chairman calls upon another person.]

If one is having difficulty in seeing or understanding something or is stopped at seeing it, is there anything that is helpful in the process?

The question, it appears, if one is having difficulty in seeing or understanding something. Is that the question?

Yes.

First, we must ask, What do we mean by difficulty in seeing or understanding something? Do we mean that we are having difficulty in understanding or seeing something because it is not in harmony with what already is within our consciousness? Is that what we mean by the question?

Yes.

Well, when we have difficulty or struggle in evolving, it reveals, of course, to all of us that we are overidentified with what we *think* we are and are losing what we truly are, for what we are is a formless, free principle that is in the constant process of expressing through varied form. You hear?

Yes.

So through the overidentification with the thought of I or what we think is self, it is the natural defense mechanism to protect that which we believe is, for that which we believe is, is dependent upon that which has been. Do you understand?

Yes.

The shadow of the past is what we have identified with. And whenever we experience fear, let us not forget, the fear is the defense of the shadow, for that is all what has been can ever be: only a shadow. It has no substance. It has no energy. It has no life until we give it life, we give it energy, we give it motion by our attention upon it, identification with it, which causes the divine, neutral, intelligent Energy to pass through our being and to the shadow, which, in turn, deceives us; and we believe that we are that which has been, which in truth is only a shadow, known as experience. Does that help with your question?

Yes. Thank you.

We have time for one more.

Yes, this lady right here. [The chairman speaks.]

Yes.

Thank you for your forecast. I wondered; you didn't mention energy in the world. And I wonder will there be a change or a discovery of a new source of energy.

Absolutely.

And how soon will it be discovered or invented?

Well, in reference to energy, definitely there is already—the technology is already there. The research is already being done in your world. Now, energy will no longer—the energy as you know energy—be dependent upon fossil fuels. You hear? That's number one. That is as comparable as the rocket ship to the horse and buggy. And so that page in your history is in the process of passing, though it certainly does not seem to be in reference to all your automobiles and all of these heating costs and things.

What source is that energy? The energy, you see, is in the atmosphere. It's right in the atmosphere. That energy is known to you as light. And so this light that is ever present, never absent or away—remember that the night is a lesser light; it's still light. The energy is in the atmosphere. It is through the crystal that it shall be captured and converted into energy for your mundane use. Now these crystals, artificial and etc., are already in process of being developed. And so how soon will this new light beam or light energy come to your world? It's in process and within the coming twenty-five years you shall have a full awareness of its great benefits. I do hope that's helped with your question.

Yes. Thank you.

You're welcome. Best give a few more, a few more moments. Yes.

The lady here. [The chairman calls on another person.]

I'm wondering if you could talk about the evolution of new forms, for men, men and women, of relationships. Is there anything—

Well, yes, but you may not like the answer that I'm about to give. Well, so many people seem to be disturbed in reference to scientific advancement. And, of course, I've spoken before on its detriment if it's not balanced with a spiritual awakening and understanding. Looking forward into what you may term a future science world—[is] that what you're interested in? *[After a short pause, the teacher continues.]* Of what the relationships between men and women shall be? Is that your question?

Yes. What is the evolutionary path?

Well, it's already well established. More and more freedom from childbirth is being offered to the women of your world. You do understand and see that, don't you?

Yes.

More and more test-tube, so-called, babies will be born. The thing is to understand that the Divine Spirit, the intelligent being, covered in what you understand to be individualized soul, enters form in keeping with the law of the positive and negative poles of nature coming together. Do you understand?

Yes.

Therefore, it could happen—it already is happening—in a laboratory, you understand?

Yes.

It is not dependent, absolutely not dependent on marriage and the family unit, etc. You understand that?

Yes.

Society is moving and changing in that direction. Will it be good or bad? That depends upon the awakening in consciousness of what you call society. It is not the first time that the species has risen to that so-called scientific advancement. It will not be the last time. For the laws of nature, creation reveal the ascent and descent. It is through the ascent and the descent that changes are brought about. Our minds reveal that clearly: that we ascend with one thought and descend with another; and ascend still with another to descend with another. And so this process takes place in a mental world, takes place in a physical world. And from that process, you have the evolution of species, you hear?

Yes.

That's what's coming. That's what you're becoming aware of. There will be what many women will feel is more freedom. There will be frustration and changes. There will be struggles, prejudices, and difficulties ever in keeping with the stubbornness of the human mind to permit the changes, that are inevitable, to take place. There is nothing to fear, as many a wise man has said. There is nothing to fear. Not even fear itself. For if you know what fear is, then fear no longer exists except by your conscious choice. If you want to experience the effect of fear, then you consciously make a decision to enter that realm within consciousness and you have that excitement or experience. And if you consciously choose not to enter that realm, then you do not have that experience.

The purpose of the Living Light Philosophy is to help the souls to awaken by a control of the mind. Remember, the soul is always awake. The soul doesn't sleep. The mind sleeps. And it is in the satisfaction or sleep of the human mind, which is an instrument through which the awakened soul is ever making an effort to express itself, that we speak of awakening. It is the human mind that must be controlled and stilled, and when that happens, there's no fear, for the conscious choice is an intelligent choice. Now we experience fear and frustration by those forms rising within the consciousness without us consciously saying, "I want you to come up so I may have this terrible experience." I hope that's helped with your question.

The question has to do more with social forms that will evolve for men and women as a result of that.

You mean the physical form?

Like, yes, is there a new social form that will evolve?

Well, the only social form—now I see in which avenue you are traveling. The only social form that is going to evolve from that, if you can call it a social form, is that what you call or know [as] a family unit is already breaking down. Do you understand that? *[After a short pause, the teacher continues.]* Pardon?

Yes.

There will be what you call more day nurseries. There will be more institutes in which babies and children are raised, you hear?

Yes.

There will be more so-called independent or single people with children in institutes being raised. Hmm?

Yes.

As far as the marriage rate, it will increase to last a shorter duration. It will be fashionable to have short marriages. Hmm?

Yes.

Like a six-month's [marriage]. Now I don't like to have to give that type of forecast, but that's the laws that have been set into motion, you see. It's kind of like picking up a novel; well, it takes you six months to read it; well, in six months you get a different novel. You understand that, don't you?

Yes.

All right. Now, but what is the good that is offered from this great license and changes that we see? The good that is there is quite simple: man is getting bored with what has been. Would you not agree?

Yes.

And in that boredom, is constantly seeking change. Therefore, as negative as it appears, the good shall come from it, for he will gradually break the back of his need to that which has been and, in doing that, will awaken to the truth that he is. One more question, only, and we must conclude.

This gentleman over here. [The chairman speaks.]

Yes, please.

Yes, thank you. I'd like to ask about the progress of mining in California and the Western states. Is it all based on the price of gold and silver?

Traditionally, yes, and will continue to be based upon gold, you hear?

Yes.

For gold is the standard that your world has been addicted to for untold thousands of years. You understand?

Yes.

Now it's been addicted to that particular mineral because that's the one that has the greatest survival rate, wouldn't you say?

Yes, indeed.

It definitely does. The very nature of it: it survives throughout the eons. And so your world will continue to base its value upon that mineral. There is no change in that respect. And in reference to gold, it went way up and it came down into some degree of balance. But, my friend, be of good cheer, if you're in California, because more gold mines are opening. Or didn't you know?

I wasn't aware of any in California, no.

You [weren't]? Well, there are, there are. Because, you know, it's so interesting. They didn't get it all. *[After a short pause, the teacher continues.]* Pardon?

Yes, that's true. I—

Oh, no, no, no. They didn't get it all. You [have] got to go deeper, see?

Right.

You know, it's kind of like looking for water. A man digs and digs and digs. He goes 20 feet, 30 feet, 60 feet, 80 feet. And he doesn't get any water. And he finally quits, doesn't he?

Yes.

Hmm. Victory never ever belonged to the quitter. Same way with mining, isn't it?

Yes.

Hmm. Dig deeper and dig farther. Thank you, friends. Thank you very much.

DECEMBER 25, 1983

Twenty-First Annual World Forecast

In speaking with you today on the twenty-first forecast, we wish first to read, from these records of cause, the economic situation [in] the year ahead for the United States. Although progress has been made with the economy and progress, though slowly, will continue to be made in the coming year, the stability is being assured for the years ahead. There will be a sharp increase in the economic situation within the United States in the early part of the June month of '85. Showing a slight slump in September, the economy continues to stabilize regardless of controversy and appearances.

On the international scene, though the meetings with the United States and the Soviet Union will in truth be most beneficial, they are under the vibration and attitude in consciousness of suspicion and caution, based on past events, based, of course, upon prevalent fear. There will, however, be a change in the so-called star-wars approach to defense by the United States in accordance with a secret agreement that will be signed in the first three months of 1986. It will be, of course, in the best interest of the planet Earth, and it shall indeed be.

A change in the location of major manufacturers now located in Taiwan, will move, by 1987, into mainland China in keeping with agreements that are already under discussion.

As we have spoken so many times before, the earthquakes continue, though in the foreseeable future for the West Coast of the United States we do not foresee any major disasters.

Weather will continue to be, in the West Coast and in other parts of your country, especially in California, will continue to be very, very, very cold. Dryer and colder in the month ahead, although it will indeed be one of the wettest and coldest winters that you have experienced in California for many years. Some time ago we spoke to you on this cyclic pattern of return and that the weather pattern for California would return to the years of the '30s. So you may well prepare yourself for the coming winter of 1985. Increasing cold in that year and not quite as wet.

Changes in the attitude of law enforcement will be known to you as we come into the November month of '85. There already is much discussion and plans, in major cities of your country, to return to the system of law enforcement by putting on far more police officers onto the streets and out of the automobiles. Indeed, a wise move that will bring about less crime, certainly far less victims of crimes. And so those changes are coming about.

A major, major overhaul of the attitudes of the judges of the courts of the land. A major change in attitude: less leniency, more discipline in respect to sentences. A drastic change of prison reform in the United States as new work farms [are] to be established come the May month of '86.

And so those are positive things that are already underway. And though there will be a continuing disturbance between the president and Congress, do not be deceived by appearances. It is only of political value and is not affecting the very principles of change that have already been set into motion.

And now I'm going to take a few moments for those of you who have questions of a national and international nature, and let you raise your hands so that you may speak forth your questions. Now, if my chairman will assist me, please.

This gentleman here, please. [The chairman calls upon a member of the congregation.]

Will there be a resolution of the Israeli-Palestinian problem in the Middle East?

Will there be a resolution of the Israeli and Palestine problem in the Middle East? *[The teacher often repeated the question for the benefit of his students in other dimensions.]* At the present time, there will be no definite results. The discussions that have been going on, that are not yet known publicly, will continue. However, you may look forward to the August month of 1987, and at that time you will see much work is being done, much will have been accomplished for peace shall come to the Mideast. That is assured and that is guaranteed. Peace shall come. War shall cease. Thank you.

The lady back here, please. [The chairman calls upon another person.]

Will there be any trouble in Korea this coming year?

In reference to any trouble, I accept you mean any conflict—Yes.

—amongst their people. There will not be any major conflict in Korea. There is a vibration that is working to be established between the communists in Korea and the so-called democrats in Korea. Now that effort has been and continues to be made over this past four years. There will be, by the end of 1988, a positive result from that effort. And great concern is held by those in power at the present time because they fear this new coalition that is going on. They fear for their present positions in a selfish way rather than to view it as a step that will bring to their country less dependence on foreign governments. And so Korea shall establish, by that time, a peace that she has not experienced in the past forty years.

This lady here, please. [The chairman speaks.]

In 1980, when Mount Saint Helens erupted, there was a lot of talk about Mount Shasta being the southern-most volcano in that particular chain of volcanoes. And I'm wondering if we could anticipate any activity in Mount Shasta?

Yes, in reference to your question concerning the volcano, which is active, in Mt. Shasta, it is not sufficiently active at this time. It is like, you might say, a boiling pot. But it has yet to fully steam. Now that we do not foresee, here in [this] record of causes, until we enter the latter part of this century. In the last year of the present century, we do see a positive, definite eruption of that volcano that's simmering at this time. Yes.

This lady here, please. [The chairman speaks.]

I'm concerned about the environment. Whether respect will be maintained as far as, like, off-shore drilling and cutting down of the rain forests.

Well, in reference to your question concerning the respect for nature, unfortunately the records do not reveal nor forecast great respect until you have passed another fifteen of your Earth years. There will be, in that time, in that fifteen-year time span, there will be eight major, major catastrophes from man's abuse of nature. Yes.

This gentleman back here. [The chairman calls on another person.]

I understand that some economists would like to see this country return to the gold standard. And on the other hand, other countries that have never gone off would have so much purchasing power that it could be a disadvantage.

Thank you for your question. In reference to the United States going back to the gold standard, it shall not happen. There is no way in the present evolution of the United States, without a total financial collapse of its economy, to return to the gold standard. Therefore, those in control of the United States shall not permit it and you need not fear it.

This gentleman here.

What will happen to the spiritual movement during the next year or two with regard to the new age? And what are our responsibilities in that?

Thank you. In reference to your question on the spiritual growth and our responsibility in reference to society and civilization, we did speak some time ago about this. We did speak some time ago in reference to man's scientific and technological advancement: how far advanced it was over his own spiritual awakening. And so you may look forward to increased scientific advancement to seemingly unbelievable technological growth. And the effect of that is, of course, an increase in man's belief in material substance. That is the great danger and detriment of scientific advancement. Not a detriment as a science and an advancement in and of itself, but a detriment because man believes in that which he judges gives him the most for the least effort expended. That's the great danger when the scientific advancement far exceeds the spiritual growth and awakening.

However, in keeping with what has been established and in keeping with what continues to be established, the scientific advancement in technology continues to grow over the next twenty-two years at a very rapid pace. However, as in all things, there is good, for in all things it takes God or good, the energy of the Light, to sustain it. And so as dependence upon machines and computers and electronic devices, as man continues with his increased slavery and bondage—a slavery and a bondage because man is granting to technology, to science, he is granting to it, unknowingly, his birthright, known as the divine right of choice.

And so you will slowly but surely begin to see that whatever man depends on for his survival, whatever man depends upon for his pleasure of his senses becomes man's god.

So the days of cloning are upon you. The days of that scientific advancement are with you now. The only thing is the masses of people know little about it, for those who are in charge and control of that scientific advancement are well aware that for the masses to know too much would not be in the best interest of their continuing with their work.

Now in speaking of this advancement, in all things there is the Light. Ofttimes we must look long to find it.

Communication with other dimensions, for over thirty-some years, has been researched and developed by the Union of Soviet Socialist Republics on a strictly material and scientific basis. Science, however, is not dependent upon the religious convictions of the human mind. And because it is not dependent upon the religious convictions of the human mind, it works for those, whoever they may be, who learn the laws that govern them. It is only within the past five years that the federal government of the United States has allotted funds for the scientific research and development of psychic phenomena in a sensible way and has placed it under the control of the military.

This is a very important thing to understand, for in understanding the laws that are being used, man is no longer left with doubt and wonder at the rise and fall of the continents of Atlantis and the continents of Lemuria. So history, like all things, has cyclic patterns. And so Atlantis, in the respect of scientific advancement, is certainly well on the rise.

However, there will be no world holocaust. There will be no destruction of the planet by nuclear cause, for those that we see not with physical sight, those that we know not are amongst us, and have been, with great interest, [working] for the survival of the planet Earth. It is their responsibility to see that what took place so long ago does not repeat itself. And so man's movement into space and his populating of other planets shall be restricted and limited to the universe that by divine law has been allotted to him, until humanity on Earth, as a whole, advances in its evolution from the bondage of belief to the freedom of faith. I hope that's helped with your question. Yes.

This gentleman over here, please. [The chairman speaks.]

Will there be any significant development or change involving women's rights in this country?

Indeed. I am indeed pleased that you have asked that most important question on women's rights. For we are in a process of growing and evolving from women's rights, men's rights, girl's rights, boy's rights, dog's rights, to the rights of life. Such an important thing. For when the mind permits itself to declare men's rights and to declare women's rights, man limits his perspective and does not view life itself, only from a peashooter sight. So so-called women's rights will take phenomenal strides in broadening its horizon in the awakening that truth needs no defense, that a change within the consciousness of each and every person will bring about the freedom that is sought, for it only exists within the consciousness of an individual. And when we permit our mind to view our freedom dependent upon that which is beyond our control, then indeed do we suffer. And so the women of the United States are awakening, indeed, to weigh out intelligently what has been gained in comparison to what has already been lost. And in that respect, great changes are ahead in these coming four years. Thank you.

This gentleman over here, please.

What will be the future outlook in regard to uniting or reuniting divided countries, like, for instance, East and West Germany or North and South Korea?

In reference to peace in North [and] South Korea, that is already in process. And it shall continue to grow and peace shall reign supreme for the country of Korea. However, we have a different situation in reference to West Germany and East Germany, for East Germany and West Germany is still a plum that superpowers are not willing, yet, to share. So in that respect, you can expect a status quo of the situation there. Yes.

This lady over here, please.

Will there be a cure for AIDS or cancer?

It is in process. First, however, increasing disaster is taking place. In reference to this seeming new disease that is attacking thousands upon thousands of people, you are at the doorstep, the doorstep of the cure. It should be known to your world as a positive, positive cure within the coming two years. Now, at the present rate of affliction, you can expect an average of 150 to 200 so-called deaths a week in the coming two years. Unfortunately, man changes begrudgingly and slowly until something affects him personally. And so from this increasing disaster, more funds shall be granted to the scientists and the research laboratories that are crying for funds in order to continue with their research and development. That will take approximately two years. Yes.

This gentleman here, please.

In regard to the economy, what imports will be increasing and those that will be decreasing as the economy improves?

In reference to the economy, the imports—you're speaking of the imports, increasing and decreasing?

[The individual may respond, but if he did, it is difficult to transcribe.]

Automobiles will definitely continue to decrease, you hear? The reason for that is because there are certain, I wouldn't call them threats from the United States, but let us say the message has been given loud and clear; and therefore, that area (automobiles) shall continue [to] decrease. However, equipment such as electronics, computers, movie machines, and all of those things, those will go into a vast increase. Now your home entertainment centers will increase rapidly within the next three years. These video machine players will more than increase a thousand percent in imports into the country and in sales. So you can look for great advancement in home entertainment as more people, from fear and various other reasons, do not wish to go out into the streets of the cities after dark. And that's where you will see increasing imports. However, you will find more and more clothing manufactured in the United States, and that indeed is good news, for you will find more quality. And therefore, it is good for your economy. Yes.

This gentleman back here with glasses.

In the next year, what do you foresee of interest rates in the United States and the forthcoming tax changes at the federal level?

In reference to interest rates within the United States and tax changes, we would like to say that interest rates are stabilizing in a most beautiful way. It is absolutely necessary for the good of the economy. So interest rates will change slightly—half a percent, one-and-a-half percent, we do not see more than that. Gold on the market, the world market, is stabilizing beautifully.

And the tax changes that are in process—and [there] will be many more—are in the best interests of all people, *of all people*. Ofttimes when there are changes and things that the masses do not understand, it sometimes takes a few years before they can see the benefit of it. The right steps have been taken, continue to be taken for the best interest of all the people of your country. Yes.

This lady over here, please.

Will there be alleviations of the sufferings in Africa?

Yes, indeed. Will there be alleviation of the suffering [of the] people of Africa? There will indeed. And it is unfortunate, unfortunate and sad, for those in authority of the various governments that such a thing would have been delayed (the help to the suffering souls) because of *political* interests. There is nothing to thank, but selfish, political interests for the millions who have waited to be freed from their starvation and their suffering. The changes are coming about. They are receiving aid, though it is approximately 40 percent of the 100 percent that is sent. But one, grateful for the crumb, manages to survive. One might like to know what happens to 60 percent of aid sent to various countries. Well, 60 percent is what those in control of it getting to the people manage to siphon off for themselves. So whatever is sent in those situations, you can expect the 40 percent to get through, and that's very good considering the many hands that it has to pass through to get there. Alleviation of those suffering souls, as we look forward in time and we come to the early part of August of this coming year of 1985, we see a vast improvement and freedom from that mass suffering. Thank you.

We have a few moments left.

The gentleman back here.

Thank you. In the same vein as this women's rights, we seem to be hearing a lot about child abuse these days. Is that a valid situation?

Well, in reference to child abuse, is it a valid situation? Why, it absolutely and positively is valid. The only difference that we find is of recent time there's been some light cast upon it in the sense of exposure. We don't find it anything [of] a new type of phenomenon. It is something that has been going on for a long time. And it's only of recent time [that it's] been receiving the publicity that it should have received twenty years ago. I do hope that's helped with your question. Yes.

There's a gentleman back over here.

Could you please speak on the situation in Central America, particularly the governments of Nicaragua and El Salvador?

Well, in reference to the countries of Nicaragua and El Salvador, if you understand the fears of what may happen to that area of your world and if you understand that those who have been temporarily placed in control are so fearful of the position that they have, they have a tendency, a weakness to disregard human rights, for their fears are so great to maintain the political positions that they think they have attained. Their positions are very short-lived. You will see positive changes in El Salvador within four months, four months from this time. I'd rather not say too much in reference to that particular person; however, you will see, like you say, a new broom sweeps quite clean. It is in the best interest of all the Salvadorians. Thank you.

There is a question here.

Regarding Afghanistan, [is] the Soviet Union going to eliminate the culture of Afghanistan? And why are those people suffering?

The Soviet Union will not eliminate, for it is not possible for them to do so, the culture of the country of Afghanistan. It is not possible for them to do so, for they have other priorities that are much higher than the little country of Afghanistan. Now, agreements reached between the Judas-Afghanistanians many, many years ago and the Russian Bear were called due, so to speak. And so when the Russian Bear came to collect its dues, those particular Afghan people in certain positions sold out. And so you have this temporary problem today.

Now five years has passed and the conflict continues, and people suffer. And it's like a chess game to those in power who could truly make the change. And you will see in these few years ahead, in reference to various agreements that are going to be brought about between the United States and the Union of Soviet Socialist Republics, you're going to find far, far down the road, for it will not be publicly revealed in these next few years, you're going to find that Afghanistan, Cuba, Nicaragua, El Salvador, and several other countries, Lebanon and several other countries, parts of Africa, are being included in reference to the agreements that shall be reached between the United States and Russia. You know, it's like playing a game of chess. It's a give and take. And so, as the United States gives a little and the Russians take a little, and the Russians give a little and the United States takes back more, you will find that this change in the star-wars approach is all being weighed out and bartered with in these coming years ahead. Be not concerned for the best is coming out of this situation.

And in reference to why do people suffer? As man is a law unto himself, man alone must ask the question, "What am I doing with the law that I am?" Now if your soul came to the Earth planet in certain circumstances and conditions, that's ever in keeping with the laws established by the ever-evolving eternal being. And so we find some evolving in Afghanistan, others evolving in Korea, others evolving in Russia, and yet others evolving in the United States.

And suffering is not limited to a particular territory. People suffer in the United States in many different ways, as they suffer in the Soviet Union. And so let us look and see the good in all things. And see that our minds, through its own bondage of belief, ofttimes makes varying degrees of suffering necessary for our mind, in order that we may be free in our faith rather than be bound in our beliefs.

Now we have time for another question or two.

This lady here, please.

You had mentioned before, when you were talking about the increased popularity of home entertainment centers being the effect of people being afraid to go out after dark.

Yes.

I'm curious if the economic times are going to be looking up, what would be the positives of this violence and how bad would it be?

Well, the thing is, it isn't a matter of increased violence; it's a matter of status quo of the present violence as the changes within the laws and the law enforcement, especially the law enforcement, [are] going to take place in the larger cities. And so in that respect, you see, those along in the suburbs and various places continue to maintain their fears of going out after dark because of experiences they'd had in these latter years. The change is coming about with your home entertainment centers, for the people have made the judgment they're freer to do what they want to do in their own home than they are in going out and watching a movie or anything, you see? Consequently, there will be a phenomenal increase in reference to people and their little home entertainment centers in their own places. And the fear continues to exist within the minds of people of going out after dark and what might happen to them based upon the experiences that so many have already had.

Thank you.

You're welcome.

The gentleman here.

Will a messiah come during this century?

Now the question, you see, requires a broader perspective than just the few words. There are those whose belief in a messiah are sufficient that their messiah has already arrived. Then we have the messiah of the Christian world, you understand?

Yes.

Then we have the messiah of the various other worlds and sects. Now I accept that you are referring to the messiah of the Christian world, is that correct?

Yes.

Yes, I understand. In reference to the experience in the consciousness of the messiah presenting himself to the Christian world, we do not foresee, for the masses of the Christian world expect the messiah—and by the messiah I accept that you mean Jesus, the Nazarene, is that correct?

Yes.

Fine. Because the masses of Christian believers have judged that the coming of the messiah shall be a full, physical materialization of a being of flesh and blood, we do not foresee it for them. Does that help with your question?

Yes, it does.

Now when they change their consciousness, when they evolve to the coming of a spiritual messiah within the consciousness, that which they awaken to, then we see the messiah in the moment of their acceptance. I do hope that's helped with your question.

[Thank you.]

You're welcome.

The lady over here.

Is there to be a liberalization or is it taking place within the U.S.S.R., such as it did in China?

Well, in reference to a liberation, do you mean more personal expression of a . . .

Less of the . . . type of government. [One word is difficult to transcribe due to background sounds.]

Well, we do not—no, no, that is not within the records. It does not reveal itself for the country of the Soviet Union. No.

Thank you.

Yes.

The lady back here.

Is there going to be a flat tax? And if so, what will it do to the charities and religions of the United States?

[It will] help them grow tremendously! In reference to a flat tax and what it will do with the religions and charities of the United States: the greatest blessing they could possibly experience.

Thank you. I'll take more than two minutes to answer that question. Thank you.

Shall I turn it? [It seems the audio cassette on which this class was being recorded is about to run out. The chairman asks if the cassette should be turned to record on the other side.]

Not just yet.

It is the greatest thing that could possibly happen to religions and charities in the United States, for it is in dire need. So when you give to anything or anyone and what you give to becomes a crip—

[The recording is interrupted at this point. It is likely that the cassette ran out of tape on Side A. After the interruption, the recording begins again, but on Side B of the audiocassette.]

Ready? Yes, I find a few more questions here. Yes, go ahead, please.

Question. Yes. [The chairman speaks.]

Recently there's been a happening where whales are beaching themselves on the beach. And I'm wondering if that species will remain thriving on the planet or if it's on the way to extinction.

Like all species on all planets in all universes, they are designed by divine law to serve a purpose, to fulfill their purpose, and in so doing, as they began, to end. In reference to the whales that you experience beaching themselves, yes, you are simply looking at a forthcoming situation. It is the way of ending that particular species. Does that help with your question?

Yes. Thank you.

And so, like [in] your world, you do not find your dinosaurs today. They came; they served their purpose, and they no longer are. And so, like with the human species, you have come; you serve your purpose, and in physical substance you no longer are. Therefore, be not attached to form, for it comes from Mother Nature, and Mother Nature shall declare her divinity and her right and that shall always return. Yes.

There are no other questions. [The chairman remarks.]

Then we'll be patient.

[After a short pause, the chairman speaks.] *A question here.*

In South Africa, there's some tremendous discrimination against black people. And I'm wondering if that will change, especially based on what President Reagan has stated about, made a statement on.

Well, in reference to the discrimination in South Africa, that is, of course, in the minds of those in control, it is being weighed out with their economy, for their way of life is a reflection of the basic principles that govern and judge their economy. Now, of course, that doesn't mean that one, necessarily, should accept that for the sake of [the] economy, we have prejudice. But, my dear friends, for the sake of economy there is all kind of prejudice, for prejudice is prejudgment. Prejudging what is necessary for a healthy economy. And so, many, many, *many* years ago, South Africa and those who got in control, they prejudged what was necessary for the type of life and economy that they wanted. And therefore, their interest and their concern was, of course, for themselves and their economy.

Now that is the law established there for a long, long, long time. And those in present control are doing what their limited minds will permit them to do and still maintain a healthy economy. The change is not coming easily. For a change to be forced, a drastic change to be forced upon them not only would that government economy collapse but the rippling effect upon the world economy would be very serious. We must not misunderstand what is to be considered by all.

For some time, the world economy and the rippling effect from South Africa has been considered. Now the pressure is on that government to bring about these drastic changes. Changes shall be given. There is no question about that. Do not expect the drastic changes that are being demanded, for the economy is not going to be sacrificed by external pressures from any government. Does that help with your question?

Thank you.

Pardon? Yes.

A question. [The chairman speaks.]

Do you see the Catholic religion changing its opinion or . . . yes, its opinion or its policies around reincarnation?

No. Absolutely and positively not. The Roman Church, in reference to your question [on] accepting the possibility of reincarnation, absolutely, positively [will not]. They will no more accept that possibility than they will accept abortion, than they will accept their priests being married and the end of celibacy. For the Catholic-Roman Church to accept those changes would be the end of the Roman Church. It would lose its power and its faithful by the millions. It cannot afford that luxury of change, for already license has crept into the very timbers of its foundation. Already so many changes, contrary to the basic principles of Catholicism, have already crept in, deteriorating the very central core of the Roman religion. If we understand that the Catholic Church is based upon a single figurehead, without the possibility of any other control, if we understand the years that it has held that solid rock of one authority, in the final analysis, for it to permit those types of changes, it would be an instrument of its own collapse. Did that help with your question?

Yes. And I wanted to add—

Yes.

—how about the other Christian churches? Will they move more toward reincarnation concepts?

Well, in reference to the Protestant churches—that's what you're referring to, is it?

Yes.

Of course, we all understand those are the churches founded from the principle of protest. We do accept that, don't we?

Yes.

And so, because they are founded under the very principle of protest, they always are seeking something to protest. *[Several people laugh.]* And they will find that, oh, yes, indeed—as well as they find everything else that they can find—to protest. Because being the principle of their very foundation, how could they be Protest-tants, if they did not protest? Does that help with your question?

Yes.

You're welcome. Yes.

A question here. [The chairman speaks.]

Yes.

Yes. You mentioned abortion. Is that a form of interfering with another soul's right? Or is it an acceptable solution to a problem?

Well, in reference to the question or statement, Is abortion an acceptable solution to a problem? Well, to many believers, of course, it is. Now, to the Christian religion—not to the Protesttant religion, but the Christian religion, the one founded under the Roman Church—of course, to them, it is an interference with the right of the soul to enter Earth, to have an earthly form.

Is it a solution to a problem? To many people, it is. Is it right or is it wrong? That's totally dependent upon your belief. And this is why there's controversy. Whatever is dependent, for its expression and its survival, upon belief comes under the Law of Controversy and is governed by it. Does that help with your question?

Thank you.

You're welcome. Yes.

The lady here, please.

Do you ever foresee a time when the president of the United States will be chosen by popular vote versus the electorate?

That is assured. You will have to be patient. For, you see, you have a system of electoral college and you have a system whereby there are certain forces that have been in control for a very long time. And so if you're willing to be patient, very patient, and you have forty years of being patient, you will see the change coming about. I hope that's helped with your question.

Thank you.

The lady in the back. [The chairman speaks.]

Is the usage of animal parts going to continue to be used by human beings? Is it right or wrong?

In reference to the use of parts of an animal's body to be used by the animal known as the human, is it right or is it wrong? Is it in the best interest of the animal [known as] human? Well, first of all, we have to take a look at the form and see which form appears to be the most evolved, capable of doing the most things. And we have to admit that we judge it to be the human animal. Therefore, is it in the human animal's best interest to use parts of an animal that are not as evolved by its own self-evidence, you see? That's a question.

Now, why should man revert to cannibal levels of consciousness for his survival? Man has scientific advancement and technology—until he turns to that which is greater than scientific advancement and technology—man, in his mind, has scientific advancement and technology available to him to make any part of the human body that he so chooses. And that will work beautifully. Many years ago, we spoke of the, truly, waste of these heart transplants in one human to another, the transplantation of the human organs, when the artificial organs, the artificial hearts, through more effort and research being put into them, will prove beyond a shadow of any doubt to be the best for mankind. Does that help with your question?

Thank you.

You're welcome.

Question here.

Yes, we've been told that seventy-two hours is the length of time to wait before anything should be done to the human body; yet in postmortem examinations, they begin immediately. Is there some kind of suffering caused to the deceased?

Well, thank you, in reference to that, "They begin immediately," only on those who permit it to be so. Is there some kind of suffering to the individual? It takes the cycle of seventy-two of your Earth hours for the consciousness of the human being to completely leave the physical body. So whatever takes place with the human body within the seventy-two-hour time span, the consciousness of the individual is well aware of it. And therefore, in that respect it is, of course, in the best interest of those who don't want to be affected by being cut and all of that to give them that opportunity to leave the physical body completely so they don't have those experiences. It's simply a matter of consideration. But that's up to each and every individual to make his own decision whether he wants them to immediately go to the butcher shop or not. I hope that's helped with the question. Yes.

The gentleman in the back.

Yes, I'd like to ask, Is the present situation of the balance of understanding that exists in the human, mankind, is that a situation that is just restricted to humanity? And is it a situation that's going to change?

Well, in reference to your question about the understanding of mankind, the consciousness within all forms is in a constant process of refining the form, which registers the impulses from the consciousness. So in that respect, all forms are evolving. Now the principle, the consciousness itself, being the principle, cannot evolve, for it cannot change. It *is*, and that's all there is to it. It *is*. Truth *is*. Truth doesn't change; however, the form through which the consciousness, truth, expresses, that form, the form changes. The form evolves. And it is the purpose of the entrance of the consciousness into form to refine and to evolve the forms. That's taking place with all forms.

Man has a great responsibility, a responsibility to all forms. But he cannot grant that responsibility, he cannot grant that understanding to the little animals and the flowers and the creatures and the critters of your planet, he cannot grant that until he first grants it unto himself. I hope that's helped with your question.

We have time for just one more. Thank you.

. . . short term predictions about, say, the next three months for people who live in the Bay Area? [A few words are difficult to transcribe.]

For people who live in the Bay Area, short term forecasts: dress warm. Warmer than you have been dressing, because, you see, no one likes to be chilly. And, in fact, it has a detrimental effect on their good attitude and their good sense of humor, would you not agree?

Yes.

So, you see, because we value so much what we call comfort, we should use a little wisdom, dress very warm and very comfortably.

Be not so concerned about [the] economy. You see, concern is such an important thing. Man prays to God to change a situation for him, a situation that he is concerned about. Now the Divine Goodness is a light which shines. Man's concern is a thick, dense fog. And so for man to concern himself about something and simultaneously to pray to God for the change is the act of a very ignorant person, for it is a divided consciousness through which no good may enter. And so when we want a change of anything, the law reveals: remove the concern we have over it and something else, the minute we move that concern, something else will move in. And we will be the recipient of experiencing what the Principle of Good, known as God, can do in anything at any time, the moment we may move out. That's my message for your Bay Area in a short-term forecast.

Thank you, friends, kindly.

DECEMBER 30, 1984

Twenty-Second Annual World Forecast

[Before 1971, the annual forecasts were often given in private homes to a small group of individuals. From 1971 through 1984, the forecasts were given at the American Legion log cabin as part of the Serenity Spiritualist Church's devotional service and were given to the congregation, which included members of the public who were new to Serenity as well as students. However, this forecast, as well as the remaining forecasts, were given at the Serenity temple to a group of students of the Living Light Philosophy. The questions asked of the teacher were often written in advance of the forecast by students and then read aloud by the vice president.]

Good morning, class, and welcome to our Twenty-Second Annual World Forecast.

Now we're going to go, this morning, on with the questions you have concerning world events, for today is the day that I have instructed my channel to show you and to demonstrate the most important pressure points on the human body for the flow of the natural divine energies for harmony, which restore the body, the mind, and the soul into a perfect balance and the effect of which is good health. *[Please see the appendix.]* And so now, we'll go ahead here with the questions that you have prepared on the events for your world.

Thank you. Are the Russian leaders sincere in their diplomatic gesture toward America with the recent sessions between the two leaders? And what will the outcome be?

Well, if you consider sincerity based on a real fear, in that respect the majority of the leaders of that particular country of the Soviet Socialist Republics are sincere, for the motivation for the diplomatic overtures, so to speak, are based upon a very real fear of their judgment on the ever-advancing technologies of the United States.

Thank you. How and when will the terrorist actions be stopped?

What you know as terrorist actions will come into a greater control in the foreseeable fifteen years.

Thank you. Is California in for a large earthquake within the next seven years?

Within five years from the year of 1985, that would bring you into 1990 and the spring of 1991, you can expect serious tremors of the earth in Northern California. You need not fear a major disaster at that time, for it will not come until you have passed the year of 2010.

Thank you. Was the reign of Stalin and Hitler planned somewhere else in the universe, like in the realms of darkness? Was it some sort of plot?

Well, what we understand as contractual agreements and what we understand, in the Great Rotunda, as contracts in keeping with the evolution of form would not be considered plots. Devices used by those who control the mental realms are very conniving, filled with deception and devices, and in that respect, of course, their planning could be considered plots. And in respect to anyone who enters the realm of belief and binds themselves to the wheel of illusion, known as mental substance, has to pay their just and fair price whenever they do not fulfill the legal and just contracts established in keeping with the laws of evolution.

Thank you. Will those of us who remain in this school be able to stay out of the mental control that is forthcoming on this planet through the use of androids and other mind-controlling devices?

In reference to that question, it takes daily effort to declare the truth that, "I am not the form nor the forms that I direct energy to. They are creations of my mind." And to the student or students who make that daily effort, many times a day, there is, of course, for them, the opportunity not to be controlled by the things they have created. Man cannot be controlled by an android until he first allows himself to be controlled by the android form which is created as his own vehicle, known as the human body. For in that respect, it is governed and controlled by set patterns that are established. And whenever man permits himself to believe that he is the form, then he is the servant of the form and, therefore, controlled by that which is basically mechanical in respect to thought patterns.

Thank you. Will peace occur in our lifetime among all nations and countries?

Among all nations and countries, you are speaking of all people and their places of residence. And so in your lifetime you will not experience what you understand as the peace and harmony that you know in truth that you are. For all people, at one time, to rise to the awakening that they are the user of form and not form itself is something that is, in your world, in the far distant future.

Thank you. Will beings openly communicate with us in our lifetime?

Well, in respect to beings openly communicating with you in your lifetime, if you are referring to forms that your physical sight and senses are not aware of, yes, indeed, they will communicate in your lifetime to those who are awakened to the vibration and the frequency on which they make themselves known.

Thank you. Will the air disasters get much worse before getting better?

Like all things that get better, they first go down in order to go up. And so, yes, there will be an increase in what you know as air disasters in the remainder of your year of '85, especially in the month[s] of May, June, and July of 1986, again in the fall and the September time of 1987. They will continue on through a fluctuation and an increase for the continuing four-year period from this time.

Thank you. Will cloning completely take the place of the family and women having children?

Well, science is advancing with their cloning and their androids, and the family, as you know family, is something that already is in a passing stage. And society is adapting to those changes in preparation for the inevitable. And so families, as you know them, will not be the experiences of the future on your planet. And as far as cloning is concerned, certainly it is in one's own selfish interest not to go through what they consider the pain and suffering and struggle for reproduction when it is so simply done in the laboratory.

Thank you. Will the U.S. budget get balanced?

Well, well, it will get bigger, if that's balanced to you. It will get larger, the U.S. budget. They're trying to put a giant band-aid on it at this time, but there is an adjustment of the world economy; and so in that respect, the budget will get larger, but its band-aid will hold it from bleeding for the next three years.

Thank you. Will world hunger end in our lifetime?

World hunger, as you know world hunger, will not end in your lifetime because the greed of man will not end in your lifetime. And it is the greed of man that is the direct cause of what you understand as world hunger.

Thank you. Will the monoclonal antibodies help those who have cancer?

They are the most important step that has been made, and they indeed will be helpful. And through that opening, scientifically, and through the effort that is being made in that area, the day of the ending of cancer is in the foreseeable future now.

Thank you. Will churches unite and become more universal in their outlook in the future? If so, when will this take place?

Well, because they are not universal in their concept, you could not and should not expect them to be universal in their application. Churches, as you know churches, the majority of them, are based upon the motivation of self-interest. And anything that is based upon the motivation of self-interest is governed by the mental world. And in that respect, of course, they could not unite for that would be contrary to the very nature of mental substance. It is not a substance that unites; it is a substance that divides as it ever seeks power and can only experience force.

Thank you. A recent air disaster occurred in foggy weather. I would like to know if a greater percent of us are not balanced within our emotional bodies or the water centers and mental bodies, air centers, will these disasters continue?

Yes, they will continue. It's like a person that's drowning, and they rise up from the ocean only to drown in the mist and the water that is in the air center.

Thank you. Will there be an end to the terrorist attacks?

I've already spoken on that question. And there will not be an end until those years have passed.

Thank you. Will the recent discoveries in genetics become detrimental to our environment if we don't put guidelines on them?

Well, indeed, of course, they will. Like anything that has such potential of force as genetics, they will become most detrimental if guidelines are not firmly established and laws [passed] governing the limits in which they may operate.

Thank you. In an earlier class, reference was made to nuclear disarmament through the intervention of a third party. Will this intervention occur in our lifetime?

You will find that France will become more active in the intervention of nuclear disasters. Now in your world there has not been much stated on the efforts of France outside of her publicized efforts to do more nuclear testing and gain more nuclear control. There are very fine, important scientists working in France, and have been for many years now, who have dedicated their life to moving from a nuclear age that could potentially cause such a holocaust for the planet Earth. They are guided by intelligent beings whose responsibility is to see that planet Earth does not interfere with their divine rights of their own evolution. So in that respect, France will become more known, as the years pass, in her efforts, her scientists and their efforts, to bring an ending to the nuclear age as far as weapons of defense and offense.

Thank you. The year 1985 is the year of the eagle. Would you please share with us what animal represents 1986 and the spiritual significance of that animal?

Yes. The coming year, the year of 1986—you are just leaving the year of the eagle. And for my students, you will understand that the year of 1986 is the year of the lion. And the year of the lion will show a great strength for those people who are turning to the Light, turning to the sun, which is the light and the life of the universes. And so the year of the lion will be a year through which any effort that is made, one should consider its continuity, especially in the coming year of 1986.

Thank you. Earth's scientists are altering the genetic structure of plants, animals, and men to make them less susceptible to disease. Is this a path of wisdom and reason? And where will this path lead in the foreseeable future?

Well, first of all, it is a path of wisdom and reason for those people who make the effort to make the changes in the genetic structure, which is within their domain and their divine right. To grant that divine right to another is not a path of wisdom or of reason.

The genetic structure of form is subject to that which sustains form. Now because you are that which sustains form, beginning with the form that you believe you are, when you believe that you are your form, you lose the ability, temporarily, to control your form. So those people and those scientists who have evolved in consciousness, knowing beyond a shadow of any doubt that they have the power to change the genetic structure of form, therefore, in that respect, are not controlled by form. However, because it is your divine birthright, your duty, and your responsibility to adjust and make whatever changes that wisdom reveals to you in the genetic structure of form, beginning with your form, then in that respect it would not be beneficial to grant that divine right, which, by the law, is your own, to grant it [to another] and to be the victim of someone else who has taken over that control from your lack of effort. And that lack of effort is revealed by your belief that you are the form and the limit. And whoever believes they are the limit cannot control the limit. And so, when you move from belief that you are the limit, when you move from the belief and the bondage that you are the form, then you will qualify yourself to control the form.

Thank you. Would you please share with us more about the light beam energy that will replace fossil fuels in the near future and how this form of energy is related to the crystal?

Well, first of all, the crystal, true crystal, because of its very nature as a mineral, is the finest possible reflector of light or frequency. It is more accurate than any other mineral available on your planet at this time. And so when it is properly cut, it will reflect these frequencies of light and be an instrument through which limitless energy [becomes] available [and] will replace the fossil fuel systems that you have today.

Thank you. What does the Book of Causes reveal about South Africa?

South Africa will continue on with its turmoil. And within the coming eight months, very important decisions, beneficial decisions, for the good of the whole shall be made. They shall not be understood. They shall take place within the coming eight months. Now over the period of the next six years, South Africa, going through its boiling point, as it has over these past years, will enter a stage of what you might understand as a simmering. And from that, the South Africans and the people and the natives of that land—natives for eons of time—will rise up in a wiser way in the sense of gaining political control in the government.

Do not expect a miracle in the next few months, for it is eight months from this time when the agreements will, some of them, become known to your world. So be patient with South Africa and its growing pains. It is, of course, understood by, I do think, most of you that the interest in South Africa is an economic situation, and it has a direct effect upon world economy. And so there are many changes and many people that are involved in bringing about the peace that shall come to pass in South Africa.

Thank you. Is there a time in the foreseeable future when housing costs for purchase and rental will return to that of the 1960s?

There is no return to those who have stepped on the merry-go-round of time. It goes 'round and 'round and 'round. It's not going down; it's just going on. And so, in reference to looking to the past and, of course, what you understand economically as the good old days, it is [a] wise path to forget it, for it's not going to return.

Thank you. Will interest rates drop back to that of the '60s in the near future?

They cannot drop back. For them to drop back, so everything else would [also], and that's contrary to the Law of Evolution. Adjust with the changing economic times. Be grateful for the bread that you have on your table. Things are not as bad, unless you insist that you gain more from believing that than from experiencing the good that is ever available to you.

Thank you. Will pets ever be accepted as legitimate family members in regards to housing and medical tax deductions?

Well, in reference to medical tax deductions, as long as medical science, in its primitive state on your planet, insists on carving up other forms in order to seemingly gain some benefit for other forms, do not expect them to be accepted as legitimate tax exemptions, for they haven't even been accepted, as yet, by medical science as beings at all. Yes.

Thank you. What is the reason for one store selling many more winning lottery tickets than others?

Well, that's a wonderful demonstration of the Law of Motivation. And so you have to go to the person who originally made the decision and the judgment to have these gaming tickets and to their belief, which permeates the particular store that has so much sales. And so if you have a person who really believes something and they completely convince themselves, they have no problem in convincing the masses. Sheep are designed to follow. And so those who believe in their limits are those who are, by their own choice, designing themselves to follow, whether it's a gaming ticket or it's anything else. Yes.

Thank you. Will the American farmer regain the lost land which was in their families for generations?

One must not look to the past to experience the good of the present. In that respect, we do not foresee any changes in the existing laws. No, we do not see that. It's filled with doubt and it's filled with cost and it's filled with economic considerations.

Thank you. Will American agriculture continue to be run by the small farmer or will they be absorbed by large corporations?

Well, first of all, as I spoke to you some time ago, the industrial days of the country of the United States has reached its peak, some time ago. Agriculture and farming. The United States of America is the breadbasket of the world. And so in order for that breadbasket to fill itself in the best way economically, of course, farmers will continue to be absorbed by large corporations. Now the balance for the United States of America, economically, is its breadbasket: its farming and the technology there that the United States is so far advanced in and especially in the fields of electronics. And so those who consider, for the United States, its own good, should consider two basic things:

the electronic industry, everything in reference to electronics, computers, and the advancing technology and the farms and the breadbasket.

Thank you. When will apartheid end in South Africa?

It will not end, as it is now known, in the early, foreseeable future. There will be a positive change eight months from this time, but an ending to that throughout the entire country is something that will come in many, many stages. And, you see, as you speak of apartheid, a separate place for these people, a separate place for that, you have apartheid in the United States of America. You have apartheid in Germany and England. You have apartheid in Australia and New Zealand and throughout your whole, whole world. You have a system of separation. You have various communities. This neighbor will not have that type of person living next to them. And economy is what balances out the apartheid. Now if you look at apartheid as an economic [system], which it truly is, it's an economic system, then you will understand that, as it is, it will be a gradual change, gradual, and it's ending will be in various stages. You have this apartheid, not as blatant, much more subtle, throughout your entire Earth planet.

Thank you. When will the black people of South Africa gain equal rights?

Not in your lifetime as you know, in your country, equal rights. And if you mean by the question all Africans, then you will not see it in your lifetime on Earth.

Thank you. Will Russia move out of Afghanistan shortly?

No. Your world, your news may reveal her withdrawal, she will only withdraw when she has set up the necessary puppets to do her bidding. And that work is not yet complete. However, it is approximately 70, 72 percent complete. And so there'll be a gradual withdrawal. She will always leave her people to keep control, but not as many of her armed forces. And the Union of Soviet Socialist Republics has made their judgment and are determined to protect their borders and to protect [them] by having these buffer states totally surrounding her. That judgment was made in the days of that Premier Stalin.

Thank you. How many centuries before man accepts man as his brother and lives in peace on earth?

Not in your world on Earth.

Thank you. Will our military ever use androids in the way intended in the movie D.A.R.Y.L?

Well, in reference to the androids and their purpose of manufacture and the funds that have supported the manufacturing and the designing and the research necessary has always been a military purpose. And, of course, those many billions of dollars that have already been invested have not been invested just to entertain the senses of man. The money has been spent by the Defense Department, and of course, they will use them for the purpose for which they have designed them.

Thank you. What steps will be taken to deter hijackings, bombings, and other forms of political terrorism? Which country will make the greatest progress in this deterrent?

The one that is the most qualified to make the greater progress is England. However, it will take much more cooperation with England and a great deal more financial support from the United States in order for that to be brought about.

Thank you. What steps will be taken to end the suffering of animals used in experiments? In the public outcry against such treatment of animals, which form of public expression will prove the most effective: the militant or the non-militant?

Well, for example, in making an impression upon the American Medical Association, because of their great pride in their achievements, because of the egos that are so convinced that they're perfect and right that are in control of that association, militant picketing and demonstrations of their headquarters would be the first step to make. Non-violent, militant marching and demonstration. That will have a tendency to infuriate and to insult the egos that they believe that they are, followed by negotiations.

Thank you. Will our medical world develop techniques of curing blindness and deafness by working with the faculties of awareness and perception?

A few medical doctors have been working on that for these latter few years. As far as [the] medical association, it will be centuries, centuries on your planet before they will accept the possibility that they have been in error in reference to the various treatments for those conditions and their judgments concerning something beyond what they consider their domain.

Thank you. In the next century, what will the average-income home look like architecturally? Will we, as a nation, be predominantly owners or renters of our dwellings?

Prepare yourself for what you know as condominiums to be dome-shape. Dome-shape is the architecture of the future. It is that way for many, many reasons, not just aesthetically. But you will find that a dome-shaped building is more economically heated. The temperature is controlled with less expenditure of energy. And [the] dome-shape is the architecture of the future for your world.

Thank you. Will Marin County and other counties with heavy traffic corridors solve the congestion problems by means of monorail or other form of mass transit? Is this foreseeable by the turn of the century?

Well, turn of the century, it only gives you sixteen years and they move very slowly in your world, especially when it's a matter of changing their judgments. So you should look more forward to twenty-five years.

Thank you. What kind of presidential administration will follow the present [A nearby telephone rings.] *administration?*

Kindly reread that particular question. We had an interruption there.

Thank you. What kind of presidential administration will follow the present administration?

Well, I would like to say conservative; however, we find one a bit more liberal. And because we find one a bit more liberal in the future there for your world, we find the budget bleeding through the last band-aid that was applied.

Thank you. Will America and the Soviet Union end the arms race in 1986?

Oh, no. No, no, no. Do not, do not be convinced that they will end an arms race in '86 with so much involved. Look forward, perhaps, to '96 and something really starting to move.

Thank you. Will the Federal Tax Reform Act be enacted in 1986?

Now that's a very difficult, difficult thing for your government because there is a 60-40 [percent chance,] at this time, of that being enacted. Now we look forward to, especially, to March-time and all the—even before the Ides of March, right at the very beginning of the March month. And we see a turnaround, which reveals to me, from this Book of Cause, that there will be a drastic change. And the chances of enactment move from that lower percent all the way to 87 percent yes.

Thank you. Will the United Nations be effective in solving disputes between countries and in solving world hunger?

[Will] the United Nations be effective?

Yes.

Oh, certain countries will be effective, but try to understand with a platform for the expression of all the world's judgments, don't expect too much. You know, a little in is a little out. And so a lot of talk goes in and a lot of talk comes out. Of course, it does serve a good purpose: it offers a forum through which those people may express themselves and vent their judgments and their emotions. But look to England, look to Great Britain for some good, positive steps being made, for the leader of that country has been working diligently to help humanity and receiving zero publicity for it. Yes.

Thank you. Will there be a victory in 1986 for animal rights?

Well, there are victories, especially in the State of California, small victories. And yes, those little victories, there will be in the coming year and there will be several before 1987 ends.

Thank you. Will there be any change in our use of nuclear power in 1986?

Not in 1986, not that which will be known to the masses and to the public. No, not in that respect.

Thank you. Will the world community find a way to curb terrorism focused on travelers?

Kindly reread that question.

Will the world community find a way to curb terrorism focused on travelers?

Not in the very near future, no.

Thank you. Will any deeper, positive results come from the increased relationships with Russia?

Yes, positive results will come. When you have great fear and you are convinced that you have an enemy and that you fear the enemy's advancing technology, necessity is the mother of invention, and the invention is coming to pass slowly but surely, if you understand the true motivation.

Thank you. What positive things are in motion and going into motion concerning the work to save and nurture nature?

Well, in reference to the work to conserve and to save nature, your environmental groups throughout the world are doing a great deal of good in that respect. They will continue to do more and more good, but, like in any organization of people, there are always the reformers and the fanatics. However, that in no way should cloud the sincere workers that are bringing about some good in that respect.

Thank you. Will there be new discoveries concerning space and the planets and our solar system?

Indeed, there will. Indeed, there will. Yes.

Thank you. How will the oil and gas supplies be affected and moved this following year?

How will they be affected? Your gas supplies?

Yes.

Well, in what respect?

I have no idea. [The questions were written in advance of the forecast by students and read aloud to the teacher by the vice president.]

Well, you can look forward to lower prices in oil, which will mean lower prices in gas. Don't expect to be the receiver of that benefit for another two years, but in that respect the prices are lowering, yes. However, for the sake of your own economy, may they not lower much more than what they [are] already projected to lower, for if they do, your economy will have a very serious effect.

Thank you. Will the missing link ever be revealed to humanity?

When you say "ever", indeed, indeed it will.

Thank you. What will happen to man with the coming age of androids?

What will happen to man is a great emotional frustration and trauma as he is forced to accept that there is something (a form) which is capable and demonstrates that it has more intelligence, that is, expresses more intelligence, [and] that it is able to perform and do things that man, in his lack of effort, has convinced himself that he can't do. And so in that respect, there will be, to many, a great competition, and it will create for man great, great jealousy.

Thank you. Will humanity have to establish itself on other planets for survival?

Yes.

Thank you. Within the age of computers, will there be a completely different social structure than we're accustomed to?

Yes.

Thank you. With the San Andreas fault running through California, would California become separated from the continent?

Yes.

Thank you. Will there be an earthquake in Marin County in the next fifty years that will cause property damage?

Yes.

Thank you. Are we now or will we be the victims of mind control through microwave in the United States?

Well, first of all, you are already the victims of mind control through microwaves. Now, you see, mind control is possible when frequencies (microwaves) manipulate the forms that a man believes he is. And when man does not make the effort to control the forms that he creates, then he makes himself a prime victim for someone operating the transmissions and microwaves to control him. And so what we make no effort to control, after we have created it, [by doing so] we simply are the victims for whoever desires to control us. So in that respect, yes, of course, the answer is affirmative.

Thank you. How soon will we have a definite AIDS test to show those who are carriers and those who will have the disease?

Within eight years.

Thank you. Will the United States engage in war in the next ten years? If so, where?

Not war as you know war. Skirmishes, yes; war, no.

Thank you. Will the space shuttles, in the next three years, pass without loss of life or major injury?

Will the space shuttles?

Yes.

Two disasters in the coming five years; that includes loss of life.

Thank you. What kind of transformation and evolution [will] the medical field go through as an effect of the AIDS epidemic?

Reread that question, please.

What kind of transformation and evolution [will] the medical field go through as an effect of the AIDS epidemic?

Out of fear great good can come. And so in that respect, there'll be more acceptance in the medical community of the possibilities of testing various chemicals and broadening the horizon a bit to accept something that has not already existed in their domain of judgments: and that is that there's more than one way to skin a cat, and there's certainly more than one way for a person to be cured.

Thank you. Am I correct in that this year is the year of the five, of faith? And because our Earth is the number five also, will there be more of a universal awakening of the truth of what we truly are?

To those who have the sense to pause in the year of the lion, the strength, yes, yes.

Thank you. Does Halley's Comet correspond with a particular number and symbol and color?

Yes, because Halley's Comet is a certain frequency.

Thank you. Thank you. It appears that more than one center is out of balance at the same time because of the simultaneous earthquakes, plane crashes, volcanoes, etc. Will our centers on the Earth become more in balance and therefore alleviating all of these disasters?

They are becoming more into balance, slowly but surely. And, of course, the nature spirits will respond, as you are a link in a chain and the link in the chain effects the entire chain. Yes, certainly.

Thank you. It has been said that technology is so far ahead of our spiritual growth. Will they ever balance in our lifetimes, or are we headed for a renaissance of Atlantis?

We're headed for a renaissance of Atlantis. It is the cycle for those who believe they are limit, for those who believe they are limit are subject to the Law of Duality: the rise and fall. Yes.

Thank you. Is there anything that you feel that we, as students, should know about, any upcoming earthquake in the Bay Area or the world?

No, I would not be overly concerned with disaster when divinity is such a joyous way of living.

Thank you. Is there one central group or government that is supporting world terrorism? If so, what is their motive and what do they hope to gain?

Middle East control.

Thank you. What effects is terrorism having on the evolution of man's consciousness, spiritually and educationally?

Most detrimental. You're returning man back to the brute realms of force.

Now I see that, hopefully, you've taken care of those questions. I may have instructed my channel if all of my students will remain, please, downstairs there in class, my channel will be down shortly and will demonstrate for you the most important major pressure points in the human body. And I can only assure you to those who are religious to their use when it is required to bring about and restore a health in their body and their mind and their soul, united, that you will not receive any finer technique, if you wish to call it that, to bring about a restoration of the natural flow of the River of Life. *[Please see the appendix.]*

And so I'll say good day at this time. I know that you're looking forward to a broader horizon of this coming new year. And accept that it is here and then you'll be prepared.

Good day.

DECEMBER 29, 1985

Twenty-Third Annual World Forecast

Good morning and welcome to our twenty-third forecast.

This year that you are facing is the year of a seven, mathematically, the year of 1987. It is the year of manifest stability or security. It is a year in which a wise person goes forth with their endeavors, either minor or major. Now in the understanding of the mathematics of the universe, that which is begun in a seven year of stability, that is the law manifest and established, is completed in a year of totality or a nine year. That reveals to you, of course, the Law of Duality, the Law of Creation, the two.

And so we'll begin here with the many questions that you have asked in reference to the forecasting of events based upon the records that are presented to us. Yes. *[Questions were submitted in advance of the forecast and read to the teacher by the vice president.]*

Thank you. What will be the condition of the electronic industry in the U.S. in the coming years?

Well, in the coming years, there is a shift of the electronic industry in the United States. There is a shift to the Far East. And you will find, to your surprise, that China will rise very supreme in the electronic industry, contrary to the mass thinking that it will all come from Japan. Yes.

Thank you. The Russian Bear has recently made gestures of reconciliation. Does this represent a change in their priorities or a change in tactics?

It represents a change in tactics. It represents a change in attitude. Whenever the minds of men fail in their endeavors with the tactics that they use, sooner or later they do change the tactics.

Thank you. What will be the circumstances and the effect on our society of our planet being contacted from outer space?

What will be the effect?

Yes.

Well, the effect, of course, will be what you would consider one of fear. Because a person has in their minds, of course, security in that with which they are familiar. Not being familiar with other intelligences, the reaction will be that of fear, for man fears what he's not familiar with because he has judged that which he is familiar with he is capable of controlling. Yes.

Thank you. What will be the immediate and long-term effect on society of the plague we are now experiencing?

Well, it will be a massive decrease in population. Looking from a positive view, one will find that beneficial to the other creatures of the Earth planet. Yes.

Thank you. What will be the primary form of expression used by visual artists in the twenty-first century?

Please restate the question.

What will be the primary form of expression used by visual artists in the twenty-first century?

Sensual. I think that's the word. Yes, indeed it is.

Thank you.

That which appeals to the functions, yes.

Thank you. Will this art depict its subject matter in abstract terms or in representational terms?

Abstract. And it'll affect the function of feeling.

Thank you. Which writer, up to now, will have the most impact and influence in the next century?

None of your present writers.

Thank you. What will be the predominant international and interplanetary languages of the next century?

Mathematical.

Thank you. In the next 100 years, what will be the major changes in the U.S. Constitution? How will these changes affect us?

Within how many years?

One hundred.

Well, within the coming 100 years, there will be many additions to the existing Constitution of the United States, known to you as interpretations. The present interpretations of what exists, known as the Constitution of the United States, will go through drastic changes because of economic, world economic necessity.

Thank you. In the year 2087, what will a typical meal consist of? Which food will yield the highest nutrition for this planet?

The food, in that time, will be taken from the waters of your planet and not the agricultural system which you are presently aware of. Yes.

Thank you. Will terrorism advance throughout the world in 1987? How will this affect U.S. and Middle East relations?

Well, terrorists would have a flux and flow. It will not increase drastically, more than it has been in the past four years. Its effect will—the Middle East—there are other factors of a higher priority than terrorism. Those factors are economic. Economy is the major guiding force or driving force, rather, in the years ahead. Yes.

Thank you. Researchers are saying that the AIDS virus will reach phenomenal proportions in years to come. Will researchers find a cure for this disease in 1987? What will be the scope of the AIDS virus in the year to come? What is the spiritual significance of this disease?

Would you like to read one question at a time? However, I'll answer the first question. When you have questions, you know, it's intelligent to read them one at a time. First of all, in reference to the first question, of course, they are finding band-aids, but all band-aids have a tendency to leak. And that's the "cure" that they've come up with and will have in these coming years. One hope, only to guarantee another disappointment. Now the second question of those several questions that you have.

What will be the scope of the AIDS virus in the year to come?

The scope? By scope do you mean what will be its increased percentage-wise of what it presently is?

I have no idea. [Again, students submitted written questions in advance of the date of the forecast and they were read aloud to the teacher by the vice president.]

I accept that that's what is meant. Well, this virus is increasing at proportions of 100 percent increase per year. When the figures are known to your world, then you will understand that it is not just a plague of your United States. It is a plague of the planet. Yes.

Thank you. What is the spiritual significance of this disease?

The spiritual significance is very positive: it is freedom from the absolute conviction that you are limit. Yes.

Thank you. How will the political situation in Central America change in 1987?

More friendly relations with Nicaragua and [El] Salvador.

Thank you. It seems—

Out of necessity. Yes.

Thank you.

Economic necessity.

It seems that the world is in a constant turmoil and confusion at present. Will harmony arise in consciousness in 1987?

Yes, it's known as the divinity of disaster. It is already rising very slowly. Increasing numbers of people are realizing that. For the divinity in this disaster of this great plague, its effect will bring about a broader and greater understanding. Yes.

Thank you. Will the African people unite in time and accept their own personal responsibility?

Well, in reference to accepting their own personal responsibility, we find, from our records, that they have accepted their personal responsibility long before the aggressors of greed entered their country. So in reference to that question, when the time comes that the greed for gold leaves their country, then the Africans, as a people, will return once again to what they have always known: personal responsibility and personal survival. Yes. It is outside influences that are manipulating the country and that is, and has been, the problem for centuries.

Thank you. When will robots be used more and will they take the place of many people in the workplace?

Yes, indeed they will take the place of many humans in the workplace. And as there is a vast decrease in the population worldwide in the most foreseeable future—thanks to the virus that is helping to awake[n] many people and free them from their addiction to the limit of the vehicle or body that they're temporarily using. Yes.

Thank you. What will be the good that comes out of the AIDS epidemic for the whole universe?

For the whole universe? A decrease in population so a balance may be restored into the universe and that the other creatures of the planet will not be totally annihilated.

Thank you. Will the test-tube babies be more aware of their true purpose from the beginning of their Earth life?

They will be; they will benefit from less attachment to what we understand as the water center of emotions, and they will be viewed, thereby, by those who believe they are the water centers of emotions, they will be viewed as more of mechanical beings rather than human. Yes.

Thank you.

That comes from the breeding, you see.

Thank you. In what direction will the educational system take in our century?

In what direction will the educational system take? Well, in reference to that, the educational system that you presently have, that is the mass educational system, is designed to guide the person to personal accomplishment and personal achievement, to guide the person in those directions and areas. Unfortunately, through that guidance, it breeds a selfishness that is most destructive and detrimental to society.

And therefore, in the coming years ahead, there will be more emphasis placed on a united effort and less of a so-called individualization of accomplishment, more of a group achievement or accomplishment. More teamwork and more unity will be the guidance of the educational system in the future.

Thank you. Will the next big earthquake coming to California be all areas of the coast of California?

No, it will not be *all* areas of the coast of California. However, we do not foresee any major earthquake within the coming three years. And several, several tremors, especially in '89 and in '88. Yes.

Are we composed of several spirit lights or one beam?

One beam. Spirit lights—when a person thinks of spirit lights, then they think of, more in a way of separatism. Man is only a beam of the one Light that is. And the beam shines as clearly as man will allow it to shine in his own consciousness. Yes.

Thank you. Will President Reagan be able to leave his office with dignity and honor?

Well, in reference to your president, for the good of your country, the full so-called story of what has taken place will not and cannot be revealed for at least twenty years in your Earth time. Will he leave with dignity? It depends on whose thoughts you're looking at. If you are looking at the thoughts of the so-called Democratic Party and some of their selfish interests, then he will not leave with dignity. If you're looking at the world population, then he will leave with dignity. Yes.

Thank you. Will there be a major earthquake in the San Francisco area?

Are you speaking of this year?

I have no idea.

Fine. Then I will accept it as the year of 1987. There will not be a major earthquake in that year.

Thank you.

Only minor ones.

Will the disease AIDS continue to spread during 1987 and will a cure be developed?

I've already stated they'll have a band-aid. All the band-aids they have will leak. Will a cure be developed? By a cure, you mean a cure? No, it will not. And, of course, it will increase. We've already stated that it is under a mass increase, and one should look at the divinity in disaster. If it takes a disaster to turn to the light of reason, consideration, and to free oneself from an addiction, then a disaster indeed contains its own divinity. Yes.

Thank you. What should we as individuals do to help reduce the tension in Central America?

Stay out of it. *[Several students laugh.]*

Thank you. Will 1987 bring any major breakthroughs or developments in energy generation?

Well, some time ago I spoke to some of you students in reference to the crystal, for energy is light. There is energy everywhere in the atmosphere, for there is light. And so it's simply a matter of advancing your technology so that the crystal may be used to absorb and to disperse the energy that is already available. However, you must understand that what is the obstruction to that advancing technology is economics, you see.

Thank you. What is the future for the animals on our planet that are being so abused?

Well, the future of the other creatures or the animals of your planet that have been, by man's selfish need and greed, so greatly abused, their future is improving as the human beings and the population is going through a decrease. Contrary to popular sight, there will be a great reduction of this great population explosion, which is reducing, and has been for some time, the population of the other creatures of the planet. However, the abuse of those creatures cannot be limited to what you see in your laboratories, for their homes are being destroyed [and] their food supply is being ruined by the two-legged animals. And so that also is a great abuse, a great abuse of their homes and their rights. Yes.

Thank you. Will we experience any land drops in our lifetime?

Any what?

Land drops.

Well, now, I've heard of many drops, but what do you mean by a land drop?

There, there was a fore—prediction some time back about part of California just disappearing into the ocean.

Oh, you call that a drop? Or a slide?

I presume that's what they meant.

Careful on presumption; it guarantees descent. However, you are speaking of descent of the coastline. Well, there already is and has been a process along the coastline of California. What you would understand as various slides. As far as the coast, your present coast disappearing completely in your lifetime, you will not view that from your Earth you know.

Thank you. In the Bible, it talks about the return of Christ. What does this mean and will it be in our lifetime?

Ask each victim of what you call the virus AIDS as they're passing on and you will awaken that Christ, in that respect, is returning. Usually on the last breath.

Thank you.

But in any other way, no. If you mean some being, known as a Christ, appearing in your universe and transforming everyone, no, that's not going to happen. That is contrary to natural law. It's contrary to divine law. And it doesn't work that way. However, when the senses suffer sufficiently, they turn to the Light. The masses usually refer to Christ in your world on your planet as the Light. Yes.

Thank you. What is the truth about the Iranian arms situation that President Reagan finds himself in?

Well, he finds himself in a position, as a president of your nation, of covering up, in a sense, or trying to protect, for the good of the nation, for the good of all of the people, various things. You see, for example, when you have someone in a position in your country or anywhere in business [or] anything and they permit themselves to rely upon assistants to follow out the orders they have given and they do not monitor them, they accept that they are reliable people and that they have interpreted the orders the way that you have given them—it is a matter of various assistants trying to make a better position for themselves and interpreting presidential orders literally, by the letter of the law, and that is the problem and that is the fiasco, if you want to call it that.

Thank you.

Yes.

Will public confidence be restored within the last two years of the Reagan administration?

Public confidence in what you call the Reagan administration has gone through various fluxes and flows. When the people finally got a little more money in their pocket, credibility in the Reagan administration improved. When they had less money, the credibility of your present president was very, very poor. And so you have to understand the masses; the thinking of the masses is very fickle. It is totally based upon selfishness and self-interest. So if you look at credibility of the masses in that respect, you will have no problem in understanding one moment they're very credible, and the next moment, they're just the opposite in the thinking of the masses. That's why masses lead nothing: because they do not lead themselves. That's why masses will never lead, for masses do not lead themselves. They are led and deceived that they are leading themselves. They are not leading themselves. They're either the victims of mass advertising or the victims of anything that they judge will feed their selfishness. Yes.

Thank you. What events on a world scale will most affect Serenity Association and its members?

Well, if you consider, if you're speaking now of Serenity Association as a group of people who still permit themselves to be influenced by what other minds think, by permitting themselves to be influenced by what their minds judge, if you're looking at it in that respect, as the Serenity Association, instead of looking at it spiritually, then you're going to find that one moment they're up and the next moment they're down, only to be up again, to be down again, because they believe they are creation. I do not consider that the Serenity Association. Yes.

Thank you. Will the Serenity philosophy ever be introduced to the public again or will it stay the awareness of a small group on this Earth?

Well, that's a strange conception there. The Living Light Philosophy is introduced daily to the world, not, however, in keeping with the judgment of the questioner. However, I see there that the questioner has asked the question based upon publicity of the Living Light Philosophy or going out to new people and in that respect, no.

[In June of 1985, public devotional services of the Serenity Spiritualist Church ended. Classes continued only for a small group of private students.]

Thank you. Is the new tax regime going to be of assistance or a detriment to the average American?

It is designed, it is designed and well thought out to be of a benefit to the average American working man. The small businessman will find it a bit difficult. Yes.

Thank you. What industries will be in the forefront in the next year or so?

Electronics.

Thank you. How will the situation with Reagan and the alleged sale of arms be resolved?

Well, I've already covered that question: it won't be resolved.
Thank you. Will there be—
To the—Excuse me—to the satisfaction of the masses. It will be resolved temporarily as one person is put up there to receive the blame, only for another one to be put up there, and another. No matter what has happened, the president of your United States is responsible. He merited assistants who were more interested in building themselves a separate empire than they were in his purpose, the president's purpose, as being president. That is what he merited and that is what he has to pay for. Yes.

Thank you. Will there be cessation of the consumption of meat in the U.S. in the near future?
No, not with the cattle industry the way that it is. It certainly will not.

Thank you. Will there be an antibody test for the two new AIDS viruses and when?
Well, there will be a test because the present antibodies that they are working on are extremely detrimental and have very serious, long-lasting side effects. The minds of men of your planet do not yet fully understand the chemical balance of the human body and how it is affected by the attitude of a person's mind. Yes.

Thank you. Will the earthquakes that were predicted in the last forecast, the smaller ones or the larger ones spoken of, affect California north of Fort Bragg?
Be not concerned. Anyone that is living north of Fort Bragg, you won't go into the ocean. *[A few students laugh.]* I hope that's helped take care of your fears. For if that's what you need, is an earthquake to keep you from making a change in your life, then I can understand that you can nurse that fear and wait until you pass to the other side to experience your quake. Yes. *[More students laugh.]*

Thank you. Will we still use gasoline to power our cars by the year 2000?

Well, now, you only have, let me see, you've only got thirteen years, haven't you? Well, the oil industry is not going to allow the water to power the cars, although an engine has already been developed. Yes.

Thank you. Will we turn to the ocean to produce the food we eat?

Yes, you definitely will. You will certainly turn to the water of the planet. Absolutely.

Thank you. Will man ever journey to the center of the Earth?

Well, he's so interested and dependent outside, that'll be the last place he'll go, is inside, including the center of your Earth. Yes.

Thank you. Will America and Russia reach an arms agreement in 1987?

Well, look to 1989. You can look to some publicity in '87 and '88. [In] 1989 there'll be some more solid agreements based upon economic needs. Yes.

Thank you. What will happen to small investors in the stock market?

Small investors in the stock market? Well, depends on how small. Small investors will be gobbled up ever in keeping with the present laws that have been set into motion over the past three years of these massive conglomerates, for it's all based on economics. Yes.

Thank you. Will the animal rights movement be successful in ending experiments on animals?

Not in your lifetime. But a great, a great deal of progress will be made in the coming fifteen years; but it will not end.

Thank you. Is 1987 the year of the jackal for Serenity, and if so, what can we expect?

Well, certainly, '87 is the year of the jackal. And what do you expect from a jackal? *[After a short pause, the teacher continues.]* Yes, I'm asking you. Do you know what a jackal is?

It's similar to our coyote, only— [The vice president responds.]

What's its characteristics?

Ah . . . [The vice president pauses as he considers the question.]

Anyone know anything about animals? Yes, good morning, [Student U].

Good morning. It survives on the efforts of other animals.

Yes. Yes, is there anything else you know about a jackal? *[After a short pause, the teacher continues.]* Yes, [Student O], please.

Well, it's spotted. Its skin is spotted. And I think it's a crossbreed.

That's all right, Mr. Red. *[The teacher addresses the church's dog, Mr. Red, and several students laugh.]* Thank you. Yes, [Student H].

It's my understanding that it's very surreptitious. It doesn't like to show itself.

Yes. And what else does it do? *[After short pause, the teacher continues.]* [Student B]. Thank you.

It runs in packs. [In a] group.

Yes, [Student R].

I think they are very beneficial for keeping the herds thinned down of the plains animals and keeping them strong.

That's true. So there's divinity in all disaster. Has that helped your question?

Yes.

Yes, good. Thank you. Move on to the next one.

Thank you. What is going to happen in Africa to the blacks and their struggle with segregation?

Well, I want to understand what you mean by *segregation*. The questioner. If you mean by *segregation*, a force which keeps you from living in a certain area and which keeps you subject to a force that you cannot, in any way, control or influence, if you mean that—you're going to find in [South] Africa that the economy is in the control of the minority, as you all know. However, the world economy has a very direct dependence upon those who are in control of the country of [South] Africa. So it is not just a matter of eliminating segregation in Africa, for to do so you are affecting many other governments. Therefore, the ending or elimination of segregation as a foreseeable event in your life is not possible without a severe, severe rippling of the economy worldwide. Therefore, those in control of world economy will not permit, for in their thinking they cannot permit, a sudden ending of segregation.

There will, however—and there is effort being made on the part of the African government, which is controlled by other world financial interests. There is effort being made to permit those black Africans into government or civil positions, as long as a guarantee is established with the black African and the white control of the government that those civil servants will not interfere with the slow, gradual process of centuries that it will take for what you understand as full [freedom from] segregation.

I do hope that's helped with your question to understand you're not speaking just about segregation of different races. You're speaking about a direct threat to world economy, and that is what [the] world economy is considering.

Thank you. Will the religious wars continue in the world or will there be a change in 1987?

As long as religion is a device for mental manipulation, religious, so-called, wars will continue. Yes.

Thank you. Will extraterrestrial visitors make themselves known in 1987?

Not in '87. Not to the masses, no.
Thank you.
No.
What recommendations can you give us for 1987 that would benefit Serenity, the Light, and the world?
Well, first of all, it would have to benefit yourself. So let's restate the question. Otherwise, you'd have no incentive. What would benefit you and Serenity and the world? Stop thinking about yourself. That's the greatest benefit. The greatest gift you can give to the Light that you are is the gift of self-thought. Yes.
Thank you. That's all the [prepared] questions I have.
That's fine. Now we have a little time or we'll make a little time—that's one thing about time, it's a delusion; so you can make it or change it, for delusion is created. So we'll create a little time here with that so-called time, and you may ask any questions that you have in reference to the classes you've been receiving.
Yes, good morning, [Student S].
I'd like to ask, when you mentioned—
That was your hand, wasn't it?
Yes.
Yes. Yes, I see.
Sorry. [The student may have formulated her question, but had not raised her hand.]
I see.
When you spoke of 1987 as being the year of the jackal—
Yes?
—was that also the spiritual animal? Because ofttimes it's different than what the—
The animal reveals the characteristic of the human beings, the mass beings. The animal reveals it.
Oh.
You see, just because a jackal or even a vulture lives off the efforts of others does not mean that the vulture, the jackal, or

the animal is a bad animal. It simply reveals that mentally it has progressed and is what you might know as cunning, you see, when it can lie around and watch and as soon as the food is prepared by someone else's efforts, it goes and eats it. But then, we know a lot of people like that. I don't know too many people, even in my classes here, that cook their own food, usually someone cooks it for them. Yes, go ahead, please.

I'd like to ask—

Of course, they don't do it to the satisfaction of the other one, but anyway, they do it anyway. Go ahead.

Is there another animal that would spiritually symbolize this year for the school of Serenity?

Yes. The jackal.

Thank you.

Yes. And I just got through stating if you see the jackal as all bad, then you've lost perspective, and it'll be most difficult for you. Now I think you can relate, as a student of mine, to the jackal. Have I not heard you say, at times, that you have made great effort to help a person, but when it comes [to] your time for a little help from them that they disappear; they don't help you at all? Well, haven't you witnessed jackals?

Yes, that has happened.

You see? Well, there you are. So, you see, one can say, "Now is the jackal good or is the jackal bad?" Hmm? Does that help with the question?

Yes. Thank you.

Yes, there's a lot of good in the jackal. In fact, there's good in all things. And so I had already stated this is the year of the seven. This is the year of the manifestation of stability and security. And when one relies on that which is within them, then one is freed from being the jackal and depending on that which they can't control. The jackal has to wait to see, "There's the food. I'll rush in and try to get it. But I might not be able to get it." You see? Go ahead. Yes, [Student S].

Thank you.

You're welcome. Yes, [Student Y], please.

Thank you. In other dimensions, other than ours, do light beings move in groups together?

Now when you speak of light beings, which are you referring to? Are you referring to a being that has existed on your planet and has left the shell and gone into their other world?

Yes, sir.

Well, not necessarily. There are some people even on your planet in the physical world, they move around in groups or they move individually or they move in pairs, etc. You see? It depends on their motive of what they have to accomplish. You may go out into your world and you may decide to take three people with you or only one person. It depends on your motive, you see. You may want them around for a time and after you've got out of them what you want, you want to say good-bye and you want them to disappear right away. So it always depends on the motive. Does that help with your question, [Student Y]?

Yes. Thank you.

Yes, it certainly is dependent on a motive. Do you want them—you know, a person says, "Well, I'd just like to have company." Company? What do they want out of the person? Now some people call it company; some people call it friendship; some people call it, "Well, I need a co-worker on this job here." But we must realize what it is that we want. Do we want to go to the store and we take a person with us—what do we want out of the person? Do we want to go to the store? Or do we want what we can get out of the person on our way to the store?

Yes, [Student M]. I mean, does that help? You see, you see, when you look at the Light that you are, there is no emotion, because if there's emotion, you're looking at the lower light, the lesser light. Yes.

Thanks. Good morning. [Student M speaks.]

Good morning.

I wanted to ask about—it seems that the banking industry for years was very—it appeared to be very secure and stable. And—

Stable? Yes, well, it appeared that way.

It appeared that way. And now it seems to be in such transition and flux. I was wondering what was creating this transition in that industry?

Well, as the masses of any country in any world become more sleepy with their satisfaction, as they become more sleepy in satisfaction, then those who have always been in control begin to rise up and become more blatant. And so you see disturbances with the banking institutions; you see so-called hostile takeovers and etc. You see, they're only beginning to show themselves. They've become more brazen in their efforts, for they have judged that the masses are really sound asleep in their own selfish satisfaction. You see, a person who permits themselves an overidentification with self becomes a person who is well satisfied and very much asleep. Yes.

Thank you.

That help with your question?

Yes, it does.

Yes, certainly. Yes, [Student O].

Yes. Would you speak on what is so-called a light sleeper and a heavy sleeper?

[The teacher laughs joyfully.] Yes. Well, I think perhaps my students could best relate that a so-called heavy sleeper is one who really becomes involved with the dreams or nightmares that he's having and, therefore, is known as a heavy sleeper. In other words, they've become so involved with the interest of what they have created that nothing else exists.

Now you've seen people, they'll sit down and they'll look at the picture box [the television] over there, and they'll become so involved they can't even hear the telephone ring. Well, they become so involved with what they are creating. Now, you sit down and you take a look at a television, and you think, you allow your minds to think, that something over there is creating and working on you. No, no, no, no, no. You are looking at a picture; you are creating that in your mind; you are working. It's exhausting to sit down and watch television, or sit down and watch anything, because when you sit down and just watch, you are creating that in your mind. That takes energy; that takes effort. Does that help with your question on light sleepers and heavy sleepers? You become so involved you believe you are that which you have created and you're a very heavy sleeper, difficult to awaken. Did that help you?

Yes, sir.

Yes. You see, the more you believe that you are what you create (attachment to the fruits of action), the more you become involved with what you create until you have extreme difficulty in leaving what you have created. Take, for example, a person who's created a thought [and] solidified it as a judgment in the water centers of emotion; and they say, "Well, now, that's not serving me very well. I don't want that judgment anymore." You just don't free yourself that way. It keeps coming and plaguing you because you believe that you are that which you have created.

Selfish people have great difficulty, for they attach themselves so quickly to the fruits of their action. So when the fruit of their action, being fruit, it rots, they have great difficulty trying to leave what they have created. Does that help you, [Student O]? *[After a short pause, the teacher continues.]* Or do you like rotten fruit?

No, I don't like rotten fruit.

Well, then don't be a sound sleeper.

OK.

[The teacher laughs joyously.] Don't be so satisfied.

Well, I, but, I accept what you say. I mean—

Don't accept what you don't want to accept. I don't think you're a light sleeper, do you?

A light sleeper?

Yes.

Well, in the sense of going to—I mean, in principle, no. No, I'm not.

Yes.

No, in principle.

By that you mean action.

Right.

By living demonstration. Fine. All right. Then your question was answered. Yes. Anyone else have a question? There's no problem at all. You do have a great need to be satisfied.

I certainly do.

Yes, well, I didn't create it.

Thank you.

Did that help you?

No, sir.

See, people who have great needs to be satisfied are people who are begging to be victims. They go out into the universe, "Please, please, help me to be your victim." Yes, anyone who has great need to be satisfied, for need is denial of what you are. And so—yes, I know. *[The teacher acknowledges a silent signal from the cameraman that the tape is nearing its end.]* And so I find in your world and as I've spoken to you many times in classes, nurse your needs to be satisfied. Go ahead and do that, because, you see, when it comes time that you awaken and you say, "I'm just a victim. I'm always a victim of circumstances." Why, certainly you are. You create that. You cry to the universe for someone to come and control you so you can have that victimization feeling as an attachment to the fruits of your action. Does that help everyone with their question? Yes, [Student R].

I'd like to ask, How will the cutting of the rain forests that exist now, how will the cutting of those forests affect the weather around the planet and especially in our—

It will have a drastic effect. It already has had and will continue to have so because you are upsetting the natural balance designed by the Great Architect for the planet. Therefore, there will be, in certain areas of the world, your world, there will be less moisture in the atmosphere and a drying condition, slowly but surely, because you are upsetting, from greed and selfishness, you are upsetting the natural balance of the planet. Yes.

Thank you.

You're welcome. Yes, [Student U].

Will there be an overall increase in the temperature of the planet to the extent that some of the polar ice caps melt?

That is already taking place. That *is* already taking place. Yes. Yes, [Student R].

It's been reported that the ozone layer at both the North and South Poles have huge holes in them.

They do.

And what will, what effect will that have on our, on the people on this planet?

Well, in time it'll destroy it, of course. Yes.

Is there any way that that may be repaired? Or will the condition worsen or perhaps get better?

Well, it will be in a state of what you would consider a pause as more of the masses are awakened. And there will be great effort not to destroy the very nature of the planet. There will be effort made, but it will only be kept on hold or pause for a time. And once again, of course, selfishness will do what selfishness always does: considers only the one thing that controls it. Yes.

Thank you.

The denial of the rights, you see, of anything that is not in keeping with its own judgment. Yes, [Student L], please.

What is the cause of the holes in the ozone?

Selfishness is the cause. Selfishness. You want to know the chemical cause? The pollution of the planet. Yes, from selfishness. Yes, yes. You see, you want to see the good in all things, including selfishness. Yes. So often a person in their experiences, if they didn't have what they judge is the original thought or the first thought, then they're not about to do anything or go anywhere. The selfishness demands that it must first have the judgment, otherwise—that's how selfishness is. Yes, [Student Y].

What would be—my mind can't see what would be the good of the destruction of the planet.

The good of the destruction of the planet is the awakening of the people upon it and in that process—because, you see, all things, they are born and they go through their aging process and they return to the source from whence they come. Now man himself is only an instrument for the final destruction of the planet. Natural causes will bring that about. Man is just assisting those natural causes. For, you see, the sun—this planet, the planet Earth, will return to the source from whence it sprung, and that source is the sun in your solar system. Though that is eons and eons of time away, man is simply assisting or speeding up the process. Does that help you?

Yes.

You see, he's speeding up the process. Yes. We have just a few moments left, if you have any final questions. Yes, [Student R].

In past forecasts, you have given a brief look at the state of the stock market for the year to come, do you have that—could you share that?

Well, I would be more sensitive about investments in this coming year of 1987 in reference to Wall Street. I would not take a breath of relief until the September time of '89.

Thank you and good day.

DECEMBER 28, 1986

Twenty-Fourth Annual World Forecast

Good morning, class, and welcome to our Twenty-Fourth Annual Forecast.

Now this morning, this being the year of the eight, numerically, you will have the opportunity [to] make yourself receptive to the stability and the security of the universal laws of life. We're going to begin our forecast today with the varied questions that you, as students, have prepared. And so I will make effort in answering your questions on the coming events, world events, as you raise your hands and speak them forth. Yes, [Student Y], please.

Thank you. What can the students of Light here at Serenity do to receive the fullest benefit from the coming year, 1988, the year of the hawk?

By accepting the possibility of the removal of the obstruction from one's own consciousness. Now all obstructions, you know as students, are created by a judgment of the mind. Therefore, it can only be removed by an acceptance of the mind to the possibility of its own removal.

Thank you.

You're welcome. Yes, [Student O], please.

I have several questions in this. What is the thinking and purpose of news medias to report mostly tragedies, the effect it has on the mass-population thinking, which, in turn, governs their behavior? And where is this type of thinking leading the masses as a spiritually-evolving group?

Yes. Well, first of all, in answer to your question, What is the purpose of news media to report and present sensational events? Profit. It has proven to be profitable to present that which stimulates the senses. Therefore, profit is the motivation of those who present so-called disasters and those things which tempt the senses. What effect does it have upon the masses, is, of course, we know, self-evident. The effect is that it directs the consciousness and the energy to things that they judge [are] beyond their control and, therefore, place themselves as victims of it. I hope that's answered your question.

Thank you.

You're welcome. Yes, [Student S], please.

Thank you. Will a synthetic blood for transfusion be found and, if so, when?

Not in your lifetime.

Thank you.

Yes. [Student M], please.

Thank you. Yes. I would like to ask, Why is education such a low priority in this country of ours and when will it change, if possible?

Because profit, financial profit, is a higher priority. And as long as financial profit is a higher priority, then that which is financially profitable, of course, will continue. When will it change? Within the coming twenty-five years.

Thank you.

You're welcome. Yes, [Student L], please.

Yes. Good morning.

Good morning.

There are more and more homeless people appearing on city streets. People with babies and some people have died there. Will homelessness in America continue to increase? And will some immediate form of help be found to help them through their crisis?

Temporary measures (band-aids) are already in process. Will so-called homelessness be eliminated in your lifetime? No, for there are many who choose to be homeless. Yes. Yes, [Student H], please.

Thank you. What will be our next presidential administration's posture toward Russia's so-called peace overtures?

Extreme caution and suspicion, for the Democratic Party is, according to the laws established, as I stated to you some time ago, it is, what you might say, their turn in office or their time. However, there is an ever-increasing possibility in this year of 1988 of a Republican president and a continued Democratic Congress and Senate. Yes.

Thank you.

You're welcome. Yes, is that [Student U], please?

Yes, sir. What does the use of laser light in various products reveal about the direction of man's evolution?

Yes, what does the use of laser light in the products reveal of man's evolution?

Yes, sir.

[At this moment, Mr. Red, the church's dog, hops into the teacher's chair and the teacher laughs joyfully. Then he guides Mr. Red back to the floor.] Well, you might ask my student, Mr. Red here. Now we have to learn to share. You share there. *[The teacher points to the floor to the right of his chair.]* I'll share here. Over there. *[Mr. Red doesn't budge from his spot directly in front of the teacher.]* Now—he doesn't like that, you see. He's not under the laser light right now. He's under the magnetic senses.

All right. It reveals that the technology is drying out in the sense that it is indeed more profitable to use that which is less expensive. Now it does not seem to be less expensive for a manufacturer to use laser as a technology; however, it is indeed much more practical. It is much less expensive after the initial cost.

Therefore—and I don't like to speak of only profit in this year of '88, but try to understand that profit is the number one priority of the world market more than ever before. The world market, of course, is a profit market. And as the U.S. dollar continues to tumble and each day man thinks it's at its lowest ebb—it's not yet at its lowest ebb because foreign currency will bolster it for their own self-interest. And so the dollar has not yet fallen on the world market to its lowest value.

Now it is true that it is a so-called secret policy of the present administration of the U.S. government to cause the dollar to go to the lowest in the history of the country on the world market. By doing so, it brings about a change in the world market which will prove to be most beneficial to the United States. Now most people are not able to see the wisdom of that type of a policy. However, within the coming five years, from allowing the U.S. dollar to drop to the lowest in the history of the country, within the coming five years, the masses of the country will see the wisdom of that so-called secret policy. That is not something that has happened by chance. That is something that has been conceived and planned by very wise financial experts in the present administration of your country. That helped with your question?

Yes, [Student K] has a question, please.

Yes, thank you. Will the U.S. economy experience any shocks in 1988 similar to that of the stock market crash last October?

No, it will experience many very loud rumbles and roars, but it will not experience again what you are speaking of. It will experience the roars and rumbles of fear as the dollar continues to drop on the world market and as the foreign countries themselves, for their own self-interest, begin to bolster the U.S. dollar. That help with your question?

Yes, sir.

Yes. Especially Japan and Germany are extremely interested and will be the first to make the changes in bolstering the U.S. dollar on world markets. Yes. Yes, [Student L], please.

Yes. Will middle class America continue to prosper?

Middle class America will continue to prosper as all classes of all people prosper ever in keeping with their own removal of obstructions, which is the belief that they are the judgments that they create. Yes, thank you.

[Student C], please.

Thank you. I understand that the effectiveness of the AIDS antibody test is very low. This being true, what is the chance of contracting AIDS through blood transfusions?

Ninety-seven percent in reference to that question. Yes.

Ninety-seven percent?

Ninety-seven percent.

OK. And what percentage of our blood bank's supply now contains the AIDS virus?

Sixty-two percent at present.

Thank you very much.

You're welcome. Yes, [Student S], please.

Thank you. Will the latex glove shortage be solved or will it impair medical and dental practice?

It is not in the financial interests of those in control for it to be solved in reference—if you mean by *solved* that there will be a sufficient amount of so-called gloves [so] that they will meet the demand. Because when you meet demand, you lower price. You do understand that, don't you? *[After a short pause, the teacher continues.]* And therefore, it is not in the financial best interest to meet demand because it lowers price. And in lowering price, it lowers profit in that respect. Now I know that sounds rather, perhaps, cruel, but you have to understand that you are dealing in a world that has the highest priority of finance. And as long as that is the highest priority, which is an effect, of course, of self-interest, then we must have this understanding of why things appear to be the way that they are. Yes, [Student S].

I'd like to also ask, Does the AIDS virus travel through latex gloves?

Well, it travels through because none of them are so perfectly made that there isn't what you might call a pinhole in them. The quality control is not that great, especially those that are presently being made. However, the greatest benefit of the use of them, of course, is the psychological benefit, you see.

You see, a person is—for example, now, say that a person makes an acquaintance and time passes, and the acquaintance reveals [themselves] to be a person who has [an] absolute high priority of a mental world. Then a person says, "Well, how did I meet a person like that?" And then a person says, "Well, let's see, now when did I meet the person?" And then a person thinks back and says, "Oh, yes. Well, I met them while I had a high priority of a mental world myself." And so when we look at it in that respect, then we see how the benefit is of the use of these latex gloves and these various things. There's a certain, of course, physical benefit to their use, but the major benefit to their use, of course, is psychological or mental. Does that help with your question?

I think so.

Well, the thing is, you see, that they're not going to not experience the disease by wearing them or they're not going *to* experience the disease by wearing them because the greatest benefit to them is their acceptance that they're going to be protected. Does that help you with your question?

Yes.

You see, if a person wears a pair of gloves and they continue to feed the fear that they are going to experience a disease, even though they're wearing the gloves, [then] they could wear six pairs of glove and still experience the disease. Does that help you?

Yes. Thank you.

You see? And so we find there are cases where people do experience the disease who have been very cautious and very careful. You understand that? That doesn't mean that one shouldn't take all precautions, but, of course, that is no guarantee because fear, you see—it's like a person [who] goes to a doctor. And they become so self-conscious. They find that there's a little spot or perhaps there's a lump somewhere, you see, on their vehicle. And they become extremely concerned about it. And so they go to a doctor with a great deal of concern. Now the law reveals that like attracts like and becomes the Law of Attachment. And so they manage to, by the law, magnetically attract themselves to a physician who is of the same kind: extremely concerned. So from the molehill a great mountain manifests itself, not just in imagination, but in the actual creation of the judgment of the fear. And that which we fear befalls us. Does that help with your question?

Thank you.

Yes. That's so very, very important. The records reveal that those who have [contracted] the disease, in reference to taking so many precautions, have taken the precautions with a phenomenal degree of fear. Pardon?

Yes.

And so even with all these seeming physical precautions, they have still [contracted] the disease. Yes.

Thank you.

You're welcome. Yes, [Student M], please.

Yes. Thank you. Is there a foreseeable future with socialized medicine? And what turn is the medical profession taking in the next—

No.

—twenty years?

No. In reference to your question, Is there a foreseeable time of socialized medicine? Absolutely not. Not under the present vibration of financial profit. You see, it is not profitable for the American Medical Association to permit socialized medicine in your country at this time. It is certainly not profitable for the American Medical Association. It is not profitable for the profit companies of insurance. It is not profitable. Yes. Yes, [Student L], please.

Will that always be? [Student M continues.]

Pardon?

Will that always be?

Well, that's entirely up to mankind. Will he always believe that the primary function is God? You see? You see, as long as we identify with the mental world, through the identification with the mental world, we believe that we are a mental world. And through the belief that we are a mental world, we are bound to a mental world. And the mental world, in the present state of evolution, has three primary functions. The god of those functions begins with *m* and you call it money. Pardon?

Right.

Yes.

Thank you.

You're welcome. [Student L], please.

Yes.

Yes.

What legislation will take place regarding AIDS patients?

Well, a great deal of legislation has already taken place and will be revealed in July and August of your year, here, of 1988. Legislation which requires a test for a marriage certificate is already easing its way into the various state legislatures. Especially legislation regarding adoption of children will be enforced in reference to blood tests and things of that nature. Those are the different legislations that will take place in this year of '88. Of course, it's like any disease, the fear and the cure is worse than the disease themselves because the fear and the cure is the domain of the mental world in the minds of men. Yes.

Thank you.

You're welcome. [Student C]—ah, no. [Student Y], please.

Thank you.

Yes.

Are we getting any closer to our goal in laws being made against the suffering and the current plight of the animals in the laboratories?

There is, indeed, much improvement in reference to the work that is being done concerning the other creatures of your planet. There will be, in this coming three years, phenomenal strides in the state legislature regarding the protection of the various creatures of your planet. Indeed, there will. It is very positive action that is taking place. And, of course, being a business world, there are increasing[ly] more corporations who find it in their best interest to announce their support of animal protection. Yes, certain corporations. Definitely. For it is in their own best self-interest, especially corporations which are manufacturing synthetic products that are not made from the creatures of the planet. Yes. Yes, [Student C], please.

Is it likely that Gary Hart will be the Democratic candidate for the presidency in 1988?

Well, if you asked him, of course, I'm sure he would have a very positive answer. We see more than a cloud of doubt over it. The little silver lining that we do see, of encouragement, is Mrs. Hart, Mrs. Gary Hart. No, we do not foresee Gary Hart as a president of your country, neither in this coming election nor in any future one.

However, in reference to that election, you may look more closely to one of the Republicans who is daily increasing in the vibration of a possible winner, even though it is a Democratic president that is scheduled. Do you understand that, [Student C]? Yes, Mr. Gary Hart you needn't be concerned about: a flash in the pan that's a double flash at present. Yes, [Student C], ah, [Student B], please.

Thank you. [Student C replies.]

In 1978 it was given in one of our classes that man had twenty years to bring about a balance between his spiritual and technological aspects. [Student B speaks.]

That is correct.

Since 1988 is the halfway mark, how is man doing in his balance problem?

Not too well. Not too well. We are not discouraged, but [man is] not [doing] too well, you see. You see, he hasn't experienced enough disasters yet. The more disasters that we experience, the better we do, you see. And be not concerned, there are disasters on their way, which are the effects, of course, of transgression of natural laws. Yes, [Student B].

Thank you.

Yes, indeed. And [Student K], please.

Thank you. Do the proposed food-help programs for Ethiopia offer any real relief or would an alternative program be more beneficial?

An alternative program would certainly be more beneficial because the present one is extremely political. Pardon?

Yes, sir.

Yes, indeed. And so when you have a so-called charitable program whose main incentive and motivation, regardless—you see, it's the forked-tongue support. And so, because it is so politically orientated—do you understand?—an alternative would certainly be much more effective and truly help the people who are in dire need of help regardless of their political affiliations. Pardon?

Yes, sir.

Yes, certainly. Yes, [Student Y], please.

Will our next president possess some of the good qualities that President Reagan has demonstrated?

Well, yes, of course, the next president will possess them. Whether or not he will have the courage to exercise them is quite doubtful. Yes, yes, but he certainly will possess them. Yes, [Student D], please.

Thank you. What can we do to help balance the Democratic administration that is coming into power?

By not believing everything you hear from them, you will help and be an incentive for some changes to come about. Though they may seem microscopic, they will be beneficial. You see, man has a tendency to believe what he has already judged about something. And so one must first question themselves of why this and why now and look at life and look at the political situation the way that it really is: that they're all human beings and regardless of a person's position in life, they're still human. Do you understand?

Yes.

And so grant them the possibility of not being perfect. Hmm? Even if you judge they're the one that's to be. Just grant them that kindness of not being perfect. Don't expect perfection out of them. Because usually we expect perfection out of another because we're so frustrated in not finding it inside of our self. Yes, I do hope that's helped with your question.

Thank you.

Yes, certainly. Yes, [Student P] has a question this morning.

Will we have a new—

That was your finger I saw going up, wasn't it?

Yes.

Yes, good.

Will we have a new system of energy other than nuclear or other than nuclear or solar energy for our homes and our cars?

Yes, certainly. A new energy—well, new, new only to the acceptance of mankind. It has always been. It will always be. It's the energy light system, you see. Although it is a slow start— you spoke earlier there of laser light. Light is everywhere present. It is never absent or away. You think when it is dark that there is no light. That is not true. The energy, the light is there; it is only lesser in the sense of your reception of it. It is always there. Light is never absent or away.

Now light is energy. Energy is everywhere. And so man's technological advancements to capture that energy that is everywhere present will come about through a technology that involves, as its very core and the very heart of its system, the crystal, the pure crystal. Yes.

Thank you.

You're welcome. Yes, [Student C], please.

Thank you. Will recession take place in this country, economic recession, during 1988 as predicted? If so, how can we prepare for this occurrence?

I don't recall a prediction of recession for '88. If I did read that from the Book of Life and the records, would you please state that to me.

Oh, I believe it wasn't—it was by analysts, economic analysts.

Oh, I see. I see. Yes, yes. Well, thank you. I did want to clarify that because I couldn't find it here in the records. We do not foresee a recession in this year of 1988. Now we do see rumbles and roars, and we do see financial changes. Recessions, we do not foresee for '88. It is true that recessions have been held off under the current administration's policy, domestic and worldwide policy, financially. Now I would be more interested in preparing for 1989's temporary sigh of exhaustion from holding recession at bay. It will not be what you will understand as a heavy recession, but it will have its impact upon the business world and the people in it. Now that's in 1989 and that's in the April month of that year. That is not in this year of '88.

OK.

Yes. And because—try to understand that as you change your president of your country, at the timing that the change takes place, in this year of 1988—do you understand, [Student C]?

Yes.

And by the time that a new president is able to bring about new policies—do you understand?

Yes.

That takes you into the year of '89. Pardon?

Uh-huh.

And so it is this change of attitude, this change of perspective by a new president that will bring about a rumble and roars and will bring about what you might consider a slight recession in the April time of 1989, not in '88. Pardon? Yes.

Thank you.

No, your present administration is far too wise to let that happen as they're on their way out. Yes. Yes, they have too much pride at stake and that serves them very well. Yes, [Student H], please.

Thank you. Will there be an event or events that will help the United States toward balancing its trade deficit?

Well, in reference to that, the rock-bottom dollar of value on the world market is doing a great deal of good. You see, the thing is there's a lack of patience. Now so many people in that financial market like to say, "Well, it's had no impact at all, our dollar falling so far on the world market." It takes time. And it takes time for other people, other countries and leaders of other countries to realize and to finally accept that it's in their own best interest to bolster the U.S. dollar on the world market. You see, it takes time for them to realize that, and it takes time for various foreign governments to change policies behind closed doors. Does that help with your question?

Yes. Thank you.

You're welcome. Yes, [Student S], please.

Who do you foresee as being the Democratic candidate and also the Republican candidate?

[The teacher laughs joyfully as he speaks.] Well, we have refrained for many years in our forecast, but if you would like to list them off on your paper there, perhaps we can see who seems most favorable on the records that are revealed. Yes. Do you have them listed?

I don't—

Well, I'll come back to you so you can list them. And in the meantime, we'll go to [Student Y], please. Yes.

Will the English ever leave South Africa and allow native rule?

Well, I don't know why everyone likes to think that it's the English who have South Africa, when I see so many Dutch and German in control down there. I don't think it's really quite fair to the English, not that there aren't many English down there. But let us not leave out the Dutch and let us certainly not leave out the German. And in reference to your question, you see, Will control ever go to the native Africans in South Africa?

Uh-huh.

Not without a bloodbath revolution because it will take at least fifty years before there can be an integration in South Africa. And the more pressure that the country experiences from outside do-gooders who don't really understand the financial picture of South Africa and its value of diamonds and various minerals on the world market, then, you see, the intent of doing good will bring a bloodbath revolution much quicker. And it does not have to be. It can be avoided through the patience of a half a century or so. Yes. Yes, [Student B], please.

Will the problems that the Philippines are experiencing be resolved?

Not as long as they have the present woman president. Not that she isn't a fine person, but she's an aggravator. She aggravates several political factions. And she has good intentions and has a tendency to speak with a forked tongue to various political factions within her own country; and promises have crumbled, like piecrusts, with certain generals and others, political heads of the country. Because her basic intent is well-meaning and good, but she is not respected, in reference to her military, because she is a woman. Pardon? Yes. Yes, [Student K], please.

Thank you.

Yes.

Will fusion power become a viable energy source in the near future?

Well, it is the step before the light energy and it certainly will. Definitely. Although it will prove to be much more expensive technology than the laser light which follows it. It definitely will be a viable technology. Yes, yes, it will. Yes. Yes, that's [Student D], please.

Thank you. There are rumblings about the Soviets pulling out of Afghanistan in the future. Will that come about in the next few years?

Well, first of all, How long have they been there?

I don't know. Quite a few years . . .

Well, they've been there as long as the U.S. was in Vietnam. You don't think those two children, a head of these two governments, the United States and the Union of Soviet Socialist Republics, are going to let one outdo the other, do you? No. So I wouldn't hold my breath for the next three years. Pardon?

Thank you.

No, they have no intention of pulling out [of the] control of the country until they've absolutely solidified it. And they will not absolutely solidify it because that country has a history, a very long history, untold generations, of battling any kind of foreign invaders, no matter how advanced their technology is. And so in that respect, the Soviet, the Bear will finally exhaust himself and take a nap with one eye open. I hope that's helped with your question. Yes.

Thank you.

Yes, [Student U], please.

In last year's forecast, it was given that the AIDS virus was increasing at a rate, annual rate of 100 percent.

That is correct.

Has that increase been altered or changed in any way for . . .

Well, if you're speaking about the entire population or if you're speaking about different segments of society, you have to clarify your question.

The general society, please, sir.

It is not decreasing in that respect, yes. Not [a] noticeable percentage. More awareness, that is true. More awareness, that is true. You see, the one thing, you see, is the wisdom of patience. You know so little about the virus. You know little about how long it takes, how long it incubates, 5 years, 10 years, 15 years,

20 years, and so you have to be patient to realize what is really going on. Yes.

Thank you, sir.

Certainly. Yes, [Student C], please.

Thank you. Is the spread of AIDS slowing down in this nation due to AIDS education?

In the communities where there is sincere effort in all segments of the society, it is decreasing. But those communities are so few compared to the increases taking place in other communities. So wherever there is sincere effort, wherever it is on the news media consistently, wherever the education is being taught in all the schools—and especially with the teenagers. There is a phenomenal increase in the teenagers and the population between the ages of 20 to 30, now, is vastly increasing. Yes.

Thank you.

You're welcome. Yes, [Student C].

Thank you. How rapidly will AIDS spread among so-called low risk heterosexuals in this country? Will we see more spread among this group in 1988?

You will be more aware of it in 1991. You will have some awareness of it in the latter part of '88, especially in '89, and definitely in '91. The thing is, you see, that it incubates for so many years. You do understand that, don't you?

Yes, I do.

And you, you see, 15 years is nothing. I said that [when I] spoke to one of my students some time ago. And I said, "Well, you talk about 5 years. Start thinking about 10 or 15 or 20." Now let's start moving on to 25 years. So, you see, what you must try to understand is these long-term incubations and they vary, of course, with different people and their chemistry and etc.

Now the spread of it in the low-income heterosexual community, you have some awareness of its spread. And they usually—of course, the ones who first are known for it are the poorest of the people, for they're the ones who go to the city and county and state operated clinics. Is that not true?

Uh-huh.

Yes. So, you see, the spread in the middle-class community far, far exceeds the spread in the lower-class communities or the poor-people communities. Do you understand? You see, it's not been and is not being reported. The cases that untold hundreds of thousands of medical doctors are aware of and do not report it. There is no law that is forcing and monitoring them to report it. Do you understand?

Uh-huh.

And this is why you do not have the statistics. The disease is spread, number wise, in the middle-class age bracket between 20 and 30, in the middle class. It has a much higher spread than in the drug community or in the low-income family brackets.

Uh-huh.

Yes.

OK. Thank you.

But they have no statistics on it because it is not being reported. And the people in that bracket go to private doctors, who, for their own personal financial reasons, will not report it [and] will not even consider reporting it. Yes. Yes, [Student M], please.

Well, when will this become public information, these statistics for the 20- to 30-year-old heterosexuals, for the public?

As the people become, the middle-class communities, become more aware of the phenomenal increase in the poor communities, their fear will force changes in the legislature, you see, you see. Pardon? Yes, [Student Y], please.

Thank you. Is there a chance of taxation on the advertisers and businesses who promote the spread of AIDS through their advertising techniques?

That will come about. It will be contested in the Supreme Court, but it will come about for the financial salvation of the countries. Yes.

Thank you.

Yes. Yes, [Student N], please.

More and more farm lands are being foreclosed on. What's the outcome of this? Are they all going—I mean, they all can't be foreclosed on.

Oh?

They can't—

When large corporations and special financial interests have a desire to purchase something, that's the system of capitalism. Pardon?

Yes.

All right. Yes. Yes, [Student K], please.

Have the overtures that Nicaragua has made during the past year towards a peaceful resolution of the conflict in that country, have these produced any positive effects that we will see benefit of in the coming year?

Now the Nicaraguan situation is a political football in the United States political arena. It is a football between the Republicans and the Democrats, you do realize that, don't you? And so Nicaragua is secondary in the interest of this football game that's being played. Pardon?

Thank you.

Yes. And so as far as the country of Nicaragua is concerned, because there are other countries in the area that are very serious in reference to revolution not spreading into their countries, there will be, within the coming four years, a settlement of that problem in Nicaragua. Yes, there will be a settlement of it. And that will come about because of the leaders of state of the countries that surround Nicaragua (Guatemala, Mexico, the Latin [American] countries) because they know—they have finally realized—that if they do not make effort themselves to get it settled, it will erupt in revolutions in their own countries. And they've had plenty of revolutions and don't care to experience any more. Does that help you with your question? So that's where the real incentive is coming from. Yes. Not from the political football being played back and forth between the Democrats and the Republicans and the Nicaraguan football. Pardon?

Thank you.

Yes. You're welcome. Yes. Yes, [Student M], please.

Yes. I'm not sure if this is true, but I believe that the Friends have said that in England the AIDS topic was publicized on the media all the time.

Yes. Very—extremely—very frequently.

Very frequently.

And Australia and several other countries, yes. It's the daily news.

Now is that because they place high value on education? Or what is the difference—

May I say this: they place a very high priority on survival, and they have accepted what will happen to their country. You must realize that they have already experienced what you understand as the Black Plague, you know, in their history. So they have some personal reference to their own history, and therefore they have a greater incentive in that respect: survival. Yes.

Thank you.

You're welcome. And [Student C], please.

Thank you.

Yes.

Why has the AIDS virus manifested in homosexuals before it will manifest in heterosexuals, the low-risk heterosexuals that we were discussing earlier?

Yes. Well, it's quite understandable that that would take place in your society. For example, it is a well-known fact, in the scientific community and in the medical profession, that the promiscuity of license is the very thing that causes a person to be more and more receptive to it. In other words, the odds are against them from the increase in the promiscuity. Do you understand that?

Yes.

Yes. Now that doesn't mean there isn't a great deal of promiscuity in the heterosexual community, because there certainly is. However, surely you realize that in the very beginnings of this disease that was spreading, those who are extremely receptive to it are those—everyone's receptive to it—those who have more promiscuity. And so, like in any segment of society, there are those who are extremely promiscuous, whether homosexual, heterosexual, or bisexual. And the ones that are usually so blatantly promiscuous are the ones who require state-supported doctors to care for them. Do you understand that?

Uh-huh.

Therefore, when this first came—[when] you became aware of it, it was from those people who were extremely promiscuous and did not or do not have the funds for private doctors. And it became knowledge of the counties and the cities. Does that help you, [Student C]?

Uh-huh.

You see? And so, what are the people who do not have the funds for private doctors? Your drug addicts, your poor people, which include many of the colored people, and the promiscuous homosexuals and heterosexuals. So to look at it in a clear perspective, you will find that it is the promiscuous people who do not have and did not have the funds for private doctors, which would hush it up, who went to the clinics where—be they heterosexuals, be they drug addicts, or be they homosexuals—who went to the clinics and got state-aid support, medical support, you understand?

Uh-huh.

And that placed it on the records and the public became aware. Does that help with your question, [Student C]?

It does.

Indeed, that's how it happened. Yes, [Student B], please.

I understand that we have the technology to survive in outer space, even to colonize on another planet.

Yes, we do have that technology. You do have it in your world, yes.

How soon can we expect man to actually go and colonize another planet?

Well, first of all, the race is just beginning between the Soviet Union and the United States. The Soviet Union never failed to be aware of the race. The United States became asleep in its satisfaction of its own accomplishments, through its own attachment to its efforts. And it is beginning to awaken again. Now within the coming six years, they will be wide awake. That's when you will see real, great progress in colonizing outer space. And so, from six years from this time, you place another twenty-five years and that will be within thirty-one years. And that will be because of the challenge, you see. You see, the ego does much better when it's stimulated with challenge, you see? Yes.

Thank you.

You're welcome. And, yes, [Student H] has a question, yes.

Thank you. What are the reasons behind our difficulty in locating and bringing back the POWs, MIAs, and do you see a positive step in that direction?

Well, there's a little effort made, but there will not be a—it is not a priority of any administration in the foreseeable future. No, but there are those who are helping. Yes, [Student U], please.

What sort of discoveries or so-called discoveries can we look forward to experiencing in the area of outer space exploration and development?

Well, first of all, what sort of advances are you speaking of? Or planets that you will be colonizing?

I was more interested in the advances, sir.

Well, hopefully, from our side of the veil, not too many. You know, we— *[The teacher laughs.]* One likes to know what neighbor's moving in, don't they?

Yes.

You know, and so there's that interest to consider. You will find the light energy, more development. You will find no nuclear holocaust on your planet. You will find what you may call defense shields, which will be made of the control of light energy. That, definitely, is one of the things that—I think you are calling those things "Star Wars"—but that is far from what will take place. You see, the protective shields of light energy, which will neutralize the magnetic effects of so-called weapons, is in process. And that will take place. That's one of the most important advances of science on your world. And that is within the foreseeable future. And the technology to protect oneself from the great disastrous rockets and things is in process. That's the most important of all of the progress for your planet. Yes, [Student L], please.

With respect to the colonization of another planet in about 30 years—

Uh-huh.

—will we be spiritually enough prepared so that we don't cause damage to others in space?

Hope's eternal and truth's inevitable. I don't know of anyone on this side that's holding our breath on that. Thank you. Yes, [Student Y], please.

Will those that participate in the colo—colo . . .

Colonization. Yes?

Will they encounter beings from . . .

Well, they will not encounter beings until their technology makes such an advancement that it becomes a threat to the peaceful continuity of those beings. Yes. Yes, [Student K].

Is it possible that in the near future, a peaceful coexistence or peaceful acceptance of this physical realm with other spirit realms will occur?

It is occurring. Will there be an increase of it? Yes, there will. You know, it's like walking through a war zone and being very careful you don't step on the mines in the minefield. Pardon? Yes. It is indeed a straight and narrow path. Yes, [Student B], please.

It's reported that quite a few of our satellites that carry communications are wearing out.

They are.

Will there be a new form of communication?

No, but they will launch more satellites, you see, because progress is slow in some areas because of the priorities of the various governments. And so there will be new satellites launched, more of them because they only, they have a certain life span and then they disintegrate. Yes. Yes, they've always had problems, you know, trying to make so many of these ships with tiles and things, but that will change. Yes. Yes, [Student M], please.

Yes. If the colonization, that you said, pushes so far and it's threatening the peacefulness of these other beings and they will show themselves, as you said, what form of communication—

I didn't say they'd show themselves. I said if they were threatened . . .

If they were threatened. What form of communication would that be?

What form of communication?

Right.

If someone is threatened that is in a higher state of evolution and technology? Probably disintegration of the offender. *[A few students laugh.]* Yes, [Student Y], please.

So—

Yes.

So that sort of answers my question. So they definitely will be able to protect themselves from this infant . . .

They are—

. . . stepping up.

Well, the offender has come from nothing and, of course, it's only kindness to return them to nothing. Yes. *[More students laugh.]* Yes, [Student B]—Do you have a question, [Student J]?

No, sir.

All right. Yes. *[After a short pause, the teacher continues.]* Very well. It seems that we got all of your questions in, and our time seems to be up here this morning. And so have a good week and I look forward to seeing you again soon in our classes.

Thank you and good day.

JANUARY 3, 1988

Twenty-Fifth Annual World Forecast

Good morning, students, and welcome to this class and, following, its forecast.

This year of '89 is the year of fulfillment.

From the heights of the Northern Sphere to the depths of the Southern, from the dawn of the East to the [dusk] of the West, all things are being called and shall respond in the Great Rotunda of Truth, where reason prevails. In the crystal-clear waters of the Lake of Harmony, its stillness is guarded by the Mountains of Unity.

And so it is that all things we have sown shall be reaped in this year of '89. There is no question for there is no doubt. The mind experiences doubt from the lack of patience, and it is from the lack of patience that we experience so much disturbance and discord in our lives.

And so it is a year to rejoice. It is not a year for new endeavor for one does not tempt themselves to sow when they are in the process of reaping. It is not a year for the sleep of satisfaction, for in so doing another, by the law, may reap our harvest. And so let us rejoice in the efforts and the opportunities that are available to us in this year of '89.

There is sufficient unto all need, the awakening to that which, at times, appears to obsess and to possess us. Without application of the various means that have been revealed to you, especially your cleansing and power breaths, without that daily application, we cannot, by the Law of Transgression, experience the goodness that we have already earned. Without the daily effort to apply and to study what has already been given, we direct, through our attention, energy to things that are already called and entering the Great Rotunda of Truth.

It is not practical nor could it be called wise to permit precious vital life energy to be used by forms unseen by physical sight and unknown by physical ears when the daily use of that which you have already received is the only protection available to you.

We know that we are indeed responsible for all that we have created with our mind. And we ofttimes desire to be free from that which we have created. However, by the laws of beginning, that which we create does not readily let its sustenance go. And so we experience what is known as the battle and the war within.

We ask, as we face this year, Where are we going? If we are honest, we know where we've been. Sometimes we think we've been nowhere. We are not so fortunate. For nowhere is no thing; that's who we are, not what we are. We are what we direct our attention to, for that is what we create; that is what we direct vital, life-giving energy to. So we know, with a moment's pause, what we are. The step to make, through daily spiritual study, is the step into awakening of who we are. Everyone knows what they are. They know it and must monitor it from moment to moment, because what we are is so fickle. If we do not monitor it, then we become very confused. And as we well know, confusion is an effect, not a cause, an effect of indecision. When one sees many things, like a child, one wants them all and has difficulty or indecision in choosing. It is that indecision that is the confusion that we ofttimes experience.

This year of '89 is the greatest opportunity that you, as students of the Light, have. The year of '89 is a year of fulfillment. You have the benefit not only of the awareness that it is the year of fulfillment—that it is the year of reaping, not of sowing—you have the added benefit of the awakening through your application of the classes and spiritual exercises that you have already received.

Before these things of creation enter the Great Rotunda, check them in your conscience, for in so doing they will not return into your aura to drain the vital energy that is necessary for your joy of living. We all know what they are, each and every one of us. Therefore, we alone, each and every one of us, have the right and the responsibility to instruct them as they enter the Light, for they are created and live in the mist of creation. Born in the errors and the ignorance of selfishness, they are forms that do not serve us well, for they are created by the error of fickle minds and, therefore, cannot, by that law, stand united and grant unto us the peace that passeth all understanding. They cannot, by their very law of creation, grant unto us the strength which is the effect of the soul faculty of unity. They cannot grant unto us the Lake of Harmony, which is the effect of the stillness of mind, the control of the water center.

This great vital energy that is necessary to create these forms, which, when they don't have their way, like little children in errors of ignorance, not only demand but create the great battle of the senses. They are not exclusive to anyone. They search the universe for like kind and in so doing, as water reaches its own level by its own weight, they find like kind for a time. But because of the nature of their creation in the ignorance of selfishness they are fickle and do not endure.

Reap your harvest intelligently. Not periodically, for the latter becomes empty by other things of which you are not consciously aware.

Now we'll spend a few more moments on obsession and possession. Whenever we create a thought and it solidifies into a judgment and we do not make the daily effort to cast the light of reason upon it, it grows; it feeds on our being. When it does not have what it judges it wants, it searches for like kind. Now it is only a created thought in mental substance. It is only solidified and becomes a judgment from the lack of daily spiritual exercises that have been revealed to you. However, once it becomes a judgment and it begins to search its realm for support or like kind, by the Law of Magnetism it attracts unto itself discarnate beings who are still bound by belief that a mental world is the only world there is. Those are decarnate beings from your Earth planet who, living in the mist while in flesh, continue to do so out of flesh, for mental substance is not physical flesh and bone.

And so when you leave your house of clay, you enter the only vehicle that is complete, that you can move in. It has always been the purpose of these classes to help you direct, through your daily spiritual study and exercises that have been given, to help you direct, in those moments daily, vital life energy, which is indispensable to creating a body or anything, to direct that energy by conscious choice to what is known as the soul faculties. Without that effort, you leave a house of clay whenever you so-called lose conscious awareness.

Now when you go to sleep, you lose conscious awareness. You are no longer conscious of your physical vehicle or your physical world. You know that reason and the soul faculties express only through a conscious mind. It is the forty sense functions that express through an unconscious or subconscious mind.

Do not tempt to bridge the gap—for you are not ready—between a conscious and sub- or unconscious mind. You are, however, ready to do your daily spiritual exercises and studies and have been ready for some time to flood your conscious mind; so when you are no longer consciously aware, that which is flooded casts its light upon the sub- or unconscious mind, where the forty sense functions express in a world of mist. That is the only intelligent and practical thing to do; for in so doing, upon awakening or returning to conscious awareness, you will be aware of what has happened while you were in so-called sleep.

Some time ago we shared with you, sleep is known as satisfaction. Satisfaction is necessary to the expression of the forty sense functions. But one cannot, by the very laws of creation itself, remain satisfied and asleep, for dawn follows darkness as darkness follows dawn.

And so in this year of reaping, this year of '89, use what you have, for you have more than what is necessary that you may not be obsessed from the effects of error of ignorance that earth-bound entities, which are decarnate souls from your earthly realm of physical substance, who are in the limits of their belief that there is nothing beyond their mind, will not be able to use you and your physical being for satisfaction that they have not earned until, through error and ignorance, you have allowed them to do so.

Now you may ask your questions on this forecast of 1989. Would you kindly raise your hands, please? Yes, [Student Y], please.

Thank you. Is the greenhouse effect that the scientists have been talking about on the news going to happen as rapidly as they predict? And if so, what can we expect in the next five years in changes in the earth's atmosphere and the earth's surface?

It will not happen as quickly as your Earth scientists are predicting. It will be longer than the five years that you have stated.

First of all, this so-called greenhouse effect is not something that is entirely new to your planet. It has happened before from what is known as natural experiences of the planet itself, long before a so-called industrial revolution was ever considered. However, man, with his advancing technology, it is true, is responsible for the effects revealing themselves so early. There has been and there always has been on all planets that are composed of the substance of your planet Earth, what is known as a natural greenhouse effect.

Try to understand, in eons yet to be, that which is born from anything by law returns to the source of its birth. Your planet Earth did not suddenly appear from some large bang, as they like to say. It is a natural growth process in your solar system of what is known as the moon, the reflector, and the sun, the source. And so I would not be concerned over the greenhouse effect, for man on your planet, as a whole, will do little to nothing. I hope that's helped with your question.

Thank you.

You're welcome. Yes, [Student U], please.

Will a successful answer be found to the war on drugs?

As long, in reference to your question, as long as earthlings insist that the limits of experience, the limit of life is the mind, then the answer to your question is not in the foreseeable future. Try to understand, whether it is an addiction to alcohol or it is an addiction to any other of the senses, there are untold millions who have left your physical world. Now the only satisfaction that they receive in the astral realms is through the Law of Magnetism, through an attraction of those who remain addicted while in the flesh—you hear?

Yes, sir.

So the battle and the effort to control or to educate the drug addicts of your planet cannot be limited to a physical world, for each effort that is made, twenty astral decarnate beings, once on your planet, come in to, once again, get their sensation or satisfaction. Try to understand that sensation is an effect of a movement in the physical body of flesh and bone. That sensation of the physical being is interpreted by the mind as something enjoyable. So astral, earth-bound beings, human beings, only in astral and mental bodies, can only experience that interpretation from that sensation by coming within the aura of someone who is using and experiencing those sensations in a physical body. Does that help with your question?

Yes, sir.

You're welcome. [Student L], please.

Yes. Thank you. Will the U.S.S.R. and the U.S.A. continue to move toward peaceful negotiation in the new administration?

Yes, there will be a few minor experiences. They will continue to do so because it is in the best financial interest of both countries.

Thank you.

Yes. You're welcome. Yes, [Student H], please.

Yes. What significant changes will be made in our country's judicial system this year and over the next decade?

In the judicial system, because your courts and your court calendars are so heavily booked years in advance, there will be an increase in the efforts to solve problems, legal problems, outside of the judicial system in the sense of mediation. And so there will be an increase in those systems in your country. Yes. Yes, [Student C], please.

Thank you.

Yes.

Will terrorism in the world continue as it has been or are we going to see a decrease in terrorism?

Well, unfortunately you will not a see a decrease for the next seven years. The reason for that is political. A united effort with European countries, especially, has failed repeatedly over the last four years. However, we do see that there will be agreement, and completed agreements, in the coming seven years, [Student C], but it will take that long. There will be some steps made, but it will take more terrorism before that happens. And we see that projected as a seven-year period. Yes.

Thank you.

You're welcome. Yes, [Student U], please.

Thank you, sir. Will there be a Palestine state in the foreseeable future?

Oh, definitely! There will definitely be a Palestine state. Those laws have already been established. Now how soon that will come about is depending on what is going to be done, which we see projected as a seven-year period, on the terrorism over Europe, which will be entering the State of New York. That is coming within the next two years. Yes. And [Student K] has a question, too, please. Yes.

Thank you, sir. In this year, we saw a number of reconciliations in the international environment, including the U.S.

and Russia, including the beginning of softening of Palestine, between Africa and in Central America.

Yes.

Is this a trend which will continue in the near future?

It is a trend that will continue as long as you have a conservative head of your government, yes. Pardon?

Thank you very much.

Yes. And the reason that we say that is because the liberal heads of your government have, over the last two decades, repeatedly demonstrated that a giving here and a giving there is their policy. It is not a wise policy. It tries to please all factions and does not work in international affairs. And the truth of the matter is, it doesn't even work in domestic affairs. You understand? And so when a change comes about in the liberal party of your country, which is in process, but will take at least another five years, then a so-called liberal head for your government could steer the ship clearly with definite direction. It is the indecision of the heads of the government trying to please all factions that [does] not work in international nor domestic affairs, you understand?

Yes, sir.

You see. You see, one must do right because it's right to do right. And in so doing those who are not in that level of consciousness have experiences that they create—[their] experiences being the effect of their own creations; they have experiences that they don't like and, through ignorance, give responsibility for those experiences to someone they cannot control. Do you understand? Pardon?

Yes. Thank you.

Yes, you're more than welcome. Now [Student L] has been waiting with a question.

Thank you.

Yes.

What will be the attitude, now that there has been a slight severance, between U.S. and Israel during the coming year? They seem to have been upset by our attitude.

Well, they may be upset. Most people get upset when they're told what to do, which is in their own best interest, by someone who is responsible for them, like little children. Children ofttimes get upset because they don't have their way; yet, they don't work and pay their bills, you understand. And so in reference to Israel, which is a child of the efforts of the United States, if you will check the history—and, oh, who received great benefit from their parents, the United States government—has entered the age of the teenager. And they will get through the growing pains, grown up, and have a little more appreciation. I hope that's helped with your question, [Student L]. Yes, [Student M], please.

Thank you.

Yes.

What way is the educational system going in this country for the children? I mean, will it get back to any degree of the old traditional with the new?

Indeed, it will, as long as conservative-minded people are in control of the government. Now by conservative, I mean intelligent people who don't try to satisfy everyone for the sake of getting a vote. Yes. Yes, [Student O], please.

Thank you. [Student M remarks.]

You're welcome.

Yes. In this year is the Earth, in this year of fulfillment, could the Earth be considered in a period of retrospin? [Student O asks.]

This is the year of '89. This is the year of fulfillment. And fulfillment is a spin indeed, not a retrospin.

[Student O responds, but his response is difficult to transcribe.]

You've just finished a retrospin, and you only have a few days to enter your spin in your world. So it's time to reap. Does that answer your question, [Student O]? It's in spin.

It's in spin.

Yes. So move ahead and reap the harvest that you have sown.

And is that a period that lasts more than one year?

It lasts for a time, yes. One has—in reference to the Infinite Divine Intelligent Spirit, that's one. Is your world a world of two or one? Does your world have opposites?

Yes, this world—Earth does.

Is that a number two or a number one?

Earth is a number two.

Well, in the sense of duality of creation, indeed it is. So you're interested in, of course, reaping. And so in answer to your question, it would seem that it must, at least, be two, wouldn't you say?

Yes, sir.

Does that satisfy you? No. That's fine. I didn't want to satisfy you. *[Several students laugh.]* You can study from there.

You know, I have watched each and every one of you as students, and I do not see what I have asked, for years, in your world: application and study of these spiritual classes. I do not see that time set aside. I do not see the spiritual studies that are necessary in order that you may continue to strengthen, through awakening, the Light that is already within you. Now if you don't do your breathing, and I won't speak to—you know, I should give you a test. I was thinking, well, this is the year of test that I might just take the time and give you a test, you see, on how you do your breathing, which affirmations are you using, and how you do your power breath and what position you sit in and how long do you take. I'm not interested in your experiences. I already know your experiences, children.

Now, next question, please. I'm well aware of those. Yes, is that—well, that's [Student B]. My! Speak right up, [Student B].

Will a solution be found for homelessness in America?

In respect [to homelessness], what has been working from our world is what you might consider very large farms. Do you hear? And it is the work from many on our side of life that the so-called homeless people would be placed in the country, not the cities, in the country where they may have supervised work on small farms and orchards. You hear? Not like what you considered in the '60s. I think you called them communes—nothing of that nature. But something that would be operated by each and every state. Now the efforts have been and continue to be from our world to impress the necessary politicians of the advisability of such a program. You will have the awareness of that within the coming three years. I hope that's helped with your question.

Thank you.

And that *is* the answer. That *is* the solution: to bring these so-called homeless away from the cities and into the surrounding country. Because then they will work and they will produce and much good will come from that. And they will have a place to live and a place to breathe. Pardon?

Thank you.

You're welcome. So each of you can do your part, you know. The spoken word is life-giving energy. And when there is something of such great import, you can always, when solicited, give the suggestion, can't you?

Yes.

Yes. You see, people have such little value for a drop of water; yet without a drop of water, there can be no oceans, none at all, let alone rivers. Yes. Yes, [Student L], please.

Is Gorbachev honest about the cultural exchanges and peaceful negotiations?

Well, I don't know what you mean by *honest* when you're referring to political endeavors. We find that honesty is something that's put on one shelf after another, ever in keeping with what the desire of the politician is at the time. Do not forget he's a politician. Do not forget that he is a Communist. Do not forget he is very satisfied and very happy with his philosophy. Politicians, my children, are still politicians. Whichever the way the wind blows, if they judge it favorable, that's where they move. And you never know which way the wind is going to blow. Thank you. Yes, [Student H], please.

Yes. Thank you. What steps will be taken by the Bush administration in dealing with the AIDS epidemic?

They will be forced to, by the health departments and by the public, to reveal more than they choose to reveal. Because that is a serious problem in your world, not just your country, in your world that has, from fear, been spreading very rapidly throughout the heterosexual community. And because of fear, because of lack of intelligent education, because so many people from that lack of education no longer consider it a problem, let alone valid, it has spread more rapidly than it would have spread had proper education been established years ago. Yes.

Try to understand the administration that is going in has much to consider. If the public is awakened too quickly to the seriousness of a plague or epidemic, then fear and revolution is the result. And that has to be weighed out constantly. Thank you. Yes, [Student U], please.

There is a new leader in the country of Pakistan. What effect will that have on that particular country and the countries affiliated with that country?

Well, in reference to the new leader of Pakistan, there won't be any drastic changes. He will continue, this new leader, with the tradition of control, more like a dictator in a diplomat's clothing, if you understand that. And so there won't be that many changes. And not only that, child, Pakistan is in a stage of evolution that it is not yet ready nor qualified for what you consider a full democracy. Thank you. Yes, [Student K] has a question, please.

Thank you, sir.

Yes.

Is the blood bank within the United States making progress towards identifying contaminated blood, like contaminated with the AIDS virus or developing a means of purifying the blood?

Well, in reference to the question, Is it making any headway with the contaminated blood that exists in the blood banks of your country and the world blood banks? There is some, yes, there is some progress in that area. However, I am sure you will agree, if you [were] president, you wouldn't get your blood from there. And so that should rather answer your question. *[Several students laugh.]* That is, if you [were] in a position to choose. Pardon?

Thank you.

Yes. And so, what I wish to say is that, you know, the years of contamination of the blood banks and the years of refusing to allow the heterosexual community to awaken of where that plague, that disease, that virus really is, has created, of course, a serious problem for everyone. However, there is some headway being made. The only answer that one can really, intelligently abide by is to have as little social activity as is possible and to make great effort to remain with a chosen partner, you hear? And so that's something, of course, that everyone can do. Because you can ask a person a thousand questions and not receive the answer that is required for your own good health. Did that help with your question?

Thank you very much.

Yes. You see, more of the community should, in order to help the entire situation, should be in the institutions being cared for, you understand? Yes. Yes, [Student Y], please.

Yes. Thank you. How is the progress going in a campaign against experimenting on animals and can we expect to see an ending to the experimentation as it is done now?

Not in your lifetime. You can expect and you will experience more and more awakening of the cruelty to the animals, which will, in turn, slowly but surely turn the tide of such brutality. However, you must not expect a miracle: you already have one. It's called survival. Survival is the miracle of life on your planet. Survival. Do not expect a miracle for the little four-legged creatures. Be grateful for the crumbs, for there are many that are helping. Yes.

[Thank you.]

You're welcome, [Student Y]. Yes, [Student B], please.

Will corporate takeovers by foreign investors continue in 1989? And if so, what sort of an effect will they have on America?

Well, first of all, they will continue. Corporate takeovers by foreign investment will continue not only from Asia but especially from Europe. First from England and then from France, especially from England. And what effect will they have on your country? Well, when you have someone—and a country is someone. It is composed of many people and each person is someone. When you have a debt owed to someone, you become the victim by the Law of Dependence in that respect. And so the effects upon the United States of America is an increasing[ly] delicate position. A delicate position that the countries to which the United States is financially in debt to do not want—of course, business is business—do not want the country not to survive or to prosper to some degree. However, those countries who hold the debt, those who hold the United States in debt, their standard of living, each year, is increasing. Their standard of living will exceed, *exceed* the standard of living of the debtor country. As that takes place, there will be drastic changes in government policy. But only 'til that awakening takes place for the country. Does that help with your question, [Student B]?

Yes. Thank you.

Yes. Already there is such an increase in the standard of living of some of those countries that there are those in government position who are well, well aware of it, yes. Yes, [Student C], please.

Thank you.

Yes.

My question is about Nicaragua and Central America. The Nicaraguan government, having experienced, the new Nicaraguan government, having experienced much stress recently, I'm wondering what the political direction of that country will be in the future and how will that effect—what will be the direction of the surrounding countries?

The Nicaraguan government is a government that must have a strong leader to survive. Do you understand, [Student C]? Without a very strong leader, the country cannot economically continue on, you hear? However, a strong leader in the view of one is a dictator in the view of another. Do you understand?

Uh-huh.

And so it will be a very delicate situation. To some, they will be considered a strong leader that is bringing the country together, you hear, and as time passes, they'll be considered, as in the Philippines, you hear, a dictator. Do you understand?

Uh-huh.

That is the situation that exists in Central America and especially in Nicaragua.

Uh-huh.

Pardon?

Thank you.

Yes.

Thank you.

And will continue on for eight years that way, yes. Yes, [Student B], please.

Are the stories about aliens kidnapping human beings true? And if so, are these aliens spiritually-evolved aliens?

Well, in reference to that question, I'm sure you're ready to understand that intelligent, physical beings are not limited to the planet Earth. Is that not correct? Are you not prepared for that awakening?

I'm prepared.

Yes. Well, intelligent, physical beings were never limited to the planet Earth, for intelligent, physical beings have been, are, continue to be in many solar systems, you understand?

Yes.

Yes. The planet Earth, being a true teenager, has been monitored for untold centuries. Because when you have a wild teenager in your house, you have to keep an eye on your house, don't you?

Yes.

You're never quite sure what they're going to do while you're working, are you?

No.

Therefore, the planet Earth is under constant monitoring and has been, as I said, for centuries. There have been some occasions when these monitors have come in contact with physical beings of the Earth planet, do you hear? However, most all of the experiences are experiences that are the effects of thought transference rather than physical experiences. I hope that helps you with your question, [Student B].

Thank you.

Yes. You know, a person who has control of their mind may project any image that they choose and a person who makes no effort or little effort in their daily, spiritual studies is receptive to the projected image and within less than a second believes that's their experience. Do you understand?

Yes.

Well, good. It's called thought transference, yes. Yes, [Student S]. *[After a short pause, during which the student remains silent, the teacher continues.]* Pardon?

Ah . . .

You had no question?

No. Thank you.

Ah. Yes, [Student M].

Thank you. What is the purpose of the country of Tibet and, like, not the purpose, but the monasteries? I know it's a spiritually-evolved country. But I would like to know, have a little more understanding of their way and what it really means.

Well, in reference to your question, I feel, as your teacher, that you should consider studying the spiritual studies that you have been given and practicing the exercises daily, for in so doing you would awaken within your consciousness their very high purpose over so many centuries. Yes.

Thank you.

Thank you. Yes, [Student C], please.

Thank you. What is the meaning or the spiritual significance of the natural disasters that we've been experiencing in the world, like the earthquake in Armenia and the hurricanes this past fall? And are we going to experience more natural disasters in the future? And why do these occur in seemingly less developed places?

Thank you very much for your question. A most important question. First of all, the nature spirits are responsible for what you call natural disasters, be they water, fire, earth, air, etc. Natural disasters, not man-created disasters. Natural disasters of which you speak.

As the human race of earthlings continue[s] to suppress desires that they alone create and refuse[s] to accept responsibility for their own frustrations, those disturbances affect the nature spirits. For the same nature spirits that are responsible for the fire center of your physical body, those same nature spirits, in principle, are responsible for the fires in the bowels of the Earth of your planet. The nature spirits responsible for the waters and the oceans and the rivers are, in principle, the water spirits (nature spirits) that are responsible for the water center that the human mind, in its ignorance, continues to disturb. So when you consider the millions, billions of human minds and, through ignorance, the lack of effort to still the waters of their own [water center] and the oceans and the rivers of their own water centers, they are affecting the water spirits.

And so it is the war and the battle between the nature spirits of the elements; the effects from those wars are so-called natural disasters, [Student C]. There are some philosophies that have revealed the direct connection between the thoughts of the human mind and the nature spirits of the planet.

And it, of course, behooves a person to do a bit more study of their spiritual studies daily. It is better to study 20 minutes in 24 hours, to study your spiritual studies, to do your spiritual exercises daily, than to spend 20 hours in one week, for there is no continuity and there is no benefit to experience. So it is the daily effort, every day, not an effort that when the need is the greatest that we turn to our spiritual studies, our spiritual breathing, and our cleansing breath. That help with the question?

Thank you.

You're welcome.

All discord and disturbance is an effect of a lack of effort of using the Breath of Life to control the entities and the earthbound forms that come to use and abuse the individualized beings still on the planet Earth.

Thank you, our time has passed. And good day, and reap the harvest and rejoice in the harvest that you reap. Remember, happiness is a thought away. Good day.

DECEMBER 25, 1988

[This is one of the last classes given through Mr. Goodwin's mediumship. He passed from this world to the higher life on February 24, 1989.]

Individual Classes

[With the Annual World Forecasts, the publication of the major categories of classes of the Living Light Philosophy is complete. However, many individual classes and sometimes a series of three or four related classes were also given through Mr. Goodwin's mediumship. These individual classes are being published in chronological order, with undated classes preceding all classes with a known date. When class titles are known, they are included, but if class titles are not known, they have been entitled based upon the date they were given. Some of these classes have not been shared, even with current students of the Living Light Philosophy, since the day they were given.]

The Lost Discourse: Giving

[The individual classes of the Living Light Philosophy are varied in many ways. Sometimes only the class has been recorded, but occasionally the preparations and exercises that preceded the class were also recorded. The preparations for this undated, but very early, class were recorded and involved many steps and different affirmations. The first affirmation, which was spoken by the few students who were present as well as Mr. Goodwin, was "The Spirit of Infinite Intelligence," which was given through the mediumship of Rev. Florence Becker, founder of Golden Gate Spiritualist Church. Following which, a mantra, based upon the word Amen, was repeated three times. After that mantra, the students first sang all three verses of the hymn "Sweet By-And-By," "Ramona," and then three verses of the hymn "Beautiful Isle of Somewhere." After the songs, the students spoke the Lord's Prayer. After that prayer, the students spoke the "Beseeching of the Angels" affirmation. Between the closing words of the last affirmation and the first words spoken by the teacher, there was a period of silence of almost forty-five minutes. The tone of the teacher's voice is quite similar to his tone of voice from the very earliest discourses, which began on January 6, 1964.]

Greetings, children.

I bring unto you my peace. Again, it is my duty and my pleasure to be with you at this time.

Children, you know how easy it is to misunderstand and to misquote another. And this evening, if I may, I should like to speak about a few of the things that we are discussing in our group on this side of the curtain.

Why is it that the giver is the one that is blessed? My dear friends, you can and will progress only to the degree and extent in which you help another on the eternal ladder of progression.

Truly are we blessed when we know how to give. There are many who are aware of this, and there are many, many more who give only for the thought of receiving. But to the many who give not with the thought of receiving, they are giving because at some time in their progression they have learned that the giver is fulfilling an absolute law which causes them to go on and on upward in progression.

Why is it that so many, having experiences of which they are not fond, are unable to release the thought and memory of those experiences? My dear children, it is because they have not yet learned to be true givers. Don't you see, my friends? If we are not true givers, then we hold things to ourselves. And regardless whether the experiences are good or seeming bad, we are unable to release them, for we have not yet learned the art of true giving.

The mental body must be educated so that it can give freely what it receives.

Please understand, I am not speaking of the giving of objects, for there are those who give of objects with such great show, for within their very being they are indeed most selfish. And this they do not want, naturally, to be known.

The giving of which I am speaking is the giving of the self, the giving of what you hold most dear. I pray that you will perceive, for, my children, the art of giving is a guarantee of the great freedom that awaits you. And I do pray that you may turn your eyes upward to learn of the things which will help in your progression.

As I had spoken to my channel, a little saying, which he was unable to understand, I shall repeat.

> Today I am an apple
> Tomorrow I'll be a tree
> And when I am an apple tree,
> I'll no longer be just me.

My dear children, you must look to the word *individualized* and that is the key to the parable.

As has been spoken before, I have mentioned to you of the many visitors who have spoken to us and the various theories and discussions that we have had. My dear children, I wish to state, as I pray at this time that you are able to bear the Light: I know that there is life in form prior to your Earth life. This life of which I speak is on a lower rung of the ladder of progression. My dear friends, you have had no birth on Earth. You are making a journey and your journey shall lead, and does lead, ever onward, ever, ever upward.

When the time is right and the winds have blown, the storm has passed and the waters are calm, I shall again speak of this matter.

Everything on your planet is in this so-called invisible world.

The mind, my friends, must be balanced with the spirit. The mental body is equipped and prepared to withstand only a certain degree of pressure.

Prepare, my friends, and build the spirit body. I pray that you will not have to have long experiences in the mental worlds. Suffer well and suffer long, for he who suffers shall learn no wrong.

Won't you, children, broaden your horizons to the great universes that await your travel?

When duty calls, may it always find you at home, ever ready, ever willing to serve and to serve well. Wise are those who know when they have served and the work is done, that they may be guided to another and another and another.

Hold not, my friends, to things and thoughts for they must and will change in the purifying processes of progression. Your path leads to God, and God is not without, but God is within.

You are, all humanity, being prepared to lead, but in order to lead, you must learn to follow. The greatest leaders in the highest realms are followers of the small voice of soul within. The greatest obstruction, my friends, to your progression is the confusion which you alone create in your mental body. Let another think and do as they will, your duty is to the soul within. Do it well and you will not see the wills and duties of others.

And now I must withdraw. In God's love and in accordance to the law, bless you.

[After a short pause and in a voice that is more like Mr. Goodwin's, he issues one instruction.]

Sing.

[The students softly sing the first verse of the hymn "Nearer, My God, To Thee," and they speak in unison a closing affirmation, which can be found in the appendix.]

Impatient Progression

[The preparations for this early, but undated, class are also recorded and involve many steps and different affirmations. The first affirmation, which is spoken by the few students who were present, as well as Mr. Goodwin, is "The Spirit of Infinite Intelligence," which was given through the mediumship of Rev. Florence Becker, founder of Golden Gate Spiritualist Church. Then all present speak a mantra, based upon the word Amen, *three times. After that mantra, Mr. Goodwin and the students sing the Serenity hymn "Spirit Working," which was given through his mediumship. The lyrics sung are different from the only surviving copy of that hymn, both of which can be found in the appendix. Following that, only the students then sing the song "Ramona," followed by three verses of "Beautiful Isle of Somewhere." After the songs, the students speak the Lord's Prayer, which is followed by the "Beseeching of the Angels" affirmation. Between the closing words of the last affirmation and the first words spoken by the teacher, there is a period of silence of over eighteen minutes. The tone of the teacher's voice is quite similar to his tone of voice from the very earliest discourses.]*

Greetings, children.

Indeed, am I honored and pleased to be with you again at this time. We have been patiently awaiting until full preparation had been made and all things had been placed in order on both sides of the curtain.

[At] this time, my children, we are about to [em]bark upon the greater universal work that is before us. As you may note, some time ago I spoke to you about my channel and that there would be but myself speaking through him at least for some time. My dear children, that time has come and the greater work is to be done.

As you know, there are many entities so close to the earth realm that in order to help them it is best that they come in contact with the gross or earth vibration in order for them to progress. I know there has been much talk of earth-bound spirits. My dear friends, they are no more earth-bound than you, dear friends, who are in your physical bodies and mundane world. You understand, my children, that they are all good souls, but they are so involved with their own small universe that they have been unable to see the broader and brighter horizons.

Now, dear friends, the spiritual work is in order and with my channel's guides and mentors, we are now prepared to permit one, or several, as be the case, of these entities to come through. The purpose of this work, my children, is to help these entities to help themselves. We have tried, that is, the rescue workers on this side of the veil, to reason with these people. You understand, my children, that there are thousands upon thousands of these poor, lost souls, lost only within themselves.

The only way that we can help them, who are so closely bound to the earth realm, is to reason with them. So many of these souls come over to this side of the curtain completely ignorant of what they are to find. Those, my friends, are not so bad off, so to speak. It is the ones who believe that they are to find such and such over here. Some of them do, as they create the worlds in which they live. However, my children, some of them do not.

The laws are very simple. And in their simplicity, to the mind of man they are so very intricate and complicated.

My dear children, as the entity is permitted to come through the channel, please be understanding. Use reason and logic to discuss with the spirit. Do not use emotion or anger, but reason, peace, and logic. We are rest assured, my dear children, that the entities will only be permitted to stay to the degree that no harm shall come to our channel. If you will be very peaceful of mind, we shall bring this about. And in each your turn, as you hear the plight of these poor, lost souls, please use reason, compassion, and logic. Do not be deceived by their ways of thinking or talking, for they are in a world of their own creation.

The universal work, my dear friends, is about to begin.

[After a short pause, a dramatically different voice speaks through Mr. Goodwin's physical form. At first, the new individual mumbles and her words are difficult to transcribe. The words spoken by this new entity have been indented and italicized to help differentiate them from the words of the students in attendance and the teacher. She speaks in a plaintive voice.]

> *Now . . . Why am I here? Why? All I do is work. Don't you see? I never, never get to see anything. I work so long, all my life. Why do I suffer from these headaches? I'm so dizzy. Why? I was such a good person when I was on Earth. Why am I here? Oh, I've always done what was right. I've had these headaches all my life, all my life. Why am I so sick? Why does everyone treat me like this? Oh, you know, I've worked so hard. All I've done—I raised eight children and not one of them ever come to see me. And that viper, that demon, that snake in the grass, he left me. That drunkard, that good-for-nothing. I had to raise all those children myself. And look what they did to me. They left me.*

> *Why do I have to live like this? All I do is work and work! Why am I here? Why do I have to work like this? And I suffer so much from my headaches. Why do I have to suffer so much? Why am I so dizzy? All I ever do is work. All I ever do is work. No one ever thinks of me. They only think of themself. Why do I have to work so hard? Why do I have such headaches? Why am I so dizzy? Oh, I'm so sick. All I ever do is work. No one ever thinks of me. All I ever do is work. All I ever do is—no one ever thinks of me. Oh, I'm so dizzy.*

My head. I'm so dizzy. Why did everyone leave me? Why did I work so—why did they leave me so? Why? Why am I here?

[Her voice trails off and she pauses for a moment before continuing.]

Why am I here? No one ever listens to me. Why am I here? Why don't you speak to me? Who do you think you are? You won't speak to me. [Although she spoke almost in a monologue, almost whimpering at times, it now seems that she is addressing one or more of the students in class.] *You! Why don't you speak to me?! Why am I here? Why am I here? Why . . .*

[Her voice trails off. The entity stops speaking and after a pause, the teacher returns.]

My dear children, I wished that you understand [you are] to question the entity as they are permitted to come through. This way, my children, is the only way we will be able to help her. Do you not see that she is in a universe of her making? And we have been unable to reach her from this side of the curtain. However, due to her strong earthly vibration, we believe that you will, in time, be able to help her. We shall try again to guide her through the channel. Please question her as she comes through. And try to gather from her, her name because she is so lost in her own vibration.

[The entity returns and, again, speaks through Mr. Goodwin's physical form. The students' questions to the entity were asked by a number of different students and no attempt has been made to identify which student asked which question. Again, the entity's words are indented to distinguish them from the words of the students who were present in class.]

Why am I like this? Why? Why doesn't anyone think about me? Why?

What is your name?

What name?

Can you tell us your name?
  Why?!
You certainly have a name, don't you?
  Why do you want to know my name?
Because then we can call you by name.
  Why do you want to call me [by] my name? I don't trust you.
We have come to help you.
  How could—if you come to help me, then you, you will tell me where that viper, that good-for-nothing, that I, that, that, that, that thing, that demon, that pig in the, in the mire, where is he?
We have come to help you.
  You can't help me 'til I know where he is to make sure that he's getting the hell that he deserves.
That is really unimportant.
  No, that is important.
Not to your universe, it is not.
  What universe?
The one you have within yourself of love.
  Love. They speak to me of love. How do you know what I did? That I sacrificed myself. I was the best-looking girl in all of the town, until that good-for-nothing came along, that drunkard. Look at me now. I'm just an old hag.
What did he call you? What is the name that he called you?
  He never called me unless he wanted something.
How can we speak to you, if we know not your name? Would you give us the honor of calling you by your name?
  Why do you want to know my name?
So we may address our answers and our questions directly to you.
  What's your name?
My name is [Student T]. May I know your name, too?

Who are you going to tell my name to?
To no one.
Would you please give us your name? [A different student speaks.]
What's your name?
My name is [Student W]. We'd like very much to help you.
You see, we all have common problems in this earth plane. We do what we can to help one another. You see, by helping others we help ourselves.
That's all I did, was—[or] ever do was help others.
Look where I am now!
Now we're going to help you to help yourself. You're important, too. We know that you are, and we want to help you. Won't you tell us your name, please? We want to be your friends. We'd like very much to be your friends.
It begins with e.
Evelyn?
No!
Ellen?
No!
No?
Elizabeth?
No.
Eileen?
No.
Is it a long name or a short one?
Why do you want to know?
It gives a little clue.
There are lots of names that begin with e. [A different student speaks.]
Would it be Emma?
No!
I bet it's a beautiful name.

It is. And too many people don't know it.
Then will you share it with us?
    I'm thinking.
All right.
    It has an r *in it.*
An r.
Irene?
    No!
No.
That begins with i. [A different student speaks.]
Would it be Erica?
    No!
Ursula?
That's [begins with] a u.
    You're not very smart. I'll tell you it has an n *in it.*
Ernestine!
    No!!
No.
[After a short pause, a student continues.] *Ernie?*
    It looks like I come to help you instead of you helping me! It has an l *in it.*
Erlene?
    No!
None of us claim to be very smart. We all just try.
    Well, I'll give you another clue. It has an o *in it.*
An o.
    I almost spelled it for you!
Oh, how nice.
Erlone.
    No.
I don't believe I've ever heard the name.
    You're not thinking!
No.

I'm thinking that you possibly could help us by telling us your name.

I almost did tell you my name!

Good.

I said it had, started with an e. It had an l in it. And it had an o in it. And it had an n in it. And it had an r in it!

How about Eleanor?

About time!

Lovely!

Thank you very much.

Thank you, Eleanor.

Don't tell anybody.

No.

I don't trust anybody anymore.

What did you do when you were here? What did you like most?

Work!

Ah, but what did you—what kind of work?

I washed dishes. I still wash dishes! And I have all this ironing to do and all those brats!

Did you know that you don't have to wash the dishes anymore?

What are you talking about I don't have to wash dishes?! That's all I have in front of me is dishes! What are you talking about I don't have to wash dishes anymore?! What are you talking about?!

What do you like—

Where do you think you are?

What do you like to do for relaxation? When you were a young girl, what did you like to do?

Dance!

Ahh.

Oh, I bet you were a good dancer.

I don't remember!
Could you try?
All I can see is dishes.
Did you wear a pretty gown when you danced?
No, I don't want to talk about it!
I bet you could teach another. Had you ever thought about teaching something that you really liked?
Where's that good-for-nothing husband of mine?
Aren't you rather glad to be shed of him?
I want to make sure he's in hell with me!
No, you're not in hell.
How do you know where I am?!
Because we are where we want ourselves to be.
If that was true, I'd be in heaven.
Hmm, yes, we earn our heaven by our thinking. [After a short pause, another student continues.]
Eleanor, will you trust us? We'd like to be your friend.
I don't know you well enough yet.
No, of course you don't.
Do you wash dishes?
Yes, I do. And you know, we teach our children to wash these dishes, too.
We each help each other.
Then how come nobody helps me?
Have you asked? [After a short pause, the student continues.] *Have you asked for help?*
You see, each and every one of us make our own mistakes. If another has injured you, they have injured themselves worse.
You believe in God.
I used to.
Oh, you still do. We all do. And one of the finest ways you can help yourself is by saying your prayers. And asking—
I said my Hail Marys all my life and look where it got me.

Ah, yes, but I'm not saying that. I'm saying to God . . .
Pray from the heart.
Would you like to be helped, Eleanor?
    Yes. I have to go. They tell me I have to go.
Thank you, Eleanor, for coming.
God bless you.
Good-bye.
Bye.
[After a short pause, the teacher returns.]

My dear friends, the entity that was permitted to come through is indeed attached to a vibratory wave of her own creation. Indeed, for many, many, many years she has remained in the same position. I do pray that through her visit this evening, which was the first one that she has been permitted to make with the earth realm, that a new thought will enter so that she may be gradually released from her self-created obsession.

And now, dear children, there are so many wonderful souls gathered here this evening. I am so grateful that the spirit was brought through because, dear children, you are the first that she has been able to hear since she has been on this side of the veil. Her passing to this world was in the year of 1897. So, you see, she has been here for some time. And now that the spoken word and another vibration has touched her universe, I feel confident that we will be able to help her on to progression.

And if I may say a few things this evening, we have spoken before about satisfaction and attachment. And now for the sake of my channel and all present, I would like to speak about impatient progression. My dear children, for weeks I have been trying to impress upon my channel peaceful progression. There is a great difference between the natural flow of peaceful progression and the impatient progression caused by the drive within. I know that it is indeed most difficult to go into a slower vibratory wave than the form is used to vibrating in. By this I mean to say that it is indeed difficult to slow the vibratory waves of thinking of an individual.

You see, my children, some people are quick thinkers, and others are slow thinkers. Now I ask you, What in truth does it matter whether you are [a] quick thinker or [a] slow thinker, if by thoughts, acts, and deeds we all do progress?

Now I do not mean to say that that can be done tomorrow instead of today. No, I do not wish to mean that. What I do mean to say is that more can be accomplished by the peaceful progression of the spirit within.

There are some things, my children, that we must be more patient with. And the most important of those things is our self. Do you not ofttimes see that the impatience that you are showing is with yourselves; not with others, but in truth with yourselves? You are not impatient at the streetcar because you have to wait for it. You are impatient with yourself because your self is not patient. Now, children, stop and think about that one thing. How can you, as reasoning, thinking human beings, be impatient at a box of steel that has no intelligence?

No, children, you are not impatient at things outside of yourselves, no matter whether you call them animate or inanimate objects. In reality, my friends, and in truth you are impatient at a part of you: your self.

And now, my friends, I must withdraw as much energy has been utilized this evening. And, if necessary, the entity will be brought back. However, I do believe that she shall now go on to a more harmonious progression than she has ever known.

God bless you in accordance to the law, for there is, my children, no other way of blessing. God is not a giver, but a sharer of Itself.

[After a pause, the students sing the first verse of "Nearer, My God, To Thee," and then speak the class closing affirmation, which can be found in the appendix.]

Control Points

[Good evening,] fellow students.

The Light is shining even though the night has not yet gone. For our discussion at this time, we shall speak on vibrational receptivity, a method of releasing the Light within, dimensional activation through pressure stimulation.

Please, my students, listen and hear well. It is for those of you who are gathered at this time. The thumbs, hearing; and, in corresponding order, the fingers next to the thumb, power, vision, breath, sound or spoken word. Place the hands with the fingers corresponding—thumbs over the ears, power finger at the temples, vision finger over the closed eyes, breath finger on the nostrils, and sound or speech finger at the corners of the mouth.

Through proper pressure you will activate the centers necessary to viewing in the various dimensions. It is only dangerous to the extent that you do not follow the rules explicitly. At the time of applying the pressure equally to each center, give forth the mantrum you have been given. I repeat: apply the pressure gently, uniformly, releasing the mantrum and releasing the pressure. Do not exceed the exercise more than three times in twenty-four hours.

Some students experience a slight itching in the eyes or ears or at other of the centers. This is not to be of great concern for it is the activation effect.

I once again repeat: do not apply too heavy a pressure too soon. My channel will be informed after [class] in the exact application.

No growth, my children, ever came to anything without pain. The disintegration processes of form are just as painful as the integration processes. You do not, at this time, recall the pain of your birth into your world, but the day will come when you shall view it; and then you shall know that life in form is continuous pain and pleasure; action, reaction; and neutrality the only peace we'll ever know.

Good night.

JUNE 17, 1971

Discourse July 29, 1971

Greetings, friends and students on the path.

At this time, we are reviewing many of the lessons that have been given. The students gathered here at this time are being permitted to ask some of the questions that have, seemingly, been perplexing to them.

However, before we open our little discussion, I would like to mention a bit concerning the last discourse that was given. *[The teacher may be referring to Discourse 29, which was given on July 15, 1971, and which was republished in* The Living Light Dialogue, *Volume 1.]* At that time, we discussed the functions and their electrical, positive, and repelling vibrations, the faculties and their magnetic, attracting vibration. In regards to your expression in form in matter, it is important to understand and to apply the balance in creation.

As you advance in varied forms, the births of these new forms will ever be from the death of the old. And this, my children, is why it is not wise to overbalance in the faculties, for they grow and expand at the expense and death, so to speak, or change in the functions. When we bring into balance the magnetic and electrical forces flowing in creation, we reach and attain this Light, this awareness, this great freedom.

When the seed of desire is born in the faculties, it does attract its kind. When it is born in the functions, it repels.

Now the question is arising in your minds, my good students, that all desires are not good. I ask you to ask the question of yourselves once again: Desire born in faculties attracts and reaps a good harvest, and desires born in functions repels and attracts its opposite. Think of that. For that that is sent forth, known as repulsion, on the positive electrical currents does not dissipate itself, but returns unto the sender on the opposite pole. This does seem, to some of you, to be contradictory to the prior lessons. You will find, my children, on close examination, it will open a new door to your understanding.

I said a bit earlier that open discussion and questions would be permitted. And one of the students has asked that question: "If our purpose in life expression is to refine the forms, why is it that such a struggle is placed upon us?" Birth and death are the eternal cycle of creation. And the forms are brought together to be refined, and refinement is friction, because without friction, there is no refinement or change or evolution. Consequently, as long as you flow through form or creation, creation or form will constantly have this friction, which is, in truth, a refinement process. But you have within you the great power to balance, to balance the faculties and functions and there rest in the eternal bliss and joy of neutrality.

Each moment, each hour, my students, is a struggle for the creation that you are in. Learn to disassociate yourselves from the form in which you are expressing. Learn to be free, for the form shall ever battle, and it shall ever struggle as it constantly, like the diamond, shows forth its great luster.

The question is again asked by one of our other students, "What is it that has guaranteed my soul expression in this particular life?" We have spoken, at times ago, that all things are under the Law of Merit. The soul's expression in your form has been guaranteed, my good students, by your prior form. So can you not see the great wisdom of learning freedom from form today? Be not attached to form and ye shall be in form and free from form and your next expression shall be one of greater expansion, of much broader horizons. It is your attachments of the past that have guaranteed your present expression and experience. Try to learn the great Law of Disassociation.

The question is asked, "In what way can I make my life more meaningful?" In regards to that question, we must first understand the meaning you wish to express, for what is meaningful to the function is not meaningful to the soul. Therefore, from which level is your question expressed? Be it from your soul and your faculties, then you will find the true meaning of life when you rise to the realization that you are in a prison of creation, and it is your purpose, as it is the purpose of the Divine, to so illumine the prison house in which you reside that it no longer becomes a prison to itself. Think on that, my children.

It is true, my students, that we have given bits and pieces of understanding concerning the anatomy and the different meanings of its parts. And the question has been asked: "We know that the feet are understanding and we would greatly appreciate knowing what the toe or toes represent." The toe, my children, represents indecision, and that is what causes us to stumble many times.

Good night.

JULY 29, 1971

The Fort Bragg Seminar

[This seminar was held in the home of a friend of Serenity in Fort Bragg, California, on March 31, 1972, celebrating the 124th year of Modern Spiritualism.]

As most of you are familiar that the Serenity Spiritualist Association has a camp here in Mendocino, eight miles northeast of Willits, it also conducts regular weekly church services in San Anselmo in Marin County. And thank you for your donations to this seminar for they go to help support the building and the continuity of the Serenity Association.

Now our seminars that we have conducted each month over these few years, usually what is done [is], we present to you our understanding of Spiritualism and after that short introduction, you're free to ask any questions concerning its science, its philosophy, and its religion, and any questions of a spiritual nature. Now the science, philosophy, and religion of Modern Spiritualism is a religion, a philosophy, and a science of self-culture. It has no dogma. It has no creed. It has no book of authority. It does, however, present a Spiritualist Manual in which are nine declaration of principles that have been brought to us over this past 124 years. This evening, March 31, 1972, is the 124th anniversary of the organized movement of Spiritualism. These principles are ever subject to change, as a greater understanding of spiritual truth dawns upon the movement of Spiritualism.

Now whereas Spiritualism is a philosophy, religion, and science of self-culture, it recognizes the individual rights of each and every soul to their understanding of God and the purpose of life itself. Through its communication with other dimensions, referred to as the world of spirit—although we recognize and realize that mediums, psychics are exposed to and do receive from realms known as a mental world, as telepathy, as mind reading, and also from the world of spirit.

Now the teachings of Spiritualism are to awaken what we term the soul faculties. Our spirit is, at present, encased in form trying to express itself according to the level of awareness, of mental awareness of the individual at any given time; [and] that is the level that the spirit is expressing itself on. The purpose of this self-culture, of soul unfoldment—which simply means an awakening of our mind to the truth, the eternity that is ours this very moment. This is accomplished through a daily effort of reeducation of what is termed the senses or functions. Now the teachings are not to annihilate the sense body in which we're in, not to annihilate our so-called ego, but to educate it that our soul faculties and our sense functions may be in perfect balance. And when they are in balance, this divine Spirit may express and free itself while it is yet encased in physical form.

I want to turn the floor over to you now for your questions concerning any of these spiritual matters. So would you be so kind, at this time, to please raise your hand? Yes.

How do we separate, Richard, what we think we're receiving and our own thoughts?

Yes. The question is, How do we separate what we think we are receiving and our own thoughts? Now it is a demonstrable fact—and Spiritualism is a religion of demonstration, personal demonstration—that as water reaches its own level by its own weight, so [do] our thoughts attract their kind from the ethereal waves. Therefore, we must first learn to become aware of what we really are, not what we think we are. The philosophers of all times have said, "O man, know thyself, and ye shall know the truth." Spiritualism says a way to knowing oneself is to become aware not only of the conscious mind with which we are most familiar but of our so-called inner mind or subconscious mind, where we have untold multitudes of experiences and belief[s], computed not only while in this form but through the hereditary factors.

We all recognize and accept that this physical form has certain tendencies of heredity. We look a little bit like our parents or our grandparents. There is a certain similarity. We understand that the physical body is merely an effect of what we term the mental body. And therefore, if we understand and accept that the physical form is hereditary, then we must also understand that the cause of the physical form is hereditary, which is the mental body.

Now how do we separate what we receive and what we think we receive? By knowing our self. Spiritualism teaches and demonstrates and shows the way that one may accomplish this through a daily type of concentration and meditation, through a way of becoming aware of the thoughts that entertain the mind at any given time. So often are we guided by thoughts of the past, by certain impulses and feelings that we, long ago, have forgot[ten] the experience that has placed them there. That is why it is termed a religion of self-culture. We must become aware that we are where we are when we are because we are who we are, not what we think we are. Does that help with your question?

Yes. And is it right to test them?

As it is right to test anything, it is indeed right to test the spirit. However, in regards to that question, I would like to say that indeed is it demonstrable that our soul is incarnated into this planet, into this form to learn the great lesson of faith. When we sit in a chair, we do not test the chair to see whether it will hold our weight. When we turn on the light switch, we do not test it to see that the light will go on. Or when we turn the key in our car, whether or not it will start. We have taken it for granted that that will happen, and therefore we have faith that it will happen. And it is also when we plant a seed in the ground, he who hath no wisdom—he who hath no patience hath no wisdom. So it is wise in our testing that we first give the seed a chance to grow before we dig it up. Thank you. [Does] that help with your question? Yes.

Does someone else have a question? Yes.

I just remembered, again. Meditation—I find it best to meditate at night, after my day is over, after I'm all through with everything that the day has to throw at me, at night when I'm in bed. I do my eating that way, too, and at night, when I have to. If I try and meditate during the day—I've tried. And I just find that I'm not concentrating on it. I'm concentrating on what I have to do when I get through here.

Yes.

Now what are your thoughts on that? I—it's [more] comfortable to me.

Yes. The question, the statement is that the person meditates while they're in bed at night because they find difficulty in concentration and meditation in the morning hours, because, while they're trying to concentrate, the forthcoming activities of the day are interfering with the concentration. Is that true?

It's true.

Yes. Now this reveals to us that we have lost control of our self. Because if we had control of our self, then we would know that although the events are to be done and they haven't yet taken place, we are either the master of our ship and the captain of our destiny or we are the slaves of the influences that we and we alone have created somewhere along the path.

Now, it's just like a person who smokes a cigarette. If they cannot educate that desire for some length of time, especially when the desire is the greatest, then the desire in and of itself has become the master, and we and we alone have become its slave. This is our understanding of what the prophets of the Bible said when they stated, "Ye shall have no gods before me. Your false gods shall be dethroned." We understand in Spiritualism that

that which we give power to in our thought becomes our master. We are free only to the extent that we are able to control our own creations.

See, God is not the creator in our understanding. Man is the creator. And man, being the creator, is responsible for all his creations. Therefore, the only thing that I can say [is] what is right for one is not necessarily right for another. However, I would instruct a student—and I have instructed students who have that seeming difficulty—that if you will make the effort to master that, you will, once again, regain the power that you are giving to things of your creation.

It is a known fact that the morning hours are most beneficial for concentration and meditation, upon awakening. It is an absolute, demonstrable fact that it is not beneficial to meditate in the prone position, but to meditate in a sitting, upright position. That is entirely up to the individual. You see, life indeed is ever as we make it and just the way we take it. We and we alone are responsible for all the things that happen in our life, for we and we alone have created them.

If it is a truth that like attracts like and becomes the Law of Attachment—and that *is* a demonstrable truth, as all truths are demonstrable—then that is universally applicable. Therefore, it simply means that all of our experiences we have willed into action. It is indeed a subtle law: that whatever happens to us has been caused by us; that if we will go through the levels of our own mind, we will find that level which is the magnet which is calling forth all of our experiences. Does that help with your question?

Yes.

Thank you. I didn't mean to give you a lecture.

Excuse me. I'm going to take my birds.

[*As the teacher was responding to the previous questions, the pet birds in the room became increasingly vocal. In response, the owner of the birds moves them to another room.*]

Certainly. You may feel free to go ahead with your questions. *[After a short pause, the teacher continues.]* [Student F], I'm sure you have some very fine questions.

Well, I have a number of them, but I'm observing more than—and listening more than—and if you ever let me get the floor, you'd never get it back. [A few students laugh, and after a short pause, the teacher continues.]

This is the time to ask your questions on mediumship, the psychic, or any of these sciences that are Spiritualistic. Yes.

Well then, when we're meditating, this question that [she] asked, we have to separate—it would be imagination, I guess, from whatever it is we're getting.

Yes, I understand your question. The question is stating, We would like to know which is imagination and, perhaps, which is reality?

Oh, well, there's another part. All right. When I'm meditating, a lot of times I know when it's imagination, right?

Uh-huh.

There are times, like, for instance, when my mind isn't even thinking about anything like that and pictures flash.

Yes.

Just, you know, they just come at me.

Uh-huh.

But I can't hold them. I can't hold them well. Then that wouldn't be imagination because you're not thinking of it at a time—

Ah—

You know, if you—

That doesn't necessarily hold true. And let me try to explain that or enlarge and expand upon it, if I may. You see, the mind is a very delicate instrument. Whatever the mind can imagine, it can and does create. Yesterday's imagination, locked deep in the storehouse of our so-called subconscious, may, years later, flash pictures to our view.

It is the mind, remember, that questions. The spirit does not, for our spirit knows. It knows. It does not question. Therefore, the thing that we are striving for is to awaken our mind that it may reflect the divine, infinite, eternal Spirit that is flowing through us. Now when that happens—but it cannot happen until we make the daily effort. How many days, weeks, months, or years that will take is very individual, because we're all different in form. We're all the same in Spirit.

Spiritualism shows one way. Transcendental meditation shows another way. Yoga shows another way. These are all paths leading to one truth, for there's only one Light; call it God or Infinite Intelligence, it doesn't matter. The thing is that when we sincerely go into our daily meditation-contemplation, when the motive is pure, the manifestation is not only right, the manifestation is inevitable. And if we'll make that effort and we'll go through those layers of mind, we'll touch that infinite Power within us that knows and does not have to be told. Then we will know what is imagination, what is telepathy, what is mind reading, what is the astral dimension, what is the desire world, and what is the world of spirit. You see, it takes our spirit to discern the spirit, for the spirit cannot be discerned by the mind. You cannot take a limited thing and discern and understand the limitless, for the spirit is known only by the spirit. Hmm?

That answered it.

Yes.

Now, the phenomena that happens when you're meditating, like the hands moving along.

Uh-huh.

Or the head nodding.

Yes?

Should that be controlled? Or should it—or should you ask for that to be sent to another power?

Well, in reference to your question, there are various types of things that happen to a person while they are in concentration or contemplation. Now some people, they seem to jump or their head seems to turn. They seem to slump over. These things do take place with many, many sincere students.

The thing is that one does make the effort to be perfectly still, for it is in the stillness that the Power truly moves unobstructed. When the mind is still, when it is no longer entertained with a multitude of thoughts, it is not possible for the body to move. It is impossible. For the body is nothing more than an effect of the image held in mind. That's all that it is in truth.

And this is why, when people pass out of this physical world, if they have become, through habit—and I mean, by habit, a repetition of a certain pattern—[accustomed] to a so-called disease or to a problem, [the problem continues]. We take our minds with us; and therefore, if it is [that] we've been crippled in a physical body, we find ourselves still crippled in another dimension, for that is what we have created. You see, God does not do it to us. We do it to our self. God is this divine, infinite, sustaining Power, like the electricity. It is used to illumine the world or it is used to electrocute people. So it's up to us. Man is a law unto himself and that is indeed personally demonstrable. Does that help with your question?

Yes.

Yes.

Richard.

Yes.

In order to hold circles, like, for instance, we thought that we'd like to hold a circle. But we do need more lessons before we start, because it is quite dangerous, isn't it?

It most certainly and definitely can be a very dangerous thing. It is a power. It is neutral. It is totally indifferent. You may use it for good or its so-called opposite. That is entirely up to the individual.

Before I myself would ever consider sitting in any circles—I don't anymore, but I used to years ago—I first, to the best of my ability, would go by the guidance from whatever I may understand to be the Divine at the time.

There are so many different levels of mind. You see, a psychic is not a medium, but a medium is a psychic. What happens in circle meetings, [is that] you come into a type of rapport. You start to become very sensitive. You start to sense feelings and emotions. A person can be smiling and you can sense if they're angry. You can sense if they're hurt or they're jealous.

Now unless a circle group is started with an understanding of how the science of Spiritualism truly works, [that is,] without an understanding of its philosophy and its religion, it cannot reap itself a good harvest. It is all dependent upon the motive. It's important to study. This is why the Divine has given us this so-called mind, a faculty of reason. You wouldn't start into a business venture without having investigated and studied the particular business that you're about to go into. And so it is in the business of religion and especially the business of communication—to study, to analyze, to investigate, to test all things that they ring true to our own spirit.

It is good for interested people to start a circle if they start it with the right motive. If they're dedicated to what they may call God or the Infinite Power and they're sitting not for self-gain, but sitting to be the channels through which a higher intelligence may freely flow and, in so doing, benefit all those with whom they come in contact. Yes. Does that help you?

That's right.

How would they sit for self-gain? [A different student asks a follow-up question.]

How would they sit for self-gain? Many people, unfortunately or fortunately, depends on how you look at it—if we understand the merit system, then it's totally neutral—many people are attracted to spiritual communication that they may receive information from another dimension or a higher intelligence on how to make more money or how to find a husband or all these personal questions evolved around self. If that is the purpose for which a group is gathering and sitting, they cannot, in all honesty, reach a very high intelligence, because like attracts like and becomes the Law of Attachment. That does not say they will not have phenomena. Phenomena is the easiest thing in the world to produce, once one finds how the science works.

But what is the motive? Is the motive to help humanity to help themselves, because that in truth is the purpose of our being in form in the first place, or is it just to gain in a business venture or to know what our next-door neighbor's doing because we feel that we don't want to impose and ask personally? If that is the motive, it's very bad. Yes.

You need to open—if you leave the circle open and are looking for a better understanding to the Infinite Intelligence . . .

Yes?

. . . is this what you mean about like attracts like?

Absolutely—

If you're seeking this, it's going to come.

It cannot help but come because the law is very clear: "Whatever I am seeking is also seeking me." Now we understand that not every flower in the garden is a rose. And God's manifestation is indeed variety. There are no two people at any given moment that are identically the same. We fluctuate through these levels of awareness.

Stop and think. What causes us misery? What causes us grief? What causes us joy? And what causes us sadness? Nothing outside of our self. The old mind deludes itself. It says, "So-and-so did such and such. Therefore, I'm miserable." We have given the power to that event. We've given our life-giving energy to it, and *it* has made us miserable. We have choice. We are never ever left without choice. We have the right, the divine birthright, to stop, to pause, to think. "That event has taken place. It is past and gone. I cannot do anything about that event, but I can do a great deal about this event." This is the only moment that we have power over. This very instant. This indeed is our eternity. Not yesterday and not tomorrow. We can do something with this moment. And in doing something with *this* moment, it will be indicative of what tomorrow will bring.

Yes. [You] had a question.

Yes. What I'd like to know is in trying to fulfill our purpose in life, you know, what should be the, say, like, the basic thing we should try and do? If we were aware of our purpose. Not aware of it in its totality—

The question is—

—but to a degree.

—if one is trying to fulfill the purpose of their being, then what is the basis upon which they should found it or start? And I would say this—what many philosophers have said before— man, know thyself. Because, you see, when we know our self, we will know the purpose of our being. We won't have to ask anyone because we will have gravitated beyond the levels of mind. It's only mind that questions. We will have gravitated ourselves individually to what is known as Spirit or Infinite Intelligence. And we have that divine birthright to express that, if that is what we've gravitated to. We will know. No one can tell us, you see? Did that help you?

Yes, it does.

Yes. Are there any other questions? Yes.

If someone has led a miserable existence here on Earth . . .

Yes?

. . . you know, like being alcoholic.

Yes.

Then they die. Are they still going on being an alcoholic?

The question is, If someone has led a miserable existence, such as being an alcoholic on Earth, and when they pass out of this physical world, do they still continue to be an alcoholic? Absolutely and positively, as long as that pattern is the predominant one in what we term mind. Because being an alcoholic or an abstainer from alcoholism—call it good, bad, or indifferent, only man makes those judgments. God is not a judge. But if we understand that to be a miserable thing, it doesn't make any difference. It's going to continue as long as it's entertained in thought, because this is a thought, a thinking world. That's what it is.

The desire is not in the piece of clay. You take the mind out of this physical body, it not only has no desire, it doesn't even move. The desire is in the mind and the body is its effect. Therefore, when we leave this piece of clay, we take mind, our mental body with us. We still have the desire, and we hover in the realms close to Earth to try to fulfill those desires. This is what you hear about haunted houses. This is what you hear about earth-bound spirits. Heaven is not a place we go to; it is a state of consciousness that we grow to here and now or hereafter. Does that help with your question?

I have one more.

Yes. Certainly.

I know that there are some people who do terrible things.

Yes?

And they don't really want to. Now this is my question, Are they going to have to go on doing terrible things after they're dead when they really don't want to?

Until they outgrow that.

But how do they outgrow it?

By becoming masters of our destiny, captains of our ship. Because, you see, we are spirit here and now. Our conscience is a spiritual sensibility with a dual capacity. It knows right from wrong. It does not have to be told. Now a person may do terrible things or seeming terrible things, and they don't want to do those things, but they're compelled to do those things. The compulsion does not exist outside of themselves. It exists in a level of mind within themselves. In time, in eternity, they will outgrow them.

No, but I've seen little children, and I know that they don't want to do these bad things.

Yes?

They do them and they can't help it.

But they will outgrow them in time.

And there are adults who do the same thing.

Absolutely. It is everywhere. God's manifestation is indeed variety. Remember that we are Spirit formless and free; whatever we think, that will we be. They'll grow out of them.

Then if you're, if you're on Earth and you're doing bad things—

You'll be still doing—

—but you don't want to do them.

You'll still be the same person.

Well then, how on Earth, how in heaven, how on the other side, are you ever going to outgrow them?

Sometimes it takes centuries.

Well, where do you get the strength, if you don't have the strength now?

We're strongest while we're here. That's why it takes so long after we leave this flesh to outgrow these things.

Gee, that's terrible!

The law is—

I mean, I always thought—

—very just.

—you know, all these people that have all these terrible fathers, and little people—and then once they're dead, they're free of these terrible things that they've got, like . . .

Oh, no.

. . . lameness or deafness or blindness or mental retard—

Not unless they have outgrown them within themselves.

Well, do you mean, they—I don't think that's fair to be condemned. After they're dead—

There's no, there's no—

—then they're free of their body.

No, they're only free of a suit of clothes. Our body is the effect of our mind and the door—

[Side A of the audio cassette that was recording this seminar ends at this point. The class continues while the tape was changed to Side B to continue the recording. When the recording begins again, a different student is speaking.]

—felt that was what she meant, but I wasn't sure.

Yes. Because, remember now, the teachings [of] the teacher that has brought about this Association have been very clear in regards to evolutionary incarnation. It is his understanding that our soul is incarnated into these varying forms according to the merit system: that whatever has come to us we have merited; that our soul, our spirit is formless and free. It [our spirit] is covered with soul, individualized soul. But this power of the Spirit is greater than all creation. Things that have form have beginning and ending, but that that is formless is free, has no beginning. And by having no beginning, it has no ending. Yes.

Well, I was reading this book, A Wanderer in the Spirit Lands. *[My friend] had some questions on it, and I've really been getting into the book.* [This was one of the many books that were offered for sale at the book table at Serenity Spiritualist Church.]

Yes.

And, you know, it's heaven and hell.

That is his understanding.

His understanding.

That is his right to his understanding. He experienced heaven and hell. Heaven and hell is not a place we go to; it is a state of consciousness, a state of mind that we grow to.

All these people that he saw, too?

That's—

These other people were experiencing this, too?

Absolutely. That is the level of awareness that he was experiencing.

This was his imagination that he was seeing these— [A different individual speaks on this topic.]

No, no. Like attracts like and becomes the Law of Attachment. People who are conditioned to believe a certain way—as we believeth, we becometh—that is what they're going to experience. So those people that he was experiencing in the so-called lower realms of spirit were of like mind and of like kind. It is an absolute demonstrable law that we are known by the company that we keep. If we look at our friends, we can view ourselves. Life and our associates are but a mirror, reflecting back to us what we're sending out to. Does that help with your question?

No, but I can just see my mother grinning away because that's exactly what she used to say to me. Birds of a feather flock together. I can just see that.

Birds of a feather flock together. Absolutely. Because like attracts like and becomes the Law of Attachment.

Well, I resented that book for the simple fact that I have never believed in hellfire and damnation. I hate to think I had— [A third individual expresses her perspective.]

Millions of people do. No, millions of people do. And they have a right to believe—

I think—

—in their savior and their heaven, their hells, and their purgatories.

Well, then there is a heaven. And you—

That they have—

—do get to go sit on a cloud and play a harp if that's what you've—

If that's what you've created. If that's what you've created, yes. Because it's right in here.

But then, I won't get to see a lot of my friends. [Many people laugh, including the teacher.]

I can understand that.

I mean, they really believe that they're going to heaven. If I don't believe it, then I'm not going to say it.

Well, I think it would be awful uncomfortable. [And still another person speaks, but the teacher seems to respond to the previous comment.]

It's a state of mind. It's a state of mind.

Well, that's what I mean. They're—

Right. That's right.

Then what you're saying is, like, for instance, I don't believe in hell. I believe that my hell is right here on Earth. I'm going to go through it all here.

And you're experiencing it at times.

Yes.

Wouldn't you agree?

Yes.

I'm 100 percent with you. I know exactly how that works.

And I—

This is my hell.

This is my hell, here.

But I have the right to change it! See, how many times a day, I can't tell you, that I say to clients, I say, "You know, I feel great and I intend to stay that way because life, she's ever as we make it and she's just the way we take it."

In other words, we can reach whatever aim we go for.

Absolutely and positively. There is no impossibilities to the Power that is all.

Then if you're an alcoholic and you really want to quit, and you—

You can!

—can't quit 'til you die, then you can be free of it.

Yes.

You don't have to go on being an alcoholic.

You can still quit. Absolutely and positively.

... did. [During this exchange, the teacher and the student often speak simultaneously, and it is difficult to transcribe a few of the student's words.]

Why, certainly! Eternal progression is the Law of Form. Eternal progression. You cannot, you cannot experience in form what is known as stagnation. Because the moment you have what appears to be stagnation, you have a breaking down of one form as it's building another. Constantly. Nature reveals divine wisdom if we truly study her. Indeed. Yes.

I, as you might think, have tested the spirit.

Have they tested you, may I ask?

They have absolutely tested me. This—

Beautiful, because that's the demonstration of the law.

... beyond a reasonable doubt. [Again, this student speaks at the same time as the teacher, and some of her words are also difficult to transcribe.]

Yes.

I wasn't afraid—a little shook to find out that it was true. Things I couldn't possibly have known, I have searched for. A long time for the answers for some, a short time for the answers for others. And within this last week I have found them. So that's why I asked if it was right to, to—

Absolutely.

—to check the spirit.

To test. Absolutely. Remember the law, she's so clear: that that we test, we guarantee to be tested by. Hmm? Yes. See, remember, that that we suppress, we guarantee to arise. That's the law: the duality of creation. That's why the teaching is, "Our adversities become our attachments;" [and] that understanding grants tolerance, and tolerance guarantees success.

My son said . . . "I don't know what you're doing, Mother, but keep it up." [It is difficult to transcribe a few words.]

Keep it up. Yes.

Then, Richard, is it true, then, that if you call upon the spirits for help or whatever or try to make contact with them, is—it isn't true that you're making these spirits earth-bound, is it?

Absolutely and positively not. Now stop and think in this way; [it] depends on what you call it. If you call upon a spirit—and, of course, I have never believed in calling the spirit. If we are making the effort and we rise to a spiritual level, they're in the atmosphere. I mean, don't you see? There they are, see? But it's up to us as channels to rise to our own spirit within. Now if we are, what they say, calling the spirits to say, "Now let's see, I need about $400 this week because I'm a little short." Well, illumined spirits—no illumined ones that I have ever, ever—at least I think they're a little illumined—suddenly dropped $400 in my lap or told me to go down to the races and put so much money on the nose of Black Horse or something. Do you understand?

You see, remember that our loved ones who have passed over, they don't all of a sudden become great physicians. They don't all of a sudden become great financiers. They don't all of a sudden become all those things. Don't you see? Now God has given his angels charge over us, lest we dash our foot against the stone. And if we are sincere in our exposure to this world of spirit and we are seeking truth—for only truth will set us free. And truth is individually perceived. He who knows truth, knows freedom and, knowing freedom, is not bound any longer by creation. Hmm?

Then we can say to some of our loved ones, "I've come to a point that I need help"?

Absolutely. And if they are in a position to help us—

I don't mean material things.

No. And it is their purpose to help us, indeed, they'll do their part to help us to help our self.

Let me understand this, that when they cross over, they're at no higher plane than they were when—

Then before they left.

So—

That is absolutely correct.

If they get a little bossy, you calm them down, right?

Absolutely and positively. We have an individualized soul, and we have the divine right to express it. Definitely. Yes.

Well, this question has bothered me because of personal reasons. But, say, what, to your knowledge, happens to a person that has always been so afraid of death, just terribly, terribly afraid of death? And then, all of a sudden, wakes up one day—and you can say this in Spiritualism—he wakes up one day and he's dead. What happens to that person?

In reference to your question, I've had, over the years, personal experience with some people who have believed that so-called death was absolutely and positively the ending.

The end, yes.

There was no continuity. And I have been privileged to communicate with some of them when they had been finally awakened. Because, you see, they've so firmly believed that it was the ending, when they left this piece of clay, they were asleep and they've stayed asleep. And some of them for many, many, many years.

But there are rescue spheres in the world of spirit. There are willing, dedicated workers trying to help all these spirits. Because, you see, they recognize, they realize, and they know that we are all one, whether we like it or not. But the oneness within us knows the oneness without. And that's what we're seeking: to find that divine Power inside of our self. Because when we find it, we will know that there's no separation in truth, that creation comes, that creation goes, to come again, to go again.

I have to put something in here.

Yes.

I was reading, just last night or the night before, and something became so very plain to me and I want to share it here. The spirit world—and we can't see the spirit world. And it was trying to explain, but they are there. And it was explained like a propeller on an airplane. That we can see it when it's stopped, but when it's going, you know, we know it's still there, but it's going so fast that we can't see it.

How beautifully put. Because when the mind is entertained with thoughts, the spirit cannot see the spirit without. Because this thing is going so fast with so many multitudes of thoughts, the spirit cannot express itself.

Don't you think that most young people, children have a fear of death? [A different student asks this question.]

Many of them do through a conditioning. Many do. Now many little children have an awareness of the other dimensions. They'll have little playmates, little four- and five-year-old children, and even three-year-olds. And they'll talk to their parents about their little playmates and their friends, you understand. And the first thing the parents do is [say], "Now that's just your imagination."

How ridiculous!

Well, how does the parent know that that's their imagination? Is the parent seeing the same image? Usually, it *is* little spirit children playing with the little spirit animals. But, you see, the sadness is the parents, in their ignorance, have automatically judged that has to be the imagination because they don't see the same thing.

That's the same way with adults with other adults.

Absolutely. A person has an experience and they try to share that with someone. Perhaps it's a very spiritual experience. Why, immediately the person's very negative. "Well, she's getting a little bit kooky. Always thought she was that way anyway; now I know for sure." That's why spiritual things, you just don't reveal them.

You know, Spiritualism is the first religion—it's the first and only American religion. In 1848, it was the first organized religious movement to put women up as ordained ministers. That had never been done before. You check our history. And I'm very pleased, because way back in 1863 the national Spiritualist movement ran the first woman for presidency of the United States. She didn't make it, though. *[Many of the people laugh.]* They ran her anyway. So they were teaching and trying to demonstrate equality long before you ever heard of these modern-day things. They always were. Yes, go ahead.

When you're interested in Spiritualism, like everything else, you want to share it.

Yes, that's understandable.

And then I come to a brick wall when I get this, "Why, that's of the devil."

That's under—you see, that's good because you will learn, in time, to go into your meditation and contemplation and ask the Divine to guide you [with] who to speak to, when to speak to them, and how to speak to them. So it's serving a good purpose. Ofttimes a seeming bad thing produces excellent results. You see? And if you ask the Divine, or whatever you want to call it, to guide you, it'll guide you to the right person at the right time.

The one's that you'd think would be least interested in it or if they—

Ofttimes they know more about it than ourselves.

I've had that experience, Richard, too.

Yes. Did the ladies up front here have some questions? *[After a short pause, he continues.]* No questions.

[After another short pause, another person speaks.] *Richard.*

Yes.

How long does it take for a person that is beginning to study now—like, for instance, we're going to have this class starting in May—

Yes. Classes start in May.

[There are no recordings of spiritual awareness classes from May of 1972. There are some records that suggest there were two or three semesters of classes that were not recorded and that predated the first recorded Consciousness Class, given January 11, 1973. Of course, without a recording, those classes cannot be included in the published teachings of the Living Light Philosophy.]

How long will it—will it take the twelve weeks to get us adjusted to understand how we're supposed to go about doing these things?

I would suggest to go through the full course, which is really a very short course. That's only three months. And after that time, if, be that in order, this Fort Bragg group is still sincerely interested, I'll be more than happy to set up arrangements for your first home circle or your spiritual meetings and share with you my understanding of the various meetings we have set up over the years.

Because there are many things involved. The reason that we have water—it's not because our throats get dry. Although that can happen, if you talk a lot. But it's because it grounds us. It brings us back down, like when you're drifting off into a trance, you see. Drinking of the water, it brings us back to what we call *terra firma*, you see. And there are reasons why, in communication, you don't cross your hands or feet. Your right side of your body is electrical. The left side is magnetic. And you're just grounding the wires, your own vibrations. Like [if] you cross these two wires that go into the lamp, and of course, it's going to ground; it's going to go out. So there are reasons why these things are done. The movement has had 124 years of experimentation and continues to, to try to find better ways for spiritual unfoldment and awareness.

Now there's one book entitled *Genuine Mediumship* we've tried to reorder. It was an old published book. I don't know if you've read it.

No.

It's in the library. I'll be happy to loan it to you. It discusses home circle groups in a very nice way. By Swami Bhakta Vishita. It's excellent. It's entitled *Genuine Mediumship*. Remind me and I'll get it out of my library.

All right.

If you're interested. Yes.

What about the yogi exercises?

Depends on which exercises you're dealing with.

The simple ones.

The raja yoga?

Just the very—

Or the hatha yoga?

I don't really have—

Well, now, the—

Simple ones.

Many of the yogic exercises are very beneficial for the health. I would certainly check in and see if they were beneficial for myself. They have all types of breathing exercises.

This is what I'm talking about.

Some of them—properly used, you see, these things are very beneficial. But it's so often, you know, a person decides, "Let's see. Two aspirin, it always cured a headache. Now my foot's hurting me real bad. I've sprained it. So I'll take six." But it doesn't work that way, don't you see? It just doesn't work that way. But unfortunately for many, it seems the mind kind of works that way. I mean, a person will sit and they'll have a few experiences, you know what I mean. And all of a sudden, swoosh! A slow growth is a healthy growth. Think of all the stuff this mind, this computer has recorded in it. We've got to get— we've got to make the effort to get through these levels and tap that spirit within ourselves.

Don't you think that we're slowed down by our guides and teachers?

Depends on—only depends on what type of guides and teachers we've attracted to us.

I've found that I have been slowed down when I was going too fast.

Yes.

By one thing or another.

Yes.

It might be a worldly thing or a spiritual thing—

Yes.

—but it has slowed me down.

Yes. Because, you see, the Power itself, as I explained, is totally neutral and impartial. After all, Rasputin used it and caused a lot of problems in Russia. Some other leaders have used it.

Wasn't Hitler a great user?

Indeed, indeed. He was really into all this type of thing, you know. Not in the Spiritualist movement, but he was in [to] astrology. And he had his prophets and he had his psychics and he had his occultists and all those things. They told him not to go into Russia. They told him not to attack England. It's in the records.

I read that in one of the books that I bought.

[They] told him not to.

Abraham Lincoln was well guided. After all, little Nettie Colburn Maynard, a little fourteen-year-old medium in the Spiritualist movement, gave the seances in the Red Room at the White House. And the spirits came through and dictated verbatim the Emancipation Proclamation to free the slaves. It's in recorded history. You might read Carl Sandburg's book on Abraham Lincoln—two-volume set. He mentions in there the spiritual seances that were taking place during his reign.

Well, isn't it true that actually most of the prominent leaders throughout history were under one type of psychic guidance or another?

Absolutely. Franklin Delano Roosevelt had many mediums attending the White House, including the late Florence Becker of San Francisco, who gave seances to thirty-three Congressmen and Senators during World War II. He was widely known to listen to—

Do you think the present administration has any of that kind of help?

Not to my knowledge. *[Many people laugh and many comment in response.]*

No, but he should.

He hasn't.

Not to my knowledge.

He hasn't.

[After a short pause, the teacher continues.] If we have no more questions, then we will get ready for our billets. And I always like to explain to those of you who haven't been to church or might be a bit familiar with Spiritualism, there is no guarantee that any medium can ever make to contact any particular spirit or to even contact the spirit at all. The only thing a medium can do is to make the effort to get themselves out of the way so that the Power, call it what you will, may move and make the contact.

Now I do ask, in this part of the seminar, that you try not to concentrate upon me and that you send out your thoughts of love out into the atmosphere to God or whatever you choose, but to a higher power than the old brain. Now to the best of my ability, I will try to get myself out of the way.

[The recording ends.]

MARCH 31, 1972

The Vacaville Seminar

[The recording begins abruptly, which suggests that the recording began sometime after Mr. Goodwin began speaking.]

—and these various tests that the scientists have been doing connecting with the brain. We understand in Spiritualism that the brain is the physical vehicle for the expression of mind; that mind, in turn, is the expression of what we termed the Spirit or Infinite Intelligence. Now in reference to brain waves and spiritual awareness, we recognize and understand the critical importance of thought, for thought is more than a thing. Thought is the cause of all things. Without thought, there is no chair. Without thought, there is no house. Without thought, there is no being.

We understand in Spiritualism the critical importance of maintaining and sustaining an attitude of mind known as peace. Whatever we entertain in thought, we create in form.

We understand that we have a conscious mind, a subconscious mind, and a superconscious. Now when the conscious and subconscious minds are in total harmony or in rapport, this divine Infinite Intelligence flows through the superconscious and brings into being whatever we set into motion.

The teachings of Modern Spiritualism are that man is a law unto himself; that whatever man sets into motion, man and man alone is responsible for. We find that the soul is encased in a form in this present journey, through this form, [and] that it is not something that began the moment it was impulsed into physical form. For that that has beginning, by the Law of Beginning, also has an ending, and whatever has form has beginning and ending. We understand that this divine, so-called Spirit, being formless and free, infinite and intelligent, has no beginning and no ending; that it flows through all things at all times.

In reference to brain waves, when the mind is stilled, it reflects what we understand as the essence of soul. When there are ripples on the gray matter of the mind, it reflects the substance of what we term the senses.

Now the soul incarnated into form is never left without choice. We may choose at any given moment to accept or reject any thought that enters this so-called brain. However, due to so-called habit patterns that we have established, we repeatedly find ourselves calling forth, to us, experiences. In regards to experiences, unless we take the essence from whatever experience that we encounter, we are going to find the experience repeat itself throughout our lifetimes.

Spiritualism attempts to show to mankind a way to find his own spirit, his own divine heritage. It does not teach that it is the only way. But it does teach that it is *a* way, that it *is* demonstrable, that we can, if we so choose, be free while yet in form, but that is entirely dependent upon ourselves.

Now I'm going to offer to you the opportunity to ask your questions concerning spiritual awareness and brain waves at this time. So would you kindly feel free to raise your hand, if you wish to ask a question.

Yes, sir.

Yes, madam.

Would there be any danger in a teacher who is experimenting with twelve- and thirteen-year-olds, quote "taking them down to their alpha level"?

Yes?

I mean, well, what happens to the children at that time?

The question is, Would there be any danger with a teacher taking a child—

A classroom.

—a classroom of children down to varying levels of mind? Is that not—

Well, the way it was told to me, it was quote "the alpha levels." Now how many of them—

The alpha, the alpha level.

—*cooperated, I have no idea.*

I understand. In reference to that question, I understand that it could be extremely dangerous. It could be extremely beneficial. That is entirely dependent not only upon the teacher and his qualifications but it is dependent upon the child and whether or not the child has any varying traumatic experiences in early life. The mind is not something that is yet fully understood by the so-called scientists or by any religionist. And therefore, when we are working with so-called mind and we are attempting to bring a child or even an adult down to certain so-called alpha states, we must be willing and ready and able to accept the responsibility of exposing the person to those levels. For man is not only personally responsible for his acts and activities and responsible for all his creations but he is indeed responsible for what he exposes others to. Does that help with your question?

Yes, sure thing.

Thank you. *[After a short pause, the teacher continues.]* Did you have a question? Yes.

I'm not sure I know what alpha *means.*

These so-called alpha brain waves—there's a great deal of experimentation taking place in regards to putting a person in a state of receptivity, a state of so-called concentration, a so-called meditation. Now there have been many experiments on this line and they have proven themselves beneficial.

Whenever you are working, as I explained to the last party that asked a question, with the brain and with the mind, then we must accept the responsibility of what we're exposing these people to.

Now there's a great deal coming up nowadays in this phenomenal wave of interest into the psychic. There are many organizations. They are teaching everything from yoga to a type of self-hypnosis. Many times the question has been asked of Spiritualism: Well, is not Spiritualism, rather, a type of self-hypnosis? Is not the trance of the medium self-induced? I would say that there are cases with certain people, psychics and some so-called mediums, who do put themselves in a state of self-hypnosis. That is not spiritual mediumship.

However, whatever the mind can imagine, the mind can and does create. A person can, if they feel so inclined, if they wish to visualize something—say they wish to see an elephant. Well, the elephant appears before my vision. That has nothing to do with the world of spirit. Imagination is the doorway to the world of spirit, through which we must pass. And a person who has a tendency to create imaginative things, they're standing at the doorway to the world of spirit, but that is not the world of spirit itself.

Now things of the mind, we understand, are discerned by the mind. But things of the spirit are discerned by the spirit. It is the spirit within us that discerns the spirit without. It is not discerned by the mind. Thank you.

Thank you.

Yes, sir.

Are you saying the danger is in what's picked up from the other people around the student?

It can be. You see, for example, a medium is nothing more than a receptive channel to vibrations. Now we understand that all things are in vibration. And a person, when they open themselves up to these other dimensions—there is the mental dimension, the telepathic dimension, the mind-reading dimension, the astral dimension, the desire world, the astral world, and the world of spirit. Now when a person is unfolding, unless they have some type of guidance from someone who has had experience in those dimensions, the person can, very easily, become extremely confused. Because if we just opened our self up to be meditative, to be receptive, we're going to be exposed to whatever vibrations are in the atmosphere. We're going to be the television set without a selector channel upon it and whatever is being broadcast is going to come through, don't you see? And that is why Spiritualism teaches the importance of concentration prior to meditation.

Yes, madam.

I read a lot about meditation, but I don't think I really know exactly what meditation is. I know what prayer is. I know what concentration is. Could you describe meditation to me and how you combine them?

Yes. We understand meditation to be an attitude of mind when there is no thought being entertained. Spiritualism teaches certain types of breathing exercises. We know that whenever the breath is held that no thought can enter the mind. When the mind is perfectly still, there is no ripple upon the water, and it reflects the essence of our soul. We understand that to be meditation, to be in tune with the Divine. Now during meditation, one does not ask for anything. When one is in tune, one knows that they are already everything; therefore, there is nothing to ask for.

You see, we experience without whatever we are within at any given moment. We accept this Divine Infinite Intelligence, known as God, to be within us. And being within us, all things are possible and all things we already have. It is the delusion of the mind, of the gray matter of the brain waves that says to us, we desire this and do not have it; we desire that and do not have it. And then we go on the struggle to its attainment. Now, for example, if we have computed in our brain that certain things are necessary to fulfill our desire—Man is a law unto himself—therefore, those steps will be absolutely necessary in order to reach the fulfillment thereof. Is that understandable?

Uh-huh. Thank you.

You're welcome. The gentleman in the back.

Is there such a thing as prenatal or cellular receptivity from external response?

Yes, in reference to your question, it is my own personal experience and understanding—and that is one of the beauties of Spiritualism. It has no dogma. It has no creed. A Spiritualist is one who believes in communication with a world of spirit through means of mediumship and who endeavors to mold his or her character in accordance to the highest teachings derived through such communication. So I will explain my understanding of your question.

When the Spirit is impulsed into being, covered with what we call soul at the moment of conception, being Spirit, a part of Infinite Intelligence, it is all things. It is all things past; it is all things present; it is all things future. There is no past and no future to the Infinite, to the Spirit. There is no time. There is no space to it. Therefore, it does in truth (its covering known as soul) register various experiences while yet in the womb of the mother. That is beyond a shadow of any doubt. And it *is* demonstrable. Does that help with your question? Yes.

Sir—

Yes.

—would you explain that last statement, "It is demonstrable"? In which way?

It is demonstrable if we so choose to study and to investigate the multitude of experiences that take place and have taken place with a child, with a person, while the mother is carrying the child. During that nine-month period, the child does react to the very emotions, to the attitudes, and to the experiences that the mother is having at that time. There is no question about it whatsoever. It is demonstrable in the sense that those who sincerely wish to investigate may prove it to themselves. Yes.

Science is now conducting, according to Reader's Digest, *they're making fantastic strides on this now. Have you read about that?*

No, I haven't.

Recently quite an article came out where the doctors are now testing the unborn fetus for its response while in the womb.

Yes.

And they're having a tendency to believe or accept mentally that the fetus does respond to stimuli, good and not so good.

I'm very happy to hear that because there's no question about it. Whatever the mind believes, it does in truth become. But so many people confuse that with the conscious mind. The conscious mind is what we understand to be the electrical mind. It is the positive mind. It is the mind in which we have reason and [with] which we're able to analyze. The subconscious mind is the magnetic mind. It is the mind that attracts and pulls things to us. It records all things and loses nothing. So when the statement is made, "As you believeth, you becometh," that, my friends, must be understood on the subconscious level, not just the conscious level. You see, when man *believes* that he can fly, man will fly. When man *believes* that he will be on the planet Mars or Venus or Jupiter, when he truly believes it, he will be there because man is creating it.

We do not understand, in Spiritualism, any power outside of our self that dictates that this is your life and this is what you have to live. You see, today we plant the seeds of our tomorrow. Whatever we set into motion, that and that alone is what we experience. There is no power outside of our self that is doing it to us, unless we believe that there is. And if we believe that there is a power outside of our self that is doing all these things, then be rest assured to us it will be true. Yes.

In other words, don't have bad thoughts.

Well—

No matter what you do—

Not unless—well, I'll tell you what my teacher said some time ago: "Our problems, they are companions as long as we love them." Love is the magnet that attracts all things to us. So if we enjoy misery and problems and things of that nature, we will continue to experience them as long as we entertain them in thought. Yes. [Does] that help with your statement?

[After a short pause, a different student speaks.]
Will you say something about reincarnation?

Reincarnation is a subject that in thirty-one years with Spiritualism I have never failed to have the question asked. It is a most interesting subject. There are those who believe in the theory of reincarnation, that they have been, their soul, incarnated into this earth plane, and this may be their twelfth incarnation or their two-thousandth; that depends entirely upon their belief. Now a part of the teaching of that theory is that, "I am experiencing a certain type of life because this is my so-called karma of my past lives." Well, if we look at this moment today, we can say that, "I am experiencing what I am today because of what I set into motion yesterday." Do you understand?

Uh-huh.

Fine. Now Spiritualism does not teach reincarnation for the reason that it has not yet been able to prove it to its own satisfaction. That does not mean that Spiritualism says that reincarnation does not exist or that reincarnation does exist. It is very neutral in that understanding. However, I do have my own personal understanding of your question. If you would like that, I'd be happy to share it with you.

Yes, please.

I am a firm believer, from my own personal experiences, in evolutionary incarnation: that the soul is impulsed into this Earth planet, into what we call the human body; that this is one of several planets on which the soul is journeying as it goes ever onward, ever upward to return to the Source from whence it has wandered. And that is my understanding of incarnation of soul. That my soul entered a certain form in a certain time under certain circumstances and conditions because that is what it had merited on the evolutionary path of expression.

Thank you.

Thank you. *[After a slight pause, the teacher continues.]* If you have any other questions, you feel free to ask them. *[After another short pause, he continues.]* No question?

No yet.

Not yet. *[The teacher laughs.]* Yes, sir.

Since you mentioned the subconscious, that's the gravity, the gravity of the premise of the gravity, so to speak.

Yes, we understand it to be the great magnet that pulls things to us, yes.

Then it's possible, then, in other words, it seems to be your soul retains everything that happens?

We understand and believe that we have what is known as a memory par excellence; that it records all things and loses nothing.

If that is the case, then there is no such thing as the differences of bad and good, then.

We understand that so-called bad is only undeveloped good. What is bad to one is good to another, and what is good to someone else is bad to another. You see, beauty and these things are in the eyes of the beholder. Some people may live here in Vacaville and say, "Oh, what horrible weather. It gets so hot up here." And others may just love it. To one it is bad; to another it is good. If you believe in an Infinite Intelligence that sustains all creation and that this Infinite Intelligence is a divine, intelligent power, infinitely manifest—Spiritualism does not believe in so-called Satan, so-called devils. It does not believe in those things.

Well, what is the cause of this destruction from this magnetic field?

Lack of balance between the positive and negative poles of Light. We understand it is only an imbalance.

Then, in other words—

That's all that it is.

Then, in other words, if this individual becomes distorted from this premise, then without his own realization, then he needs other guidance to . . .

The guidance is available to him because the guidance is within him. It is only a matter of being receptive to his own spirit.

But these people that don't understand this activity because of the distortion.

Yes?

Or, you know, their state that they cannot perceive the idea of opening themselves to—

I understand. But Spiritualism teaches the law of eternal progression of form; that the doorway to reformation is never closed against any human soul here or hereafter. What we do not learn today, we shall learn tomorrow here or hereafter. We are not this suit that we are wearing, this so-called piece of clay, this body. We are only expressing in this dimension through it and at the same time we are expressing in a mental dimension, in an astral dimension, and in a spiritual dimension, here and now. We are spirit this moment as much as we will ever be spirit, here and now. We may not be expressing as much of our soul qualities as we're going to be expressing, but we are spirit as much as we will ever be spirit.

And we must stop and think; if someone seems to be expressing what we understand to be bad, then we have become the judge of that person. Therefore, if we have become illumined, we no longer are able to judge, for he who judges another in truth is judging himself. Does that help with your question?

Not quite, in the sense now, you see, when I discuss prenatal . . .

Yes.

. . . receptivity . . .

Yes.

Now this, this soul that's entering through this new life . . .

Yes?

There's a thing that's angry in him, you know, certain responses that he's sending to this child. And they are not aware of this, you might say, this, well, this language barrier, say, and they have a distorted idea of the concept of things that they have heard and they bring injury to themselves through this anger, you might say, through the exterior response that they have . . .

Yes?

. . . that they feel. And they are not responsible for this particular distortion, you see, or ailment or whatever you call it.

The soul is incarnated into a form with that so-called ailment. Therefore, if we understand and believe evolutionary incarnation, then we understand that so-called deformity that the soul has incarnated into has been merited by the soul on its evolutionary path of incarnations. Yes.

Are you saying, then, sir, that each soul voluntarily chooses the time, the vehicle, and the circumstances under which it will be born into human form?

In reference to your statement, I would like to say that whatever we experience today, we have chosen at some other moment. We are sitting here this moment because we chose, at another moment, to be sitting here. Therefore, in reference to that—Does the soul choose to enter this particular form and these circumstances and etcetera?—at some path in its expression along the journeys of life, indeed, the choices have been made.

Now the soul may not have said, "Ah, I wish to be born in South Portland, Maine, at such and such a time on such and such a date." No, we do not understand that. But we do understand that it has made a multitude of choices in various incarnations as it goes up the scale of evolution. And then, when it reaches a certain point, it is impulsed into being according to the choices that have been made along the pathway. Does that help with your question?

Yes.

Yes. *[After a short pause, the teacher continues.]* Did you have a question? Yes.

I'm not sure if I know how to say this, but after a person passes over, if it has been what I call a shock death—that might not be the right term—but suicide, a car wreck, or an immediate [passing], something to that effect, do they have a more difficult time adjusting or does everybody adjust the same?

Well, in reference to your question, whether or not—depending on the type of a transition a person has when they leave the physical body, do they all have the same type of readjustment or do they have varying experiences with their readjustments? We understand that when we leave this physical body, we take our mental body with us; that our mind goes with us into this other dimension. And therefore, all minds have different experiences. And a so-called suicide or anything of that nature, there is no escape. We cannot escape from that which we've set into motion. We find ourselves, if we're suicides, we find ourselves out of the physical body, but we find our self in our astral and mental body. We still have the same problem and we have to face it. We cannot escape it. If a man commits suicide because he can no longer tolerate his wife's nagging, he leaves this physical body and he finds his wife in a mental world and the experience remains the same. We understand those type of souls to be the earth-bound spirits. There are many of them. However, they do not stay there forever. Yes. [Does] that help with your question?

Thank you very much. Uh-huh.

Yes.

Another part of her question, How about—oh, she mentioned auto accidents.

Yes.

A totally unexpected death.

Yes.

Or soldiers killed in war who resent the fact that they died so young.

Yes.

They have problems. I'm assuming they would.

Depending upon the individual. Resentment brings no good harvest to any soul. And if a person—there are rescue, what we call, rescue doctors and rescue workers in the world of spirit, and they do try to help those souls who have gone on from accident or from war or things of that nature.

And one of the greatest shocks to most people that go on is that they still have their body. They still have their same thoughts and their same emotions, their same feelings. And they have not been prepared for that. They don't all of a sudden change. They just leave the physical body. They still see themselves. They still have the same feelings. It's just like if a person has been a long time ill prior to leaving this physical world: if they have entertained it in thought and that has become a habit with them, then when they leave the physical body, they don't all of a sudden find themselves healthy because they've taken their mind with them. And they have to go to these Halls of Learning to be reeducated.

I remember, years ago, when this lady appeared in a wheelchair in one of my counselings. And she was very sad and upset because she'd been over there for twenty-some years and she was still crippled. Well, I talked to the gentleman at the counseling and he said yes, that was his mother and she was crippled while on Earth. And I explained to him if he cared to send out [to] her a thought and explain to her that she no longer had a need for that—do you understand?—that that obstruction was strictly in the physical body; she no longer needed that wheel chair; she could be free. But she took that with her, don't you see? She had become programmed to the need for it. Yes.

Oh, yes, like a lot of people seem to be of the opinion that as soon as you die, you're perfect, you're healthy, you're whole, though this is not so. And that's what—

That has not been my experience in communication the past thirty-one years.

Well, sometimes I have a hard time explaining myself on that.

Yes. You know, hope's eternal, but truth is inevitable. And I'm sure it's a nice thing to hope for: a heaven where the angels play their harps eternally, [but] to me, that would be its opposite because, though I like the playing of harps, I wouldn't like to hear them forever. But that depends on the individual's right, if that's what they wish to entertain and believe. Untold multitudes are waiting for their savior, but that is their divine birthright to do so.

Yes, madam.

On the other side of the coin, let's take an example of a patient who is in deep pain, is religious, believes that after they leave their human body—

Yes?

—that they will find peace and be free of pain. Then—

Then, indeed, they shall, according to the laws of merit. Indeed, they shall. If that is what they have merited, that is what they believe, that indeed is what they shall find. So few people realize that there are so many spheres in the world of spirit; that there are spheres where you have every religious denomination there. You have churches in the world of spirit in certain realms, all kinds of them. But you keep sending people over there that believe that way. And they believe [in] the need for them; so therefore, they have them. Yes.

Do they eventually come to disregard the church atmosphere or the wheelchair atmosphere?

Indeed, they do.

To where they're all . . .

They're free.

... evolved or whatever you call it.

They're free from that. Yes. A long time ago a teacher said service, selfless service is the only path they've ever found to spiritual illumination. To serve is to free, when the service is not self-related.

I have another question. You're talking about the souls progressing to other planets, which brought to mind the word astrology in planets and reverse. Do you—what do you feel about the belief in, practice of...

Present day astrology is approximately 6,000 years old. It's a Babylonian theory. It is based upon the seven planetary system. That is not the teachings that I have received, for I have received a basis of a nine [planetary] system, not seven. Astrology is indicative, but there is an Infinite Power that is ever at the helm. And it is indicative, as the moon has an effect upon the tides or water of this planet. And, after all, there's water in our brain and it does have an effect upon us. Sometimes when the moon is full, you notice certain people [are] highly sensitive and emotional. Sometimes people that have a tendency to be psychic, they become extremely psychic. Now it doesn't mean they have to go out and see whether the moon is full or not or know anything about it. It just happens to be that magnetic pull. And that's what happens. And I'm sure that most everyone in the sound of my voice has had some experience of how certain people they know, or even themselves, feel when the moon is full. Yes.

You see, that is not a matter of belief, you understand. That is a matter of these planets having certain influences on this planet.

Well, that's all I meant about—

Yes.

I do believe that there is a little bit of influence exerted by the various planets.

No question about it. But our spirit is greater than those influences because, you see, Truth, Spirit is formless and free. And that that is eternal, formless, and free is greater than that that is created. And all the planets and stars are created. And they have come and they shall go, but our spirit shall go on forever because it has forever been. See, this is not—this moment—we weren't born just all of a sudden: we were born and we're so many years old and that is it. The only part of us that is eternal has ever been eternal. We have always been. There is no separation in truth. What we call our spirit is a part of the Spirit that flows through you, that flows through the plant, the tree, and the blade of grass. It is the one and the same Spirit. The separation is the illusion of so-called form, yes.

Yes, madam.

Do you know of or believe—do you know from actual experience that some people have more vibrations than others?

In reference to vibrations, some people, depending on—that's a very good question. Now in my experiences with communication and with these spiritual dimensions, I have found that need is a catalyst which releases energy from the human aura, and that those who have the greater need receive the greater fulfillment or demonstration. Now it is not a matter, in reference to vibrations and communications, it is not a matter of believing. It is not a matter of disbelieving. But it is a matter of need, do you understand?

Uh-huh.

Because that is energy. Communication is strictly—it works on energy. No medium, no honest or genuine medium can ever guarantee a communication with any dimension because it is beyond their powers. The only thing that they can do is to try to get themselves out of the way long enough for the power to flow. That's all they can do. Yes. Otherwise, you get into this—sure, you can get into this telepathy and all those kind[s] of things, but that has nothing to do with mediumship. It has nothing to do with communication, no. Yes.

So, I misinterpreted something that you've said, but I believe I thought that you said when the spirit takes the form of soul to incarnate into this perception that's going on, I almost got the connotation that eventually, when we've progressed far enough, we might even break through this shell of a soul and no longer need it. We'll be true spirit again.

That is my understanding.

Yes.

Yes, that is my understanding. Absolutely. That it returns, in time, in eternity, the soul, individualized, to the Allsoul from whence it has come. To go out again, to come back again. That the spirit—

Once they were pure Spirit, then they would—

We are pure Spirit, but it is only in form, which is what we call the covering. Soul is the covering through which the divine, infinite, formless Spirit expresses itself through form. That it is evolving through these various graduations through evolution and that in time, in eternity, it returns to the Source from whence it came. Yes.

Then the soul itself will be no longer necessary, you say.

That is correct. But it comes out again. You see, the soul does garner up a multitude of experiences on its journey. And I understand that it returns to the so-called Allsoul from whence it came out in the first place.

Well, it would if that's . . . [The student speaks very softly and it is difficult to transcribe the remaining few words.]

To go out again, to go back again. See, to lose and to gain, to be or not to be; it is the same ageless question. Until we learn to separate truth from creation, we will never find freedom, for creation is governed by the laws of duality. Look at any form: it's positive and negative. No matter where you go [or] what you see. And this is why the mind is not truth. It is a reflector of the Divine Spirit. Truth *is*. It is not governed by the laws of creation, the laws of duality. It just is. And that we understand to be Spirit.

The mind accepts one thing, and in the accepting thereof, it guarantees to reject it at some time, sooner or later, only to accept something else [and] to reject that at a later day. And it goes on and on and on and on. And once a man said, "When of thy mind thou seekest to know the truth, / On the wheel of delusion thou shalt traverse." *[The Wise One said those words in Discourse 1, which was republished in* The Living Light Dialogue, *Volume 1.]* It is our spirit that knows truth for it is our spirit that *is* truth. And our mind is reflecting back and forth. Yes. Does that help?

Yes. [The individual speaks very quietly.]

Pardon?

Does this mean that you're talking about, through a person's aura on a conscious level? [A different individual expresses.]

Is the what, sir?

Is the need on a conscious level that you were talking about?

The need?

Right.

No, it's on a subconscious level. And many—in reference to communication and energy?

Right.

No. Many times people think they have a phenomenal need when they don't have one, really, at all. It's up here being entertained, but it's not on that inner, deeper level which releases the energy that is necessary for the communication. Yes.

Did you say when the spirit enters the body—at conception or at birth—or did you say?

The moment of conception, when the positive and negative poles come together. That is our understanding, yes. I know there are others who have a multitude of different understandings, but that is my understanding, yes. Remember, that that comes is guaranteed to go, only to come again and go again. This is why Spiritualism tries to show a way to find the eternity that we really are this very moment. Yes.

You mentioned that spirit enters at the moment of conception. But we question—what about the doctrine of performing an abortion—or a murderer—

Yes?

Where does his guilt lie? Would he be considered a murderer? And would he have to face that responsibility to—

I would have to ask, "Who would be doing the judging?" in order to go further with your question whether or not he would face some type of responsibility. Now man is responsible unto himself unto all his acts and activities and creations. Now, for example, when we truly understand that Life herself—there is no such thing as death. There is only eternal life. There appears to be a change of form. You see this form come into being and you see it pass. It returns to the elements (the body) from whence it came, only to come up again to go back again. That is creation. Do you understand?

Now if a doctor performs an abortion, the doctor himself has certain beliefs and [a] certain understanding. Now we do have a conscience. Everyone has a conscience. We understand that to be a spiritual sensibility with a dual capacity. It knows right from wrong. It does not have to be told. So therefore, we cannot say or would not say whether or not a doctor who performs an abortion is right or wrong.

He's aware of his own conscience or consciousness.

Absolutely and positively. And the person that requested it. Definitely. Personally, I do not believe in a God that's in form or a God that is a judge.

Thank you.

Yes.

What if this doctor believes in Spiritualism?

If the doctor believes in the Spiritualism that I understand, because I have my right to understand my religion in my way, as all Spiritualists do—

[At this point, the audio cassette recording this seminar ended and the class continued as the tape was being turned to the other side. A portion of the discussion was not recorded.]

—with energy in what might be termed good. And that can be balanced out either here or hereafter. That depends on the individual. But there is balance and there is no escape from any of our acts and activities. There is no escape, no. Not in my understanding. We can only hide from our self for so long. Thank you. Yes.

Yes, but then, how do you determine what's good and bad? If it's within your own conscience, then who's determining whether it's good and whether it's bad?

You. Your spiritual sensibility, known as conscience. And that's very individual. You have a right to your understanding. And you have a right to your expression, to what's good or bad for you. You have that divine birthright.

But then, for instance, in different cultures, [they] might have an altogether different idea.

That's most understandable.

From what I would think was, maybe, completely wrong would be a completely right thing merely because of the culture that the person lived in.

He who respects the rights of his own freedom cannot help but respect the rights of another's freedom. That's very individualistic. Absolutely and positively. Definitely.

Spiritualism has not come to preach to the world. It has come to share its understanding with those who are seeking it. It is not concerned with converting members to its churches. It is not concerned with building cathedrals. It is concerned in serving what it understands to be the Light of Infinite Intelligence. Many people come to Spiritualism and many people go. Spiritualism in and of herself is not concerned with those things.

Yes. Someone had a question? Yes.

What about the type of person who's plagued with second thoughts, you know, "Maybe I will; maybe I won't", "Should I or shouldn't I" or "I just don't know?" With the doubt in the mind, working at a positive answer and a negative answer, [how does one] get separated?

In time, in reference to your question, in time, if a person makes the daily effort to tune in with their own divine Spirit, they will know beyond a shadow of any doubt what is right and what is wrong for them. And sooner or later these so-called doubts that plague the gray matter of our brain, they will disappear as we go on. But if we give power to things outside of our self, if we ask someone else, "Am I right or am I wrong?" and we continuously rely upon influences outside of our self, we're only going to become a cripple. Because if we take that someone away, we can't make decisions anymore because we haven't had the years of practice to make them. Does that help with your question?

Uh-huh.

Thank you. We have a few minutes left for your questions, and then we'll get on to the other part of our seminar.

Would you explain spirit guides?

You wish an explanation of spirit guides. I can share with you my understanding of spirit guides. Everyone, to my understanding and awareness, has guides and teachers. These spirits that have left the flesh are attracted to people through like attracts like and becomes the Law of Attachment. You have certain interests in certain things; you attract to you people of like interest. You not only attract from this dimension, this physical world, but you attract from the so-called invisible world. And they come into your universe as mentors and helpers. Now there are guides and teachers whose specific purpose is to help mankind to awaken to the Light within himself.

Remember that the spirit guides and teachers can be no greater illumined than our own soul's aspiration. The prophet is never greater than the prophecy. And so it is with spirit guides and teachers. They are no higher, they are no lower than our own soul's aspiration. And we cannot expect to have some great, illumined master as our personal guide unless we are demonstrating, through the laws of effort, to be just that. [Does] that help with your question on spirit guides and teachers?

Thank you.

Yes, madam.

So, does that mean, then, that with a change of attitude, you will change your spirit guides as you grow here on Earth?

That is correct. What happens, in reference to that, as we change our attitudes for the better, what we consider to be the better, whatever it is to be, our guides and teachers, they either grow or they go. One of the two. And if they don't grow, as we are growing, if we're growing, then they will go because like attracts like and becomes the Law of Attachment. They have no longer a rapport with our aura, and they disappear. Yes. And so it is if we are not growing and they are, they will not, they cannot stay in our atmosphere. No, they can't.

We are never, we are never conscious of them, are—well—

Of our spirit guides and teachers?

Uh-huh.

Some people are. Some people are aware of their guides and teachers while they are at sleep. Sometimes they're aware through a certain feeling, almost like a telepathic experience taking place. But remember what Saint Paul said: test all things; hold fast to that which is good.

[After a short pause, the teacher continues.] Are there any more questions before we finish?

Would a clairvoyant dream of an impending, well, I don't want to say disaster, but some unhappy event? Would [there] be a warning to you through spirit guides?

Yes, a clairvoyant could. A clairvoyant could see that condition while yet in the waking, conscious state. Some clairvoyants, some psychics, some mediums receive many of their messages in the dream state. Many do. Some of them receive them through symbology.

Well, how about, oh, once in a lifetime, not a known clairvoyant, but just—

Yes?

—one of those snap dreams that come and are probably never repeated?

Absolutely.

That would be an example of your spirit guides helping you or warning you.

It could be, but not necessarily so. It *could* be, but not necessarily so. It could be your own spiritual faculties. It could be your own psychic abilities. You see, every human being is psychic, but not every human being is mediumistic. A psychic looks into realms that are the psychic realms, not into the worlds of spirit. A medium is one who looks into these realms of the spirit and who is also psychic. Yes.

[After a short pause, the teacher continues.] If there are no more questions, we will get to our psychometry of the billets.

Now I do ask one thing during that part of our seminar: I do ask that you place your feet flat upon floor and not cross your hands or arms. You only—

[The recording ends.]

APRIL 28, 1972

Discourse June 5, 1972

Greetings, students of the Light.

Although a phase of our work has indeed been completed, we shall carry on and serve the Light whenever we are called to do so. *[The teacher may be referring to the publication of the first book of teachings, entitled* The Living Light. *Discourse 65, which was given on May 29, 1972, was the last discourse to be published in that book.* The Living Light *was republished in* The Living Light Dialogue, *Volume 1, in 2007.]*

As you know, the lessons that have been given are brought forth in an ever-unfolding and expanding way. Such is the Law of Progression and such are the laws of merit. And so it is, at this time, that we're speaking on some of the techniques, so to speak, that have been given to you to free yourselves from certain levels of disturbances within your being. You will recall that a certain way of breathing was given to you to help you. And now the time has come to expand upon it.

When you feel that you are receiving disturbing vibrations, which you have opened the doors to, place pressure upon the receptive side of your anatomy. For example, as you inhale through the left nostril, stand upon the left foot, for that part of your anatomy is your understanding.

We shall, in time to come, speak more on these parts of the anatomy and how they are controlled by these patterns of mind.

We are indeed grateful for whatever growth and whatever steps forward have been made. We are grateful for our channel, for, as you know, the channel cannot step any higher than the students which are being served. And so it is in all dimensions at all times. And we are indeed pleased to note that there is, level by level, step by step, greater, ever greater selfless thoughts and selfless service.

Whether or not we enjoy growing is not important, for we shall indeed grow. There is no other way that we have found. And to our understanding at this time, there is no greater life than the life of freedom.

Good night.

JUNE 5, 1972

Discourse June 12, 1972

Greetings, good friends.

We have been discussing selective concentration, freedom from emotion. Now in reference to the discussions that we have been having, we should like to review with you a bit about concentration. You have been given the technique of spiritual concentration, placing the mind upon one thing.

As the students unfold and begin upon the path of Light, there appears to be seeming difficulties and disturbances to grow through. Once the Law of Concentration has been set into motion, it is easily opened in the day-to-day activities of the mind. To concentrate is to be one with a thing. Unless there is daily practice, the selective principle of concentration, the mind will hold to any thought wave that enters it and will be unable to release it.

A wave of thought held in mind, the electrical part of mind, moves from the conscious to the emotional body or subconscious mind. This is known as being grounded. The way to release is as simple as the way to hold or to concentrate. Whenever the mind, being concentrated, holds on to a wave of disturbance, it can, through the selective principle, transmute the wave of thought and rise the spirit within to a greater level.

Many exercises have been given to you as students to help you to be free. You may, by placing the appropriate fingers upon the temples, with pressure, transmute any thought of disturbance held in mind.

As you continue to unfold, to become more and more receptive to these dimensions around and about you, it is ever-increasingly important that you use the selective principle of concentration. Without freedom [derived] from concentration, you will burn out, so to speak, the electrical body and become the self-inflicted victim of the emotional body.

The path to the Light is inescapable. Our spirit and our spirit alone places us upon it. The necessity of freeing the spirit from the self-preservation realms is critically important, for without freedom from those levels within, the spirit cannot serve its purpose through the form.

Use, don't abuse, the pressure technique and you will, in time to come, transmute this power, this energy when it enters on disturbing waves of thought.

Good night.

JUNE 12, 1972

Discourse June 19, 1972

Greetings, fellow students.

He who seeks to gain the freedom of his soul shall pay the price in the coinage of his goal.

So often the students on this side have asked, "Why is it necessary to give up so much to gain so little?" My good students, that which is forever can never be known by that which is passing in the illusions of so-called time. It is [not], and never has been, what must be gathered to be free, but what must be removed that the spirit may once again return to its home.

So many exercises are given and so many words are spoken to help the students to free their eternal being. And again, the words are spoken, like the voice in the wilderness, the eternal cry to free our spirit from its bondage to Mother Nature.

When the soul is ready, then it is willing to give up what it seemingly values to be free. How, I ask, can we know what we in truth value unless we're willing to make the daily effort to be free? My good friends, you cannot be free as long as you insist upon holding to these passing so-called values. To become aware of what we value is to awaken the form in which we are encased this moment.

Many, many, many times, my good students, it has been asked to think, to ponder, to become aware of what you insist upon holding to. There is no teaching, there is no way that I have ever found that can free the soul that is not ready to free itself. Unless we're willing to give up what we're insisting upon holding to, there is no true Light and no freedom of our soul.

Become aware, children, of what you're really doing to your spirit, to your soul, [by] the bondage and the darkness that you insist upon keeping yourselves in. Awaken to the freedom, to the peace, the love, the joy, the purpose of life itself.

Good night.

JUNE 19, 1972

Discourse June 26, 1972

Greetings, friends and fellow workers.

He who bears the Light shares the Light.

We are discussing at this time the soul's journey through the form's evolution. And in review, we should like to speak on your planet Earth. As you know, it is the fifth planet in your solar system: the planet upon which the soul's incarnation is earning and learning faith. In the soul's journey, passing through the other planets of your system, they come to your earth realm from different planets with various experiences that they have merited. And indeed is your planet the so-called melting pot of the universes.

You will find, my students, in time that that which has met before shall meet again, though it knows it not. There are just reasons for this.

And from your planet to other spheres, we all shall travel. Whatever it is that you have to learn, to earn, be about the Father's business, for it has been said this and this only, this moment, this eternity, is what you have, my good students, power over.

Indeed, does it seem difficult to overcome the temptations, the patterns of mind stuff. But that, too, has been earned and merited, so to speak.

However, there is a greater way and that, my good students, you have indeed been given. The student in time is destined to be the teacher, for the teacher and the student, in truth, is one and the same, for he who is a student on one level is a teacher on another.

And so it is with the passing of this evolution of time. Go deeper into your being. You will find the Light in ever-increasing degrees.

I am permitted to say that this is not first time this class has met, and by that I mean the first time in incarnation.

The purpose shall be fulfilled and I beseech you to do it now. Free your mind from so much of passing creation. What is it that you can lose that has value? Only your soul, my children, is eternal. All other things have come to you and all other things are passing from you. Take greater value of the formless and the free. That is truth to you and truth to me.

Someday I shall return. That is known by a greater power than I. And when that day comes, we shall indeed meet again.

Good night.

JUNE 26, 1972

Class July 20, 1972

Greetings, students.

Indeed, it is our pleasure to be with you in this way. We will be grateful to share with you our understanding at this time. Please feel free to ask your questions.

The first—it's not a question. We all thank you for all the help you have given us. And the first question would be, If you have any prejudices in any manner, how would you work them out?

[Students prepared written questions in advance of this class, and those questions were read by a student.]

Thank you. For the benefit of our other classes, I shall repeat the question. If one is entertaining in thought certain prejudices, in what way may they be freed from that level of expression?

Prejudices, so to speak, are born and given birth in the darkness of ignorance from lack of understanding. If it is one's sincere desire to be freed from them, through greater effort in seeking understanding, their spirit within shall rise to a greater level of awareness, and in so doing they shall be freed.

Thank you. How do you find out if you see or, if what you see or hear is imagination or real?

The question is, In what way is it possible to discern between imagination and reality? We should like to add to your question, truth. Reality, my good friends, is but a conscious realization of any passing event. What is real to one in one dimension is not real to one who is in another dimension.

Discernment of what is imagination and discernment of what is truth can be accomplished through a greater awakening of one's own spirit. There is a level within us known as the creative principle. In that level, imagination is the ruler. Beyond the level of creative principle is the level of truth. It is beyond the illusion of form and forms. It is the great peace. It is the great oneness that knows itself. And in so knowing, truth is made manifest.

Thank you. How does a person know he is on the true road to spiritual growth?

The question is, In what way is it possible for a person to know beyond a shadow of any doubt if they are on the true path of spiritual growth? My good friends, through the laws of evolutionary incarnation, we have indeed merited the experiences that we are encountering each moment and each day. That that we are seeking is in the very process of seeking ourselves. If the motive is that of Spirit, then, in time, according to the law, it shall manifest itself. Therefore, it behooves us to first find our true motive. Not the one that we entertain in thought on one day and change in another, but go deep within ourselves and there we will find the motive and the cause.

Thank you. Is there anything wrong with sitting for phenomena?

The question is, Is it beneficial to sit primarily for so-called phenomena? Let us have a greater understanding of what we mean by that word. If we mean by the word *phenomena,* science not yet fully understood, if we mean by that word, laws not yet revealed to our being, then it can be beneficial to sit for greater understanding of those laws. The motive to serve the Divine is the only motive that is eternal, that is permanent, and that is truly useful.

Thank you. What happens to those souls who have no idea of an afterlife and then cross over?

The question is well put. What happens to souls who have no belief in the continuity of life and pass from your dimension of the earth realm into this other, so-called invisible realm? My good students, without belief, there is no creation, there is no form here or hereafter. Therefore, there is no soul that passes from your planet to ours who does not have, in their very being, belief. In time, this belief is stimulated and they are awakened.

There are times—and sometimes it is centuries—that they remain asleep, unaware of their very being. But that cannot, and is not, an eternal state of being.

Thank you. What is ahead for a soul who has committed suicide?

What is the destiny of those who come to other dimensions by their own choice and will of their mind? The cause for leaving the form shall ever be fulfilled. If a person leaves one form because they cannot endure its trials and tribulations, they take with them those very experiences. And it is much more difficult, students, on this side of the curtain to work out those trials and so-called tribulations.

Whatever experiences that we encounter, they are only effects of causes. But study wisely these effects, for in them is revealed their cause.

Thank you. What is the difference, if any, between being in divine order and that what you've set into motion by one's will power?

The question is, Is there a difference between what is divine order and what is set into motion by the individualized will? Indeed, my friends, there is a great difference. Expression of the will may or may not be in divine order.

There is a realm, a level of awareness within us, where Spirit reigns supreme. And when we release our desires and aspirations to that divine level, known as divine order, where Infinite Intelligence reigns, then we are freed from the mental level of cause and effect.

Thank you. Why is the principle of combined life chosen over reincarnation?

The question is stated, Why is the principle of combined life stated over reincarnation? Is that your question?

Yes, but there's a second question. What evidence have you seen to prove reincarnation, if any?

The question is also stated, What evidence, [if] any, is revealed to substantiate [the] so-called theory of reincarnation? If you mean by that word a return of the soul back to the planet upon which it has previously expressed, we have and do see untold millions of people waiting to once again reexpress in earth form. It is our understanding, from untold time, that the soul passes through planet upon planet on the evolutionary path. We do not and have not definite evidence of a return to your earth realm for the masses of people. There are rare occasions when a spirit, highly illumined, to serve the higher purposes of the Divine, is returned to your realms. This is not the general rule to our understanding at this time.

Thank you. Will you elaborate on soul flights and restrictions of movement involving the silver cord?

The question concerns so-called soul flight and restrictions involving the silver cord. My good students, I believe from reading upon your ethereal waves that the one who asked the question is concerned with this so-called silver cord, which is attached to what is termed the astral body.

The astral body is one of the many vehicles through which your spirit is expressing at this time. When one has an experience of soul flight, which indeed is not a common experience, there is no cord connected to the soul. When the astral body leaves the physical body, there is a cord that connects the vehicle. Soul, my good students, is inseparable. It is one expressed through many. If it is an astral flight, then, if the cord is snapped from the astral vehicle, the soul is freed. If it is truly a soul flight, there is no vehicle, my children, for the soul.

Thank you. Is there life on another—other planets?

The question is, Is life expressed on other planets than the earth realm? Indeed, my friends, it is.

Thank you. Can one spirit communicate with another at will?

"Can one spirit communicate with another at will?" Only those spirits who are on similar or equal levels of expression can communicate with each other.

Thank you. How can one learn the names of one's guides?

The question [is], How can one learn the names of one's helpers or guides? My dear children, form is bondage. And names are tags. Many times I have been asked, From what realm do I come? What name do I bear? We have striven for centuries to free ourselves from the bondage of creation. Concern not your beings with names and things, and ye shall be free.

Thank you. What is the basis for Spiritualism in the Bible?

The question has been asked, What is the basis for Spiritualism in that book they call the Bible? Our understanding of your word, *Spiritualism*, is an awakening and an expression of the divine Spark within all. And when that spirit within is awakened and expressed, Spiritualism shall reign and fulfill her purpose.

In reference to that book, the Bible, it has many errors and some truths. It was brought into being by a few who tried to serve the greater Light. Many times it has been changed to fit the needs of the people. Concern yourselves, my good friends, with the divine Light that is within you, and then your soul shall indeed fulfill its purpose.

Thank you. Should some students work on healing and developing healing?

The question is, Is it advisable for everyone to unfold what is termed healing? The divine Spark within, known as Spirit, covered with soul, is the greatest healer you will ever know. Therefore, it is the divine birthright of all souls to heal themselves.

Good night.

JULY 20, 1972

Class July 27, 1972

Greetings, students.

Once again it is our pleasure to be with you. You may feel free at this time to ask the questions that you have prepared.

Thank you, again, for helping us to open spiritually. The first question is, How can we best guide our children towards their own spiritual unfoldment?

The question has been asked, In which way does the spirit express itself fully in the so-called body of a child? My good students, children are children only in form, not in truth, for the soul, when it enters your earth realm, is not new; it is indeed very, very old. In the guidance of children, we have found that an appeal to the spirit within them, in more of an adult, so to speak, way is indeed most beneficial. The problem seems to be that parents or so-called adults in form have not yet recognized or realized that they are speaking to a soul that is not new. There are ways to appeal to the soul within, and that way is to reach the level of soul first within ourselves. Children, like so-called adults, need and respect proper discipline. However, proper discipline is not given from a level of emotionalism, but it is extended from a level of logic, of reason and compassion.

Thank you. Why do some philosophies claim seven planes, while others describe nine planes? Which is correct?

The question is asked that there are teachings amongst you of seven planes of consciousness, and there are also teachings of nine planes of consciousness. The question is also asked, Which is correct? My good friends, what is correct to one is not necessarily correct to another. The teachings of the seven, the mystic, or the occult, is relatively new. It is not of ancient, ancient origin. However, there are many, by far the masses of earth men, who still express through what is known as the level of mysticism or superstition. Therefore, the understanding of the seven and the seven planes of consciousness would indeed appeal and be correct for them.

When we rise our spirit to a higher level of understanding, when we in truth know that all is law, that there is no exception to divine law, then we will have a greater understanding and see and know the totality, which indeed is truth.

Thank you. Why is it that people who have entered the spirit world whom you were close to on Earth do not try to contact you on Earth?

The question is asked, many times there are friends we have while yet in the flesh. They leave their form for other dimensions and no longer, seemingly, attempt to communicate with those who remain in the flesh. As you look over your lives, you will find that many have come into your life, so to speak, and indeed many have gone. Ofttimes it is said that we make an acquaintance which is useful.

Just because a person leaves the physical body does not in any way guarantee a change of their attitudes. There are many factors involved that are so little understood in so-called communication. The problem of communication is with those who are yet in the flesh. For some unknown reason, they refuse to make the daily effort to become more receptive to these various dimensions and worlds of spirit.

As our thought goes to the Divine, the Divinity within us expresses itself. If we think of our friends, so to speak, who have gone to other worlds, now and then and we do not make a sincere daily effort to establish communication, to learn the laws, the science of communion, we cannot expect to communicate with them.

Thank you. As we progress spiritually, do our guides remain with us or do they change as we change?

The question is asked, As a student unfolds and awakens spiritually, do their guides and teachers remain with them? The guides and teachers that have been attracted will remain as long as they are in rapport with our own levels of awareness. If, for some reason, they cannot or will not grow with us, they will indeed be left behind. But usually, my good students, it is indeed the other way around.

Thank you. How do you establish rapport with our guides? And have our guides been with us from conception or birth?

In reference to your question, In what way is it best to attempt communication or rapport with our guides and teachers? And have they been with us since our soul's incarnation on [the] earth realm? As the soul enters form in the physical dimension, a part of itself, commonly known as a guardian angel, enters form in an ethereal being. This guardian angel, the other half of our self, is with us throughout eternity.

Remember, my good students, form is not possible without the poles of opposites. Our guides and teachers are attracted to us at various times in our lives. Sometimes they will come in our early life and remain with us. Usually, they do not. If it is the sincere desire of the student to establish communion with their helpers, their teachers, and guides from the realms ethereal, then they need but make greater effort in selfless service and daily communication. For when self is set aside, God the Divine, the Light herself, flows freely and brings indeed heaven in your being.

Thank you. Is there any such thing as bad luck or can a person always do well if they apply the right principles or laws of nature?

The question is asked, Does superstition or so-called bad luck control our lives or [do] the laws herself control our lives? My dear children, man is a law unto himself. Let us ask in sincerity, What are we doing with the law that we are? Whatever happens to us is not superstition or so-called luck; it is the setting into motion of various laws. There is no cure without the cause, and the cause lies deep within our being. The greatest thing I know to free oneself (their eternal spirit) from the prison house, the bondage, the slavery of creation is to pause and think, to reeducate the so-called brain, to feed it new information, for there is never or ever a cause outside of our own universe. It is the delusion and the illusion created by the lower self. No matter where you wander, no matter where you go, no matter what you do, you will never be free until we learn and demonstrate the Divinity of which we are in truth.

Thank you. How related is the self to the conscious mind and subconscious?

The question is asked in reference to the relationship of the so-called self to the conscious and subconscious minds. The conscious and subconscious minds *are* creation. As long as the spirit flows through the levels of conscious and subconscious mind and the two minds are not in harmony or, so to speak, in rapport, man shall eternally face problems and disturbances. When man makes the effort to go deep within himself to learn the habit patterns established by himself, to educate them to permit so-called pride to bow to the soul faculty of humility, to place his faith in the only power that never fails, then and then only will man truly be free.

Thank you. What are the effects of alcohol or drugs, meat, etc., to the unfoldment of awareness in man?

The question is, What effect, if any, does so-called alcohol, meat, and drugs have upon the unfoldment of one's soul? We understand that the effects of these chemicals change the form through which the soul is striving to express itself. Anything that blocks, so to speak, the soul's expression or light while yet in form, in that respect, is detrimental to it. There is a power greater than all chemicals. There is a power greater than form. To those who have reached that level and are able to demonstrate it, no longer have need for food for their form, for all the chemicals necessary for the so-called good health of the form is in the air you breathe.

Thank you. What is the purpose of personality?

The question has been asked, What is the purpose of so-called personality? Personality, so to speak, is the individualization of so-called form. Its purpose is to be the vehicle of expression for the soul. The soul, on its evolutionary path of expression, has merited a certain form or personality in order that it may express itself according to the laws of merit that it has set into motion. There are those with so-called personalities that are most difficult, it seems, to tolerate. However, if a person is enabled, through that so-called difficult personality, to unfold a greater level of tolerance, understanding, and compassion, then the greater good is indeed accomplished.

Thank you. Good rules for recognizing and maintaining your own purpose.

The statement is made, good rules for sustaining and maintaining one's purpose. Rules, my children, are form. They begin, they change, and they end. We are concerned with the spiritual awakening of the students. When man is honest with himself, he can only be honest with the world. In reference to your question, a rule set into motion may help one soul somewhere, or two or more, depending upon their level of awareness. And this is why we have no rules to offer. We have no set ways. My good students, you have the potential of eighty-one levels of awareness. What level are you in and when? Your spirit knows. Go to the Light within you. Be honest with yourself and you shall indeed find the way.

Thank you. Ways to avoid depression through seeming slumps or standstill periods.

Are there ways to avoid depression? May we ask the question, What lesson is perceived and being learned during the depression? Is a greater awareness, a greater freedom being given birth during the struggle? "O God, I am grateful for all life's experiences, for I know they are in truth my greatest blessings." *[Another version of this teaching, which is from The Serenity Game, is "O God, I am grateful for all life's experiences, especially the difficult ones, for I know they are in truth my greatest blessings."]*

Thank you. Best method to have total dream recall.

The question has been asked, Is there a method, beneficial, for so-called dream recall? Be ever the dreamer, my children, and not the dream herself. In reference to your question, there is a way that we have found [that is] beneficial: by a reprogramming, so to speak, of the mind. It is not possible to reprogram a level that refuses to be reprogrammed. When we are peaceful with our soul, that is the time to set laws into motion, for peace is the power. So when you are peaceful, pause and think and speak your word forth into the universe, knowing that it shall not come back to you void, but accomplish that which you send it to do. Then speak your word, and the day will come when you will dream and you will be aware of your dreaming and you will be aware that you are the dreamer dreaming the dream. And when that day arrives, my good children, you shall awaken.

Good night.

JULY 27, 1972

Common Sense Meditation Part 1

We are indeed so grateful to once again share with you our understanding.

The interest appears to be, at this time, concerned with meditation. We have found that the true purpose of meditation is to still the mind in order that the soul, the Light, the Spirit may express itself through the vehicle of form in a clear, unobstructed way. We find that this is possible when there is a great peace over the brain waves. When the mind, its energies, no longer express themselves, the soul within rises to the level known as conscious awareness and illumines the so-called mind, which is expressing through the brain.

You know, my good friends, that meditation is not something to be taken lightly. The stilling of the mind is not an easy task for many students simply because they have not practiced for a sufficient time.

The nature of mind is constant activity, releasing a great amount of energy. But when the mind is still, this great Power, known as God, stills our being in a perfect peace, which, my friends, you know is indeed the Power itself.

All things move and be in rhythm. Seeming discord or disorder is a rhythm that we do not, as yet, understand. Many are in harmony with the instrument known as the piano. Others with the drum. And still others, the violin. And so it is in so-called discord, it too has a rhythm, a beat, a vibration. Students on the path will consider wisely what their rhythm or natural beat really is.

To find oneself is to find truth. To find oneself is to be perfect harmony. This, my good children, is accomplished through your daily efforts.

As the sun arises on your planet, so let your soul arise. Be in harmony with Nature herself. She holds the greatest secrets of the ages. Study her effects and you will learn the causes of your being. Let your spirit rise each morn. Let it become aware (your mind) of what you really are. Be not tempted by the passing panorama of things, for, my good friends, things always come and things always go.

In true meditation there is a great stillness, a great silence. There is no thought. There is no act. For God, my children, is indeed silence.

Garner up the powers within your being. Place your attention on the oneness which *is*. We are ever, my students, what we entertain in thought. Can you not see the wisdom and the benefit of being without thought for at least a few moments in a day?

You may put your house in order before confusion sets in. I mean by that statement, declare the truth in your daily meditation. Not your will, but divine will. Be receptive to its flow. But remember, we cannot be receptive to that which we are not in rapport with. Feel the freedom, the peace, the love, the light of your spirit. Still the mind. Will the thoughts to stop, and you will find your real being.

You may feel free at this time to ask whatever questions you may have.

In going into the deep silence in your meditations, what is all the noise, the noise of the silence?

That indeed is [a] good question. And for the benefit of my other students, I shall repeat it. What is the seeming noise and sounds and disturbances during one's effort to find silence? My good students, the experiences of noise, so to speak, of sounds is a level that we are tapping within ourselves. It is the door before the silence. It is the outer silence. And the sounds, my dear friends, are the sounds and the motions of your so-called body. Each part of our anatomy is playing its tune. And if we listen intently, we will know beyond a shadow of any doubt which part of our so-called physical anatomy is out of tune or out of harmony. My good friends, you are a great symphony, a great orchestra. Each part of your body is playing its tune. Think, think, and think more deeply. You are becoming aware of your being.

During the manifestation part of the meditation and we have a question to ask and we do ask the question and we get the answer back through an inner feeling or an inner thought, does this come from our spirit guides or does this come from our own spirit knowing what's right or wrong for us as an individual?

Thank you. The question is asked, During the part of meditation known as manifestation, when we receive impressions, feelings, sights, or sounds, are these received from our own spirit or are they received from so-called guides and teachers? Like attracts like and becomes the Law of Attachment. Whatever guides and teachers that are attracted to us, my dear children, they are equal to us in spirit, in spiritual awareness, and on spiritual levels.

Many people are unable, so to speak, at this time, to be in rapport or in tune with their own spirit. There are decarnate entities who, according to laws set into motion, have been attracted to us. They are enabled, at times, to impress our minds through telepathic communication. Therefore, usually, but not always, the impressions, feelings, sights, and sounds that we receive are from our so-called helpers.

You understand, students, that for most people a thought impression is more quickly understood than a soul impression. However, as you go deeper and deeper into your silence, this great Light shall rise from level to level, until you become consciously aware of your own spirit. When that day comes, you will know beyond a shadow of any doubt what is from your spirit and what is from other spirits. Remember, my children, that there is no separation in truth. Therefore, indeed are we all one, and one indeed is all.

Thank you.

Sir, I have a question. My question is, What are the dangers of meditation and how can we avoid them?

The question is well put: What are the dangers of meditation and how may they be overcome? The dangers, friends, exist within ourselves. In order to reach the spark known as Divinity that is within us, we must go, layer by layer, down through the subconscious levels. There are many pits, so to speak, many psychological traumatic conditions that have been suppressed since early childhood. To go into the deeper, inner levels of mind without guidance is not recommended.

Who, shall we ask, is so illumined to know this moment every thought they have ever thought, every act they have ever done, every feeling they have ever known? My dear children, all of those things lie waiting in the memory par excellence. And through that dimension we must pass in order to enter the levels known as Light. Do not feel that there is some type of magic wand that will protect you from all of the experiences that you have encountered in a lifetime. For if there is, my dear friends, I have yet to find it.

Guidance is critically important that when you open these Pandora boxes, known as psychological traumatic conditions of your past, that you will have someone who has tread [trodden] the path to help guide you through them. All of those feelings must be brought to the conscious awareness in order that you may be free and touch the Light herself.

Sir, I have another question. There is, among different psychic channels, differences of opinion concerning meditation. And each psychic channel, who are very good people in themselves, profess these differences and believe in them very strongly. Why is this? That they—there seems to be a great deal of belief in higher guidance from the spirit world and yet, there is difference in opinions on the subject matter of meditation.

The question, once again, is well put. It is not new to our understanding. The question is, What is the variety, what is its cause amongst varying channels? The teachings differ so widely concerning meditations and spiritual endeavors.

Yes.

There are many levels of awareness on your earth realm and on ours. We are always grateful to share with those who are seeking the understanding that we have found at this time. Think, my students, we cannot be receptive to that that we have not grown to. We cannot be receptive to the language, for example, of Chinese, unless we have made the effort to study and to apply it. For example, if we are seeking the guidance of the Divinity, then the Divinity must be made manifest in ourselves.

As like attracts like and becomes the Law of Attachment, so please bear with me in this understanding. If an individual has severe traumatic experiences and they have been suppressed beneath the conscious level of mind, the traumatic experiences must be brought to the fore—in other words, our house must be put in order—in order that our conscious mind may tap into what is known as the superconscious level.

When the student, level by level, is uncovering those experiences, like attracting like, they will attract, at those times, entities from the astral realms who are in harmony or rapport with the experience of the past that they are reviewing and expressing. This is one of the major reasons why we teach do not open yourself to a receptivity of meditation without guidance [from] someone in your dimension [who] may benefit you in their understanding and experiences.

Many, many people are good. In truth, my friends, we all are good. A man may be an excellent mathematician; however, he may be very poor as a musician. And so it is with the various channels that the worlds of spirit have to work through. A little light in the night is ever better than no light at all.

And so it is, indeed is God's manifestation variety. And there is ever-varying understanding and teaching from the realms of spirit, for in truth there are eighty-one levels, planes of existence.

Thank you.

[After a short pause, the teacher continues.] There appears on the ethereal waves the question of technique. If the student will sincerely do his part in being still, in doing the breathing that has been given, when the motive is pure, the manifestation is inevitable. It is so simple, in truth, to be still, to be silent, to let the great God of all flow freely. Speak to the levels of mind and declare the truth of truths:

> I am Spirit, formless and free;
> Whatever I think, that will I be.

Good night.

OCTOBER 4, 1972

Common Sense Meditation Part 2

Greetings, students of the Light.

Indeed, we are grateful to visit with you again. You are free to ask your questions at this time.

Old Man, we're trying very hard to put a booklet together on meditation. Could you give me a direction—I'm supposed to write it—as to which—how you would like it done? I was thinking of asking you personal questions. Or should I just confine my questions to meditation? And is it possible to have another meeting with you after this time?

In reference to your questions, let yourself be guided by your light and be it in order, we may meet again.

Thank you. Well, all right, sir, one of my questions, then, is on meditation. And I would like to ask you, Why meditation was chosen as a communication between the here and the hereafter? From what law it arises? And why are some people unable—or why must some people live their entire lives without the use of meditation?

The questions are varied and of great import. Meditation is a form of receptivity to higher dimensions than the mind, in its activities, usually encounters. The laws under which meditation is expressed are very, very simple. It is our spirit, covered with soul, that must be permitted to express through the vehicle known as mind. There is nothing new or old to Spirit, for Spirit is timeless and formless. When the Light or Spirit dawns upon the so-called mind, it awakens it (the mind) to the truth that all is one; that there are no beginnings or endings of the divine flow.

Some souls have merited in their evolutionary incarnation an understanding and expression of the Law of Meditation. Some, at this time, have not. When proper meditation is practiced, you will find a greater freedom, a greater understanding of your being. It improves all of our acts and activities, for it awakens the mind, so to speak, which controls our actions.

Thank you, sir. The next question is, Can you please tell us what plane you are from and who are your guides and councils?

My dear students, to speak of myself or my plane of expression is to limit myself in your understanding. That that is form is limitation. With your kind permission, we prefer to be formless.

Thank you, sir. Anybody else have questions? [The initial questions were asked by one student, who now addresses the other students in class. Another student asks the following question.]

Can you, perhaps, prescribe some techniques for children? What age should children begin to meditate? And how can one teach a young child—or counsel a young child towards meditation?

The benefits of meditation are beyond number. And in reference to meditation for children, it has been recommended, by many who have practiced it, that children may start in their third year. They may even start earlier, depending on the evolution of the child. A child placed in daily silence to think only of peace for ten minutes a day will indeed help the child to remain and sustain a rapport with the Divine.

Thank you, sir. The next question is: There are certain, what we call, prophets who have come to us—Mohammad, Christ, and Buddha. Are their teachings that varied or is it only the interpretation? And are these people on your plane? And could you dissertate on that a little bit? Do you understand?

The question in reference to the prophets who have visited your plane of expression is not a new question in the minds of the masses. The divine Spark known as Truth, Eternity is one. It is the misunderstanding of the receivers who find a contradiction and doubt in the teachings of old, which are the teachings of new. Truth is simple and unconcealed.

When we receive truth, our minds, which are guaranteed to be dual, start the opposing forces into motion, and we experience what is known as confusion. The teachings of a Buddha or a Christ or any of the prophets is one and the same teaching. There is one Life, one Law, one Love. It is unbroken and eternal. We are not going to God; we already *are* God. It is our minds which need awakening, and this is possible through proper meditation. The tendency of mind is to hold, to form, to bind. And this is why we ask your cooperation in not attempting to bind us, for our freedom has been a long, long climb.

Thank you, sir.

[A different student speaks.] *Excuse me, sir. Could you tell us what are the dangers and [the] very big problems with meditating for too long of a period of time in one day?*

The so-called dangers in extended meditation is the tendency of the mind to create. The mind not only creates but it possesses. And when we are in meditation, we are highly receptive to whatever level we are expressing at that time. Therefore, we have found to extend a receptive or meditative period beyond thirty minutes in any given day is extremely dangerous, for the majority of people are not in control of their vehicle known as mind, and they can and ofttimes do become possessed by a predominant, insistent thought from their own subconscious mind.

Thank you.

Sir, when we encounter entities in meditation, can they misrepresent themselves to us by saying something like, "I come from God," instead of, "I come by God"? I mean, I heard that there was a way in which—that God had certain laws and that they could identify themselves by—well, is there any way an entity who is not the correct—or [not] a very high entity could misrepresent themselves to us as a high entity, as a guide?

Thank you. We understand that the laws of God are one, and only Spirit or God is one. That the laws of mind are two;

they are dual; they are creation. Therefore, be awakened, my children, and do not presume that the minds of men may know the laws of God. The spirit is known by the spirit, and the mind is known by the mind. They are two separate things, not one.

So-called spirits may enter a person's aura or universe and be from the realms of deception; they may not be what they pretend to be. And therefore, it behooves us to judge the tree by the fruit that it bears. But we cannot, my friends, experience a deceitful spirit unless we have expressed energy, at some time in our lives, into the realms of deceit, for that that comes from a realm *is* the realm. That that is indeed within us is indeed attracted to us. And this is why we teach know thyself and you shall be free.

Sir, if you could pick one lesson, what would be the greatest lesson that we should learn while here—or strive to learn?

My dear children, in reference to that question, I would say self-control.

Thank you.

Sir, are there certain foods that we should eat that would prepare us for a better body for meditation? Is there anything you would suggest that might have a slight value?

In reference to the question, it is entirely dependent upon the computations of your inner mind. If somewhere in the inner mind there are programmed patterns of belief that dictate a certain type of diet would be beneficial to the finest possible purification of meditation, then for those who have those patterns, it is not only wise to use those diets but indeed is it necessary, unless they can change the patterns of mind that they have entertained and, therefore, believe.

The mind, my friends, controls the body. And therefore, that that controls a thing is greater than the thing that it controls. Work with what is known as your vehicle of mind, then you shall be receptive to the Divine and control what is known as so-called matter.

Sir, should one discuss one's meditation experiences with someone who is interested? Or should one refer the person to a teacher and proper guide and not—and keep his own meditation experiences to himself?

The greatest counsel that man can ever have is the counsel known as silence, for silence is indeed the power itself. However, there are those who need an expression of the experiences that they have in meditation. Choose wisely, my friends, who you express those experiences with, for you will trigger certain levels of mind known as envy and jealousy, and in so doing ye shall rob yourself of future beneficial experiences.

This envy and jealousy that we incur, sir, is it from people on this plane or on the hereafter?

It is from people on both planes, for you are in truth living in many planes, though you may not be consciously aware of it at this moment.

All right, sir. Is there anything in particular you would like for me to stress in the booklet on meditation, other than the dissertation you gave us in the past? Any particular point?

Stress, my child, the importance of thought. Become aware of all your thoughts for your thoughts are creating your lives. They are the seeds that you are planting in fertile soil. And you will make a garden of beauty or a jungle of so-called hell.

Sir, my mind is a blank now. I don't think I have any more questions. But I haven't written up the booklet yet. Is it possible to ask—I'm going away for about a week or so—Is it possible to ask another time when you might come to us?

We shall return. So-called time and date is something, my friends, that no longer governs us.

Good night.

OCTOBER 9, 1972

[No copies of the booklet referred to in this class have been located.]

Class October 19, 1972

[Greetings], students of the Light.

Again, we are pleased to visit with you in this way. You may feel free to ask the questions that you have at this time.

What is the purpose of meditation?

The question has been asked: the true purpose of meditation. We understand the purpose of meditation to be an attunement, a oneness of the spirit encased in form with the universal Spirit. It is a process by which the mind, the vehicle expressing in a mental level, is stilled that the soul may express itself in its fullness while yet encased in form. It is expressing the Divine, the God that in truth we all are.

Thank you. What will be the end result for us by constant meditation?

The question is, What is the inevitable result from continuous or constant meditation? When one is truly meditating, they are at one; they indeed are the Silence, the Truth, the God. The result is freedom. Freedom to know that which is right and to know it and to do it beyond a shadow of any doubt. It is a fulfillment of the soul's incarnation into form, the one and only purpose of its true incarnation.

Thank you, sir. What is the difference between meditation and the dream state of sleep?

The question is asked: the difference between meditation and the dream state of sleep. Sleep, my children, is a lack of conscious awareness. Most people think that conscious awareness is an awareness of the things that their mind records, the things that they see, the things that they hear. That is not, in any sense, true awareness. When the mind is stilled and no longer entertains a thought, that that is all, known as God, is aware of all things in all places at all times. We are not aware during a so-called sleep and dream state. We are not aware of the eighty-one levels in which our spirit truly is. We are, however, aware of the things that the mind creates during what you call a sleep state.

Thank you, sir. From where did the meaning of color come from, sir?

The question is asked: From where cometh the true meaning of color? It has often been stated, my friends, that color is vibration. We know that when colors are perfectly blended that they produce what is known as purity or the color white. White is the highest vibration there is. It is the color of purity, of perfect harmony, of peace herself. When this color known as white, when its vibration is activated or disturbed, it produces varied colors or different notes of the symphony of life itself.

The lighter the color, the higher its vibration or, one might say, the greater its spiritual expression. You all know that colors are lightened, so to say, by the color known as white or by purity. When you purify a thing, you raise its vibration and you change or lighten its color. For example, when the aura is perceived, when we see it in the darker shades of color, it is because it is in more of a discordant or inharmonious state of expression.

There are many colors. There are many vibrations. We move through them from moment to moment, depending upon the thought that is being entertained in mind.

Each word has its color. Each color is the essence of the thing itself. For example, when you truly speak forth the word *peace*, you will encompass yourself in the divine white Light, known as God, the Peace itself. Therefore, it behooves the student, before speaking, to become aware of what the color is they are expressing.

There is an affirmation that goes: "I speak my word forth into the universe knowing that it shall not come back to me void, but accomplish that which I send it to do." When you speak the word from the level known as a pure heart and a clear mind, an open soul, then indeed shall it manifest before your very eyes.

Thank you, sir. How do we get away from the mundane problems of everyday life and get into the feeling of peace during meditation?

The question has been asked, In what way is it possible to become in rapport with God or Peace when our minds are so filled with the so-called mundane problems and experiences of the plane in which we are expressing? I know of no law greater than the Law of Effort. If one will truly make the effort and one will truly have the wisdom, which is patience, the faith, which is strength, then the student shall indeed enter the peace that passeth all understanding. The reason that it is difficult for some is because the mind is filled so very full with the thoughts of the passing creation in which so much time, my children, is being spent. To still the mind is to attune oneself with the Divine. It is in the silence that God does his greatest wonders. In all your getting, get self-control.

Thank you, sir. In meditation, is it advisable to try to communicate with our spirit guides and, if so, how?

The question has been asked, Is it advisable to attempt communication with other dimensions during meditation? My good friends, meditation is a total stillness; it is not a matter of communication. There are three parts to the so-called daily meditation; and that is concentration, meditation (or stillness), and manifestation (or communication). All things in their proper way. A house well-ordered is well expressed.

Thank you. When, in meditating, you fail to meditate at the exact time, is it possible to make it up at some other time? And another second part to the same question, Does this harm you in the unfoldment process in any way?

The question has been asked, Is it more beneficial to meditate at a set time or to meditate when one feels so inclined? I am sure you will find that is the essence of the question itself. My good students, the law is very clear: indeed, do we get from a thing what we put into the thing. Therefore, when God the Divine is the most important thing in our thoughts and in our acts, then God the Divine shall guide our lives and they shall indeed be well ordered.

We know that like attracts like. And if one does not feel the value of system and order, then one shall not find system and order in their acts and activities. Ye shall indeed attract from the universes those entities that are as reliable as you are yourselves. No higher, my dear friends, and no lower shall your experiences, your guides, your teachers, your helpers, your mentors be.

Thank you. What is the recommended time period for meditation?

In reference to the length of time for meditation, it has been recommended strenuously, so to say, a twenty-minute maximum for beginning students and not to exceed a half an hour in any given twenty-four-hour period.

Thank you. In meditation should we concentrate on our chakra centers? And what does meditation do to the opening of the chakras?

The question has been asked, During meditation, should one concentrate upon the psychic centers of the psychic body? My dear children, it is indeed most detrimental to most people. When we concentrate upon a thing, we become the thing concentrated upon. And what is more important than God, than Peace, than the Divine? Many students try to find a shortcut to going back home because that is what we are doing in truth. To concentrate upon activating the various psychic centers of the psychic body can, and ofttime[s] does, trap us in so-called psychic-astral realms. Not only, my friends, while you are in the flesh but when you leave your earth realm. And it is much easier to grow through those dimensions while yet in flesh than it is when you have left the so-called clay.

Thank you. In meditation, should you feel more than just the peaceful state of vibration?

The question has been asked: Should one feel or experience more in meditation than God herself? My dear children, there is nothing greater than the true, eternal spark of Divinity that you are this moment. Meditation is meditation, and manifestation is manifestation. Put your attention upon what you want to become. Become the Divine that you truly are.

Thank you, sir. Is there any assistance that we could obtain in order to achieve the state of peace?

In attaining the state known as peace, become godly in your day-to-day thoughts and you will become godly in your acts. And whereas like attracts like and becomes the Law of Attachment, the peace that you are is the peace that you experience. There is nothing greater, my friends, than peace itself. Remember that the key of wisdom unlocks the door of tolerance through which we must pass to gain our freedom.

Good night.

OCTOBER 19, 1972

Journey of the Living Light
Discourse 1

Greetings, fellow friends and students of the Light.

Indeed, it is a great pleasure for us to continue on with our Earth class and especially the continuity of the Light in this way.

Some time ago we mentioned to broaden your horizons, to expand your consciousness, to awaken, my dear children, that, in so doing, you may receive a greater degree of Light, of freedom. Remember, friends, freedom comes as we willingly and gratefully let go of whatever we hold in mind, for he who releases is freed from all his created things. Entities are things that bind us and chain us to ourselves. Free your minds, my dear children, that you may free your spirit that your soul may go to greater awakening, to ever-expanding freedom. Man receives freedom as he receives anything: ever in proportion to his ability and willingness to endure. And so it is with the lessons that we continue to share with you. Remember, if the Light is too bright, 'tis best to give it not now. And so we ask that you may be receptive to greater thought, to greater freedom.

The soul's journey, the Living Light, as it sails on the seas of so-called creations. Remember that your present expression is on the planet known as five: to serve the purpose of awakening and demonstrating the great power known as faith.

Now we all know that nine is the number of totality. And we all know that nine is the number of service. And so it is that our soul expresses in the cycle known as nine. You Earth children are on the bridge, waiting to cross to greater and greater understanding.

In the soul's journey, there are nine visitations in each galaxy. There are, in truth, nine visits to each planet. Do not misunderstand; the soul evolves through time, so-called. It does not return in the sense of payment, but there are nine great lessons to each expression. Faith is learned on your planet that you may go on to the next, the next, the next, and the next.

My dear children, you are not new to me nor am I new to you. Where you presently are, you have indeed been before.

Remember that lessons are given to various levels of awareness in various ways. Our purpose is to raise the souls to greater and greater understanding, to, yea, even greater freedom.

Once the journey of the soul has passed through the nine visits to the nine planets of the galaxy, it returns to come again to another planet in another galaxy. The final visit, my children, on your particular universe will be the sun.

Good night.

DECEMBER 1, 1972

Journey of the Living Light
Discourse 2

Greetings, class.

It is good to speak with you again at this time.

We are discussing the soul's journey through time and its evolution through the solar system. Often we have requested that you broaden your horizons, that you consider expanding your consciousness that you may be receptive to, yea, even greater Light than has already been given.

Now you know that totality, fulfillment is the number, mathematically, of nine. You know that your soul, in its present journey, is expressing through the fifth planet. Now, my dear children, I am sure that you have perceived, by now, that there were four expressions prior to your present incarnation and that there are four yet to be.

My friends, we indeed are the children of the sun, that plane, that planet of illumination. As the soul journeys through the solar system, it expresses in form on each planet. The allotted time of expression is 1,000 [years] of your Earth time for each planet expression. The planets are sun—illumination; Jupiter—knowledge; Saturn—understanding; Venus—love; Mars—war. And on and on through space. The rest of the planets will be given to you at the proper time. Neptune—emotion.

Now, my friends, the normal life span for each expression on the planet is 900 years and 100 years in the gravity pull of that particular planet. Due to errors of the past, eons of time ago, your expression has been greatly shortened, so to speak. This is not the first time your soul has expressed on the fifth planet and it will not be the last. The circle ever completes itself.

That that has been shall be again, as that that comes from a thing shall return to the thing. As the soul evolves, it learns many, many lessons and, in so doing, merits varying experiences, so to speak.

As you awaken within, you will personally become aware of varying influences within your being. That, my children, is known as the solar consciousness of which was spoken before. When you awaken to that consciousness, you will know your present, as well as your past, so to speak, as well as your future. Not just the identity of the moment, but the awareness of your totality of the different beings that in truth you really are.

The indicativeness of so-called astrology—and it can be indeed more indicative when it is based upon the great Atlantean Astrology of truth; that is, the nine planetary expressions—will reveal to man which identity is predominant at his moment of conception and which is the ruling power at his moment of birth.

Remember the exercises that have been given to you. Use them wisely. Do not go with the speed of light, for expansion in any area guarantees, my children, contraction in another.

We shall continue on with our discussion at another time.

Good night.

DECEMBER 8, 1972

Journey of the Living Light
Discourse 3

Greetings, friends and students of the Light.

Again, we come to share with you our understanding of life, her purpose of expression. At our last meeting we spoke a bit on the soul's journey through so-called time and space. As you will recall, we mentioned at that time that the soul is passing through the form and forms that it has merited as it continues to evolve and to return to its true Source.

In reference to the soul's incarnation into the form and forms that you have at present, those forms of which you are aware and the forms of which you are yet to be aware, broaden your horizon a bit more, open your mind, expand your conscience, and you shall indeed awaken to a fuller and a greater expression and freedom of your Light. It indeed is difficult for some to become aware of their eternity, especially when, through belief, identity is yet the master.

There appears to be some interest in the soul of man and the soul of the mouse. There is in truth no difference in the soul of the tree or the soul of man. The apparent difference is in the evolution of the soul; it merits progressively more refined vehicles of expression. As the power goes out from itself, it expresses from the lowest forms to the highest, known and unknown. As this journey continues, the soul is enabled, through expression, to create greater and greater and more refined vehicles of expression. The soul's purpose, my children, is the redemption of nature, of creation. In time on all planets, this purpose shall indeed be fulfilled.

How sad it appears to be to see, through error and ignorance, that man has sold his divinity. The greatest power of the universes waits quietly inside your being. He who continues to deny it continues to suffer on the wheel of so-called time.

Birth and death are ever inevitable until man awakens within. Then, my children, he shall no longer know death, for he shall no longer know birth. This is not the first time we have met, and it shall not be the last.

Awaken your solar consciousness and you will see beyond a shadow of any doubt your journey through space and time. And in so awakening to that eternity, you shall know the reason for your present lessons, the reasons why you are in the school that you are, and where, indeed, you are going.

That that comes from the thing shall return to the thing. Think what thoughts you may, life is the circle. There is no escape from the true self. No matter what we think, no matter what we do, we shall be what we be and we shall continue on the circle. There is no separation in truth. And if it is truth, my children, that you seek, then accept the unity of all, accept the simplicity of Truth herself.

We have spoken of the planets—some of them—and their meanings or names. Remember, they exist within you, as well as without. You are a universe much greater than the one of which you permit awareness to yourself. Its experience, this universe, is waiting at your door. When less energy is spent in the minimum and more is spent in the maximum, you will be receptive to greater love, to greater life, to greater understanding and freedom. You will know that you are, have always been, will always be. You will know and live and demonstrate the greatness of the great. So broaden, once again, your horizons. Be not limited by the limiting. Be limitless by the truth.

Good night.

Thank you.

Thank you.

[After a pause of more than one minute, the recorder is stopped. At some point later, the recording begins again.]

He who knows the Light and loves it not shall lose the Light and find it not. For love is the magnet, located in the heart of man. It is the tie to the Divine; it is the lifeline of eternity. And man shall not live long without it.

To still the mind is to make the mind a clear reflector of the Light herself. It is of great importance, my children, that you spend more time in peace and less time in deciding what is best for your soul, for the soul knows what's best for itself. And indeed, does it know better than that which has been temporarily created from mind stuff.

The journey is long. It is worthwhile. And that that comes to the mind also leaves it in time. And yet the soul, timeless and ageless, goes on and on and on. In all your searching, in all your seeking, seek sincerely that of value. And the greatest value, my dear children, is your own soul.

Good night.

DECEMBER 15, 1972

Atlantean Astrology Part 1

Greetings, workers of the Light.

We shall continue on with our discussion at this time concerning the journey of the Living Light.

We have spoken of its visits on the various planets and we have discussed the meaning of most of those planets. And at this time, we should like to state that the planet known as Pluto is ignorance; the planet known as Mercury is wisdom.

In the soul's journey through space and so-called time, it incarnates, so to speak, on each planet. When the soul enters the planet known as Earth, which is the planet of faith, it comes to fulfill and to learn the lessons of the experiences that it has had in its prior incarnations.

Now, my good students, bear with us as we try to present to you as clearly as possible which identification, which life experiences you bring with you into your present life. You know that that with which we identify we become attached to. And so it is in the soul's journey. For example, if you have become attached to a life experience on Jupiter or Mars or Venus, then your soul will be incarnated under the influence or influences of those planets. This in truth, my children, is the essence of your so-called astrology. For example, if your life experience on Mars was one with which you became attached or strongly identified, then your soul in its journey would incarnate in the earth realm under the influences of that planet, for that that we identify with we become attached to, here and hereafter on the eternal circle of truth.

Remember that we spoke of the final journey, the journey to the solar, to the sun, where there is true illumination, true Light, and true freedom. And so it is in your present experiences, as your soul rises through the many levels of awareness, once it enters the center, the nuclei, the core, the solar plexus, illumination dawns in your universe and true freedom is indeed expressed. This freedom, my children, must not only be sustained but it must be maintained through self-control. One cannot experience the peace that passeth all understanding unless one has the willingness, the ability, and the strength to control that which is distracting, that which retards one's growth, that which keeps them from the Light itself. And so it is as you travel in space, in eternity, as you are indeed doing at this very moment.

Think and think, my children. Broaden, indeed, your horizons. Be greater than the mundane thoughts that you entertain. You are indeed on your planet to serve a purpose. You have the awareness and you know the way. Be strong. Be one with the Divine.

All these things, as we have spoken before, are constantly passing before your view. Be not tempted to be trapped in them, for if you do, my children, you will not learn the lesson that you have incarnated to learn.

You may, by checking your birth dates, become aware of the planetary influence that you are under, which is indicative, for you, of the identification you have had with that life's experience. And in so doing you may find even a better way of freeing yourself by learning the lesson today, this moment more fully and more completely.

You know we have said many times that if the Light is too bright, it is best that it be given not now. And so it is, my good students, that some come for a time and then they go. Hold not to form, hold not to things, for they bind you with the chains of so-called creation.

Be free and be at peace. You are not new. You are not old. But you *are* you, eternally and forever the great freedom, the great, eternal One.

We shall speak more at a further time of the purpose you are serving not only on your present experience and expression but in the solar system of which your soul has passed already many, many times.

Good night.

Good night. Thank you.

Thank you.

[After a pause of almost two minutes, the teacher continues.] Time was made by fools who cannot find eternity. So be at peace and find yourself beyond time, beyond space. One and only one is truth.

Good night.

DECEMBER 22, 1972

Atlantean Astrology Part 2

Greetings, students.

We will continue on with our class in our discussions of the solar consciousness and the journey of its expression through the universes.

Now, as has been stated, the soul is passing through the nine-planetary system expressing itself nine times on each planet. In expanding on this understanding, we wish to state at this time that recall of the past experiences is possible when the consciousness has been broadened and expanded, so to speak. Now the expression on the planets is nine times in each species or form on the given planets. For example, if the soul in its evolution is incarnated into a certain species, animal or otherwise, it continues through its expression through the totality of nine times in that particular form or level of expression. As it continues to evolve, it grows or expands itself and gains greater and greater awareness. And so it is that your last experience and expression may be reviewed according to the planet under which you were born on your present Earth expression. That was the last of your soul's expression prior to your present one.

The lessons are many and can be perceived if you will be at peace and think, my children, and think more deeply.

The question arises in the minds, Why is it necessary for the soul to pass through these many, many, many forms? My dear children, the soul is not the spirit, but it is the vehicle through which the spirit is individualized that it may express in form. It evolves through many planets and many, many forms. This is why we have stated that the so-called missing link of man will not be found on your planet because on your planet it never existed.

As you learn the lessons that you have merited, as you study more thoroughly what has been given, you will change, to some extent, your next expression in form, for once the lesson has been perceived, it shall not be repeated. And so it is, my children, if you have entered your present form with the lesson to be perceived from your prior expression, which is the law, then learn it now that you will not have to repeat it again, again, and again.

Remember that peace and peace alone is the power, and the only power there is in truth. Be pure of heart and sound of mind and you will not eternally evolve in this little solar system.

Good night.

Good night.

Good night. Thank you.

[After a pause, the teacher continues.] Remember, my friends, that man cannot gain when he is not willing to lose.

Good night.

DECEMBER 29, 1972

[Please see the appendix for additional teachings on Atlantean Astrology.]

Discourse January 12, 1973

[Greetings], fellow students.

Once again, we've come to share with you our understanding of the soul's journey. And so it is from planet to planet, Life indeed is expressing herself.

Now we have spoken of the planet sun being the final journey in your soul's travel. And so it is, my children, that the sun can be referred to as the planet of Light, the home of the soul, the Allsoul. That is the planet on which the multitudes of experiences and lessons are deposited, and that is where true awareness dawns in our soul.

At our last meeting we spoke of the ability, within your soul, to awaken to its many journeys. When the allness of life becomes the purpose of your being, oneness will manifest and you shall awaken to this great eternity and know where you've been and, in so doing, know where you indeed are going.

Now, my good friends, all souls are not equal in their expression, for they come from different planets in your solar system with different experiences, with different lessons. And upon your planet, known as Earth, it could be referred to as the so-called melting pot, for here we find the souls entering from all the other planets of your solar system to learn their lessons through the great power known as faith.

Astrological forecasting can be more than indicative; if you will remember when the planets are in certain positions in the solar system, you may check the controlling planets in your life and it will reveal unto you the influences that they have at any given time. Remember that those influences are simply the identification and attachment that you have to the life expression that you had on those particular planets.

If your soul has merited going to the planet of faith with the lesson to be perceived, for example, of understanding, then through the power of faith, understanding will indeed be learned. And you shall not have to again repeat that particular lesson.

My dear children, what is it that is so important to entertain so much of your thought in such mundane things? Does it not behoove you, as students, to awaken more to your own divinity, to your own divine purpose?

Try to be more receptive to your own sun, to the Light that is within your own being. Remember the laws that govern energy. Be more discreet with its direction and then you will find greater freedom coming from within your own being.

If your soul has entered the planet of faith to learn the lesson of knowledge, of wisdom, of emotion or, yea, even war itself, learn it now and learn it well for this is the only moment that you have any power over. Yesterday has gone; tomorrow is not yet here.

Have greater value, my students, for the power known as peace. Feel that great awakening within yourselves. Choose more wisely your associates. Try to choose more wisely where you are spending so much of this great, life-giving power.

At this time, I should like to share with you some of the experiences on the planet known as Saturn. Those whose souls have merited that life expression are given great opportunity to understand, to live, and to demonstrate the universal laws governing Life herself. Many are able to learn them and to demonstrate them. Some are able to learn them and to demonstrate them for a time. The greatest difficulty with the lessons that that planet has to offer is the will, the determination to stick, so to speak, with one thing long enough for it to manifest. Therefore, failure in that particular planet is simply, my dear children, a lack of patience.

Good night.

JANUARY 12, 1973

Discourse January 18, 1973

Greetings, travelers to the Light.

Again, we come to share with you our understanding of the soul's journey. We are speaking at this time on the reason and the purpose of the soul's incarnation on the particular planets. As was stated before, your Earth planet may be likened unto a melting pot where the souls from the other planets have all gathered to learn the lessons they came to learn through faith. For example, my students, the planetary influences under which you are born on your planet reveal, as was stated before, the last soul incarnation.

The birth number under which your soul has incarnated reveals the incarnation prior to your last one. For example, if you have entered the earth realm under the planetary influences of Saturn and have entered under the number two, that simply means that you have come to the earth realm because of a failure in your understanding from lack of learning the lesson that Neptune, the planet of emotion, the number two, had to offer. In clarifying this understanding a bit further, from Neptune, when the lesson has not been learned, our soul sends itself to a planet for understanding. If on the planet of understanding, from lack of patience, the lesson has not been learned, our soul goes on to the earth realm where, through faith, we may gain understanding and balance.

The soul's incarnation applies to all souls, to all planets.

There was some concern in the mind of my channel this evening that we had requested a special meeting. My good students, the reason for the request is because at this time my channel is most receptive to the influences of the planet Moon, which is gratitude.

As the soul journeys through space, it enters the planet that it has merited. It comes with a dual purpose: to learn the lessons of its last failure and the ones prior to that. This is revealed by your birth number and by the planetary influences under which you have been born.

As you journey through life, you will find many experiences that repeat themselves. The reason that they repeat themselves has been revealed to you if you will study more thoroughly the Diagram of Destiny, which has been given to you. *[Please see the appendix.]*

When certain planets are in certain locations in the so-called heavens, according to the identity, you become influenced, to some extent, by them. This is the essence of what you call astrology. If you will study, you will find at what time is the most opportune for you to venture into any endeavor, for according to the influences is your identity with that life experience on that particular planet awakened.

If you enter your earth realm under the vibratory influences of the seven with the birth number of two, that reveals to you that you are twice from the planet under which you are born. For example, if you enter your realm of faith in the planet of nine and your birth number is three, that reveals to you that you have the ninth time incarnated through that planet and the third time in the planet that is revealed by your birth number, which has been simplified for you by the Destiny Diagram.

Think, my children, and think more deeply. You have the great opportunity to free yourself, to gain greater understanding, to use the divine laws that are revealed by your various soul incarnations.

You know that on your diagram the sun has not been placed. You know that on your diagram the moon has not been placed. But if you will study more deeply, you will find that Uranus is self-awareness, individuality and it is number one. If you will study more thoroughly, you will find that Moon is number two or eleven on your diagram.

My dear friends, Neptune is not the last number on the diagram by chance. It is there because it is the last of the planets before returning home to the sun. When a soul comes anew from the sun, it is governed by the divine love from the Allsoul or Sun. Its second incarnation is the Moon. And ever onward do we pass through the universes.

We have been given the divine right. We have been given nine opportunities in this particular human form to learn the lessons that the planets have to offer. Learn them well, my children, that you may be freed from the cycle again and again and again. For example, if, on the planet of Neptune, you have passed through the nine soul incarnations and have not learned the lessons, that simply means that in time in eternity you'll return to the Allsoul or Sun to come out again, again, and again. However, if you will broaden your horizons, your soul will be freed into a greater universe and truly awakened.

Remember, the lesson that is not perceived guarantees its own repetition. In time in eternity, it shall be perceived; it shall be demonstrated.

Remember the power of the spoken word. When you do your mantra, if you will tune its expression to middle C, you will have the power of balance and it shall reveal itself.

Whenever you think, you open the door to awareness, but in so doing you also choose to be guided by eternal experiences or to be blinded by self. Choose wisely, my students. We are not here by chance. We are here by the laws that we and we alone have set into motion.

It is very important that you understand the reason of your soul's incarnation on to your planet of faith. It is so simple to understand, if you will only ponder wisely. You may look out into the world, my students, and know how many times any particular soul has expressed on any particular planet. Study what has already been given you and be free.

Good night.

JANUARY 18, 1973

Discourse January 19, 1973

Greetings, on the path of Light.

We shall continue on at this time with our discussions concerning the soul's journey. We are indeed pleased to note that, through your efforts to attain, you have perceived the simple keys that [were] given to you at our last meeting. Remember, my good students, it is not our purpose to deprive you of your divine right to attain that which you may value. And so it is that the teachings are designed in as simple way as possible and, yet, so presented that they will not take away your rights of effort and attainment.

Remember to think and to think deeply is to awaken your own soul.

As was stated at our last meeting, that a soul incarnated on Neptune is driven by its own laws to the planet of Saturn to gain understanding. We had hoped, in the time that had lapsed, you might perceive that all planets go to Saturn for understanding, for that is what Saturn has to offer. And so it is, my children, that you find the center, so to speak, planet located on the number seven in your Destiny Diagram. *[Please see the appendix.]* And remember that you have been given the meaning of the seven and where it is located in your human anatomy, for you indeed are the small universe of the great universe. For example, if a person understands, they no longer find themselves going to Uranus and finding need, for once understanding dawns in your universe, you know that you have, and therefore there is nothing to gather and nothing to gain.

And so it is, my children, that with understanding, you pass the lessons that you have to learn, for understanding frees your soul and awakens the mind. When, for example, man truly understands the principle of so-called love, he never again will entertain the thought of need for anything, for we cannot need what we already have.

There has appeared on the ethereal waves some questions concerning the keys that were given. And for the benefit of those students, we should like to clarify the teaching that was given at our last meeting. To find your planet, you know; that is the one that you are born under. To find your destiny, you know, for that is the number of your birth.

The question appears that the keys to one's finding is not the same key to another. That, my good students, is not a contradiction. It is simply a greater awareness. Each planet offers its many, many, many lessons. Totality is the service number, and it serves any planet in the universe that it comes in contact with. Nine is the planet of Pluto. And because of its darkness, it becomes controlled by any planet that it touches if it forgets that one and only one brings it to the Light.

Each planet has its strengths. Each planet has its weakness, for that is the Law of Creation everywhere, my children. For example, if man desires to understand faith, in the moment he entertains the thought, he denies finding it. For understanding is everything. Total, whole, complete, and one. It is within you, has ever been, will always be.

Look at the teachings with the simplicity of a child, for, my children, they indeed are simple. Be simple in your thinking. Be humble in your heart and you will know beyond a shadow of any doubt where you are, why you are, where you've been, and where you're going. Study them daily for at least a few moments.

Remember, this is your eternity. Look wisely and see where you've been. You will find your weakness. You will find your strengths. Use them wisely; don't abuse them, and free yourself here and now. Remember that all creation is receptive to the planetary influences. At any given moment you may know where you are and how you got there, and in so knowing, find your way back home. And so it is, my children, that all planets respond and are balanced in understanding.

At a future time, be it in divine order, we shall reveal the location of the planets in the human anatomy. And therefore, through a greater awareness, you may express a more perfect being.

Good night.

JANUARY 19, 1973

Discourse January 26, 1973

Greetings, friends on the path.

We come again to share with you our understanding and expansion of the teachings that have already been given.

As you look upon the destiny chart that has been brought forth, you will find in Pluto the word *concern*. And so it is reading on the horizontal path, concern of self guarantees emotion. Reading upon the vertical path, you will see that concern of love guarantees aggression. The direct opposite to Pluto is Jupiter or the planet of knowledge, where the Light waits to serve you and bring understanding. *[Please see the appendix for the Destiny Diagram.]*

Some time ago we spoke of the nine states of consciousness and the eighty-one levels of awareness. My dear friends, the nine states of consciousness are the nine planets of the solar system upon which you have identified, your soul. The eighty-one levels of awareness are the nine lines or experiences recorded in those planets. The solar consciousness within your being is gradually awakened as you use the mantra that has been given to you with the nine power breaths, which have been designed to awaken your mind to the solar consciousness.

The question may well be asked, as it has been asked by others in times past, "Of what benefit is this understanding in my day-to-day activities?" My good students, understanding is understanding, and that that we understand we free from the bondage of mind; we awaken to a brighter light. He who knows the path on which his soul has entered, he who knows the reason that his soul is upon that path has a greater benefit, a greater awakening and, using and applying the knowledge gained, may free himself from the constant repetition of experience upon experience.

As you study your destiny, you will find, yea, even greater perception awakening within your own being. The only thing that blocks, so to speak, the awareness of your great eternity is the insistence of the mind to hold to its present identity. It is indeed difficult for most students to broaden their horizons, to awaken to the great Light that eternally waits to show a broader, a straighter, and a better path.

He who knows the purpose of life fulfills the life. He who knows it not searches century after century in the error and the darkness of the laws ignorantly set into motion.

When a lesson is to be learned, wisdom dictates to learn it. Only a fool would postpone the inevitable. Why not use the tools wisely that they may serve their purpose and, in so doing, grant unto your souls the peace that passeth all understanding? Why stay in one place when all places in truth are your birthright and your destiny? The purpose of the soul's incarnation is to awaken the forms. Awaken them well that you may not have to eternally return and return and return to lessons repeating themselves again and again and again.

A few moments [of] study and application daily of what has been given will gradually brighten the Light of your own being. He who stumbles in the darkness is in no position to lead others to the Light. So let your light shine forth into the universe through application, through demonstration. Be about the business of your own divinity.

I listened attentively with our other students to your discussion concerning what was given on the planetary relationship to the human anatomy. And it shall be broadened, my children, in accordance with the laws that have been set into motion. Remember that man only limits man. We are ever permitted to give what is in accordance to the laws already set into motion by yourselves.

From this moment to the eternal moment, it is not a step; it is simply a change in thought. Why hold to that which limits you when the limitless, the freedom, the greatness, the allness of the universes waits sleeping within yourself for your own recognition of it?

Remember that understanding is the broadening of the horizon. Because others may not think or do what you are struggling and striving to think or do does not necessarily, in any way, dictate wisdom or light. You are you, and they are they. All have their right to their slumber. Be not entrapped by the Law of Satisfaction, for it is satisfaction that stunts our growth and retards our progression.

He who is not willing to change a thought can never change a life. The wisdom of teaching is the Law of Expansion, for truth is not stagnant; it is broadening and expanding to those who truly are seeking it.

One cannot say that freedom is this or that, for freedom to one level of awareness or state of consciousness or planetary experience is different to another state of consciousness or planetary experience. And therefore, freedom of one level is not equal or necessarily in harmony with the freedom of another level. And so it is, my children, that the word *freedom* is so gravely misunderstood. Freedom to one is to do what they desire to do; that is a level of awareness. And upon another level, that so-called freedom is total bondage. You will know within yourselves that freedom is control, as was spoken before. Control of error that the experience may not repeat itself. Control of ignorance that Light may shine more fully.

Remember that each planetary experience offers its strength and its weakness. You know and you know well, my students, the reasons why you have entered your earth realm. You know the lessons that you have to perceive. And you also know why you have to perceive them. It has all been given to you. Study and apply. Become the demonstration of that that you are destined to be.

Good night.

JANUARY 26, 1973

Discourse February 2, 1973

Greetings, children.

We shall continue on with our discussion. What happens to the tree whose desire tells the wind, "Cease to blow"? And so it is that man stands ever in his own light as he refuses to accept the divine natural flow of infinite and eternal Intelligence. And so it is that we continue on through these cycles of life and experience until the day dawns in our universe and we say, "I am indeed at peace." And becoming that great peace, we flow with the natural and divine order of things in all places at all times and in all ways.

Now the question arises, How did we fall—if *fall* could be the term—so far from our natural abode? My good students, as often has been spoken, the soul is on its journey through time and space. Time and space being created of mind stuff, it is only recognized and accepted by mind. It cannot be known by Spirit for there is no distance, no space, and no time to the infinite divine Spark known as Spirit. It is the mind and the form, the covering of your spirit, that experiences and, from it, constantly expands itself, redepositing in the great universal bank, so to speak, a multitude of experiences.

We try, in our way, to help you to find this great power known as peace, that you may reside in it and be it more often than you have been. For in all our journeys and in all these times, the day indeed does dawn that we are this peace any moment that we choose to enter it. Only through self-control and self-discipline can we attain this understanding and this freedom.

And so, my friends, we travel onward, ever onward, ever upward. Again and again, again and again. Be not a part of the cycles. Witness them as you would a passing scene. Be free while yet expressing your divinity.

The destiny chart that was given to you is to help you, through education of the form, through awakening in your memory the multitude of things that you have already been through. That, my dear students, is creation.

There is no escape from the prison house of form or creation, but there is a way of being free while yet in it. And that, indeed, my good friends, is the true purpose of us coming to speak with you in these times. You cannot change that which is infinite, immutable law, but you can flow through a higher state of consciousness. You can indeed be fulfilled and not be disturbed by the opposites of forms. When you reach that level, that state of consciousness, you will indeed prefer to remain on it. You can do this if you will learn the Law of Separation, the Law of Division. Then, though it is a thin and straight path to God, you can still be fulfilled and serve your true purpose.

Good night.

FEBRUARY 2, 1973

Spiritualism and the Christian Bible

[This lecture was given by Mr. Goodwin before the Spiritual Frontiers Fellowship, an interfaith, nonprofit movement of individuals interested in higher states of consciousness.]

Mr. Chairman, ladies and gentlemen, it is indeed a pleasure to be here for the first time, as a member of the Spiritual Frontiers Fellowship, and to speak to you on the topic that was chosen, "Spiritualism and the Christian Bible."

And before speaking on that topic, I should like to give the definition of the word *Spiritualism*, as understood by the National Spiritualist Association of Churches. Spiritualism is the science, philosophy, and religion of continuous life, based upon the demonstrated fact of communication with the world of spirit.

And in keeping with that understanding and definition of the word *Spiritualism*, we turn to that great book known as the Christian Bible. Page after page we see a living demonstration of events that took place nigh two thousand years ago. There is no part in that Bible that we do not find a recorded history of spiritual communication.

It is often spoken, by some, that the Bible warns us against communion with the so-called dead. And indeed, that is true on certain passages of that book and [is] most understandable. Mediumship or communication with other dimensions is no respecter of persons. Communication and psychic phenomena in and of itself does not lead us to the Light of eternal truth. It can be instrumental in doing so, if that is the aspiration that we ever keep before us. And so, due to the many abuses of communication in biblical times, prophets of the time forewarned many disasters and many different events.

And so it is today, my good friends, when we look at that book of history, we once again see the tides turning. Again, the masses of people are interested in so-called psychic phenomena. Their interest is once again awakened to that great truth that there is no dead and there is no death.

Indeed is the Nazarene a living demonstration of what we know today as mediumship. There is no question in our minds, if we are believers of the Bible or certain passages therein, that he demonstrated the phases which are known as clairvoyance, clairaudience, and clairsentience. There is no question, if we are believers, that he stated, "The things I do, ye too shall do and, yea, even greater."

There seems to be an apparent gap, so to speak, between what is known as Spiritualism and Christianity. In truth there is no gap, my friends. It is in truth one and the same thing. The demonstrations that took place in those times have always taken place. Psychic phenomena and communication is not new to the world. It has been with the world ever since there has been men on Earth. There is no question that it has been and [is], even today, gravely misunderstood and, sadly but true, ofttimes abused.

The purpose, to my understanding, of communing with these other dimensions is to learn, through communication, what this so-called other life is like. My good friends, whatever life is like now—and we indeed take a mind (our mind) with us [when we pass on]—then it cannot be much, if any, different. Again and again, the teachers have spoken that heaven, or its opposite, is not a place we go to; it is a state of consciousness that we grow to. It is ever within us. And once having found the great power of the Spirit, the Light within our self, then we will find that Light wherever we go and wherever we seek.

Let us pause in our thinking and let us unite for the common good. All religions are in the world to serve one God, for there is only one God. There cannot be 10 or 20 or 30. And so it is that we are seeking to serve this great Divine Spirit, that the Spiritualists call Infinite Intelligence, that other religions call by different names. It's the same Spirit. There is no separation to truth; and so there is no separation to God itself. Spiritualism, in its presentation, has strived, through over 125 years as an organized movement, to share its understanding of the purpose of life.

That great Nazarene, who walked upon this earth realm so long ago, gave his life to bring to mankind a greater way, a better path, that man may recognize and realize that whatever happens to us has been caused by us. Did he not say, if you are stricken, then turn the other cheek? What does that mean? And so few of us are willing to apply. My good friends, to us it simply means not to get into rapport with that which is disturbing and of no benefit.

We understand that forgiveness is the greatest blessing known to man, for when we forgive, we free from the bondage of our own minds. And so who or what is it that we should consider in forgiving first? He who cannot forgive himself is not capable of forgiving another. One cannot grant unto another what one is not able to grant unto oneself.

I spoke to our chairman prior to this meeting and stated that I would try to keep the lecture to a minimum that those who have come may have the opportunity of asking whatever questions of a spiritual nature that they may have. And so at this time, my good friends, if you will raise your hands, I will be happy to serve as the instrument to answer whatever questions you have concerning spiritual matters.

Yes, the gentleman in the front row, please.

In the book that you wrote, called The Living Light, *I read in there that, according to the book at any rate, God was neutral, that He would not help either the good or the wicked, which is a little bit different than I was taught as a young boy when I went to church; although it is an interesting, a very interesting thought. And I was wondering if you could elaborate on, if God is neutral, how do we explain God's love of mankind? Is there a benefit for God to be neutral? I hope I don't have too many questions all in one.*

Thank you very much. I will be more than happy to share with you my understanding in reference to the teachings of the Living Light of a divine, neutral Power known as God. The moment we attempt to define a thing, we limit that very thing. We put it into form of expression. And so it is, my good friends, if we believe in what we call God, a divine, infinite, limitless Power, then we do not believe in God that has limitation or form. It is our understanding that this divine, neutral Power, known as God, expresses through all form; that it is known as the spirit of Divine Love. Throughout the untold centuries man has attempted to define what we call God. In his attempt to define this Infinite Power, he has created in his mind an understanding of God. Consequently, God is in a constant change, a constant process of evolving.

It has been stated in these teachings that man's God is ever equal to his understanding. And so the greater our understanding, the greater our God. It is also our understanding that God is everywhere present, never absent or away; that good is in varying degrees, and so-called bad is what we understand to be a lesser degree of the same power. For example, if we say that God is good and the devil is bad, then we are admitting to ourselves that there are two powers at work in the universe. If we believe that God is all powerful and if we believe that God is a creator, then it only follows that God has created this so-called devil.

Now there are some teachings in the world that teach that there is this other power, and that is placed into the universe in order to tempt mankind, to help keep him on the path of Light or Truth. If that is true, my good friends, then we must question the all-encompassing love of the God that we believe in. For if we believe in a God of divine love, that has no partiality, then is it not a bit difficult to accept that this great, all-powerful divine love of God would send unto us a so-called opposite power to tempt us to leave him?

No, my good friends, that is not our understanding. But I do want to state clearly: we respect the divine right of all religions, of all philosophies, of all teachings to worship God in the way they find it in their heart to do so. For is it not better to worship God than not to worship God? And so it is, with a little tolerance and respect, we're all striving to find what we call God. Does that help with your question?

Thank you.

Thank you. The lady in the next row, please.

Jesus says, "Blessed are the poor in spirit for theirs is the kingdom of heaven." Could you comment on that?

Yes. The statement is from the Bible. Blessed is the poor in spirit for theirs is the kingdom of heaven. My good friends, man does not value that that is easily attainable. Man does not value the element water, until he is thirsty. Man does not value the element air, until it is so polluted it is difficult to breathe. And so those who are poor in spirit seek a greater expression of the spirit. And in their seeking and in their effort, a greater awareness dawns in their life. And indeed shall they inherit what is known as heaven. Does that help with your question?

Thank you.

Thank you. Yes, please.

Mediaeval mystics talk of the companioning presence of Christ. Cayce, Edgar Cayce describes [it] as the Christ-consciousness. Saint Paul describes it as being in Christ. How do you see the ongoing presence of Christ as a reality, say, in a community of believers?

Yes. In reference to your question, I understand the presence of Christ to be the presence, the awareness of the presence of the Divine Spirit. There is no question in my mind that that Nazarene, who is ever amongst us in spirit, as all great spirits are, was the living demonstration of the Divine Power itself.

There is no question in my mind that whenever there are two or more who seek, in the spirit of sincerity and truth, God, there is no question in my mind that they [rise] to a level of awareness within themselves and are receptive to what is known as the Divine Presence.

To me, it does not matter whether they call that the Christ-consciousness or the Buddhic-consciousness or Nirvana. There is one Divine Presence. There is one truth and one truth alone. And whoever is truly a seeker cannot help, by the very law of seeking, [but] find the Divine Presence that the Christian world calls the Christ-consciousness, that the Eastern world may call the Buddhic-consciousness. It is the one Divine Consciousness. I see no separation in words to define it. Does that help with your question?

[Thank you.]

Thank you. Someone else had a question? Yes.

In some of the editions of the Bible prior to the King James version, such as the earlier codex editions, Jesus is described as being in a temple at one time and when some people tried to stone him to kill him, he disappeared. He did a disappearing act, like a magician. Jesus did this several times in older versions of the Bible. He would disappear in one place and reappear in another. When we had the King James version and other versions, they took away all these references to these superhuman abilities of Jesus and made him into a plain, simple person. Could you explain some of the purposes that they would do such a thing?

Yes. In reference to your question of the living demonstrations of the Nazarene, known as Jesus the Christ, of his disappearance, we would understand that in Spiritualism as dematerialization and rematerialization at another place. It has also been stated by the questioner, What is the purpose of that being deleted in one translation and having the Nazarene made a very simple being? Is that the basic question?

[There is no audible response on the recording.]

I can only comment from my own views concerning your question. In simplicity lies truth; however, in complexity there is achievement. But truth indeed is simple and unconcealed. Ofttimes [with] the masses, because of a certain type of emotional shock that takes place during certain psychic demonstrations, there is a tendency to confuse the mind and lose the true, lighted path. By that I mean to say that there are those, seeing the phenomena and being confused and awed by it, [who] do not go onward to find the true purpose of their soul's incarnation and have a tendency to put the phenomena before the Divine Spirit. To my understanding it is better to present a teacher of truth as a simple and uncomplicated man than to present him as a great wonder-worker. Does that help with your questions? Thank you.

The lady in the red, please.

I was wondering—my sister's part of the Pentecostal movement. She's very concerned about my concern in Spiritualism and reincarnation and things. And she really feels that I'm really being, you know—that the devil's working through me and I'm part of the occult. And she's always quoting Scripture to me, like I'm practicing necromancy and this sort of thing. And I was wondering, are there any Bible passages I can quote back at her . . . [Many audience members laugh, which make a few of her words difficult to transcribe.] *the devil's work and so forth.*

Thank you. There is not a passage in the Christian Bible that does not directly or indirectly refer to what we understand as Spiritualism or communion with other dimensions. And in reference to your question, in First Corinthians, Chapter 14, it says exert your utmost to obtain love and especially to commune with the spirits. *[The text from the Greber translation is, "Exert yourself to the utmost to obtain love. Also be eager, of course, to enter into communication with God's spirits. Above all, strive to become instruments through which God's spirits speak to you in your mother tongue."]*

We have a translation by the late Father Johannes Greber that is very well done, based on the ancient codex manuscripts from the Vatican in Rome. I would be more than happy to show you a copy. And you can refer to any Bible and see where repeatedly, again and again, Saint Paul, in his letters to the Corinthians and in his letters to the Galatians, had warned them about their disagreement in reference to the teachings of the day. It is our understanding, from recorded history, that the first 300 years of the Christian movement was a living demonstration that what we understand as sensitives, psychics, and mediums today were practicing and demonstrating their talents in the first 300 years of the Christian era.

If a person truly believes in the Bible and they believe it literally and they believe every word and passage, then they cannot help but set it down perplexed and a bit confused. Now if we choose certain passages from the Bible, then, my good friends, we can support any religion, any denomination that we choose to support. But if we go beyond the words of the Christian Bible, we go into the spirit that was behind it and we tune ourselves into the great inspiration that unquestionably has flow[ed] from the Divine, then we will find the truth inside ourselves. Does that help with your question? Thank you.

The lady over here, please.

Yes. Would you please give us your understanding of the fall of man?

Yes. The lady is asking in reference to, perhaps, a sharing of understanding of the fall of man. I would first have to question and ask, From what has man fallen? If we mean, by the fall of man, that he has fallen from spiritual awareness, that he has fallen from a true peace that he once had, then I can only say that energy follows attention, and thought is the vehicle through which energy expresses itself. If our thoughts are imbalanced in the sense that they are primarily on mundane, material things, then it is most understandable that we would not have an awareness of the spiritual things.

The teachings are a balance in all things. The material world is here to serve a purpose. And indeed, it does serve its purpose, in a temporal way. We're in the material form or flesh for how many years we know not. But we are eternally spirit, have always been and will always be. And so a wise man chooses to spend some thought or energy in spiritual matters in order that he may maintain an even balance while yet expressing in a physical dimension.

My understanding of the fall of man is simply that he has denied his own divinity for he has looked out into the world of form and he has permitted a material dimension to become his master. And in so doing he has become the slave. How unfortunate, but how true in so many cases. Does that help with your question?

Thank you.

Thank you. The gentleman in the front row, please.

In view of the ongoing life of the spirit and the evident thought that we always were spirit, what do you perceive to be the purpose of the individualization of man by the Creator?

An excellent question. It is my understanding that: that that has no beginning has no ending. And therefore, to me, God is something that has always been and will always be. If God had a beginning, then by the laws of beginning, it would have an ending. And I do not believe in that kind of God.

And the question is, What is the purpose, if any—I believe that was your question—of the soul's incarnation into form? Is that correct? *[After a short pause, the teacher continues.]* It is my understanding that this Divine Spirit, covered in the form of soul, enters creation at the moment of conception, when the negative and positive poles of Nature herself come together. When that happens, this Divine Spirit is impulsed in soul into form. Its purpose is the evolution and the evolving of form itself, and in so doing it brings about a spiritualization of all creation.

My particular understanding is not that of God [as] a creator, but it is that of God, a Divine Power, an Infinite Intelligence, the sustainer of all things at all times and in all ways. Does that help with your question?

You know, I'm afraid I didn't make the meaning quite as clear as I would like. If I understood you to say that the poles, the positive and negative at the moment of conception or creation, that the soul is individualized...

That is—

Is that what I—

That is my understanding.

If then—in other words, at conception, then you would put away the thought of reincarnation, that the soul takes with it its individual characteristics and may come back again as an individual characteristic, that the man and his striving, perhaps strives to no purpose.

Perhaps I should make it a bit clearer, my particular understanding, if I may interrupt for just a moment.

Please.

It is my understanding that the individualized soul is impulsed into being according to laws that it and it alone has set into motion. It is our teaching of evolutionary incarnation: that this earth experience is simply a grade of school through which we are passing. It is also our understanding that whatever happens to us has indeed been caused by us, according to laws that man and man alone sets into motion. Therefore, we see, as we look out in creation at the human race, we see those souls who have entered incarnation into wealth; we see souls who have entered into poverty; we see souls who have entered into so-called very healthy bodies; and we have seen souls entered into so-called opposite bodies. We do teach the divine merit system.

What we set into motion this moment becomes our destiny of tomorrow.

However, the Divine has not left us without choice. We may choose, at any given moment, what it is we wish to set into motion. But once the choice is made, we and we alone have set a law into motion; that law shall be fulfilled. Does that help with your question?

Thank you.

Thank you very much.

[Does] someone else have a question now? The lady in the back row, please.

Humility is mentioned in many places in the Bible. And I would like to know what you think true humility of the spirit is?

It is our teachings that humility is a soul faculty, inseparable from faith and poise. Faith, poise, and humility we understand to be a triune faculty of the soul. When our divine spirit expresses through the soul faculties, we understand that to be the expression of the Divine itself. We also understand the opposite, known as the functions. And when there's an imbalance of this divine energy expressing primarily through the functions (not in balance with the soul faculties), we have so-called disturbance, discord, and disease.

On speaking of the word *humility*, I would like to say this: I believe beyond a shadow of any doubt that God is the greatest servant of all servants; that God is indeed the true spirit of humility. When we express humility, we also express total consideration. A humble man does not think of himself first; he thinks of the allness of the Divine. He knows beyond a shadow of any doubt that he is merely an inseparable part of the Divine Spirit and that God speaks to man through man. When we have an expression of a humble spirit, we are open and receptive to learn and to receive wisdom. Does that help with your question?

Thank you.

Thank you. The lady next to her, please.

Will you please tell, according to your understanding, the planes or levels of consciousness or awareness?

The lady has asked in reference to our teachings [of] the various levels of awareness. And we understand that there are eighty-one levels of awareness or states of consciousness; that a person may express through any of them at any given time. I do feel, however, for this particular lecture that, perhaps, there would be more questions concerning the teachings of the Bible, whereas that was the topic chosen for discussion. However, I will be happy to discuss that with you after the lecture is over.

Thank you.

Thank you very much. The lady here, please.

Can you please tell us the meaning, as you know it—in the Bible it says, "In my Father's house are many mansions: were it not so I would have told you." And I have struggled with this because of my understanding of the oneness. And also, the statement they parted his garments—they gambled and parted his garments and the robe was seamless at that time. Would you tell us—

Thank you very much. In reference to your question on the teachings from the Bible of the [saying], "In my Father's house are many mansions," yes, we understand that this vehicle, known as a body, is the Father's house, for it is God the Divine Spirit that is expressing through it. Without God the Divine Power, we could not speak, we could not move, and the body would not be. And so it is that in my Father's house are many mansions. In each and every body there is eighty-one levels of awareness and that is our understanding of the many mansions of the Father's house.

In reference to your question concerning the seamless robe, my good friends, what is a seam? If you have a garment that has a seam in it, then there is a separation of the two materials, and it is put together. But it was a seamless robe, a living demonstration that there is only one; that God is one and one is everyone. Without separation, there is but one truth expressed throughout the entire garment, but [it is] not separated. Does that help with your question?

Thank you.

Thank you very much. Are there any other questions? Yes.

In reading the Bible, I've been often confused about the Trinity: the Father, the Son, and the Holy Ghost. And I've talked to quite a few ministers and they have been confused about the Holy Ghost. And then I read a book on Spiritualism and they said that the Holy Ghost was a very simple thing to explain. Could you explain some of the things of what you could say was the Holy Ghost?

I'll be happy to share with you the understanding that I have reached at this present time. Remember, he who is not willing to change is not willing to grow. And so it is that God has placed before us divine, ever-expanding universes. The question is concerning the Trinity: the Father, the Son, and the Holy Ghost. I understand that this, called the Father, is the Divine Positive Power in all universes at all times; that the Son is its creation, what it is receptive to; that this Holy Ghost is the divine Power that is everywhere present, never absent or away. My good friends, let us entertain the possibility that there is no place that God cannot be, for if God is truly God, then it is everything and everywhere.

And so it is that the Father, the Son, and the Holy Ghost is indeed the manifestation of the Divine Spirit itself. The Holy Ghost is here this moment. The Holy Ghost is on the freeway. The Holy Ghost is everywhere, for there is nowhere that God cannot be. Does that help with your question? Thank you very much.

Are there any other questions? Yes, the lady here, please.

There is a part in the Bible about the Syrophoenician. And she comes to Jesus to ask that this demon be struck out of her daughter. And she says—and then he says to her, "Let the children first be fed, for it is not right to take the children's bread and throw it to the dogs." And then she answers him, "Yes, Lord, yet even the dogs under the table eat the children's crumbs." And he said to her, "For this saying you may go your way. The demon has left your daughter." I don't understand that.

The passage says that, "Let the children first be fed." Is that not true?

Yes.

We have to go to it bit by bit. What does that passage mean? I am sure it means many things to many people because we're all on different levels of awareness. There are times, however, when we're in rapport or on the same level. But my understanding and my impression is—"Let the children first be fed." What is one's child? My good friend, one's children are their responsibilities. And so he says, in my understanding, "First take care of your responsibilities." Read the next line, please. I'm sorry, if you want my understanding, you'll have to give it to me line by line.

OK. "For it is not right to take the children's bread and throw it to the dogs."

For is it not right to shirk one's responsibility while we entertain the pleasure ground of the senses. Next line, please.

But she answered him, "Yes, Lord, yet even the dogs under the table eat the children's crumbs."

Yes, Lord, but even the dogs, even my friends, hidden, take the crumbs or entertain their senses of pleasure and do not face their personal responsibilities.

"And for this the demon was cast out of her daughter."

And for this, a recognition of one's responsibilities, that they and they alone are responsible for all their acts and activities, the so-called demons were cast out.

My good friends, we cannot experience demons unless we are demons. Like attracts like and becomes the Law of Attachment. Man cannot experience that with which he is not in rapport.

And so it is, my friends, if we are fearful of entertaining demons, then we may be rest assured, "The thing I fear the most has befallen me." And demons and demons shall we attract unto our universe and experience. Because what we have done to our self, we have entertained in thought a certain level of awareness. And through our faith—remember, my good friends, fear is only faith in the negative—and through our faith we have attracted so-called demons to us. Fear is our faith. And faith is our fear, for it is nothing more than an energy.

As you believeth, you becometh. If you believe that the world is headed for destruction, then for destruction the world will head if there are a sufficient number of people believing in its destruction. We have a great responsibility, those of us who have some feeling for this Divine Power known as God, to entertain in thought that to God all things are possible; that God is a God of love; that God is a spirit of joy. And if we truly believe in that God, then there is no so-called power that can rob us from the peace that passeth all understanding.

To the degree of our faith shall it ever be made manifest unto us. If we do not have faith in God, we cannot expect to experience the Divine Presence. To the extent that we have faith in God, to that extent alone, my good friends, shall we experience that Presence. Does that help with your question? Thank you very much.

The gentleman here, please.

It brings up a point which I've often been puzzled about and it's more a technical point in work such as you do. When you go into trance, your personality moves aside, assumingly, that is conscious personality, and that other entities may speak through you, using your body and your voice, your vocal cords, to communicate with the material world, such as we are. Are you conscious of or have you ever been conscious of a place or a position where you and your conscious mind goes when the entity comes and speaks through you? Where are you, the soul?

In reference, to your question, that is dependent upon the degree of trance that the channel or myself, in this case, is experiencing. I can say that at times I am aware of other dimensions when I'm, supposedly, supposed to be lecturing in my church.

Now what dimension does the medium go to if they have that type or that phase of trance mediumship? That, my good friend, is entirely dependent upon what the particular medium has gravitated to. For example, we could not go to one of the higher spheres of the so-called world of spirit if we had not merited and gravitated to that state in our being while here, yet in flesh. In other words, man's heaven is ever in harmony and in accord with his heavenly expression. Does that help with your question?

I wasn't thinking of gravitating to other spheres as much—are you conscious of being at another spot at the time you are—I assume you go into deep trance or just—

That depends. There are different degrees of trance.

Yes. If you go into deep trance, are you ever conscious of your own personality being at a different place that you may recall when you come out of trance?

Yes, I am at different times.

That's what . . .

Thank you.

Thank you.

I don't know how our time is.

We still have some time. [The chairman of the organization responds.]

We have some time. Yes, the gentleman here, please.

What does spiritual—what is your belief concerning Christ died for our sins? That's what Christianity is based upon.

Thank you very much for your question. And I would like to make it clear that the national movement of Spiritualism has basic principles. Nine of them to be exact. Each Spiritualist expresses Spiritualism according to his or her basic understanding. And when I speak for Spiritualism, I speak for the Spiritualism of the Serenity Spiritualist Association Camp and Church, and I speak for the understanding that I have received.

The National Spiritualist Association does not accept or believe in what they call the vicarious atonement of Jesus the Christ; in other words, that he died on the cross for our sins. The national association teaches—and the Serenity Association is in accord—that man and man alone is responsible for all of his thoughts, acts, and activities. There is, personally, no question in my mind whatsoever that if a human being believes that Jesus the Christ died for the sins of the world, according to his belief he may indeed be benefited and, indeed, has the divine birthright to that belief. That is not the present understanding of Serenity Spiritualism. Thank you very much.

Anyone else have a question?

On the . . .

Yes.

On the matter of the belief of Christ dying for our sins, I've known a great amount of people who took advantage of that and they said, "Jesus died for my sins." And so they figured they had free license. I could never find any place where the Bible said that. I've found a great many religions that have told me that, but I can find no place in the Bible where Jesus intended that to be. As far as I can find out, he just said you had to have the belief and the understanding. But to me, it taught personal responsibility: that if you did something, you're responsible for what you did.

Yes, indeed. It is our understanding that—[and] my personal understanding—if anyone feels that Jesus has died for all of our sins, and continues to do so, as we continue to sin—and my understanding of sin is nothing more than an error of ignorance—to me, that is not my understanding of a Christian or of Christianity. I do not believe that Christianity, sincerely, would teach that man can continue to sin as Jesus will continue to forgive them. There is no question in my mind that if we believe that, we're going to experience, of course, what we believe to some extent. No question at all. But we do have personal responsibility. And indeed have we been given choice. We can choose to be happy or we can choose to be sad. The choice is ever up to ourselves.

I sincerely pray with all of my heart that it may be in the divine plan that I can live in this physical dimension to see the unity of all churches; that the Holy Spirit may enter and demonstrate its presence to the skeptic. And if the skeptic needs the living demonstration of so-called psychic phenomena, then let it be, if it leads them to God. If it leads them to a better way of thinking, if it leads to a world of peace, to a mind of tranquility, then indeed I will do all within my power to bring what understanding of psychic phenomena that I have to any church in any place that is sincerely interested. But remember, my good friends, it is not the end. It is only a means to the end. Do not be confused by communication. Do not be deceived by so-called miracles. Because if you forget for a moment and you think that you have some power that is truly your own, then we're only deceiving ourselves.

I would like to share with you at this time a few words that [were] given to me last year from the Spirit. *[This saying is part of The Serenity Game.]* And it said:

> O man, you little god, what wisdom hath you found
> O man, you little god, what power can you keep
> O man, you little god, know that I am humble,
>   but never sound asleep.

And so it is, my good friends, let us ever remember, regardless of the seeming miracles, regardless of demonstrations, let us ever remember and never forget that there is a great Divine Power; that our conscience is a spiritual sensibility with a dual capacity; that it knows right from wrong. It does not have to be told. There is a part of us—of all of us—it's our spirit. It knows the difference. It knows what's right or wrong for us at any given moment.

The Spiritualism that I know is not interested in building cathedrals of stone and mortar, but it is indeed interested in building cathedrals of the soul. Those, my friends, are the cathedrals within. Because if we cannot be a living example of the path to God, then we are not serving the purpose that we have been designed to do. Thank you.

Are there any other questions? Yes.

In the Bible, it explains where, at one time, they had thousands of people and they were hungry; so Jesus fed them with a couple of pieces of fish and a loaf of bread. And I've had a great many priests and ministers explain to me that is merely a parable. They were merely making an example. Whereas in studying some of the ancient books of the Bible, they really meant it. They meant that Jesus actually did this manifestation of food for the people. What does the Spiritualist church think of a passage like that?

I will be happy to give you my personal understanding of that particular passage. There is no question in my mind, from the demonstrations of the Nazarene, that he indeed fed the thousands; that he indeed used the powers of the Divine to multiply whatever sustenance was present. There is no question in my mind, from the many years of experiences, that it is not only possible to move physical objects but that it is possible to multiply them. And therefore, I take that passage literal. And I believe beyond a shadow of any doubt that he not only multiplied that, that he not only changed the water into wine, that it was not some type of a hypnotic trance that he imposed upon the people, but that it was an actual demonstration of the Divine Power moving to the extent and degree of his faith. Yes. Thank you.

In other words, the Spiritualist church actually believes in Jesus Christ as much as any Christian church.

Richard Goodwin, of the Serenity Spiritualist Church, absolutely and positively does. As a person, I do not accept that he has died and continues to die for my personal sins or errors. I respect the Nazarene as a great teacher. I respect him as I respect the Buddha. And I respect any of the spiritual leaders that have come to the world to awaken [people] from their lethargy and from their sleep. That does not mean that the Serenity Spiritualist Church believes in the vicarious atonement. I can only speak for myself when I say that I do not believe in the vicarious atonement, but I respect the rights of all people who do. And I also respect the rights of those who come into Spiritualism with that faith and that belief.

[Side 1 of the reel-to-reel tape recording this lecture ends at this point. The class continues on side 2.]

My good friends, it is better to have a little faith in God than no faith at all. Now, however you worship is a personal thing to all people, because we all find our way to the Light in our way. There are times when there are some people with similar understanding, and so we have churches in the world. But remember, religion is in the world to serve God, not to dictate what God is. Let us ever keep that in mind. Thank you.

Yes, the lady here, please.

Many people have read the Christian Bible and believe that they will meet Jesus personally after death. Is this possible, in their state of consciousness when they leave, that he will be there to greet them?

Thank you very much for your question in reference to those who believe that they will meet Jesus after the change known as so-called physical death. There is no question in my mind that those who have gravitated to an expression of spirituality that the Nazarene has obviously gravitated to, even before leaving the physical body, indeed, according to the divine merit system, they cannot help but meet the Nazarene. But how many people, let us ask ourselves, are expressing such great spirituality that upon the moment of transition are going to fall into the arms of Jesus? Let us ask our self the question. But let us not deny the right of those who believe it, because if that belief leads them closer to God, then it serves a very good purpose. And who is to say? For I believe in a God to which all things are possible. I do believe in that. Thank you.

Yes, the gentleman here, please.

As I understand Jesus' childhood, he demonstrated perfect love when he was very young. And then he disappeared and the record of him ceased for many years. And he reappeared again and demonstrated the same perfect love. And I wonder what was the need, if, as a child, he understood and was able to demonstrate perfect love, why must he disappear for many years only to demonstrate the same love when he appeared again?

Well, I would like to answer your question, if I may, in this way: if you have a child that is demonstrating a great deal of love and then the child starts to grow up and you must send them out into the world for their education, there is indeed a question how long they will be able to continue to demonstrate that great, perfect love. Would you not agree? My good friends, it is my firm belief that the Nazarene, demonstrating perfect love as a child, went away somewhere, in order to continue to demonstrate this perfect love, into some type of a retreat or shelter until such time as he may be fully awakened and strong enough to sustain it under all trials and tribulations.

If you take a child that is extremely sensitive and you send that child out into the public schools—and I don't mean to speak despairingly of them, but let us face reality of today and it's not that much different today than it was then—then it is most difficult for the child to maintain and to sustain their innocence and their pure love. And so it is that many religions, recognizing that, have retreats, and they have schools for their children.

Does that help with your question? *[After a short pause, the teacher continues.]* Thank you kindly.

Yes, the young lady here, please.

Do you believe that Jesus Christ is God's son?

I most firmly and absolutely do. I believe that you are the daughter of God; that he is the son of God; that all people are the sons and daughters of God. Because I do not believe that there is any power outside of God; therefore, all people are sons and daughters of God. Thank you.

Yes, the lady here, please.

I would like to ask the question, If people believe that Jesus Christ came to save the world, then what happened to the people before Jesus Christ was born? How could he save them?

That's a very good question. And if we study religious history, we will find that there were other great spiritual leaders prior to the Christian era. There were other savior gods. After all, there was the Mithrain religion, which was very popular at that time. There are many religions prior to the Christian era that promised salvation through faith and belief. And so it is that man, he's never left without the opportunity to serve the Divine: that there are ever amongst us teachers, somewhere, to show us the way. All people are saved because all people are of God. Therefore, there's no place to be lost because there's no place that God does not express itself. Thank you.

Yes, the lady in the back, please.

Jesus' statement, "Lo, I will be with you always, even to the end of the age."

Yes—

There are different words or different interpretations of that statement. Different words used for "age." What do you think?

"Lo, I will be with you always," is a very clear statement to me. We are inseparably the same Spirit, the Holy Spirit or God or whatever you wish to call it. Therefore, Jesus the Galilean is also that same Spirit. Therefore, Jesus is eternally with us when we are eternally in Spirit. Therefore, all people in Spirit are ever with us. Does that help with your question? Thank you.

The lady here, please.

Yes. Could you give me the spiritual interpretation of the Ten Commandments?

The lady is asking a question of the spiritual interpretation of the Ten Commandments. My good friends, I cannot give you the Spiritualist interpretation because to my knowledge the Spiritualists have not yet attempted to give their own particular interpretation of the Ten Commandments.

I would be more than happy to share with you my personal understanding of the Ten Commandments. I believe that the Ten Commandments were brought to the world to help the people to rise to a more humble, a more awakening level of consciousness. I believe that they were direly needed at the time they were brought to the world. There was so much barbarianism in that particular time and era. I believe that they are, beyond a shadow of any doubt, from a divine source to help mankind at the time they were brought into being. If one truly studies the Ten Commandments, then one cannot help but see the wisdom that flows through each and every word; that they came to this world to serve a spiritual purpose at the time they were brought. Thank you.

Are there any other questions? [Mr. Chairman], you have to call time on me.

I believe it's time. [The chairman replies.]

Thank you very much. *[Mr. Goodwin addresses the chairman.]* Thank you, ladies and gentlemen.

MAY 6, 1973

Class November 15, 1974

Good evening, friends, and welcome to the Living Light Philosophy class.

In keeping with the principles of Spiritualism, we're presenting this class to help you with your understanding of Spiritualism. And especially to those who are new to the religion and philosophy and science of Spiritualism, we'd like to state that Spiritualism is the science, philosophy, and religion of continuous life, based upon the demonstrable truth of communion with spiritual realms. Now a Spiritualist is one who endeavors to mold his or her character in accordance to the highest teachings derived from such communication. And so it is that over these past ten years a philosophy has been brought to us from the world of spirit. And our purpose here this evening is to share this philosophy with you.

So if you will just kindly place your feet flat on the floor, I'll be more than happy to give the introduction that we are scheduled for.

The teaching of the Living Light, and in keeping with our religion of Spiritualism, is one of personal responsibility. Our understanding is that the soul evolves and is evolving at this very moment.

Now we all know, I am sure, that that which is form, called creation, is dual; it is both positive and negative. Whatever is individualized, therefore, is dual because it is form. Our teaching is that the soul is individualized; that the Divine Spirit, known as God or Infinite Intelligence, is expressing through this soul; that our soul entered this earth realm according to laws that it and it alone has set into motion. Our teaching is that man is a law unto himself; that all experiences in life are but the direct effect of certain levels of consciousness, known as rates of vibration, that we and we alone have set into motion.

Life here and hereafter is a continuous school. We have a golden opportunity at any moment to choose whichever path we wish to trod. Now once we set a law into motion, we will follow that law to its fulfillment. For example, How does man set a law into motion and what is a law? A law is the effect of directed energy. How does man direct energy? Man directs energy through the vehicle called thought; therefore, in keeping with the ancient teachings, as a man thinketh in his heart, so he becometh. Now why is that teaching as a man thinketh in his heart he becometh? Because, my friends, it is not just the thinking of the conscious mind that sets laws into motion for us. It is the thinking of the patterns of mind in the depths of our own subconscious. However, we have never been left without choice, and at any moment we may choose which experience we care to have in life.

Our teaching is self-control, for only through self-control will man experience what is known as freedom. When man becomes truly aware of his own patterns of mind, then he is in a position to consciously choose which patterns of mind or levels of consciousness he wishes to express. And that, my friends, is known as freedom. But man cannot experience this great freedom, this great peace that passeth all understanding until he makes the effort to become aware of his own levels of consciousness.

Spiritualism is not simply interested in what happens to you after what is called death or transition. We are interested in what is happening this moment, for we know, once we become awakened and control the eternal moment of the now—for only the moment of now can we in truth control—then we will not need to be concerned about the hereafter or where we are going. We understand that heaven, or hell, is not a place that we are going to; it is a state of consciousness that we are already growing to. And so it's entirely up to us how we want to make the life and the experiences that we have.

Now the question may well be asked, Then why does one soul enter a form and certain experiences that are so difficult for it? Well, that is the law that that soul has set into motion on its evolutionary path. Remember, my friends, that something cannot come out of nothing. And so man's soul did not come out of the nothingness, but it evolved and is evolving in its own individualization.

Our teaching is that God, the Divine Intelligence, is ever equal to our understanding. And so, as we broaden our understanding and we broaden our acceptance in life, our God, the Divine Intelligence in our consciousness, begins to expand. But that, of course, my friends, takes a multitude of experiences for a multitude of people. It is easy to use the word *self-control*, but it is not possible to apply it until we awaken to what it is we're supposed to be controlling.

All of the experiences in all of the universes are only a mirror that are reflecting our own level of consciousness. It is nothing greater nor is it anything smaller. So let us think about life and let us think a bit more deeply. Where are we this moment? Let us not be so concerned about the tomorrows, and let us not think so much about the yesterdays, for all we do, in that attitude, is entertain it in mind and cannot in truth do anything about it.

Now in our classes, usually, we offer an opportunity for the students to ask whatever questions they have. And so at this time, in reference to this philosophy, I encourage you to ask any questions you have on Spiritualism and the Living Light Philosophy, [if] you'll be so kind as to raise your hands. Yes, the gentleman, please, in the front row.

Just one question about the law. You spoke of the law being the effect.

Yes?

The direct . . .

Directed energy through the vehicle of thought. Yes.

Ah . . . [After a short pause, the teacher speaks.]

For example, man may choose to direct his energy through a level of consciousness that is not beneficial for him. For example, he may be angry at another person. Now if we choose to be angry at another individual because they did not do something that was pleasing to us, what we have done in truth is given the individual power over us, for each time we think of the individual we become angry. Therefore, we have lost control of our own emotions; we have lost control of our self. Our teaching is the personal Law of Responsibility. If you do not like what someone else has done, is doing, or about to do, remember that that is their divine right to express. Now if it is not pleasing to you, it simply means that you have got into a level of consciousness and have attracted that experience to you; but you have the divine right to change your thought pattern and, therefore, regain this divine peace, which is your own power. Does that help you with your question? Hmm? *[After another short pause, the teacher continues.]*

Now, of course, you know, when we're in rapport with someone, when we like them, the next step, of course, is attachment; we become attached to them. And when that happens to us, our next step up the ladder is possession; we want to possess them, you see. And when we open that door, we have nothing but problems, because, you see, the Divine expressing through form has its own expressed individuality. And that is the divine right of that particular soul to express. Thank you.

Yes, the gentleman in the second row, please.

I understand there's a teaching of faculties and functions—

Yes.

—in this philosophy. And I wonder if you could explain exactly what is a faculty and what is a function.

Thank you very much. Our understanding is that expressing the Energy, the Divine Energy, through what we call the soul faculties directs this energy into the building of a spiritual body within our physical body. Most people think that they automatically have a spiritual body, and of course, that is the farthest thing from the truth. We have the essence of it, but it takes directed energy to build it. And so our teaching is to balance, through expression, this Energy through the soul faculties: the first being duty, gratitude, and tolerance; and the second being faith, poise, and humility, etc., etc., etc. Each faculty has an opposite sense function. When we direct this energy through the soul faculties, we are freed from the reactions of experiences.

Now we all know, I am sure, that one experience in life calls forth another experience of like kind unless we take the essence from that experience, which is necessary for the reeducation of our own senses. And so it is, the teaching goes to balance the soul faculties with the sense functions.

Also, in keeping with that teaching is the teaching of faith and fear. Our understanding is that faith is a positive expression of the Divine Energy and fear is a negative expression of the Divine Energy, but they are both faith. For example, man has fear if he puts his hand in the fire that it will burn. What man really has is a complete belief and conviction that that is what will happen. And so that is what does happen because that is how great man's faith really is.

Now many people don't think they have any faith because they associate the word *faith* with religion. Well, the atheist has faith because they have belief. They believe that there is no God or anything outside of them. Well, that is their faith. We have faith when we put the key into the ignition in our car that it will start. And when the car doesn't start, we get very upset. The reason that we get upset is because that's how great our faith is directed in that particular area, of course, of starting the automobile.

And so it is that man in truth is the effect of his own beliefs. And God in truth is ever equal to our own understanding. And so, when through acceptance, total consideration and total acceptance—acceptance of the divine right of all of creation to express itself, for expression is in truth the Divinity itself. It is the purpose of all form to express itself. And when we decide that this form or that form is not expressing itself the way we think it should, then we become the judge. And he who becomes the judge also becomes the victim. The victim, of course, of his own judgments.

However, when man has total consideration, to consider all life's forms, to consider all people, to consider the right, the divinity of all form to express itself, then man is on the path to freedom.

In keeping with that philosophy, our teaching is that selfless service is the only path, the *only* path to spiritual illumination. For it is when man's attention, which is his directed energy, is freed from the self that he expands his consciousness, and this so-called God is freed in his universe, then life takes on a new meaning. It takes on a new purpose. And then we begin to see our true responsibility for coming to this Earth in the first place.

Remember, my friends, this is not your first awareness of the world. And by that I do not mean to imply what is commonly referred to as reincarnation, for our teaching is evolutionary incarnation. All of nature teaches us that all form evolves. We all, I am sure, will agree that our soul is an individual soul and that that is individualized by the Law of Individualization is form. Therefore, all form is evolving. Our soul is form and therefore, according to the divine immutable law, it too is evolving. And so it is the Law of Spiritualism which teaches eternal progression. Everything is returning to the source from whence it came. For that that came from a thing, by the law of coming from the thing, is destined to return to the thing from which it came.

And so we agree, I'm sure, that from the Divine we have gone out into the universes and to the Divine we shall indeed return. But let us not think of returning to the Divine, to our own divinity, in some far distant time because time, my friends, is only an illusion. It is a conscious awareness of passing events. And so it is that when a man is truly interested in anything, when his attention is directed to something that pleases him, he has no conscious awareness of time, for that illusion called time and space no longer entertains his thought.

Our teaching, of course, is also that concentration, that oneness, is the key to all power. So remember, whatever it is in life that you want, accept that you have it. And when you accept that you have it, you will move in the illusion called time and you will indeed experience it. For, you see, my friends, we can never experience in life what our mind has not first accepted. And so, what sense does it make that we chase a rainbow repeatedly telling our self that we don't have it yet, and go on through the centuries ever chasing.

You know the Bible prophets said, many centuries ago, in all of your getting, get understanding. They didn't say, get understanding. No. They very clearly and distinctly said in all of your getting, get understanding. They were very wise men. They knew that the nature of the human mind was to get. That get, get, get was its very nature. And so they said, "Well, we can't stop the natural process of the human mind of getting. But let's direct the getting to the only thing that will free the human soul." And that is known as understanding. And understanding, to us, is the foundation stone upon which the soul faculties are built. Without understanding, there is no true acceptance. And without acceptance, there is no true consideration. And without consideration, there is no true experience. So let's think about that for a few moments.

Let's stop and ask ourselves the simple question, "Why am I here and where am I going?" And when we ask our self that question, we'll go to a level of consciousness inside of our self where peace reigns supreme. We understand that peace is the only power. We understand that peace is God. And so to God, of course, all things are possible. But remember that God is as small or as large as our understanding.

And our purpose in Spiritualism is not to convert the masses to any dogma or creed. We are not concerned with numbers and building cathedrals of this world. Our interest is in building cathedrals of the soul, and that is built through our own consciousness. The greatest temple that man will ever know is not made of stone and mortar. It is made of a mind of peace. There, man has freedom. There, man will see the Light of eternal truth. He won't have to spend his hours and his years in getting, getting, getting substances that will disintegrate into the nothingness. Not that he will not use them, but remember, when the tools, the tools in life no longer serve the worker, the worker begins to serve the tools. That's when we become the victims of our own creations.

You see, life is like a game, and we are her victim, if we permit ourselves to be so. What is there in all of the universe that is worth seeking when it is not lasting or eternal? What we sought ten years and fifteen years ago, ofttimes today it has no value to us. So what does that in truth reveal? It simply reveals a level of consciousness, a tape in our so-called computer that kept on playing until finally we fulfilled that desire.

You know, we do not teach the annihilation of desire. We try to teach its education, not its suppression. We know that desire is a vehicle through which great energy is expressed. And if you suppress desire, the day will come when you will experience frustration and disappointment and discouragement. That is not our teaching. Our teaching is to educate the desire or to fulfill the desire.

And the question arises, well, Is desire a man-made thought or is desire a Divine principle? My friends, think and ask yourself the question, Does God desire?

We believe in an Infinite Intelligence, but desire is one of the five steps of the principle of creation. And, of course, without desire there would be no expression. And where and what would the Divinity be, if there were not forms through which it is to express?

And so, you see, we all desire. We desire to express our own spirit, our own soul. But because of the tapes of the acceptances of the past—that that is accepted in mind is experienced in life, when it is truly accepted. And so we have, over the years, accepted many thoughts and many beliefs. And so as we go along in life, we're controlled by those accepted thoughts and beliefs. And it's difficult to make change. Yet change is the Law of Progression. Without change, there is no progress. Think, my students.

Now you're free to ask any other questions you have. Yes, the lady on the third row on the right, please.

You spoke of self-control and freedom. And could you also tell me if that is related to understanding? Is self-control directly related to understanding?

Yes, in reference, you see—we cannot understand what we cannot control in mind. For example, if you have a moving object in front of you, you cannot understand the principles by which it moves until you can control it. And so it is in life that when you control yourself, your mind, [then] your understanding is expanded because your acceptance is broadened and so indeed is our consideration. Does that help with your question?

Thank you.

Thank you. The gentleman in the second row, please.

I wonder if I could be pardoned [for] a personal question. I wonder to what extent your present state of consciousness is related to spiritual communication.

Well, if that is important to you, I'll be happy to discuss it after the class. If that is important to you, yes, I'll be happy to discuss it with you after the class. Yes, the lady in the back, please.

Yes, would you please express the laws and responsibilities governing leadership?

Thank you very much. In reference to your question on the laws and responsibilities governing leadership, first we must consider the responsibility of those who are following us, as leaders. A sincere leader makes great effort to be a good follower, for man cannot lead until he can follow something that is greater than himself. And so if it is the thought of leading and leadership with which we are concerned, then let us express through the soul faculty, the second soul faculty, that is known as faith, poise, and humility. Because unless we can be receptive to a higher guidance, a higher intelligence than our own brain, our own mind, then we're not going to be good leaders on a spiritual path in life. A good leader has the responsibility to all of the people that choose to follow him. And a good leader also has the great responsibility to have an open mind, to be a willing follower of an intelligence, an inspiration that is greater than his own computed brain. Does that help with your question?

Yes. Thank you.

You're more than welcome. The lady, please, on my left.

OK. You were talking about not becoming involved in a situation or, like, if there's a person that you didn't agree with their actions, to not be, that if you did become concerned, that you'd become a victim of it, of this . . .

That, yes, is absolutely true. Number one: we cannot have an experience in life that we have not first in our own consciousness become receptive to. Now a person may say, "Well, I have someone that calls me every day and they're always in a low level of consciousness." Well, my dear friends, if we were not in a low level of consciousness, we couldn't attract that person to call us every day in a low level of consciousness. Because one of the basic teachings of Spiritualism is that like attracts like and becomes the Law of Attachment.

Now, you may say, "All right. I'm having these experiences in life, and I choose not to have them anymore." The place to go to work is not outside, for that is not where the cause is, for Life herself is a mirror reflecting where we are at any given moment. The place to go to the cause is inside our self, to find out what level we are on and, once finding that out, to raise our soul consciousness to another level. If we do not do that, then we continue on with experiences that are distasteful to us because we have lost control through a lack of awareness. Does that help with your question?

But what if that lady calls again? What do you say? "I'm sorry, I don't want to listen to you." Or, you know, what do you do?

Well, no, my dear friend. My dear friend, you have what all souls have: the divine right of choice. You may listen and yet hear not. In fact, even the Bible prophets said, "You have ears to hear and hear not. You have eyes to see and see not." So, you see, if you go to work on you, that person will not call you in that level of consciousness again. Do you understand? Now give it, if you wish, give it a try. Because, you see, it works. Like attracts like and becomes the Law of Attachment.

So if we are not happy with the experiences that we are having, if we are not happy where we are in life, all we have to do—it is so simple. You see, truth is simple and unconcealed; 'tis falsehood that is complex and deeply hidden—all we have to do is stop and think: "I do not care for this experience. Therefore, I will change my attitude of mind concerning it. I will rise to another level of consciousness." And then you will no longer experience that experience. Does that help with your question?

Yes. Thank you.

You're more than welcome. Yes, the lady on my left has been waiting, please, in the third row.

Oh no, no.

The lady across from you, please.

You say that awareness is a way to self-control. Are there other ways? Or could you expand on that?

Awareness, a way to self-control, it is the only way. We cannot control, my good friend, anything that we are not first aware of. When we become aware of the laws that govern any experience in life, then we are in a position to control them.

Now, it's just like a man and his wife. They may be having difficult problems and a wife may say, "Well, he has a drinking problem. He has this problem. He has that problem. And I just cannot take that anymore." Yet, there is a bond of attachment because there is a rapport on certain levels of consciousness. It is a very simple process for the wife or the husband to change their level of consciousness to not let the experience affect them emotionally. And one of two things will happen: the husband or the wife, whoever has the seeming problem—of course, a problem, we all understand, I am sure, is only a lack of faith in the power of God, the Divine Intelligence. However, if they change their level of consciousness, the husband or the wife, whoever has the seeming problem, they will either grow or go. Because, you see, like attracts like and becomes the Law of Attachment. If the one that has the seeming problem is unable to control themselves and the wife is able to control herself, like attracting like, he will either stop what is the problem for her or he will disappear, but life will carry on. Does that help with your question?

Yes. Thank you.

You're welcome. Yes, the gentleman in group two, please.

I don't quite understand how form is both positive and negative.

The Law of Nature is dual. It is a positive and negative. All form is both positive and negative. Whether that form is the human being, the animal, the plant, or the rock, it makes no difference; that is the Law of Creation. Now this positive and negative—and I'm glad you've brought up the question. We understand that the mind, the conscious mind, emanates electro energy, electrical energy; that the subconscious mind, which is the great magnet, emanates magnetic energy. Now when, you see, our conscious mind (electrical) is in balance with our subconscious mind, which is the patterned mind, when they are in accord and in harmony, they then become receptive, through this perfect balance, to what is known as the odic, the divine, neutral Energy called God. And that channel, through which it passes, is known as the superconscious.

And so it is that when you are in balance, you speak your word forth into the universe knowing that it shall not come back to you void, but accomplish that which you send it to do. But first, my friends, we must become aware. We must become aware of what our patterns are of our own mind. Because, you see, we have a conscious thought, an electrical impulse, and when that triggers the subconscious pattern, they're not in harmony; they're not in accord. And so man becomes a house divided. And then, you see, he speaks his word, but he experiences failure because he does not believe his word. You see, our subconscious is the believing mind. That is the mind that you work with because you must have that balance in life in order that you can have freedom.

For example, a man says, "Well, I'm going to go to college and I'm going to study this particular profession. And I'm going to become that." And so he's going to college and his grades are so-so. And here, back in his computer, is a fear mechanism that is triggered because his grades aren't too well. Now what is this fear mechanism? Well, it's a pattern of mind called experience. Perhaps when he was five years old, he tried to do something else and he only got halfway. This is what we're talking about, my friends. We're talking about awareness within our own being so that we can become free.

Now what is the technique through which this awareness is brought to our students? Well, it's known as concentration and meditation. But if you want to be free and find your true purpose in life, then it must be very high on your priority-desire list. It must be number one. Our teaching is: When God is first, all is well; when man is first, all is hell.

And so I am sure everyone within the sound of my voice will agree, when they put their faith and their belief in another human soul, they are destined to experience what they call hell. The reason they are destined to experience that level of consciousness is because they have put their faith in an individualized soul that is not identically the same as themselves and, therefore, will guarantee a difference of opinion, and the experiences go on.

So remember, you and you alone with God, which is called Infinite Intelligence, are a majority in any endeavor that you choose. But you are only a majority with the Divine when the Divine, in all your acts and activities, in all of your thoughts and feelings is number one. Remember that God's work is not limited to churches and temples. A man that digs the ditch, an electrician, or a plumber is doing God's work if God is in their thought. Now what do we mean by that? We mean God, Intelligence, Divine, Neutral, Impartial, we mean good and goodness. And so when you have a job to do, whether it's for you or another, and you do a good job, then that is God's work.

Remember, let us never want for another human soul nor an animal nor an ant because in truth in the Living Light Philosophy, we see no difference between ants and angels. They're all one and the same. You see, the plant has its love and its feelings, and so do the insects that crawl upon the ground and so do the so-called human beings. But let us not look at creation as though we and we alone wear the crown. How long do you think that we could exist, how long do you think that we could survive if it was not for the trees and the blades of grass, the insects and the animals that are our associates and our friends on this earth realm? My good friends, we would not long be in this form if it was not for the rest of creation.

So, in truth we are an inseparable part of one Divinity. And if you want to communicate with someone, learn to communicate with yourselves. If you want love from another, then first set the law into motion and experience love from yourself. If you want another to forgive you, first forgive yourself. Man—you see, it is in keeping with the teachings and the philosophy—man cannot experience what he has not first accepted. So how can you experience an expression of forgiveness from another if you have not first forgiven the level of consciousness within yourself that set the law into motion in the first place?

Now, we have a little time left, I'm sure, if you have any other questions. *[After a short pause, the teacher continues.]* You know, I don't want to do all the talking. After all, it's a philosophy class and you should feel very free—now isn't that a nice little ant crawling on that table. Do you see him, Mr. [Vice President]? *[Many students laugh.]* You should feel very free to ask whatever questions you have because our philosophy is not a dogma nor a creed. It's for your own questioning and awakening. The gentleman over there in the black sweater, please.

Yes, sir. Could you share your knowledge with us about astral surgery, please?

Well, thank you very much. And there has been interest in astral surgery and the piercing of the aura. Now I have experienced in life certain types of what they call psychic surgery and healing and etc. We must not think that psychic surgery is such that it does not make an incision in the body, because it does in truth. It makes an incision in the astral body because usually that's what they're working on in psychic surgery. They're working on the astral body. And so it is not recommended nor is it advisable to expose oneself to psychic surgery or what we call astral surgery unless you can be rest assured that the healer or physician or whatever they choose to call themselves is well informed and applies the law by knowing how to close the astral incision that he or she has made.

Now, you know, there's no greater healer, you'll never find a greater healer than the healer that is within you, for that is the greatest healer of all! That is your divinity! Your divine right is perfect health. Your divine right is full abundance and wealth. That is your divinity! And so we, as intelligent human beings, should deny our own divinity? My friends, all lack, all limitation, whether it be of material supply called money or it would be of our health, which is only the effect of harmony—when our mind, our conscious mind, our subconscious mind are in harmony, there is a perfect healing constantly taking place inside of our bodies.

Now what is the purpose of the Spiritualist healers? Their purpose, number one, is the great responsibility to *first* be in balance themselves. Because if they're not in balance, then balance, divine, neutral Energy cannot pass through them, as channels, into the patient or the recipient of this energy. So the number one responsibility of a healer, be he named a Spiritualist or other, his number one responsibility is balance. Balance of his own consciousness here in his own mind. Then he becomes an unobstructed vehicle through which the Divine energies may flow into the patient.

Now what is the patient's part? Well, that's quite simple: they must make the effort to be peaceful so that they can be receptive to this divine Energy. Will the healing last? Usually, it doesn't. And why doesn't it last? Because the patient is not doing their part. Oh, yes, they were brought into balance at the time of the healing. It might last a week. Why, it might even last a year or ten. But usually there's no follow-up. Usually, they come in with pneumonia or a cold or this or that or something else. They have an experience. They feel fantastic, and they go on about in their own, old levels of consciousness and they go right back to where they were when you first met them. But that, of course, is the divine right of the individual. But if you want a healing, my friends, bring your mind into balance, accept the eternal truth that you are perfect: perfect peace, perfect poise, and perfect power. Because that's what you are in truth, and anything else is a denial of your own divinity. And that denial is nothing more than the effect of ignorance.

You see, so often in life we try to do what's right. But, you know, there's a better way: just to do it. Stop theorizing about it. Stop saying, "How hard I'm trying to do this or that." And just go out and do it. You see, there is a difference. There's a great difference.

Now you're free to ask any other questions you have.

Thank you.

You're welcome. Yes, the lady in the back, please.

As a Spiritualist, I am interested in the Declaration of Principles that are set out in our philosophy. Could you give us your understanding about the doorway to reformation never being closed?

Thank you very much. It states in the Spiritualist Declaration of Principles, as stated by our national association, that the doorway to reformation is never closed against any human soul here or hereafter. And indeed! there is no power outside of us that closes the door to reformation. But be rest assured, my friends, we, with the divine right of choice, are constantly closing the door to reform in our own head. Now we have that right. What those principles mean, and I'm sure our pioneers were very sincere, was, at that time in the 1800s, there was no God out there on a throne that closed the door to reform, because there isn't. We close the door to reform through our choices as we are the victims addicted to our own taped experiences of acceptance of the past. And so it is that the door to reform, why, we're closing [it] all the time. Of course, some of us open it up a crack and we look inside and say, "Oh, it's too bright." And they close it again. *[A few students laugh.]*

You know, that's what life's all about, you see. If the light is too bright, it's best that you see it not now, you see? That's in keeping with what we call the womb of satisfaction. You know, there's nothing that keeps a man where he is, except satisfaction. When you're satisfied, you certainly don't make any effort to do anything different. So, you see, the teaching is "Irritation wakes the soul and satisfaction lets it sleep." So let us not be so satisfied and so pompous in what we have or have not.

Let us be a little irritated because then we'll be about the business of the Divine. Then we will not look out into the world and say, "Oh, there's a sugar shortage. There may be a depression and there's a shortage of this and there's a shortage of that." Well, what was it? Last year there was a toilet paper shortage. There's always some kind of shortage in the consciousness of the human mind. But is there a shortage? Where does it exist? I assure you, my good friends, it is not the time of year for our annual forecast, but I can assure you of this: there is no sugar shortage. There is in truth no paper shortage. And you will never be short of anything you desire if you will accept that you have it. All you have to do is to learn to control your mind. Accept that you have whatever you desire.

But do not desire what another has, for that is a transgression of the divine law. Whatever another has, you may desire from the universe, which is limitless, but do not desire to remove it from another human soul, for if you do that, you will set a law into motion guaranteeing all the experiences necessary to understand why that person has it and you have it not.

So let your desires be directed to the Divine. The Divine is the only one capable—believe me!—of fulfilling them. You see, through an error of ignorance, of course, our mind says, "I have this desire and it's over there. And I must move over there and

I must go through a certain path in order to fulfill it." As long as the mind has accepted that as the way, then it has set that law into motion. But isn't it better to sit at peace to see, in full visualization, all that you have desired and to say, "Thank you, God," [and] to accept it in your consciousness?

Remember that gratitude is the first soul faculty: duty, gratitude, and tolerance. And it is through the soul faculty of gratitude that man's supply and abundance constantly flows. And so, accept what it is you desire, and don't tell the Divine Intelligence that you have to do a certain thing in order to have it. Because when you do that, that's the law that you set into motion. You descend from a spiritual realm where all things are in the eternal now, and you descend into a mental realm where you must go through the necessary mental gymnastics of what your tapes are dictating in order to experience it. Now which is the best way? Which is the simplest way? Which is the easiest way? But that takes a slight dethronement, a slight dethronement of what they call the unbelievable, tenacious human ego. That's what that takes to accept an intelligence in the universe that is greater than our brain.

Look at life. Is there one man, or has there ever been or will there ever be, who can create all of the universes and sustain all life? That's what the Divine Intelligence does. Now if it can do that, and that is a demonstrable truth that all men can see, if it can do that, do you think for one instant that it cannot move any mountain, called obstruction, that your mind has accepted?

Why, my friends, it's not a matter of faith. You already have faith. It's simply a matter of direction. So let's direct our divinity. And let's live a life that is enjoyable, that is fulfilling, and that has a true purpose, so that we will not, upon leaving this old universe, have to enter the realms of regret. We've already, many of us, entered those realms, for they exist in consciousness. And we look back at life and say, "Well, if I'd only finished school, if I'd only had done that. But I couldn't do that because of this person or that person." How ridiculous! We couldn't do this and we couldn't do that because we had no self-control. We gave it to somebody else. You can't blame God for that.

But now remember, my friends, don't live in regret. A guilt complex is the most destructive attitude of mind you could possibly entertain. Let us encourage ourselves. And when we do that, we'll be enthusiastic in life. And you know, enthusiasm means to be in God. But you can't get enthusiastic, my friend, no matter who you are until you can get a little encouragement. You know, you can't encourage somebody else until you can learn to encourage yourself.

You know that old saying is that God helps those who help themselves. And how true that is. Man cries and complains and gripes and says, "This is all I've got. And I want to buy this, but I don't have the money." And he declares those laws with his mouth, you see. The mouth opens, the law is set into motion, and the tongue moves and the key is turned. And there's the door, you see. Well, man says, "Well, this is all I got. And I don't have no money. And I don't have this and I don't have that." The Divine looks down, and God says, "Well, if that's all you will accept, then that's all you're ever going to get." Now think about it. If you want a stingy God, don't expand your understanding. And your God will stay as stingy as you're permitting your mind to be with its own understanding.

So let's look inside. That's the only place we're going to make a change, if we're ready to make the change. You can go to a thousand churches; you can join a hundred thousand religions, [but] you're not going to change unless you're ready. The church won't do it. You know, there's a poem here, months ago we put in our little Sentinel magazine. It's very beautifully titled. It says, "It's not Your Church, It's You." *[Please see the appendix. At the time of this class, Serenity published a monthly magazine entitled the* Serenity Sentinel.*]* So let's think about it. It's not the world. It's not the government. It's not the people. It's not the stock market. It's our self, you see? Who causes depressions? People's attitudes cause depression, and their ego has to blame someone else because they don't want to face responsibility.

But, you know, there's something within the human mind; just take a look. If you have a man preaching on the street corner about God, there might be four or five people. But just have a twenty-car pileup accident on the freeway and you [have] got a thousand people. Well, just take a look, you know. What does that? One thing excites the senses, and the other is whispering to your soul. So let's think.

If you, in your spiritual search in life, are fascinated by the philosophy or experiences that you have, then remember, you're on the function-sense level. You haven't yet triggered to the spiritual.

Because that that fascinates us—and I'm glad, perhaps we have a few moments to speak on this psychic business, on the science of Spiritualism. A psychic is not a medium, but a medium is psychic. And so many people attracted to the religion and the philosophy and the science of Spiritualism are fascinated and excited about the possibility of seeing something in a so-called invisible world. My good friends, that is not Spiritualism. It is not the Spiritualism that the Serenity Spiritualist Association knows. That's not what Spiritualism is all about. We're a philosophy. Our science sustains that philosophy, and that's how we find the religion. Don't touch the doors of Spiritualism seeking to be a medium or a healer, seeking to see visions in the sky. If that's what you want, I tell you, it's much more advisable to buy a color TV set. I happen to have one myself. Just buy a color TV set; you would be much wiser.

Look, the prophets, the psychics, the mediums, their guides and so-called teachers are no greater, nor any lower or lesser, than the mediums, the prophets themselves. So let us judge the tree by the fruit that they bear.

And let us use common sense and reason in our investigation of Spiritualism and its philosophy and its science. Let us think. If you go into a meditation, do you go there to hear a voice talk to you and tell you how great you are? *[Several individuals laugh.]* Believe me, my good friends, if you want to know when you're in delusion and illusion, remember, when these so-called entities tell you they come with such great light and you're doing such fantastic work and you are so great and you're such a wonderful medium and healer, be rest assured you're locked in to delusion and illusion. Because those kind[s] of entities are not from very high realms of light or they wouldn't be saying such things.

The workers win. All of life proves the workers win. So let's go to work. And let's just do something. And let's not be fascinated by the science of Spiritualism. Its one and only true purpose is to help you open the doors of receptivity, that there is a greater intelligence in these universes, that life is one eternal journey, that it does not begin, and therefore it cannot end. That's the true purpose of communion: that you can be receptive to your own divine spirit. And according to your receptivity, that's the kind of helpers that you will merit. You will not merit anyone so great, so far beyond your level of consciousness, unless, within your consciousness, that is your true aspiration.

Time, please.

It is a quarter to eight.

Thank you very much, my good friends, for attending. Your church services are starting. Thank you so very much.

NOVEMBER 15, 1974

Stardust

Greetings, children of promise, principle, and reason; body, mind, and soul.

We have come to share this ancient truth with you in bits and pieces as the Law of Eternity dictates. All has been given in the philosophy that has been revealed to you. You, children, are now being given an expansion of that great truth in simplicity instead of allegory.

Long ago we stated when the lips speak as the heart feels, words become the savior of the wise. We also stated that the spoken word is life-giving energy. And now, my children, do you not see that the divine life force is released by the spoken word? And so choose wisely the words you speak. Choose even more wisely the thoughts you think.

We also stated that concentration is the key to all power, for concentration is placing the vehicle of mind, through which the life force is released, upon the object of your choice until only the essence remains, for the essence of a thing is the principle of the thing. And principle is the awakening of your soul, the freedom of your spirit, the fulfillment of your form.

Now in reference to the teachings given to you of recent date, those teachings, my children, are from the ancient time of Atlantis. Cloaked in many garments, they, in truth, are still with you. Remember that the Divine Light, which is the life force, is controlled through the vehicle known as thought. As man reviews, he directs the life force to creations, to gods and goddesses of the past, of form, of bondage.

As man previews, man establishes principle, through promise, and principle awakens the soul and frees the spirit. Through faith, reason transfigures your being.

Now, my children, use the Light you have received wisely. Use it; don't abuse it, for it is the principle of life. It is to be used in all areas of expression. And so, my children, the boat (your soul) sails through eternity in your own consciousness, which is in truth the God of gods, the Light of light itself.

And so, awaken your souls by the effort of demonstrating principle that you may be freed from personality. My good students, do you not yet perceive that personality is the control by the god[s] and goddesses below the fifth center or state of consciousness?

When all things flow freely, for truth is like a river, it continuously flows, the gods and goddesses above the fifth center are the angelic gods and goddesses that bring you all goodness and fulfillment of life. The gods and goddesses below the fifth center serve their purpose in rising the river that it may reenter its true source. Now when the ship, your boat of destiny, rises in the river to the higher centers, your soul experiences the consciousness of those centers. You hear? And in so doing you free your soul from the limit and bondage of so-called form.

Without promise, man does not live, for promise in the consciousness is called hope. You hear? And without hope, there is no life. We stated before that man does not hope for fulfillment. Do you remember? It's in the book. *[The teacher may be referring to the first book of teachings published by Serenity, entitled* The Living Light, *which was republished in* The Living Light Dialogue, *Volume 1.]* For he scales the mountain only to descend and scale again. You hear? And so, my good children, though hope serves her purpose—you hear?—promise is the divine principle that frees your soul.

And what is promise? The constant revelation that all things in form are subject to and demonstrate the Law of Evolution, called change. You hear?

We have also given to you what change in truth is. And do you not remember that it is in truth expanding consciousness? You understand.

And so, my children, you, your souls, have journeyed far. The journey in truth is not ending. It is in truth beginning, for now you stand at the gateway to demonstrate faith in reason, the power that transfigures thee. The transfiguration is the true freedom of your own soul.

Long ago we stated that the soul can and does all things create. And now, my children, think. Your souls established a law. That law dictated what form your soul would enter, you understand? Ever in keeping with the Law of Attachment and Adversity, you hear?

Yes.

[The student speaks in a whisper. It may be that the students present also responded to the teacher's previous questions, but spoke so quietly their words were not recorded. In addition, all subsequent responses from students were spoken so quietly as to be whispers.]

Those souls attached to form enter their next form contrary to their soul's natural vibration, you understand. And so an electrical soul enters a magnetic body; a magnetic soul enters an electric body. And that is 90 percent of all souls on your Earth planet, you understand. This, my good children, is the divine will and mercy of God, that man shall free his soul from his own suffering of form from form. You understand.

Yes.

And so attach not that you adverse not, for God's laws are immutable laws, and they are destined, my children, to free your soul.

What has been given to you, the Truth of truth, the Light of light, abused by man, destroyed the continents called Atlantis, you hear? And so, my good students, use it; don't abuse it. Remember, your words are your saviors. When they speak as your heart feels, they create the life force, [which] creates angelic gods and goddesses, you understand?

Yes.

And the war within finally is won by the greater Light, for the lesser light must bow. And that is the law that the souls may be free. There is never a day, my children, that God, in his infinite love, does not reveal to you in the sky his eternal promise. You understand?

Yes.

So look to nature and be closer to God. For without God, nature does not exist. You will be inspired from within. The little bits and pieces, you hear?

So listen to your souls. They have already awakened. The brain does not know soul. The heart is the instrument through which the soul gently speaks and brings all goodness, all God, in Life herself. You understand?

Yes.

And so, my children, remember and ne'er forget: God lives in laughter. He dies in despair. For laughter is an expression from a bay of joy. You hear?

Yes.

Now it is true that many things cause a person to laugh. You understand?

Yes.

But look not at the expression of what causes man to laugh. But look at the center from which it does in truth come. You hear?

Yes.

Now your efforts in helping the souls to be free can best be accomplished when you—for you all know, intuitively, your center of soul consciousness expression at any moment. Knowing your soul expression in that moment by the power of will, the love of God, speak the word and it shall not return unto you void but accomplish that which you send it to do. Don't you see, my children? When you speak the word from the fifth center of soul expression out into the universe, it cannot return to you void but accomplish that which you send it to do, for the life force, God, leaves your universe through the spoken word and it does in truth return unto you.

Study well the teachings you have been given. Organize them and unite them. They're in bits and pieces. If they were otherwise, they could not be received by mind. You understand?

Yes.

For the ship moves to different bays. And we pray each day it will move more freely. You hear?

Yes.

And so, my children, study and truly perceive the fifth center of consciousness, for there, my children, at the gate of eternal truth you demonstrate divine principle. God's promise never faileth.

Good night.

JULY 23, 1975

Review #1

Greetings, my good students.

We are pleased to return and share with you a bit of my life on Earth in the year 6000 B.C. During that time, I have spoken before about my duties as a magistrate. It was during the time that your recorded history, long lost to you, calls Atlantis [ət'-læn-tis] and calls it incorrectly. The proper name of the continent at that time was, and is in truth, Atlanis [ət'-læn'-is]. I will someday give to you its true meaning.

I resided on your Earth planet during the transition time of that great continent. By transition, I mean during the time that the joy and beauty of life was being expressed and gained control by the few and was beginning its descent.

Now the early days of Atlanis, similar to the days today of the Land of the Double Serpent, similar in many ways to the early days of the Earth continent. However, as the functions known as greed, as the great power became locked in the bays below, the descent of the continent began.

In those days, my good children, there was no need for mechanics or machinery, for everything was guided and controlled by what you call the life force. This control was within the powers of all people, was harmonious, beautiful, and joyous; however, as the law dictates, in form or creation, evolution and devolution and evolution is the eternal law of the duality of creation.

Now, my good children, the innocence or purity of love is the freedom of expression. This was the first law that the people on the Earth planet forgot as they began their descent. Due to the powers they had awakened, as that power surrounded and encompassed their entire universe, and because they would not remain innocent with what you call the life force or love, that power, they demanded to control others; no longer satisfied with the goodness that they were able to experience. And so the dangers are ever present: what man will do with the power that is.

When man closes the door of the soul faculty of humility, then the descent begins. But humility, my children, what is it in truth but the acceptance, the recognition, and the truth that each man is a part of the whole; that the whole is the greatest of servants and the parts can be no less.

And so Atlanis, from the abuses of the council that controlled it in its descent, as they used the power to direct the masses to build and build and build, never satisfied with the buildings that they built nor satisfied with their temples that ever increased in size, that the people were the bondage and slaves of the few, that the life force was totally imbalanced from abuse, destroyed themselves.

We will speak again on the law that governs life and how they lived in my continent of old.

Good night.

JULY 29, 1975

The Dog of Destiny

Greetings, my good student.

Again, in response to the request and great thirst of your soul for understanding, I have come to share with you the principle that governs the dream of life.

We spoke before, "Dreamer, dream a life of beauty before your dream starts dreaming you." Now what is the principle that establishes the dream of life? My good students, the principle, which in truth creates form and experience, is the principle known as rejection. As man rejects, he establishes, in the Law of Principle, the direction of divine Energy which in truth creates the dream of life called form. For example, the soul, striving to express itself through the form or dream of its own creation, which is the effect of its own rejections or denials, creates the dream of life, and that is why we have stated that your denials are in truth your destinies.

And so, my children, the formless, free Spirit will ever strive to express itself as the form, which is in truth the dream, strives to preserve its own dreaming. This in truth is the illusion and delusion or veil of creation which man must separate from eternal truth or principle in order that he may be free.

Look at life, your life, in the eternal moment called now. Is your life the same as yesterday? No, my good student. It is not because yesterday's laws are today's fulfillments. As you, the formless, free spirit moves in the stream of consciousness, the dreams continue to view themselves in mind stuff.

When the spirit regains its rightful throne, it sees creation, the dream; it declares its divinity, establishes its rightful laws, and sees truth through the veil of illusion, known as creation. And so the eternal soul, descending from freedom through the dream process, guarantees its own ascendancy home in consciousness through the dreams of life to its own home and its right and just freedom. This process, my good student, is taking place this moment. As it continues, the question you asked earlier is being fulfilled. In reference to the degree on which it has already ascended, we are able to view, happily, that there has been a 16-degree movement, you hear?

Yes.

Now the dream, my children, the effect of directed energy, called rejection or self-will, is the right granted to man, you hear?

Yes.

That he may choose his dreams wisely. Without the dreaming process, there would not or could not be individualization—you understand?—

Yes.

—or form. And when the dream becomes greater than the dreamer, man suffers from his own dreams and in truth is freed, you hear?

Yes.

And so, once again we say, "Dreamer, dream a life of beauty before your dream starts dreaming you." Remember, God, the formless, free Intelligence, denies none of his children. And destiny, in truth, is at your command. You understand?

Yes.

So be not discouraged with dreams of yesterday, for they are only dreams. Be not encouraged of dreams of tomorrow, for they too are only dreams, you hear?

Yes.

But take the eternal moment of now, the moment of peace, poise, and power, establish the divine principle of freedom, and enjoy the dream of life and all its beauty.

Good night.

JULY 30, 1975

Special Discourse - The Path

Greetings, students of Light.

I have come at this time to share with you the laws of attainment that you may gain principle and freedom in your eternal moment of now. We have spoken much on creation's laws of attachment and adversity. We have also spoken to keep faith with reason for she will indeed transfigure or transform thee. We have also stated that reason is, in truth, perfect balance.

Now think, my children, and think more deeply. In each attachment is the ingredients, the essence, of its own adversity. When man transgresses the Law of Balance, he guarantees in truth an adversity to his own attachment because of his own imbalance. When man, having adversity and not balance, [the adversity] guarantees its own attachment. So look wisely at your attachments and your adversities, for when you look wisely at them and apply reason, which is the Law of Balance, your adversity will meet its own attachment. And when it meets, you then are granted the opportunity, as balance is achieved, to view and to attain principle, which is in truth freedom.

Now the divine Energy directed by the thought of man is the creative process. And so it is that each thought you entertain in mind stuff is building attachments and building adversities. Take stock of your life and see the laws that you have established. And in so viewing them, bring them into perfect balance in consciousness, and there you will be granted, within your own being, the opportunity of balance, reason, and transformation. There is no escape from the divine, eternal laws of life. So view wisely your attachments for you in truth are guaranteeing the law to be fulfilled.

So often the mind says, as a self-preservation, defense-mechanism expression, that it in truth has no adversities; that it in truth has no real attachments. This, my children, is the delusion of mind stuff in order to preserve its dream of Life herself.

And so each and every one of your experiences is presenting to you your attachment-adversity experience, for there is no experience in life that does not in truth reveal that Law of Duality.

Now I want to speak for a moment on the direction and creation of your bodies. We stated long ago that man views the realms of spirit with spiritual sight, which is the effect of a spiritual body; that man views the mental world with mental sight and experiences the physical world with a physical body. And so, my children, seekers of peace and truth, think more deeply what body you are directing the divine energies to. Is it your physical body that entertains your mind or thought process? Is it your mental or emotional body? Is it your vital body, your astral body, your spiritual body, your soul body, your universal consciousness? What you are entertaining in thought you are binding your own eternal soul to.

You cannot see principle when you insist upon blinding yourselves by so-called form and creation. As you view form, you are controlled in mind stuff by the Law of Duality, known as adversity-attachment. And not until that dual law comes into perfect balance in the soul faculty of reason can you in truth be freed.

Now many times this simple Light is taken by what we call the brain, the king brain. It spins in the gray matter and uses and abuses the light of peace and joy. The reason that it does that is because the soul consciousness is locked in the bay of self. And he who entertains thoughts of self guarantees the continuity of the duality of consciousness in expression.

It is the oneness, my children, that is the path to paradise. The oneness of your consciousness, the perfect blending and harmony of the nine bodies in which your soul is now expressing. So bring totality in duality and free the form and free your soul.

Good day.

AUGUST 10, 1975

Special Discourse - Bee

[At the beginning of many of the class recordings, the vice president of the Serenity Association, who served as recording technician, identified the date and often the title of the class. His identifying comments are not typically included in these transcriptions. On this recording, he also recorded statements that may be relevant to the teachings. In this volume, as in later volumes, a series of five asterisks indicates that the tape recorder was stopped and then restarted.]

The bee is the greatest worker in the insect kingdom and stands for wisdom. He gathers all the honey.

*****

Greetings, students of the Light.

We shall discuss at this time the Destiny Diagram and the twenty-eight-day of cycle influence in your lives. *[Please see the appendix.]*

You will note by placing the double serpent over the Destiny Diagram that the points are as follows: three; six; eleven; eight; and return to three. And so it is, my students, that Saturn moves along those patterns. Now to clarify that for you, the other point at the top of the diagram may be traced in the opposite direction. You hear? *[As of the date of publication, no image of the double serpent has been located.]*

Yes, sir.

When you have totaled the numbers that the serpent follows, you will note that they equal 1 and 1 for each serpent. You hear?

Yes, sir.

That is the God of the formless, the God of the form. You will also note that a twenty-eight-day cycle equals 1. And so it is that you may perceive the beneficial influences of those planets during those cycles. Also, those influences are your life experiences of centuries ago, which we mentioned once before, a bit. You hear?

Yes, sir.

And so, my children, view the Destiny Diagram well. Use the beneficial influences of those past life experiences and all will be peaceful and well, as you continue to awaken your souls.

I am so happy and grateful that my prize graduate, so to speak, from our school, has come to you to work and help to free the souls of God's children. His work on Earth is just beginning. You hear?

Yes, sir.

But he comes to you well qualified to accomplish the task that he has chosen and good works shall be done.

Good night.

AUGUST 11, 1975

Private Class 1

Greetings, seekers of truth.

Peace I bring to your soul and balance to the mind.

As we move along in this great river of consciousness, we view many things that pass our sight. Let us, O seekers, view the eternal truth of this eternal moment that we may know and be the freedom that we in truth have sought for so very, very long.

The soul, as we have stated before, may be likened unto the ship of destiny, a ship that moves along a river of consciousness called God. Now this ship, my good students, is well equipped to take your little soul to heaven's heights. It has a sail that moves by the gentle breeze of peace, known as God. It has an engine, which is the force of Nature herself. And it has oars that also move this ship of destiny, called your soul. Now these oars are seventy-two in number. And they are composed of what is called mind stuff. And when the oars are used to move your ship of destiny, your soul, unless they move in perfect rhythm and harmony, your little ship gets stuck along the way.

And so it is that we have given you an affirmation that reveals this great truth, that nature teach[es] to all who seek the truth: that Life, the River of Consciousness or God, is perfect rhythm, perfect harmony, perfect balance, and perfect peace. *[Please see the appendix.]*

These oars, when used to move your soul consciousness, are ofttimes out of balance. And when a few oars are moving the ship, it doesn't move upstream to God and freedom. It moves to the bays along the way. And so it is that we have taught that freedom is the direct effect of self-control; that self-control is a balance of mind stuff. And that balance, my good students, is known as reason. *[Please see the appendix for a diagram of the bays.]*

And so, if you make greater effort to flood your consciousness with balance, which is reason, and principle, which is law, you indeed will have the kingdom of heaven, which waits for you to arrive in consciousness within your own being. Without the effort to control the oars which move the ship, when it is not being moved by the force of its engine nor by its sail, moved by God's eternal peace, if you do not make that effort, then you, your soul, no longer serves its true purpose, for the oars that move your soul have become your masters and control you, your eternal being.

We have spoken before on the Law of Review, the Law of Preview, and the Law of View. The eternal moment of now—view; the dreams of yesterday—review; and the dreams of tomorrow—preview. Now think, my students, what you do when you permit the patterns of yesterday, the dreams of the past to control you. It simply means those oars that move your ship of destiny continue to move it in the bay of their own choosing. And their choosing, my good students, becomes your eternal destiny.

We stated long ago, "When the tools no longer serve the worker, the worker begins to serve the tools." And so it is when the oars of your ship no longer work in harmony and perfect rhythm, you, your eternal being begins to serve those oars. That is not the path of illumination. It is not happiness, joy, or freedom. But it is in truth bondage, my good students. Someday the bondage will be so great that you and God will meet in truth, and those oars will start to move in perfect rhythm, balance, and peace.

And so it is that we have taught, "When of thy mind thou seekest to know the truth, / On the wheel of delusion thou shalt traverse." Only when your mind is sound, when all the oars are functioning properly, will your heart speak, will your soul express itself, and then you know the joy of Life herself.

And so, my good students, think more often and think more deeply what is controlling you, your life, what is denying you your happiness. Nothing outside, my children, has ever done it. Nothing outside can ever do it.

The dream is simply the Law of Identity, for you are in truth Spirit, formless and free. The moment you think, you identify. When you identify, you conceive. And when you conceive without perception, you deceive yourselves, until the day comes that the deception becomes master and you become its slave. It's known as the sleep of satisfaction. But someday all souls awaken. And ofttime[s] the irritation is so intense that their bodies shake. It's known as the fear of God. For those created dreams fear their own death, for they have not soul and cannot live eternally.

I shall speak with you again. Remember to do your part. No one needs to tell you what it is. You already know that.

Good night.

AUGUST 7, 1975

Private Class 2
The Fountain of Youth

Greetings, children of Light and Life.

It is our pleasure once again to speak with you. And at this time, we should like to discuss the fountain of youth and how to perceive and become it. You all know in truth that Life herself, which is God, is a stream of consciousness in perfect flow.

And so it is in order to help you, your soul, to help yourselves, I should like to give at this time an affirmation to help you to flow in consciousness, which is in truth God. The affirmation is:

> Rhythm, Harmony, Balance, Peace.
> Hold, release. Hold, release.

Now, my good students, whenever you have a thought which is with you at all time, declare the truth in, "Rhythm, Harmony, Balance, Peace. Hold, release. Hold, release." That is the Law of Demand-Supply. And so it is that the magnetic mind holds, as the electrical mind releases. When these two minds are in perfect balance, which is reason, which is peace, which is soul perception, which is truth, which is the joy of life, you indeed will be Life herself.

My good students, long ago we stated, "Dreamer, dream a life of beauty before your dream starts dreaming you." And so it is because of the dreams of yesterday that you persist on holding in consciousness, you, your soul, cannot move in the perfect rhythm and harmony along the stream of life.

This ancient truth is revealed in your world today in many, many ways. One of those ways is what is known in your world as acupuncture; that is, the placing of needles in the human body in order to redirect the current or life stream. It is known by those who know well the science of acupuncture that harmony can be restored in the body by the proper directing of the life stream or energy. It is not necessary, my students, nor is it desirable to use needles to direct this current, which is the stream of consciousness. This current may be directed in perfect balance by the affirmation that has been given to you.

When something disturbs you, it controls you because you, through the power of thought, have directed the current to a dam which you yourselves have built. Using this affirmation in perfect rhythm, you will release what you are holding. You will free the river of life, the stream of consciousness, within your universe and be free, be happy, and be joyous.

Now, my students, it is time to apply what you have already received. When you are concerned, you hold. And when you hold, you dam up the river of consciousness. When you do that, you create an obstruction. The soul, moving along the river, views many scenes. Do not become the scene itself. View it for what in truth it is.

The eternal moment is the only moment that you have power over. Take control of your mind and demonstrate the Law of Harmony, and you will have the fountain of eternal youth. The only reason that your bodies experience an aging process is because of your mind, which has blocked the flow of God-consciousness through it and within it. When you hold, release, hold, release, the river will then flow freely, and you will not need to be concerned about your aging processes for they are only the effect of your self-will, which insists that it knows more than divine will, which in truth sustains it in the first place.

My students, many dreams you have been, and many dreams yet you will become, for the soul can and does all things create by the electromagnetic Law of Life itself. It is only in neutrality that you express your divinity or godhood, which is goodness. That neutrality is when the magnet holds and releases in perfect rhythm and harmony all thought, all feeling. That, my good students, is called surrender of the self to the truth of life.

And so it is man, consciousness, God, is ever and forever moving upstream to heaven and paradise in the eternal moment, which you choose to capture and to release that your ship may move, unobstructed by your own mind, to eternal truth in the moment of now. All things to the left, magnetic, to the right, electric, are conceptions and deceptions. Only perception, the view of the now, is your happiness and eternal joy.

What will it take, my students, for you to make that simple effort each moment of each and every day and night?

Now the question may be asked, "I can take conscious effort of my thought while I am consciously awake. But what can I do with my thought when I am not consciously awake?" My good students, when you demonstrate the divine Law of Conscious Control of your thought while conscious, you will not have to be concerned about your thoughts while you sleep, for you will be conscious of them, and yet, you will rest.

Sleep is not something that you should be seeking, for sleep is satisfaction. Rest is what the body needs, and that is not truly accomplished by sleep. It is accomplished when you, your soul, perceives the truth of the eternal moment and is rejuvenated by that perception; [and] the vitality is restored in your body.

Your dreams of yesterday demand their constant playing. And so it is you sleep. The question may well be asked, Then why does the soul in the babe sleep so much? My good students, the soul has entered the form on your Earth under the Law of the Sleep of Satisfaction, for that is how the soul entered Earth: by the law of its own dream.

Good night.

AUGUST 14, 1975

Private Class 3
The Principle of Getting and Giving

Greetings, children.

How good it is to be with you again in this way and to bring to you a bit, perhaps, more light on the Law of Getting, the Law of Giving. For untold ages the teaching has been taught, in all your getting, get understanding.

Now, my good students, we have brought to you the teaching that God is equal to your understanding. Now what does man do with his understanding, which is in truth equal to his God? My good students, wisdom is the way. And what in truth is wisdom? Wisdom is the application or expression of understanding. And so in keeping with eternal truth, in all your getting, get understanding; in all your giving, give wisdom.

And so, my good students, without giving, there is no gain. When you, as students, in keeping with the Law of Solicitation, give to another from a level of understanding, you are in truth the channel through which wisdom helps to free the human soul.

And so, my students, do you not yet see the great responsibility having got so much understanding that it is indeed time to give a bit of wisdom? Now the mind may say, "I do not have the opportunity." And if the mind says that, then you may be rest assured it is not coming from a level of understanding and, therefore, is not giving to you wisdom.

For when the student is ready, the teacher appears. And when the teacher is ready, the student appears. And so, my students, your spiritual duty is the duty to your own eternal soul. And the Law of Harmony dictates perfect balance, which is in truth its beauty. So as you gain in understanding, you must give in wisdom. Do not tell wisdom what wisdom is. The mind does not know wisdom. The mind has knowledge. The soul has understanding. The soul gives wisdom.

And in speaking on the soul, I should like to say this: you perhaps have heard before about the individualized soul. Now what does *individualize* truly mean? It means indivisible, inseparable. And indivisible from what? From the Allsoul of which it is in truth.

Remember the Law of Creation. Remember the law governing individualization. And remember, what you seek is seeking you. And when you feel in the depths of your being what you call a lack or emptiness, it is simply the eternal drive of your soul to the fullness, the wholeness, and completion of itself.

And so, my students, look inward for truth. Look inward for the Divine. You will find the spark. And once having found it, the fires of true illumination shall never again cease to burn. For the journey of the soul, like the circle, is a continuous process of dream upon dream upon dream.

You all know that the body is the temple of your eternal soul. You know the meaning of many parts of the human anatomy. And so, look with reason and light at the little house in which your soul is striving to express itself, and do not deny the toe because it is not the eye. Do not deny the hand because it is not the foot. But look at your little house, which is designed by the master designer of all design, created in the image, *in the image* of what you call God.

And remember that the temple of your soul is in truth an idea of the Godhead; that the idea is without fault or defect; that it is a perfect design to serve the eternal purpose of your heavenly soul. And remember that God and God alone is the sustainer, the designer, but not the creator. That job was given to the gods and goddesses of creation.

And so whatever you think, you and you alone create. And what you create, you are not only responsible to but you are its god. And the children of your own creation shall demand their continuity. And you and you alone will pay the price of sustaining them. Choose more wisely what you think. Choose more wisely what you speak, for you are directing God, the infinite Life Force, energy and love and life to create so many things that are not things of beauty, love, and joy.

Rob not yourself of the peace that passeth all understanding. Remember well that the conscience of wisdom, that spiritual sensibility that knows right from wrong, is the love of understanding; that the love of understanding is the conscience of wisdom, and that truth is not within your human mind. It is in your soul and your heart.

Long ago we stated, "The soul can and does all things create." It created, by the laws that it established from the dreams that it dreamed, the temple in which you now reside, your eternal soul. And so your house is the direct effect of the laws of yesterday established by those dreams. And so, my children, if your hair is blonde and your eyes are blue, do not think it is by chance. If your face is freckled and your height is short, do not think it be by chance. For your house is the effect, not the cause.

And so when you truly perceive, when you truly love understanding, you will give wisdom, and in so doing be the joy of life expressed. I cannot grant you understanding nor wisdom. I can only share what I am receptive to. And I can only be receptive to that which I have made some effort to attain. But in the sharing of what God has granted me by natural law, it may awaken within your soul and understanding rise and wisdom flow.

Now it is stated that truth is like a river for it continuously flows from the Mountain of Aspiration. And so you know the lips represent aspiration. So let them be the aspiration that God has designed them to be. Let them express from the heart, the soul, and you will no longer be concerned with all those foolish mundane things.

Good night.

AUGUST 21, 1975

Private Class 4
Sanity and Self-Concern

Greetings, students.

Again, we are pleased to speak with you in this way and should like to discuss at this time sanity and self-concern.

Now I am sure that you will all agree that a sane mind is a balanced mind. And whenever a person is concerned with self, it simply reveals a concern with the entertainment of their own dreams.

This evening you spoke forth the eternal call of your soul, and that call may be likened unto the seventy-two oars of your ship of destiny, known as your soul. *[The teacher may be referring to an affirmation that can be found in the appendix.]* We have taught many times a balance between the conscious thought and the subconscious, taped experience or dream. Only when you make that great effort to first become aware of the dreams that control your soul and put them to sleep, when, in reason, you view they are not beneficial in your present moment, [will you move toward balance.]

It is often stated that man views life through rose-colored glasses. How beautiful it would be if that were true. But we find that man views life through black glasses, not rose or pink ones.

And so, my students, any moment that you concern yourself with yourself, you are entertaining the dreams of your own subconscious mind. We have often spoke that selfless service is the only path to spiritual illumination. That means service of your soul without the interference and obstruction of your dreams of yesterday. How does man free himself from the constant concern with himself? Man, so doing, stands in his own light and cannot find God or peace, freedom, or fulfillment.

My good students, in this the final private class given at this time, it is of the utmost importance to your own true self—your own true self is your soul, not the multitude of dreams that it has created—it is of the utmost importance that you make greater, yea, even greater effort moment to moment to bring yourselves into balance, into sanity, and free yourselves from the insanity of self-concern.

Think, my students. "When of thyself thou thinkest most, / Thine heart is closed to angel host." They cannot enter your universe, my good students, when these multitude of dreams insist upon being entertained and fed. Someday you will be free, but that freedom, which is the eternal moment, only comes through great effort. View more clearly what you are in truth doing to yourselves. Of what benefit is any philosophy, if the students of the philosophy are not applying it? Make greater effort, my students. Freedom is worth the price, the payment of some of your little childish dreams.

You ask what principle is; then ask what God is, for principle is God's law. It just is. You don't need to balance it out with mental gymnastics. Use—stop abusing—the laws of nature. Use—stop abusing—the principle of Life herself.

You know, my students, when you leave your earthly flesh, you live, your little soul, without the dense physical body. That other body registers greater pain and greater pleasure. It's known as the astral body. Now, my students, build strong bodies, be they astral, mental, spiritual, or celestial. Build them solid, my good students, with kind thoughts and kind deeds, for the kindness that you give is the kindness that you get. No more and no less.

You, my students, cannot dream your way through eternal truth. You can only view eternal truth. You cannot, my good students, go around, over, or under. You must go straight ahead in consciousness. Many obstructions lie in your path. Those obstructions are only your own past dreams. They are only obstructions, my students, to your self-concern and your self-will. No will of man can free the eternal soul. Only the will of God can free the soul. So give it more thought and give it more act in your own consciousness.

It is wise to study. And it is wiser still to apply what you study. For the application thereof is the reaping of the harvest, and it is time to reap the harvest for the seeds are well sowed in the fertile minds of my students.

Now it is time, long past time, to stand firm on the rock of eternal principle to make greater effort to leave a soul better than you found them. And in so doing your own soul is ever bettered.

It may seem that I speak a bit strongly to you, for some of you feel you are such new students to the light of this philosophy. My good friends, you have traveled through centuries and multitudes and multitudes of dreams and experiences to get to this point in consciousness. And so it is you are ready to be firm with yourselves. You are no longer the little babes of yesterday. You have grown beyond that point in consciousness. And it's well past time you did something with what you have received.

Good night.

AUGUST 28, 1975

Special Discourse - Class AAA1
Human Relations

Now we will unite in thought and motive as we speak forth our "Total Consideration" affirmation.

[The teacher and the students speak the affirmation in unison. Please see the appendix for that affirmation. After a short pause, during which Mr. Goodwin goes into a trance, the class continues.]

Greetings, students.

We have brought about this special class in order that you, as students who have already received so very much, may be inspired to yet greater effort in demonstrating the laws that have already been revealed to you. And so we shall begin this class with a discussion on human relations.

Before speaking on that, let us first view the teachings that have already been given in that respect. Some time ago we gave to you the functions of the second soul faculty of faith, poise, and humility; and those functions of that faculty being money, ego, and sex. And so it is that the triune rulers of the astral depths of hell represent what you call money, ego, and sex. They represent those functions because man has created with his mental consciousness the need thereof.

And so it is in human relationships, as man entertains in mental consciousness the need for one or all of those three functions, he comes under the control of the Law of Creation, known as duality, and is governed, his eternal soul, by the rulers of those depths. Man, in his sexual relationships, because it is governed and controlled by his mind and not free to be expressed by his eternal soul, man accepts and rejects the experience at the same time. A part of man in its rejection, another part of his consciousness in its acceptance causes man nothing but a continued misery and disaster.

When the thought concerning those functions is not permitted to be entertained by the human mind more than thrice at any given moment, then man has a fine opportunity to express and yet be free. The bondage of the functions, because they are entertained and controlled by the mental substance of hell, is revealed to man by the great magnetic pull of those functions.

The expression, in its pure and simple spiritual simplicity, designed by the Great Architect of the universe, is designed as a spiritual exchange of energy and soul amalgamation. But that does not exist for those souls who are bound by the need created by their mental substance.

How does man free himself from the bondage of his mind in those functions? Only through a constant and sincere prayer to the Divine Light that he may not only see the Light of eternal truth but that he may not be deceived by the illumination caused by the second center of your being, known as the fires of lust.

And so, my good students, whenever you have that experience, as you frequently do, then view what is really taking place. Because your soul has entered Earth under the control of the second center, known as the fire center of lust, whenever you have that expression, you are under the control and the influence of the experience at the time your soul entered your earthly body at the moment of conception. Therefore, the experience magnetically pulls you, your eternal soul, into the continued duality of creation until finally the day dawns in your eternal consciousness and you free your soul from it forevermore.

Should you, in your efforts, be sincere with your eternal soul and pray without ceasing for that freedom to see what is truly taking place at that time, then it is within the realms of possibility that you may rise to higher levels of consciousness. You will know when you have risen to higher levels of consciousness for you will no longer dictate how it is to be, when it is to be, and where it is to be, for you will have no thought nor concern. And then it will be guided by your eternal soul and you will be free.

My good students, have you not already had sufficient experience to realize the constant acceptance and rejection concerning that personal function? As a wise person once said, it is hell if you have it and it is hell if you don't. It is hell because, my good friends, your mind has taken that which belongs to the divine, eternal Intelligence.

Your soul left the divine Allsoul and when it left, it entered creation. Now when a soul enters into the dual Law of Creation, it separates in order to enter the duality of the law. That is known as the Law of Division and Multiplication, the law that governs form. And so it is, your soul, when it left the Allsoul, left a part of itself, and that other part of you, commonly referred to as a soul mate, is what your soul in truth is seeking to find. Because your mind knows it not and because it is not something created by mental substance, your little soul urges you ever forward to find your better half. If you concern yourself mentally with it, then you will be disturbed by it, for that that you insist on concerning yourself with takes control over your eternal soul.

The true purpose of expression is to release, as an instrument of the Divine, God's infinite, intelligent energy. Man has decided how God's energy will flow and because man has decided how it will flow, man is controlled by his own decisions.

My good students, much water must pass under the bridge before you will open your eyes and apply the spiritual laws that are so simple and true to all areas of your life. As you continue on in those functions, which are a part of your form, you will experience the pain and the pleasure thereof.

Some time ago we stated to our class to separate truth from creation. The separation of truth from creation is the separation of your eternal soul from the created tapes of your temporal mind. You are not the tapes you have accepted. You are not the tapes, so to speak, of mental experiences that you have rejected. But those tapes or experiences, rejected and accepted, offer to your eternal soul the necessary lessons to free you. My students, look wisely at your rejections, for those rejections are the very lessons that you need to free your eternal being. Look at them in the light of reason. Because they are your created rejections, they are your denials of God, his divine right of expression. It is your denials and your rejections that bind your eternal soul.

All of your acceptances lift your little soul to heavenly heights in the here and now. It is your denials and your rejections that are the chains that bind you to hell. The rulers of the depths of the abyss of darkness are rulers of judgment, and judgment is rejection. There is no judgment, my good students, in the Law of Total Acceptance. Judgment exists solely, wholly, and completely in the depths of hell, for judgment is rejection. And this is why you have what is known as heaven and you have what is known as hell.

Now a person may say, "Well, if I accepted everything, then where would I be?" My good students, how can you know? You've never done such a thing. God accepts everything, and where is God? In God's hands is all the universes. In God's hands is the smallest creature that crawls your Earth.

Now think and think more deeply of this journey of your eternal soul. You have already had so many lessons. You have already had so many, many experiences. Your soul is passing through the universes and you have come here to Earth. What are you doing with the lessons that face you? What are you doing with your own rejections of life? Those are the things, my students, to view. To view them, accept them, and move on through them. What is it, you must ask yourselves, that keeps you in your bondage? Is it not your own steps of justification? Is it not your own excuses? Is it not your own procrastinations that you may not face your true eternal being?

There is [not], and cannot be, any peace, true love, or harmony in sexual expression until your mind is taken out of it. Do not deceive yourselves, my children, surely your experiences are already without number. It is your mind that has taken control of that which belongs to God. And because your mind has done it, the dual Law of Creation is ever fulfilling itself.

The soul knows its own expression. And it knows what its mind, the created substance, is doing to it. And so the guilt rises within our own minds and the conscience sheds the light upon the path.

Where can man find peace when he spends so much time denying God? Where can man find truth or freedom when his mountains of rejections build greater and higher each moment that he spends in his own thoughts.

Look at the journey that has brought you through eons of time to this moment in consciousness. Look at the many lessons that you have already had. And think, my students, where you are and where you are going.

There's only one home. And you enter that home, your heaven within, by bowing that vehicle through which your soul is expressing, that vehicle called the human mind of judgment.

The steps down to the depths of eternal hell are known as the steps of judgment. The rail upon which you lean as you descend is the rail of pride. And so whenever you permit your mind to experience judgment because of pride, for judgment and pride are handmaidens to eternal hell, [you descend]. That is the true cause and the true problem with human so-called relationships.

Ascend the steps to a heavenly experience. But that, my friends, takes two ingredients: honesty with oneself and acceptance of God's divine, eternal right to the expression of all of life.

Good night.

SEPTEMBER 2, 1976

Special Private Class 1

[This class is a rather informal class, but it is representative of the type of classes that were given when students would meet with Mr. Goodwin in the kitchen of the temple for coffee, after the scheduled work had been completed. Many, many informal classes were given, but not many were recorded.]

Did you release it? *[The teacher may be inquiring about the tape recorder.]*
It's going.
OK. Fine.
Now we started to discuss, downstairs, when the question was brought up, we started to discuss money. Money is what we discussed. And I told you at that time that you had already been given that truth that time and money was one and the same. Because the others weren't present then. And therefore, that time, being an illusion, that is exactly what money is, an illusion.

[The church office and workshops were downstairs at the temple, while the recorded classes were generally held on the main floor. This conversation seems to have begun downstairs, before the recording began, with only some of the students present. The other students were working in other rooms of the temple. The teacher may be repeating the teaching for the benefit of the students who were not present when the teaching was originally given.]

Now what is an illusion, [Student S]? Do you know what an illusion is? Do you know how it's created?
By a judgment.
[Student R]? *[After a short pause, the teacher continues.]* The question is—
Well, I would say just by a thought. [Student R responds.]
By a thought.
Yeah.

Anything else?

It has to have a reference.

What is the law through which an illusion is given birth?

I don't know.

OK. [Student P]?

I would say—wouldn't it be just the power of belief and faith and the creative law. Because if you believe in something, then it's real. If you have a thought . . .

What is the law which is necessary in order to believe?

The creative law is the will, the will, the faith, the belief, in action. [Student P continues.]

And you have to accept before you can believe. [Student R remarks.]

Right. [Student P responds.]

OK. [Student G].

And I think it's the Law of Identity.

The Law of Identity. You cannot—the law of the birth of illusion is the Law of Identity, created by the thought of man. Now, you cannot have identity without the thought of I. So when you work to eliminate the thought of I, you are not identified with illusion. And when you're not identified with illusion, then you're not controlled by illusion. Do you understand that? *[The teacher addresses Student R.]*

Uh-huh.

So now, you know that in the teachings, [it] is recommended to work to free yourself from the thought of I. For only by freeing yourself from the thought of I can you free yourself from the mental Law of Identity and from the illusion of creation. Now as you, by the thought of I, establish the Law of Identity, you give birth, through the creative principle, to the illusion, whichever illusion it is that you are creating. And by so doing, you become bound by the illusion which is your own creation.

Now how does a person free themselves from the thought of I? That was already given to you in a class. [Student S].

By just redirecting the energy to something else.

Well, say that you have a stack of bills—

Uh-huh.

—and you feel emotional and a lot of pressure and etc. concerning this responsibility that you have. You would have to first think of you before you could have the feeling, wouldn't you?

Right.

Then all of the rest would follow—

Right.

—the created illusion. Correct?

Right.

All right. Now how would you free yourself from that experience and still have responsibility?

Well, like, reaffirming the truth that God is the true and only source of our supply.

That's a step towards freedom. What does that do?

That ...

What does it do for you in that moment?

It opens up the door for all these possibilities.

Ah! It opens a door of possibility beyond the judgments which the mind already has. Is that correct?

Right.

All right. Now you see the benefit of that step of declaration. It opens the door of possibility. Something beyond the limits of what information is already within the mind. Is that correct?

Right.

What does it take to make that step? What faculty has to be used in order to make that step to that declaration that God is the source of your supply? What is necessary?

Acceptance.

And? *[After a short pause, the teacher continues.]* What else is necessary?

Faith that it's there.

Faith in the declaration.

Right.

Uh-huh. So you already have faith. So it isn't something that you're trying to gain. So it takes a directing of that soul faculty.

Uh-huh.

And that takes on a new identification. Is that correct? Do you understand that?

Right. Uh-huh.

In other words, you begin to identify with something; you don't know what because it's beyond the mind. And because it's beyond the mind, it's beyond illusion. And being beyond illusion, it is the cause that you then begin to work with, and not the effect.

Now, you see, those are the steps of going beyond the illusion. You have to go beyond the mind. You already know what the mind has already offered you. Therefore, you can very clearly predict what is going to happen from past experiences of what the mind has to offer. You see, if you know yourself, your mind, then you know your tomorrows—

Uh-huh.

—as long as you permit yourself to identify with the illusion that is created by the thought of I, for you already know what your thought of I has to offer. Do you understand that, [Student A]? *[If Student A verbally responds, her response is not audible.]* Is there anyone who doesn't understand that? *[After a short pause, the teacher continues.]* [Student A]?

Hmm.

I couldn't hear you.

I'm not sure why they're doing this to me. [Student A remarks.]

Yes. Well, I didn't think that you did understand it, but do you know why you don't understand it?

Because my mind was wandering. [Student A speaks very quietly, almost in a whisper.]

Pardon?

Because I wasn't paying attention.

Do you know why you [weren't] paying attention? *[After a short pause, the teacher continues.]* What was the subject matter we were just through discussing here?

Money, faith, and acceptance that it's there.

Money, faith, and acceptance that it's there. But you did pay attention to know enough that that's what we're discussing?

Yes.

Right?

But that was when . . . [The last few words are difficult to accurately transcribe.]

Yes. Why do you feel that you didn't pay attention to the rest of the discussion?

Because my mind didn't want to hear the answer.

All right. Now, class, why do you think that our minds do not want to hear the answer? [Student R].

Because they will lose control. [Student R responds.]

They will lose control. What is it that will lose control?

The emotions—the levels of judgment will lose control of the soul through the emotions. Because the emotions are the, are what the levels use to maintain their control. So if whatever is being done is taken above the realms of the mental judgments, then they will no longer be in control of the effect.

There. Now do you see how very simple, how very simple it is and how very difficult we make it for ourselves? In this creative process of the illusions, each judgment is the law that binds us to the illusion. The identity, the thought of I, the identity takes us to it, gives it birth. Judgment keeps us in it.

Now, we were discussing, well, people, you know, you make out a budget. You know how much money, how much illusion, is coming to you. You know that. All right. Now because your mind says you know that, you are controlled, then—and all of your experience in that respect—to what your mind dictates that it knows. Therefore, what is actually taking place is a thought in the mind of yesteryear has grown to have full control over you.

Now, how does one get free of the control of these thoughts of yesterday, which have become strong judgments? By going beyond the mind. You cannot be free in mental worlds, for mental worlds, thought worlds, have form and, therefore, have limit. You cannot be free in form. You can only be free when you are no longer identified with form or the mental world.

Now, many people think that the physical world has form. The physical world has no form without the mental world. You see, you perceive what we understand is a physical world. You perceive it by a mental world. It is your mental world that gives it form. Now you think that a tree has a certain shape or size. Your mind sees it. It is your mind that makes it; that creates it. Therefore, the physical world does not have size, shape, or form. Only the mental world, which is perceiving your physical world, has size, shape, or form. Because your mental world creates that.

Yes.

Well, how is it, then, you get hit in the back of the head with a baseball when you didn't see it coming and you get knocked out? [Student R asks.]

Your mental world knocks you out. The sensation is not to your physical world, your physical body. You think your sensation is taking place in your physical body. Your sensation, as all sensation does, takes place in your mental body, not your physical body. So what you perceive, you perceive from sensation in your mental world.

How about the damage that it causes? [Student R continues.]

It only causes the damage that your mental world, through its thought, judges is damaged.

But the breaking of bone and such.

The breaking of bone and such is what the mental world views!

All right. [Student S] has a question. [Student R remarks.]

Because, you see—for example, it's just like in spiritual healing. If the mental world of the patient cannot make necessary adjustments in the mental world, then there is no so-called physical cure. The changes must take place in the mental world because the mental world is the only world of form, of limit.

Yes, [Student S].

I thought it might help [Student R], like the people that can walk on coals and not be burned, then they haven't accepted that in their mental world; so they don't—you know, there's no physical sign of it. But for us, if we did the same identical thing, we'd be burned.

Uh-huh. Very true. Same as walking on water. It's in the mind. Created by the mind. It is an illusion. Now I know that it is very difficult, in your mental world, in your minds, to make this step forward: that the physical world is not form or shape.

Now, here, the truth's been told for centuries: Beauty is in the eye of the beholder. But what does that mean to you? What does that mean to you? What does it mean to you, [Student R]?

Well, it— [Student R begins to speak.]

What does that great truth mean?

It just means that the person judges what he sees. Therefore, if he judges pleasant, it is pleasant.

And he can—

If he judges it's ugly, it's ugly.

That's right. *[Student R continues talking as the teacher speaks, but the student's words are difficult to transcribe.]* So it has nothing to do with a physical object that only exists in mental conception. It is your mind and its thought processes that conceives—

Yeah, because—

—that this is; that this exists. *[The teacher may be referring to a physical object, like, for example, his coffee cup.]*

It's only electrical impulses that go to the brain that make it in the first place. [Another student offers.]

It's what the mind does with the electromagnetic impulses that it receives that causes you to see an object with a shape or substance. This is why some people are able to walk through so-called solid matter. Solid matter is a matter, but it is formless and it is shapeless. And whenever the mind has fully accepted that, then you will be able to move through it. And not before. Yes, [Student Q].

So actually, a sickness, then, that we form as a sickness is all in the mental world.

It is in the mental world and must be worked on in a mental world. Absolutely. Definitely. But you must understand that the mind, through eons of evolution, has created an illusion that is very real to it, for its faith and its belief is so great. Yes, [Student V].

But in order to gain that acceptance, don't we have to work on, first, as, I think, as I understood, physically, mentally, and spiritually?

Yes. How do you work on it physically? Do you work on it physically by moving some physical object? Or do you work on it physically by moving some mental object which you believe is affecting a physical object? *[After a short pause, the teacher continues.]*

You see, you can pick the chair up and move it from there over to the corner. But unless you believe mentally that you are doing that, then, for you, you have not done it. You must first believe that you are doing it. And you can't believe you are doing it unless you're in the thought of I, which therefore follows your identity to this whole process of illusion. Yes.

In referring to the word beauty, *there's that exercise in* The Living Light *book. And I have been working on it, but so far, I haven't really been able to—perhaps I haven't said the word properly. But, by repeating it, say, thrice in the mind or twice in the mind and then thrice—*

Thrice.

—speaking the word forth. Is this to help us in that, as what we're talking about now?

Yes. Well, you see, it's been given in the classes several times. You must follow very carefully what this really means. "I," it begins with "I." "I speak my word." All right? Now what is that saying to you? You have identified, right?

Yes. [Student R responds.]

My word.

Yes.

"I"—begins with "I."

Uh-huh.

"I speak my word forth into the universe, knowing, *knowing* that it shall not come back to me void, but accomplish that which I send it to do." How do you do that knowingly?

Now, [Student Q] said earlier, you know, we were discussing budget and things, "Well, I *know* how much I have coming in." All right? How does she know it? What is that knowledge based upon? It is based upon experience that has been accepted. Would you agree?

Sure. [Student Q responds.]

Fine. Now when you say, "I speak my word forth into the universe knowing that it shall not come back to me void, but accomplish that which I send it to do," now how do you know that it's going to do that, unless in this realm of illusion you have created it? There's your key. Now if [Student Q] knew this great truth as she knows her budget, then she would speak her word forth into the universe and it would not return unto her void, as the same for everyone else.

You see how simple and clear it is?

But, you see, when we say, "I speak my word forth into the universe knowing that it shall not come back to me void, but accomplish that which I send it to do," it's in the computer and it takes a look around, in the mind, and says, "No, I don't know that at all, for I have no reference. None at all." And therefore, you speak your word and you say the statement and it does not happen.

So therefore, we must use the creative principle in order for that to work. We must use what has been given to you so many times, what is so very simple: image. Imagination. The doorway out of the mind into the great world of truth. The doorway. For that's the only way that that can become a truth for us in a world of illusion. This is why, you can take many years of study, many years of effort, but until you have created, in your world of illusion, these things, it cannot be.

Now a person who says, "Well, now I have—this is exactly what I get coming in. I know that." I agree that the illusion is in full control. I'm trying to show you, in a world of illusion, how to create illusions that are more beautiful and more harmonious and bring you more benefit. For the very same law that created the illusions that you now have, which you call reality, through the very same law, you may create that of your own conscious choosing.

But you must remember that you have to put equal energy, through the Law of Attention, into the birth of a new illusion that you have put into the illusion or illusions that you already have that are contrary to the new illusion that you are trying to create. Yes, [Student V].

In order to, say, to image something that you want to accomplish, is it necessary, like, in the Law of Creation that we should have, say, a dual law or a—

You have to put it into the now. All illusion is duality. All illusion. Truth is single and simple. All illusion is dual. Now when you image, you use this process through the door of imagination to go beyond this mental realm, this doorway—it's an actual doorway you go through—you have to put it into the present.

Not that something is going to happen; not that something is going to take place, but that something *is*. Now the reason that you need to put it into the present is so it can be created, and you can experience the effects of the creation in the building of the new illusion.

You see, if you have—and we all have—many, many thoughts in our mind that we know absolutely. Now when we know absolutely, then we know that we know we have really created a potent illusion. Therefore, you've got to work very hard if you want a new illusion. For it must have equal energy just to bring about a neutral balance in the mind. And if you want this new illusion to take over, then you've got to pour more energy in than the one that you already have. Yes, [Student Q].

So imagination or image, then, would be, like, you visualize it actually happening.

Yes. Visualization is one of the processes. It must take place—see, concentration is the key to all power. Therefore, it takes concentration to hold an image in your mind. For example, I see a pink polka-dotted elephant here. Now I have this elephant before me. I have created this elephant. For me, it exits. Now for anyone that is on the same level of consciousness at this moment that I happen to be on, they will see this pink polka-dotted elephant that I have just created. Now for me to keep that elephant in existence in that realm, I must use the power of concentration, you see. Now, contrary to popular belief, though concentration is placing your mind pointedly and fixedly upon the object of your choice, you can do other things. For example, I'm talking to you, but my elephant has not yet disappeared. Because I still have my mind fixed upon this elephant sufficiently to keep him in form. Do you understand?

Uh-huh.

All right. So when you are creating these things, you have to give it form and substance. Do you understand?

Yes.

In that realm. Otherwise, it dissipates, you see. Now you will notice whenever you have a real strong emotion about something—in fact, especially this time of year, they call it impulsive buying. Something just happens and comes over you, and you just have to have it. And every obstruction within the mind disappears in that moment in order to attain it, you see. So you must have, in the creative process, you must have the fullness of desire.

Now it might be, a person might say, "Well, I certainly don't have any desire to be on a limited budget." But, you see, that's the furthest thing from the truth. It is because it is so long ago that the desire set that thought and that form, you see, that it has consciously forgotten it. But there is desire that keeps energy going to it. It has taken on a new shape in the conscious mind. It's been covered over with a whole forest of obstructions. But when you clear the forest in the mind, you see, "Oh, yes. Yes, there was a desire connected with that judgment."

Now, you have to be still a moment and ask yourself what was it you experienced in your mind when we started to discuss the non-existence of a material, physical world; that it is only created by a mental world. The things that took place in your mind, the perplexities, the reactions. Because I sit here and I witness these reactions. All emotional. None really expressed, outside of what I discussed with [Student A]. What do you think it is inside of you that reacts to such a simple truth? [Student R]?

Well, my mind went racing around for reference, first.

Reference.

And the first thing I thought was how scientifically it's explained that we see. You know, the electrical-magnetic impulses on the brain and all that. Well, that's fine. But then it gets to a—

[This class was recorded on a sixty-minute audiotape cassette. At this point in the class, side A of the cassette ended, and the class continued as the tape was changed. Side B begins with the teacher speaking.]

Put the ninety-minute [cassette] in now.

OK. [Student R responds.]

Thirty minutes went by awful fast. Or a two-hour tape. All right. Then?

OK. So— [Student R begins.]

Yeah.

I, I sit here.

You see the recorder.

And I see the recorder and everybody else sitting here at least believes that they see the same recorder that I do. And . . .

But do they?

They believe they do.

But don't you believe that they believe they see it a little bit different than you?

I know that from experience that no two people see the same thing the same way.

All right, now fine. We even got a toe in the door here. We now admit that no two people see things the same way. Go ahead with your discussion of this material world.

Well, these things are racing through my head, when it was first mentioned that all form is merely an illusion.

Uh-huh.

That it doesn't really have form or substance.

Uh-huh. You're just now evolving to this class being given.

So—

Think of that.

Now, when that statement was made—

Uh-huh.

—my mind went through all those little trips. And I know that it dealt merely with perception. What I see as form is a perception.

I'd like to say something at this time. What you see as form is a conception.

All right.

It is something you conceive. Perception is what your soul views. Go ahead.

OK. Well, I didn't realize this.

There is a difference.

OK.

The soul perceives; the mind conceives. Now, does anyone know the difference between perception and conception?

Isn't conception something that, it's like with a judgment of? It has something with the thought. [Student P speaks.]

[Student R].

A conception is created through the creative principle. [Student R responds.]

And perception?

Perception is beyond it.

Well, all right. Now, we'll let you see what Webster has to say after a while.

OK.

You go ahead with your thoughts. When your mind received, you believed—

Yeah.

—a statement—

Uh-huh.

—that the material, physical world does not exist without the mental world.

Yeah.

It does not exist. It is only through the mental world that conceives it. Go ahead.

Yeah.

Which science is gradually, very slowly but surely proving.

But—

So-called material.

So I thought of those things and there was just a very small seed of acceptance.

Uh-huh.

But very small. But then the next thing, you made the statement regarding money and budgets. And when I began entertaining that thought, I looked, of course, for reference in my own situation. And the tapes rose and the emotions started to rise, and immediately when that happened, it just kicked out the whole works.

Now what does that—what does that prove to you?

Well, it revealed—

Identification.

—the level of control of a particular judgment.

Through i—

Through the identification of self.

I-den-ti-fi-ca-tion. Break the word down and you'll learn a lot. Go ahead. There's no such word as we-dentification. *[A few students laugh.]*

No.

There's only i-dentification.

Yeah. Well, that's what happened. And . . .

Didn't you find that a lesson in itself?

Yes, it was. It was very interesting [As Student R speaks, the teacher makes a comment that is difficult to transcribe.] *to feel it come up, because, I hope, gratefully, it went back down. But it didn't disappear, but, at least, it went back down. And—but it was interesting to see it happen.*

Uh-huh.

It showed the degree of irritation that the level felt at the mere thought of something beyond it.

Now, do you see how we're only affected by that which we identify with?

Yes.

You see. Now, if we did not identify *[The teacher gently taps the table.]* this table in our mind—

Uh-huh.

—then this table, for us, would not exist; and therefore, you would move through it. Because, for you, it would not exist. Now it does not exist just because you see it.

No, it exists because I've accepted its existence.

It exists because you have created it.

I have created the illusion of it. And I have accepted the illusion that I've created it.

You have accepted the illusion as a reality.

Yes. That I've—yes.

You see, the experiences we have in our lives, being illusions created by our mental world, affect us only to the degree that we have identified with them. Now why do these illusions only affect us to the degree that we have identified with them? *[After a short pause, the teacher continues.]* For example, in the discussion that the physical, material world is an illusion, there was a seed of possibility that it *could* be. You see?

Well, you see, there is some reference to—

Possibility.

—to the other side.

To the other side. But when, in the discussion, it got into the money—

Yeah.

—and budget and these illusions—

Uh-huh.

All emotion rose up.

Uh-huh.

And kicked out this possibility completely.

Uh-huh.

Because at the present time, you are overidentified with that particular illusion.

That's correct.

Now [Student A] is so overidentified with it that she just didn't even hear the class, she said. But when I asked her a few questions, oh, it registered. So, you see, our so-called problems, which, of course, is in the mental world—its illusions—affect us ever in keeping with our own identity. Hmm?

Yes, [Student H].

Well, then this explains this phenomenon that was discovered: when certain photographers thought that they could win the friendship of tribesmen in certain cultures, they'd take photographs of them. And the tribesmen could not identify anything in the picture. And they showed them their reflection—they could identify with a pool of water, but not in a photograph.

Uh-huh.

And . . .

Because they had never conceived it.

Right.

The tribesmen had never conceived it.

And also, then, [they] had never conceived their image of self as we know our image of self.

That is correct. That is correct. It'd never—that illusion, they had not yet created. They had not yet created that illusion.

Right. So then, therefore, they were not as attached to form as we are.

That is—not as attached to their form.

Right. Right.

Because they had not identified, through a creating illusion, to it.

Yes, [Student R].

Wouldn't it be more correct to say that they were not identified to our conception of their form? For the picture reveals our conception of it. But yet, their conception of their form is, maybe, altogether different than we see them.

No, the conception of their form does not have the rigid stability of our conception of our form. Because we have identified, through reflection—

Uh-huh.

—with this illusion. We keep building this illusion.

Uh-huh.

We look in mirrors and we look in any things that reflect back to us this illusion. And therefore, it has this great effect upon us.

Uh-huh.

It does not have effect—the tribesmen, the primitives, they don't stand at a pool of water and look at their reflection.

Uh-huh.

You see, they've never been known to do that, you see. They do not have that created illusion. You see, when they look in a pool of water, they may see the fishes passing by or the reflections of the tree, maybe possibly even themselves. But that is taken into a general reflection. Do you understand? There isn't the "I" identification. The so-called civilized world has the "I" identification with the reflection, you see.

You see, remember in *The Living Light* book, he finally came and he thought that he'd reached the, [in] this golden chariot, he reached the Gates of Truth. And what did he see, but a body of water: it was only a reflection. You see, long ago way back in 1968, you were given the simple truth we're discussing today. Eleven years later. Eleven years later. It's being told in different ways. Again, it's being told, you see. But the same truth was given that long ago: the reflection.

Now you were also given that truth is individually perceived. As long as you are in the mind, as long as you are identified with self, as long as there is an "I," your truth will always be individually perceived. Because, you see, the soul perceives, and it perceives through the limit of the vehicle through which it is expressing. So truth is individually perceived. If you only let this much light through your window, then that's all the light that can get in. But if you pull your drape *all* the way open, then *all* the light can get in. But you can't pull the drape *all* the way open until you free yourselves from what you believe that you know.

I will have a little more coffee, [Student S].

You see? I'm trying to show you that we are in the mind, we're in the thought of I, God only knows, much more often than we're out of it. And therefore, we are moving, breathing, and living in an illusion. But this illusion can be a beautiful illusion. It does not need to be a difficult and struggling illusion. As he said long ago, "Dreamer, dream a life of beauty before your dream starts dreaming you." Now, our dream starts dreaming us—in other words, we become the victim of that that we have dreamed. Now, we become the victim of that that we have dreamed when the dream, you see, [when] the dream takes control.

Now what do we mean about the dream and the dream taking control? For example, if you say, "Well, now I *know* that that's exactly what is," then that that is saying that is the dream! Do you understand? That's the dream. That's not you with all the possibilities beyond limit.

Possibility is beyond limit. Do you understand? Now because possibility is beyond limit, then there is nothing that your mind can say that it knows and that is absolutely true. Because if it does, then that is the dream created by the I, the identification, which created the experience and experiences, returning to you and speaking through you and has you as its victim.

It's like a person saying, "I can't change." There is a dream that you have dreamed that you can't change. And whenever you say you can't change, then that old dream is speaking through you. And you are bound and you are in bondage and you are totally identified with the illusion created by your own mind.

And so you're given many, many affirmations, which are stepping-stones to step beyond the mental world into the doorway, which is imagination, to bring back to you new illusions.

Now, you see, because what you call the spirit world—the essence of life is the spirit world. The essence of life itself. You must go through this doorway of imagination to enter the essence of life that you may bring back with you the essence, the necessary ingredient, to create a new illusion for your life's experience. Yes.

I'm not clear how you can image without dictating. [Student G speaks.]

It's very simple, [Student G]. You must dictate in order to image, in order to enter the doorway of imagination. But, you see, as you enter that doorway, this is where you enter into the Light essence, the cause of all things.

You see, for example, you come into this world. You bring with you a mental body. Now this mental body can already speak. It already has the knowledge of untold eons of evolution. But it is limited by its new illusion. And its new illusion is a little, teeny physical body. And so it tries to speak, and the larynx, the tongue, and everything isn't developed yet. And so the words do not come out. It tries to run, and this illusion isn't yet ready to run. It has to go through the illusion of a growth in a so-called physical world. Yes.

In relation to [Student G's] question, if a person images, imagines— [Student R speaks.]

Can you image without an I?

No.

Right.

The thing is, it is a mental—the image, whatever the image may be, is a mental form with limit.

But, don't you see, you must have the essence to bring the illusion into reality in your life.

I don't think we're talking on the same thing.

We are. But you go ahead.

When, when we imagine something, it is a form with limit. And we may go to the limits, but not beyond the limit.

You can only go beyond the limits when you leave the world of illusion.

But you cannot leave the world of illusion in an imag—in an—in something you have imagined because it is . . .

I said earlier and I'll say again, imagination is the doorway, the doorway to the world of spirit, to the essence itself. It is *not* the world of spirit. It is *not* the essence itself. But it is the doorway. Now what does a doorway mean?

I accept that. It means a passage, an opening into something else. But it's beyond the limits of the illusion.

It is the essence of the illusion. It is the—

Can you explain that? [Student R speaks simultaneously with the teacher.]

It is the essence that gives anything life. *[After a short pause, the teacher continues.]* All right, we'll try to make it a little more clear for you. You came to Earth.

Uh-huh.

You came with a mental body.

Uh-huh.

It had gone through multitudes of experiences.

Uh-huh.

And you entered the little embryo.

Uh-huh.

And your mind slowly but surely, through a thought of I, began to identify with a new illusion.

Uh-huh.

And as you identified with this new illusion, you became more constricted, more limited.

Uh-huh.

And nine months later, approximately, you came out and your little eyes opened to this new illusion that you had created.

Uh-huh.

Do you understand?

Uh-huh.

All right. So from one bondage, you left to enter another one.

Uh-huh.

Right?

Uh-huh.

All right. Now as you move out of the I, out of the bondage that you now have in your illusion, you pass through the doorway of imagination, you enter the total lack of I, of identification. You are formless and free Spirit. Then you return, you understand, and in the doorway itself, the I rises and you identify with your new illusion, the one that you create in the doorway of imagination.

Now, you see, entering the doorway of imagination and entering the essence of life is not something that takes place just because you pass from this illusion of the physical world. This takes place many times in your life and you're not even aware of it. Do changes come into your life?

Sure. Some changes do come into my life. It's inevitable.

Why is it inevitable?

That's the Law of Evolution.

All right. Now, you tell me that changes do come into your life and bring you new experiences?

Yeah.

All right. Now these new experiences—do you agree?—are an effect, not a cause, but an effect of a new illusion that you have created?

Yes.

Ah! How did you get this new illusion? How did you come about this new change that brought you new experiences, that brought you new illusions?

Because there's still reference. You see, there is reference all around.

Ah, there's still—now, just a moment. There is reference and associated reference.

Yes.

And so, the silver thread runs throughout eternity. When you are here, identified, through the Law of I, identity, with the illusion that you presently have, to stay in that space and create a new illusion is very difficult. Would you not agree?

Uh-huh.

You have to enter—perhaps you might call the—you might relate better if I say enter a world of fascination. There you can create all kinds of new things, though they are associated to old things.

Uh-huh.

Right?

Uh-huh.

All right. Now the truth of the matter is we'd rather work with the realm of imagination, but it's the same process that's taking place. So you move on up into this realm of imagination and here, through the laws of association, you create new illusions, though there are similarities to past experiences, correct?

Uh-huh.

All right. You cannot bring changes into your life without the thread of association.

Uh-huh.

Because it is contrary to the nature of the mental world of illusion. You must have something to tie it to.

Uh-huh.

And so, have you not received in the, in the teachings, "Broaden your horizons" [and] "Expand your consciousness"?

Right.

You understand?

Uh-huh.

All right. Now if you have a little, small house, you have a reference to this small house.

Uh-huh. But you can imagine a bigger one.

But without the power of imagination, you cannot enter a bigger one. For if you have a little house and you are identified, through the Law of I, to the little house, then a big house cannot come your way. You may think about a big house, but you will never enter a big house until you move—no matter how little you may move—until you move out of the locked-in identity with the little house that you are already in. Therefore, you see that some people, they move ahead and some people, they just don't seem to move at all. They are moving, but they are moving so slow you can't see it. Do you understand?

Everyone is changing their illusion. Some are changing their illusions at a much more rapid speed than others. But everyone is in the process of changing their illusions. Now, usually a person, in the process of changing their illusions, becomes very emotional, gets very upset, and it takes a terrible toll upon their life. The benefit, the benefit to changing your illusions with a greater rapidity or greater speed than changing very slowly, very slowly, is very simple: in the slow changing process of your illusions, a great deal of energy is dissipated. Energy that could be so wisely used to create the new illusion.

Now, for example, like with [Student G]. I have spoken to her and spoken to her and spoken to her about getting this china painted. *[Painting the china was a spiritual responsibility that Student G had merited. When more formal dinners were held at the Serenity temple, students would dine on that hand-painted china. Each set of china, which included dinner plate, salad plate, cup, sauce, demitasse, and dessert plate, featured one type of flower. There were twenty-five complete sets.]* Now she said to me today, she was in some kind of space where it took no time at all. She couldn't believe she got so much accomplished. What does this prove? It's simply another proof that it's an illusion of the mind. It's not a physical movement of a brush and etc. Do you understand? It's our conception and our judgments, you see.

The slower we move to make changes, the more energy we dissipate to the emotional realm of all these forms created by past judgments. There's the difference. That that is to be done, let it be done right and quickly. Now you understand what they mean when they say he who procrastinates is lost. Lost in the sense that in the process of thinking about what is to be done, the energy to get it done is dissipating in the thought illusion.

When you decide to do something, do it well and do it quickly. If you permit your mind to think about it, then you will utilize a thousand percent more energy in finally getting the job done than if you did it quickly. Surely, this house is a demonstration of that great truth. *[The teacher refers to the Serenity temple, which was built with remarkable rapidity.]*

Any questions? Yes, [Student H].

OK. There are certain people in our society, whom we have branded as mentally ill because they live in a world of delusion. That's the term that's been put on them.

Yes.

They—in other words, they create roles from themselves. They frequently change those roles. Many of them are quite happy that way. And for them, that's real. Well, what I'm about to ask is, is the age-old question: Are they crazy or are we?

What is the difference between illusion and delusion? Do you know?

No, I don't.

Do you know? *[The teacher now addresses Student R.]*

Delusion was defined in this month's Sentinel. [The *Serenity Sentinel* was a monthly magazine that was edited by Mr. Goodwin and published by the Serenity Spiritualist Association.] *And it is illusion that man has taken . . . how was it put? I don't recall the exact quote.* [Student R responds.]

Someone get the *Sentinel* and let's—[Student G], do you remember the quote?

I don't.

Please get the *Sentinel*. Let's get the quote exact. Because I would like to know if anyone knows the difference and then we'll finish up our class because about forty minutes have passed.

It's not the one that's been printed already. It's the one being printed. [Student R calls out to Student G as she leaves to retrieve a copy of the *Serenity Sentinel*.]

It's the one just typed. [Student G responds.]

Yeah. [Student R acknowledges.]

Ah, yes, put it on pause.

[The tape recorder was paused at this moment.]

Yes.

Delusion, the definition, Living Light definition of illusion is—or delusion is, "When man takes illusion and uses it for his personal self-gain, it is known as delusion." So an illusion— [Student R reads the definition, which was published in the *Serenity Sentinel* of January 1980, Volume IX, No. 1.]

Now—

—taken for self-gain is delusion.

No, please read it correctly, taken for personal self-gain.

Yeah.

Now think. Do you see the difference between illusion, which we're in, and delusion?

I see—when he puts his stamp of ownership on it. When he puts his stamp of ownership on it, it becomes a delusion. Is that correct? [Student R responds.]

What does everybody else think? [Student H], you asked the question.

Yeah, I would agree to that.

And what is the stamp of ownership?

It's total self. [Student R responds.]

One word. Begins with *d*.

Denial. [Student R again responds.]

Denial! And so, the stamp of ownership in a realm of illusion is the denial of the right of anyone else to have it and creates what we know as delusion. Now you have your answer.

Now, I'm trying to reference this to a student who recently went through experiences. [Student R continues.]

Yes.

And to my mind it was a delusion.

Take a look at the tape. How much tape do we have left? It's a very important class.

We've only got a minute or two. [Student R responds.]

Well, take a look. I don't—I think we got more than that.

Is there, [Student S]? I can't see it from here. [Student R asks.]

It's almost gone. [Student S confirms.]

Well, what's all that tape right there?

One is backwards. [Student P remarks.]

Well, the counter— [Student R remarks.]

Yeah, but there's this much tape over here left.

If it started at zero it should be— [Another student comments.]

Oh, and we're running— [Student S remarks.]

It's going from here—

We're running it from right to left. [Student R comments.]

You run it from here over to here.

Uh-huh. [Student S remarks.]

So how much is left on this hub over here?

Almost none. [Student S responds.]

Stop the thing. Put it on pause and let's look at it. [Student R declares.]

[The sounds on the recording suggest that the recording was stopped. Then, the recording continues.]

Right. It always goes [the way] the arrow goes. This is a wonderful class. It's very informal, but it's a very important class. It's not going to be edited. No, there's no reason to. Go ahead. You understand now the difference between delusion and illusion?

Yeah. Yeah. [Student R responds.]

You see—

The table is an illusion. [Student R interrupts the teacher.]

Yes, and we're in an illusion.

But my table is a delusion. [Student R declares.]

[The recording of this class ends at this point. Although all recordings were searched thoroughly in an attempt to locate the remainder of this class, no additional recording was located.]

DECEMBER 9, 1979

Special Class 1

I realize to some of you this is the first time you've been to our classes and I will share with you what the Spirit gives to me in reference to this philosophy.

Now I am happy to announce, before we start this special class today—is there anyone who can't hear me?—before we start this special class today that our classes will resume on Thursday nights here at the house. They will be limited to the people present, who wish to attend them. There will not be the set fee of $150, which has always been our policy for our classes. It will be a donation. Classes will begin as soon as the students and friends of the church are able to get the necessary tables and stools together so they can begin. So, of course, it's entirely up to you people. [Student S] and [Student Q] will explain that. Because there will not be a $150 set fee, the cassettes will be available, of course, for purchase. The classes will not be available to the public. They are definitely limited to the people present who wish to attend. However, attendance is a regular process. No one is allowed to be in and out of class. So, while classes are in session, unless prior arrangements are made, due to work for their livelihood or to actually calling from the hospital because of so-called illness, no other excuses are acceptable. And people who are attending class will not be able to resume in that semester unless it is work or illness in a hospital.

Now we will begin our special class for today.

Many of you are aware of the various sayings in what we call The Serenity Game. One of which is, "A half a soul with God is better than no soul at all." And, of course, many students have wondered, What could a half a soul possibly be? When you understand the laws of creation, which are division and duality, then you will understand that a soul in creation, to God the Infinite, is a half a soul. Now what does that really mean? We understand that we are in truth formless, free Spirit. The only time we become form is through what is called the Law of Identity. Now it is the thought of I which is the birth of the Law of Identity. Without identity, there is no form.

Now the benefit of making the daily effort to gain some control of our mind is that we may experience the peace that passeth all understanding. Now in order to have that experience, we must first free our self from the Law of Identity, which is the Law of Limit, which is the Law of Form, which is the Law of Creation.

Now we all know that there is, and we have experienced that in our lives, that there is something that seems to be missing. Our minds know that the power that sustains the mind is something beyond the mind, and the mind is not able to conceive it. The difference between conception and perception is the difference between the spiritual essence and the mental substance.

Now if you feel that I'm talking too fast, do not be concerned, for it is being taped for your benefit. *[Some students may have been taking notes.]*

Out of the formless, free Spirit, there is what is called a movement or motion. Now to understand that which we call void, we have to be freed from mental activity. It is not possible to experience peace as long as there is activity in a mental world.

Now we are all seeking something. The moment that we find the something that we're seeking, we are seeking something else. Because the moment that the mind gets it, the mind goes to work to get something else. The mind is never satisfied. Our mind can never ever experience fulfillment. It only experiences, by its very nature, the constant gathering and [garnering] of information and things. Because it cannot gather the very thing that sustains it, it can never ever experience fulfillment. That does not stop the mind from seeking that something that it knows is missing for it.

In all of our life's experiences, we must understand someday that a thought is the birth of a law. Now as we continue to place our attention upon any thought of our choice, we increase, for us, the law and the destiny that we must follow. For example, we already know that there are times in our life that a thought enters our mind; it repeats itself in our mind, and we cannot seem to be free from it. That experience, which happens to us rather often, reveals to us the lack of control we have over the mental world.

Now we understand that thoughts are forms, but we've yet to understand that law is form, for law is limit. Now when we, in our evolution, identified, when we awoke to the mental world, the first thing offered in a mental world is the Law of Denial. Now the Law of Denial is the Law of Destiny. And what is the Law of Denial? The Law of Denial is not the I; it is the thought of I, for that that limits denies in order to limit. And because that which limits denies and is the Law of Destiny, we have, through a lack of understanding and awareness, become the victim of the Law of Duality, called creation.

Therefore, we are experiencing here, this moment, in this life what is known as half a soul. Now we say to our self, if we are expressing what is known as half a soul, Where is the other half? Well, the other half is when the faculties of our soul become in perfect balance with the functions of our body (mental and physical and astral), then we experience, in that amalgamation, a whole, complete soul.

Now soul, of course, has form in the sense of awareness to the mind. It is when the mind forgets who is the ruler in our universe that we become the half a soul, governed by the laws of creation. Of course, it is in our best interest, and I'm sure we will all agree, to be free from the laws of creation, for the laws of creation are the laws of give and the laws of take. The laws of creation are the laws of an eye for an eye and a tooth for a tooth.

When we fell, what they call in many religions and philosophies, the fall from grace—the fall from grace, so-called, is nothing more or nothing less than the thought of I, which established the mental world of creation over the formless, free world of the Divine Spirit which we are. When we reach that state of consciousness, when our soul expresses fully when we are in creation, no longer a part of creation—for we are a part of creation when we identify with it. Now to be in creation, to use creation for the vehicle for which it was designed and to express through it without the bondage of it, we must make the effort to be free from the thought of I, for the bondage that we experience only takes place when we permit our mind to think of the I. That does not annihilate the I, but it does remove control of the mental world over our eternal being. For example, without the illusion, as creation is an illusion, without the illusion of the thought of I, man is freed from all duality. Man is no longer experiencing lack for he cannot experience limit.

Whenever you entertain the thought of I, you experience fear. Now we understand in this philosophy that fear is the mind's control over the eternal soul. You cannot experience fear without the thought of I. It is not possible to experience fear without that illusion. That illusion is absolutely necessary to experience fear. Now whenever we permit ourselves to think of ourselves, we experience fear because that illusion, those judgments, which are experiences of past events, use as their defense what we know as fear.

Man does not make change readily not because he does not want to make change, but because he fears what his mind calls the unknown. Now when the mind experiences that which, to it, is unknown, it faces a choice: it must choose either to remain in control in a mental world or to, what most minds would say, take the chance, the possibility of something happening that it cannot control.

My good friends, stop and think. You all have experiences and circumstances, you call [them]. Already your mind is not able to control them. We are already, moment by moment, having experiences that we permit our minds to say is beyond our control—"That's the way the economy is. That's just the way the situation is."—until we start to apply the Living Light Philosophy, which clearly teaches and demonstrates the Law of Personal Responsibility: that everything that happens to us is caused by us; that we are constantly setting ourselves up to prove how right we are. We are constantly experiencing one disaster after another so that—you see, my friends, it is not important to the mind whether you experience disaster or its opposite. What is important to the mind is that it prove to you that it is right. Because if our minds do not make the effort to prove to us how right we are, we will not long permit our minds to stay in control. Therefore, it is our mind, as clever and devious as our minds are, that set us up repeatedly with failure or success; it is not important—only important that it prove to us that we are right. I assure you, my good friends, anyone that has to prove to themselves that they are right are [is] serving a realm of consciousness that can never bring any good.

It's like a person asking someone to prove God to them. You cannot prove that which is. And that is why truth needs no defense, for truth does not have want, need, or desire. That that is does not need. Therefore, that that is, being truth, you cannot defend. It is foolhardy to waste your energy to try to defend that which cannot be defended.

Our minds express our opinions. Our minds express our judgments. Our minds are filled with facts. And they serve a purpose in a mental world. Without our minds, our eternal being could not express in this the mental world.

You see, my friends, we think, our minds, that this is a physical world. Because our minds have made that judgment, for us, we experience physical obstructions, for we have established the Law of Identity and, therefore, must serve the law that we alone have established.

Some time ago we shared with you that simple truth that, "Man is a law unto himself. Therefore, what are you doing with the law that you are?" Well, we all know, of course, what we are doing with the law that we are: we are serving the obstructions that we identify with.

Some of us have had the experience of people walking through walls or walking on fire, and they have no harm done unto them. It is a very simple process. It is what the individual identifies with. He who sees the obstructions in life shall never find the way because the law is impartial. When we identify with an obstruction, we become the obstruction. It's like a man and his wife. As long as the wife, or the husband, identify with the obstruction that they view in the other, the day is guaranteed, by the Law of Identity, that they will be, for them, the obstruction to all good that is waiting for their experience.

Whenever we place—there is a part of us in consciousness where peace reigns supreme. That part of our consciousness is the Law of Harmony. It is when we place form in that space in consciousness that we begin to serve the Law of Form, known as creation.

Now we place, at various stages of our evolution, different forms in that space where peace passeth all understanding. We place the form of a wife or a husband. We place a bank account or the lack thereof. We place food or the lack thereof. We place many forms at various times in our evolution in that space of harmony. And in so doing we pay a very dear price. Sometimes people in their marriages and relationships, they will keep a form, the form of the person, in that space for X number of years, then they will divorce. And they will feel better until the next form comes along and takes the same space in consciousness.

That is a mental world in its effort to interfere with what we truly are.

We all realize, I'm sure, that in our great evolution, for we have evolved through many planets and many times, we are not a new soul except, most of us, to this particular planet. We have come to this planet, the fifth planet, to learn once again the Law of Faith, for we have fallen from the grace of divine harmony. The only time we fall from that grace is when we permit that illusion, that thought of I, to take control in our mind.

Now ofttimes a person will say they've had a great problem. And they just went to sleep and they woke up with the answer. They were fortunate for in their sleep they lost that illusion, and in losing that illusion, they found the solution. And so it is, of course, with all of us. As we make the effort to encourage our self in our daily efforts, be rest assured, things get better for we get better.

That that is around us, that that affects us, we must understand someday, is that that we are in rapport with. So all we have to do, to know what is controlling us at any given moment, is to become aware of what affects us. If the trees affect you, then they control you. If people affect you, then they control you. If you have limited it to one or two people, then they become your god. Now those are known, throughout time, as the false gods with clay feet, for they are the gods that have been created in a mental world.

The lessons in life that we have to learn are not nor have they ever been limited to the few short years that we spend here on this Earth planet.

Stop and think of the various emotions and experiences you have had since you were informed that there would be a special meeting here at the house, for there would not be a church service this Sunday. *[This class was held at the Serenity temple on Sunday morning, at the time when devotional services were normally held at the American Legion log cabin.]* As we came closer to the hour and closer to the day, various emotions rose up in the consciousness of many people. Not because of being here at this house, but because there was a change in routine. And so it is, my friends, that we experience our trauma whether we move from one house to another or we change our particular dining habits. Or any change that takes place, we must pay the price with our emotional realm, which is our magnetic realm, because of what is called attachment to the fruits of action.

If you want to know how attached you are or are not to anything, remove it from your consciousness and you will soon find, in the effort to remove any form, any object, you will soon find the degree of attachment. And the degree of attachment that we have permitted our self to make in anything is also the degree of control that the thing, the form, the person, has over us. None of us, of course, appreciate an awakening of things, of people controlling us.

We all know deep inside our self that we are formless and free. Whether we call it a spirit or anything else is not important. We do know we are formless and we do know we are free. And because we do have that inner knowing deep inside of us, we are constantly doing whatever our minds permit us to do to experience that formless, freedom and truth that we are. The only sadness is our minds cannot give it to us. Our minds can only go out into creation to gather and to garner, to do this and to do that and always be left empty after the harvest.

So what, of course, is the alternative? If you say God, well, *God* means one thing to one mind and I can assure you that *God* means something else to some other mind. And the meaning of *God* in our mind is in a constant process of change. If we give God the credit for bringing the good and we experience what we judge to be good, then God is great. But God help God if we don't get what we want when we want it. Now those are the gods of creation; those are the ones that our minds have created. And

I can assure you, from forty years of experience, they exist in a mental world in which we are moving and breathing. They give a little and they take a lot. Stop and think. It's a very poor bargain that we have put our self into, for I can assure you they take a lot more than they ever give. And that's the way it is in that realm.

But above and beyond that is possible for all of us in this moment. It's not something we're going to get by doing certain things. It's something that we really are when we stop long enough and we are in a moment of stillness to experience.

It's like our health, the effect of the Law of Harmony. Whenever you have what you call disease, known in truth as discord, How does one free themselves from disease, which is the effect of discord? Well, it's quite simple: you must move to the opposite of what is called discord or disease. And what is the opposite of discord or disease, but harmony. And how does man attain harmony? The body cannot move without the activity of the mind. Without activity of the mind, it is not possible for the body to move. Therefore, to attain a healing of discord or disease, one must experience the greatest power in the universe: and that power to our minds is known as concentration. When we are perfectly still, when there is no movement, then the mind, you see, is stilled.

Remember, become aware of your breath, for without your breath, you cannot think. So when you hold your breath, your thought is nonexistent. It is totally and completely dependent upon movement. So when you are perfectly still, when you breathe not, then you are in the Law of Harmony. And so when you place yourself in the Law of Harmony, in those moments you are healed. But the healing does not last unless great effort is made. Because, you see, my friends, you take 5 degrees or 5 percent, say, of healing to 95 percent of disease. You have to work at it. You have to make the effort every day in every way.

When you find, in creation, experiences that you feel you no longer can bear, become the observer that you may not be the observed. But one cannot become the observer until one is freed from the Law of Identity. When you free yourself from the Law of Identity, you, in that moment, become the observer and are no longer the observed.

I know, and everyone that has animals know, that they have the same thing that man has: it's called self-conscious. Now none of us like to entertain the thought that we're being watched, but being watched we are, twenty-four hours day and night. Oh, how wonderful it would be if it was only the eye of eternity that watches us, but it's much more than the eye of eternity. Say, for example, you have an animal and you feed the animal. What happens to the animal? The animal, his mind, becomes dependent upon you for the source of his or her supply. And so the animal watches whenever it has desire for sustenance. And anyone who has animals knows that very well. It has a much better time clock than all the clocks man has devised. The animal knows. It has a desire for food. Its little mind goes click, click, and it looks for you and it watches.

Now, my friends, let's go to thought. We have a thought; say that we think, "Oh, it's a nice day. Yes, I [will] go to the beach." Is it a new thought? Of course, it's not a new thought, for it is a strong desire. It means that past experiences have reinforced the thought. Now we say, "Why, there's nothing wrong with that thought. I have a thought to go to the theater. And so there's nothing wrong with that thought." It is not a right or wrong that we are discussing; it is what we are doing that we are discussing.

So we have a thought and we feed *[The landline telephone rings.]* —let it ring—we have a thought and we feed a desire. And so— *[The telephone continues to ring.]* Just take it off the hook, please. *[The teacher addresses a director.]* You disconnected it first, didn't you? Somebody's on the other line. Just hang it up and then leave it off. Leave the receiver off. *[After a short pause, the teacher continues.]*

So we understand now that we have a thought and in the thought we feed a desire. All right. We understand that in some realm of consciousness somewhere that is some type of a form. It is the form that we have created in our mind. Now that form we have mothered and fathered, of course. And so we follow the form and we go to the theater, we go to the beach, we do this, or we do that. And so the form that we have created in a mental world is fed. It gets some sustenance. Like the dog who watches; [he] has the desire to eat and watches the person that usually feeds him. And so the form we have created is fed.

And then it comes the next day. It's hungry again and it wants itself fulfilled. And we say, "No, we can't go to the theater today. You'll have to wait." Unfortunately, however, we have not separated, yet, truth from creation; we don't realize that this thought rising in our consciousness is a form that we have given birth to. And so that gets pushed out [and] suppressed by our mind. And it rises the next day and maybe the next week and the next week. And it appears to us that this desire is getting to be almost a compulsion; that we must, *we must* fulfill it.

Now we think, unfortunately, that that is some free choice that we are making. No, we have already made the free choice. We chose to go to the theater or do this or do that. We already made that choice. The form has already been created. It is hungry and it needs energy. And because it's the child that we created, it goes to its creator to be fed. And so it watches us day and night. As it gets more and more hungry, from a lack of being fed, we begin to experience this compulsion and this possession that we've *got* to do this or we've *got* to do that. And if we don't do it, we become not only frustrated but we become an emotional wreck.

Now is that, I ask you, free choice? No, it is bondage. There is something watching us. All of the forms we have created are waiting to be fed. Because there is a lack of controlling our mind, it entertains a multitude of thoughts and forms. They become great armies before we're five years old, demanding their sustenance. As the dog watches his master when it registers a need to eat, so the forms we have created watch us whenever *they* decide they're hungry.

Now, my friends, where can peace be when there are so many demands upon our vital body, when there are so many forms that we not only have already created but there are so many forms that moment by moment we continue to create?

Now we face the Law of Evolution, which we all know is the Law of Change—[Student M], please, no sleeping—which we all know is the Law of Change. What are we going to do when these forms of yesterday—they are created by our mind. They have all of the intelligence of our mind. They have access to our total mind. And they take a look, and they see that we are just about to create a new form. They rise up and they look and they know, because they have all the intelligence of our mind, they *know* that energy that they desire for their sustenance is now going to be directed to a new form, to a new army. And so it's called the war within.

And yet change, the Law of Evolution, is inevitable whether we like it or not. And so we can clearly see, clearly, the greater the struggle and difficulty for us to change, simply reveals the strength of the armies that bind us to yesterday.

And your church and your school has offered, ever since its beginning, change upon change upon change. It is in a constant process of change. For without its effort to introduce, to sustain, and to maintain this constant process of change, its people cannot be free. And so we find one trauma after another. We find what we call in this philosophy the forces of the emotions.

Remember, the more you suppress desire, the more the armies, someday, will rise, and you will indeed be its victim for a long time to come. Never suppress desire. Educate or fulfill desire, for your mind is dealing with the Divinity. It is dealing with the divine expression, which is the expression of God, the Power itself. And your mind, and no mind, is greater than the very power that sustains it.

How can man educate, if not fulfill, the multitude of desires that he entertains? It's simple. It's a word known to all of us as *communication*. Why do you think we have such great difficulty in communicating? Because when you communicate, you reveal. And when you reveal, your armies become defenseless. Now by your armies, I mean the armies of all humanity. We all have thoughts. We all have desires. So we all have the armies [that] the ancient philosophies taught so many centuries ago. You reveal when you communicate.

Whether you communicate truth or falsehood is not important to the principle of communicating, for in communicating you reveal, and the light within shall rise. As truth crushed to earth shall rise again, so through communication are you freed.

Now we know, most of us here, that exposure frees the soul. Without communication, there is no exposure. And so you find in the world, in your world here today, people with great difficulties in communicating. It is because we have become the victims of the armies that control us that we reach a stage in consciousness that we rarely grunt a morning hello, let alone a full sentence of communication. Think, my friends. Let us also, in our understanding and in this class, let us also look to the bright side if our minds have judged it looks so gloomy.

No, *religion* means, in the ancient Greek term, it means to bind, to bind back. Now we are interested, in this church and in this philosophy and in this school, to free our self from bondage. We already have faced the bondage that we have, whether it's the bondage to a judgment that wants us to sleep, at whatever time it is this morning—and I'm so happy to have classes that I can have my eyes wide open because I can see very clearly, and I don't have to rely upon the Spirit to tell me your chairman's asleep. But let us wake up! You see, my friends, it's not our soul that is asleep. That is not sleeping. It's ever awake. It does not sleep. There is no sleep to our soul. Do you know why there's no sleep to our soul? *[After a short pause, the teacher continues.]*

Our soul does not experience satisfaction. It is our mind that sleeps in satisfaction; it's never our soul. And believe me, no one is ever satisfied for long. It's not possible. You're fortunate if you can experience satisfaction for a maximum of five minutes because it doesn't last any longer. And if you think satisfaction lasts longer than five minutes, you have not yet awakened to the demonstrable truth that you are only reviewing an event that has passed.

So satisfaction, friends, is not where it is, because you'll never have enough. No one ever did. Take a look at how we dine in life. We eat and eat and eat and eat and eat. And then we feel, oh, we're so stuffed. And then we go and eat again. So, you see, even our eating habits prove to us we're never really satisfied.

The human mind is an empty vessel that we are constantly trying to fill, that has no bottom. There's no bottom to that vessel. We are constantly pouring energy into that vessel. We are constantly pouring all these new forms and thoughts, and then we have all of these thoughts and forms of yesterday demanding their sustenance.

You know, I would much prefer, myself, to be constantly watched by one single eye of eternity than ten thousand armies of those dudes around demanding that I feed them. So it not only behooves us to gain control of our thoughts but if we want to rejuvenate ourselves, if we want to be transformed, then we must be transfigured. And in order for that to happen, we must enter in consciousness the realm of reason, for only in the realm of reason can we transfigure and be transformed.

Remember, it's never too late. It's always a beginning. Each moment is a beginning, moment by moment. But to make a new beginning, that's beginning again, to make a *new* beginning, we must stand firm at the portal of thought and not permit the armies of yesteryear, the forms created, to take control of our new beginning.

We have, indeed, we *are* very, very fortunate, whether our minds realize it or not, for our minds, created from mental substance, shall return to mental substance. To mental worlds, there's birth and death. How long does a thought live? Only as long as it drains your energy that it may survive. For all forms created by the mind and the mental world, all forms have beginnings, and by the Law of Beginning, they all have an ending. So we feed the life-giving energy we need for the abundant good experience of the moment, we feed it to the shadows, which are the past.

That that has gone has in truth gone. We cannot change it. We can only feed that which has been. Now to feed that which has been is to feed the archangel of death, for there is such an archangel. Whether we know it or not is immaterial. So, you see, whenever you permit your mind to direct energy to that which has been, you're dying inside, for you're giving the life-giving energy, which is *the* power itself to that which has died. And you cannot give it rebirth, for it will never again be. You will never again be what you [were] a moment ago. Do not try to be that which was.

Be that which *is* by control of your mind. And if you will be that which is, there will be no concern, there will be no suffering, there will be no struggle for there will be no lack for there will be no limit. Lack and limit cannot exist in the eternal moment of now. It can only exist when you permit the shadows of yesterday, that which is dead, to rise by the vital life energy which you direct to it.

That which we place our attention upon we are destined to become. So if you want to know what you are becoming, be aware of where your attention is going, for that is what we become. What we become is not what we are. What we become is the illusion known as error. That is what we become; that is not what we are. What we are is above and beyond all creation. It always was and it always will be. We cannot (our mind) control that which we are. We can only control temporarily that which we think we are. Because that which we are is beyond limit; therefore, cannot be controlled by limit.

Thank you. We will have brunch now.

MAY 17, 1981

APPENDIX

The Divine Healing Prayer

I accept that the Divine Healing Power
Is removing all obstructions
From my mind and body
And is restoring me
To perfect health, wealth, and happiness.
My heart is filled with gratitude
For the Divine Law of Acceptance
That is healing both present and absent ones
Who are in need of help.
Peace, the power that healeth,
Is guiding my thoughts, acts, and deeds
As God and I go hand in hand
Living a life of joyful abundance.

The Total Consideration Affirmation

I am the manifestation of Divine Intelligence. Formless and free. Whole and complete. Peace, Poise, and Power are my birthright.

The Law of Harmony is my thought and guarantees Unity in all my acts and activities, expressing perfect Rhythm and limitless flow throughout my entire being.

Without beginning or ending, eternity is my true awareness and sees the tides of creation, as a captain sees his ship.

As the Light of Truth is sustained by the faculty of Reason, I pause to think and claim my Divine right.

      Right Thought. Right Action. Total Consideration.
                    Amen. Amen. Amen.

Divine Abundance

Thank
(Gratitude)

You
(Principle)

God
(Divine Intelligence)

I'm
(Individualizing)

Moving
(Rhythm)

In
(Unity)

Your
(Realization)

Divine
(Total)

Flow
(Consideration)

The Controlled Spiritual Environment Affirmation

You are in a controlled spiritual environment of truth and freedom
Where peace and harmony reign supreme.
Be awake, be aware, be alert.
Your purpose of being is freedom from what has been.
Thoughts of self are foreign to this environment.
Take control of your mind and experience the joy of living.

The Laws Be

Our being is the consciousness, Truth.
Holy be the identity
The joy of Life
The totality of Acceptance
In mind as it is in heart
Grant us the Light
Our daily sustenance
And forgive us our has-beens
As we forgive those has-beens who tempt to steal our joy
Free us from the romance of self-love
Deliver us from the service to the false king of shadows
For Light is the kingdom
And the power and the glory forever
Peace be, the order of Divinity

The All That Has Been Affirmation
From A/V Class Private 12

All that has been cannot be
That's not Good and I'm not free
Until I give then I be
The joy of life that sets me free.

The All That Has Been Affirmation
From a Recording of Affirmations

All that has been cannot be
That's not God and I'm not free
Until I give then I be
The joy of life that sets me free.

The Beseeching of the Angels

[The version below is as it was spoken on the class recordings. The alternative fourth stanza is from a printed version.]

O ye who once were mortals,
Enrobed like us in clay,
Come down from heaven's bright meadows
And be with us today.
Instruct us, loving angels,
The way your glory came
And wreathe about our foreheads
Truth's glowing ring of flame.
Come down, O blessed angels,
Make earth and heaven one.
And when our paths are shadowed
Be ye our rising sun.
Unfold us in God's wisdom,
His beauty and his love,
And may the earth life fit us
To be like you above.

[An alternative ending to the last four lines is:]

Enfold us in thy wisdom,
Thy beauty and thy love,
And may the earth life fit us
To be like you above.

The Class Closing Affirmation

[This affirmation was recorded on The Lost Discourse: Giving and on Impatient Progression. In one recording, the word power *was not spoken or spoken so softly it was difficult to transcribe. However, in the second recording of it, that word was clearly spoken.]*

We thank thee, O Infinite Power, for the blessings we have shared in this hour of holy communication. And we pray that we may be guided each and every moment with the hands of loving angels from the realms of Light. Amen.

[The poem below is referred to by Mr. Goodwin in Class November 15, 1974 and was transcribed from the Serenity Sentinel *of May 1974.]*

It Isn't the Church—It's You

If you want to have the kind of a church
   Like the kind of a church you like,
You needn't slip your clothes in a grip
   And start on a long, long hike.
You'll only find what you left behind,
   For there's nothing really new.
It's a knock at yourself when you knock your church;
   It isn't the church—it's *you*.

It's really strange sometimes, don't you know,
   That things go as well as they do,
When we think of the little—the very small mite—
   We add to the work of the few.
We sit, and stand round, and complain of what's done,
   And do very little but fuss.
Are we bearing our share of the burdens to bear?
   It isn't the church—it's *us*.

So, if you want to have the kind of a church
   Like the kind of a church you like,
Put off your guile, and put on your best smile,
   And hike, my brother, just hike,
To the work in hand that has to be done—
   The work of saving a few.
It isn't the church that is wrong, my boy;
   It isn't the church—it's *you*.

[The teacher refers to an affirmation in both Private Class 1 and Private Class 4, but does not specify which one. It is possible that he could be referring to the following affirmation, which is sometimes called "The Call of the Soul" or "The Eternal Call of the Soul."]

The Call of the Soul

Rhythm, Harmony, Balance, Peace.
Hold release, hold release.
Thank you, God, I am at peace.

Oh, Love Divine

Oh, love divine, a servant be
'Til selfishness imprisons me
And warps the reason of my mind
Into the madness of the blind,
When truth cries out, "Not mine but Thine"
And frees my soul with love divine.

Spirit Working

[The song entitled "Spirit Working," was sung as part of the invocation for the class entitled Impatient Progression. The version below is as it was sung, and it is followed by a version of the song that was printed.]

The harvest is ready, the laborers few
God's minist'ring angels are waiting for you
To open the door through which they may work
And bless all the workers who never do shirk.

> *[Chorus]*
> Spirit working through the conflict self-imposed
>   upon the mind
> Tells the weary to be cheery we have earned our
>   state and kind.
> Workers, workers, you are winners when you serve
>   the selfless way
> Be then fearless, ever ready to serve God and Truth today.

Open your heart, your head, and your hands
To the glorious goal in heavenly land
Share all with another, the blessings received
Fear not of the cross when the crown is relieved

> *[The chorus is repeated.]*

The angels of Light have waited so long
To tenderly guide your footsteps from wrong
The time has come, the hour eleventh,
And angels of light . . . from heaven.

> *[The singers seem uncertain of a few words and hum the melody.]*

> *[The chorus is repeated.]*

O courage, my brothers, fall not away,
The Spirit is working, we're progressing today.
Keep ever the spirit that knows no retreat
For God's blessed angels there is no defeat.
[The chorus is again repeated.]

[The version below is the printed version.]

The harvest is ready the laborers few
God's minist'ring angels are waiting for you
To open the door and enter within
Blessing all the workers who selflessly win.

> *[Chorus]*
> Spirit working through the conflict self-imposed
>   upon the mind
> Tells the weary to be cheery we have earned our
>   state and kind.
> Workers, workers, you are winners when we serve
>   the selfless way
> Be then fearless, ever ready to serve God and Truth today.

Open your heart, your head and your hands
To the glorious kingdom in heavenly lands
Share one with another, the blessings of love
And take up the cross and the crown from above.

God's angels of light are ready to stand
To show you the truth upon this low land
The pathway is straight yet onward we climb
And faithful hard workers reach heaven sublime.

Oh courage, my brothers, Oh courage with God
The Spirit is working wherever we trod.
Keep ever the Spirit with never a why
The angels are telling, "We never shall die."

[The following text is from the personal notes of the vice president of Serenity, a man who also served as the recording technician for these classes. This procedure is referred in A/V Class Private 29, which was given on January 5, 1986. The exercise may also be the one the teacher refers to in the Twenty-Second Annual World Forecast, which was given on December 29, 1985.]

Acupressure of Circle of Logic

This procedure, as given by the Friends, is to help students restore balance in their universe, as long as effort is being made by the student who is the recipient of the procedure.

Procedure:

The student who is seeking help should sit, with back perfectly straight, on a stool or low back chair. Hands in lap, body completely relaxed.

Student to be helped, and one who will administer the pressure, should do the cleansing breath, three times. *[Note: A/V Class Private 30 also recommends that the person administering the pressure have clean hands and that their hands be rinsed with water immediately before and after the procedure.]*

The student who is to administer the pressure should stand behind the seated subject. Referring to diagram, place the index finger on top of middle finger. Be sure your finger nails are short enough so they won't dig into the other student's neck. Place the middle finger on the spot, point "A" on diagram, press firmly, and rotate tip of finger in small circle to the right, clockwise, 14 revolutions. Change fingers so that the middle finger is on top of the index finger, see diagram. Press index finger firmly, on same spot and rotate counterclockwise 13 revolutions.

Find spot "B" on diagram, and repeat procedure. Rotate middle fingertip 14 clockwise, then rotate 13 counterclockwise with the index finger. That completes the procedure.

APPENDIX 497

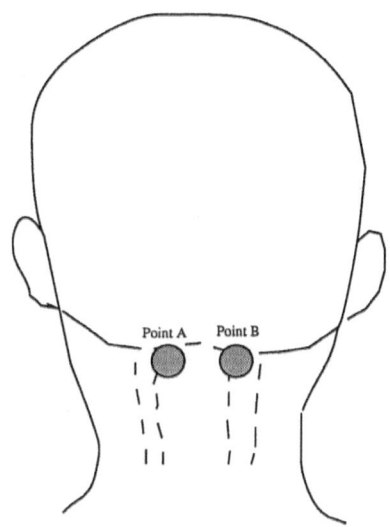

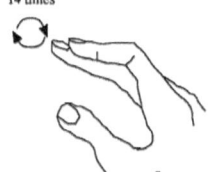

Step one

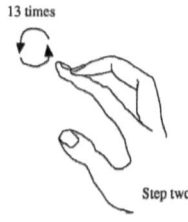

Step two

[In A/V Class Private 48, as well as in a few other classes, the teacher refers to a pamphlet that was published by Serenity many years earlier, entitled, "The Celestial Marriage." The title published on the cover of the pamphlet is "The Descent of Man," but the title page has two titles, "The Celestial Marriage" and "The Descent of Man." Here is the text of that pamphlet as it was published. An asterisk indicates a page break.]

THE CELESTIAL MARRIAGE

OR

THE DESCENT OF MAN

A FABLE
FROM
THE BOOK OF LIFE

*

GIVEN IN HUMILITY
TO ALL
HUMANITY

*

One day in great **ASPIRATION GOD** sent forth from itself **WILL**, and the sons of **WILL** became. Now the sons of **WILL** were of **GOD**, yea, they were **GODS** sent into form, but knew not because of form. The sons of **WILL** roamed the universes for eons and eons of time ever seeking other forms. After much searching they met to consider what they must do. For seven days and seven nights they discussed, and at the seventh hour **ILLUMINATION** fell upon them and said, "Behold, sons of

WILL, within thyself is **COMPASSION**, know it, and unto thee shall be given." Alas, the sons of **WILL** knew **COMPASSION** and that night the daughters of **DESTINY** became.

In the morning when the daughters of **DESTINY** awoke to the sons of **WILL**, the **GODS** and **GODESSESS** of nature danced in jubilee.

Now the sons of **WILL** married the daughters of **DESTINY** and all nature wept with joy.

One day in **TRUTH** a son was born, his name was **INEVITABLE**, and the sons of **WILL** were greatly pleased. Now the daughters of **DESTINY** were quite unhappy for they **HOPED** for a daughter, and so that night in **DESIRE** a girl was born, her name was **LUST**.

Now **INEVITABLE** grew in the warmth and sunshine of the day. Oh how he loved the sun, for to him all **LIFE** was **LIGHT**.

LUST grew up to be a beautiful and lovely woman with a great fondness for the moon and darkness, for had she not been born in the night of **DESIRE**.

Time passed on, and one day **INEVITABLE** felt he would go into the night to find **LUST**, for he had heard so much about her, and had sent her many messages asking her to come into the **LIGHT** so that they may know more of each other. **INEVITABLE** went down, down into the darkness of night, and as he descended a great **FEAR** overcame him, but he found **LUST**, her face glowing so beautiful by the reflection of the sun. From the shadows where the **LIGHT** of the moon shone not, a voice spoke unto **INEVITABLE** and said, "Behold the beauty and the glory thou hast found, is it not worth the descent into our realms?" But from within, a voice spoke to **INEVITABLE** and said, "Take her to the realms of **LIGHT** that you may see more clearly in a day of **REASON**."

The senses won, and that night in **DESPAIR** a child was born, her name was **GRIEF**. The years passed and **GRIEF** could not be comforted, for she had been born of **LUST**, in the night of **DESIRE**, by the promptings of **PASSION**, and knew not of **TRUTH**.

INEVITABLE wandered on and on with the daughter **GRIEF**, hoping to return to the realms of **LIGHT**, but no, the centuries passed and only **SORROW** did they know.

Then one day a bird from the realms of **LIGHT** landed on his shoulder and sang this song, "In **SORROW** doth thou stay for self-pity knows no way."

INEVITABLE thought and thought of the meaning of those words, then he thought of his homeland **TRUTH** where he had been so very, very happy; and in **CONCENTRATION**, he found himself leaving the realms of darkness, passing through the lands of **IGNORANCE** and **EXPERIENCE** to return to his blessed land.

LOVE ALL LIFE
AND KNOW
THE LIGHT

*

OH MAN THINK HUMBLE
YET WELL OF THYSELF
FOR IN THY THINKING
IS CREATED
THE VEHICLE OF
THE SOUL

The Diagram of Destiny

[The Destiny Diagram was referred to in Discourse January 18, 1973, in Discourse January 19, 1973, and in other classes. The text below, as well as the hand-drawn diagram, is from Mr. Goodwin's binder of Diagramology teachings.]

Atlantean Astrology

1. Destiny number or primary lesson is total of month, day and year of birth.
2. Birth planetary or secondary lesson is planet under which you are born.
3. The fulfillment of your destiny is revealed by adding your destiny number to the six of Venus, which gives you the planet of your fulfillment.
4. Destiny number is the number of times you have been through the planet under which you are born, also the planet prior to the one under which you are born.
5. Adding your planetary number to any planet, subtract from 9, gives you the number of times you have been through the planet and the lessons to be learned are revealed by the planetary number remaining.

Example:
Neptune 2 to Venus 6 = Earth 8 or secondary lesson.
Earth 8 from Pluto 9 is Uranus 1 Sun or primary lesson to be learned.

Man loses gratitude when he is out of balance in Neptune. When his [our] emotions are no longer passive, we lose gratitude and go to Uranus where self drives us to Pluto where we become unaware.

Last planet you came from is your birth planet. Destiny planet is the one you identified with on the path.

APPENDIX

	MARS AGGRESSIVE		MERCURY PEACEFUL		JUPITER CAREFREE	
SADNESS	3	FEAR / INDIFFERENCE	4	FREEDOM / JOY	5	FAITH
	REACTION POSITIVE		INACTION NEUTRAL		ACTION NEGATIVE	
	VENUS NEED		SATURN CONFIDENCE		EARTH SUPPLY	
DISAPPOINTMENT	6	PERSONALITY / RELIANCE	7	PREOCCUPATION / EXPECTATION	8	PRINCIPLE
	REACTION POSITIVE		INACTION NEUTRAL		ACTION NEGATIVE	
	PLUTO CONCERN		URANUS SELF AWARENESS		NEPTUNE PASSIVE	
AQUIANTANCE	9	REGRET / STRANGER	10	RELEASE / FRIENDSHIP	11	REWARD
	REACTION POSITIVE		INACTION NEUTRAL		ACTION NEGATIVE	

APPENDIX   503

[The diagram below is from the personal notes of the student who served as vice president under Mr. Goodwin.]

DESTINY DIAGRAM

Atlantian Astrology

(red-orn) **MARS** CELESTIAL 9 WAR heaven AGGRESSIVE SADNESS — 3 — FEAR REACTION POSITIVE	(yel) **MERCURY** ETHERIAL 8 commo WISDOM PEACEFUL purification INDIFFERENCE — 4 — FREEDOM INACTION NEUTRAL	(med-grn) **JUPITER** ODIC 7 understanding KNOWLEDGE prana CAREFREE JOY — 5 — FAITH ACTION NEGATIVE
(dk-gry) **VENUS** MAGNETIC 6 love LOVE NEED DISAPPOINTMENT — 6 — PERSONALITY REACTION POSITIVE	(pur) **SATURN** ELECTRIC 5 balance UNDERSTANDING CONFIDENSE RELIANCE — 7 — PREOCCUPATION INACTION NEUTRAL	(dk-grn) **EARTH** AIR 4 mental discussion FAITH SUPPLY EXPECTATION — 8 — PRINCIPAL ACTION NEGATIVE
(blk) **PLUTO** EARTH 1 body (self preservation) IGNORANCE CONCERN AQUAINTENCE — 9 — REGRET REACTION POSITIVE	(lgt-grn) **URANUS** FIRE 2 lust SELF AWARENESS INDIVIDUALITY STRANGER — 10 — RELEASE ⟨1⟩ INACTION NEUTRAL	(lgt-gry) **NEPUTNE** WATER 3 emotion PASSIVE EMOTION FRIENDSHIP — 11 — REWARD ⟨2⟩ ACTION NEGATIVE

[In Private Class 1 and in other classes reference is made to "bays." The diagram below is from the personal notes of the vice president.]

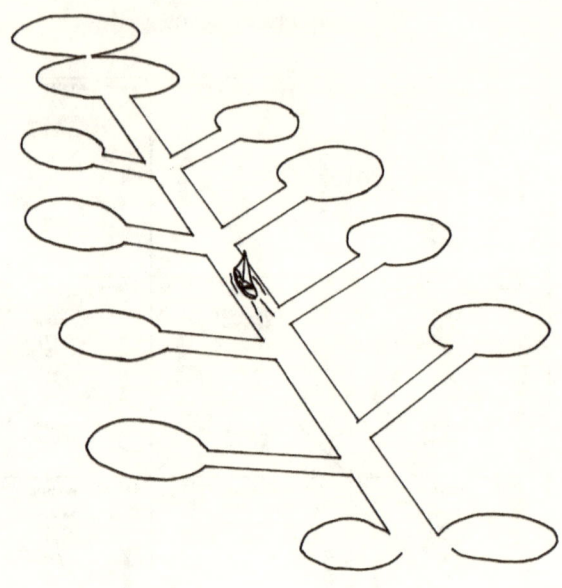

Cover Image of 1972 Edition of *The Living Light*

[The cover image of the 1972 edition of The Living Light *is displayed on the frontispiece of this volume. Reference to the symbolic image is discussed in excerpts from the following volumes of* The Living Light Dialogue:*]*

[Volume 2, Consciousness Class 44, pages 480-481:]

"And we'll begin with the outside of it, *[The teacher refers to the cover image.]* which is the snake, representative of wisdom consuming itself. Now why does the symbol of wisdom consume itself? Does anyone know? Does anyone know why wisdom is self-consuming? Because, my friends, if it's wisdom, then it can gain nothing from outside of itself: it already is wisdom. So all that wisdom is—you understand, you don't gain wisdom and neither do you give wisdom. Wisdom is self-sustaining. When you rise to a level of consciousness where wisdom expresses itself, then you will become it and it is self-sufficient unto itself. So the snake consuming itself is representative of wisdom, in comparison to what one might call knowledge. Now, knowledge is something that you gain. It's something that you put into your brain and you feed back at your discretion—but not wisdom.

"The next step is the interlaced double triangle, which is a very, very ancient symbol. It is the meeting of the spirit with matter. It is the power above that meets the forces below. And at that junction, when those two triangles meet, that's the negative and the positive poles come together in creation and the divine spark, the rays of light, life is so-called born into matter.

"Now you all know that all poles are triune. The negative pole is triune and the positive pole is triune. In fact, my friends, as we've stated before, all things that are manifest are triune and that is why three is the number of manifestation.

"Inside of the interlaced triangles you'll notice on the top of the pyramid in the rays of light is the all-seeing eye. Now the all-seeing eye is that that is not distracted, because it sees everything and so nothing gains its attention. And that is why it is the all-seeing eye. The triangle itself, the pyramid upon which all knowledge, the all-seeing eye, all wisdom, and all life rest, is the pyramid of manifestation. All things in all universes (physical, mental, or spiritual) are triune. There are three parts to all things: that is an absolute fact of physics and it is a truth of the universe."

[Volume 4, Consciousness Class 78, page 172:]
"Then, we'll be happy to share our understanding. The serpent so designed—consuming itself—is the ancient and eternal symbol of everlasting and eternal wisdom. The double triangle, with its apex downward, is the manifestation of the Divine Power and the balance of nature, its own creation. The pyramid with the all-seeing eye on the top is the eternal Light that never closes, that sees all things, that knows all things, and that ever is and ever has been."